CLARENDON ARISTOTLE SERIES

General Editor
LINDSAY JUDSON

Also published in this series

Categories and *De Interpretatione*   J. L. ACKRILL

De Anima   CHRISTOPHER SHIELDS

De Generatione et Corruptione   C. J. F. WILLIAMS

De Partibus Animalium I and *De Generatione Animalium* I   D. M. BALME
New impression with supplementary material by Allan Gotthelf

Eudemian Ethics Books I, II, and VIII   MICHAEL WOODS
Second edition

Metaphysics Books B and K 1–2   ARTHUR MADIGAN, SJ

Metaphysics Books Γ, Δ, and E   CHRISTOPHER KIRWAN
Second edition

Metaphysics Books Z and H   DAVID BOSTOCK

Metaphysics Book Θ   STEPHEN MAKIN

Metaphysics Book I   LAURA M. CASTELLI

Metaphysics Book Λ   LINDSAY JUDSON

Metaphysics Books M and N   JULIA ANNAS

Nicomachean Ethics Books VIII and IX   MICHAEL PAKALUK

On the Parts of Animals I–IV   JAMES G. LENNOX

Physics Books I and II   WILLIAM CHARLTON
New impression with supplementary material

Physics Books III and IV   EDWARD HUSSEY
New impression with supplementary material

Physics Books VIII   DANIEL GRAHAM

Politics Books I and II   TREVOR J. SAUNDERS

Politics Books III and IV   RICHARD ROBINSON
New impression with supplementary material by David Keyt

Politics Books V and VI   DAVID KEYT

Politics Books VII and VIII   RICHARD KRAUT

Posterior Analytics   JONATHAN BARNES
Second edition

Prior Analytics Book I   GISELA STRIKER

Topics Books I and VIII   ROBIN SMITH

Other volumes are in preparation

ARISTOTLE
Topics

Book VI

*Translated
with an Introduction and Commentary
by*

ANNAMARIA SCHIAPARELLI

CLARENDON PRESS · OXFORD

Great Clarendon Street, Oxford, OX2 6DP,
United Kingdom

Oxford University Press is a department of the University of Oxford.
It furthers the University's objective of excellence in research, scholarship,
and education by publishing worldwide. Oxford is a registered trade mark of
Oxford University Press in the UK and in certain other countries

© Annamaria Schiaparelli 2023

The moral rights of the author have been asserted

All rights reserved. No part of this publication may be reproduced, stored in
a retrieval system, or transmitted, in any form or by any means, without the
prior permission in writing of Oxford University Press, or as expressly permitted
by law, by licence or under terms agreed with the appropriate reprographics
rights organization. Enquiries concerning reproduction outside the scope of the
above should be sent to the Rights Department, Oxford University Press, at the
address above

You must not circulate this work in any other form
and you must impose this same condition on any acquirer

Published in the United States of America by Oxford University Press
198 Madison Avenue, New York, NY 10016, United States of America

British Library Cataloguing in Publication Data
Data available

Library of Congress Control Number: 2023932758

ISBN 978–0–19–960975–8 (hbk.)
ISBN 978–0–19–960976–5 (pbk.)

Printed and bound in the UK by
Clays Ltd, Elcograf S.p.A.

Links to third party websites are provided by Oxford in good faith and
for information only. Oxford disclaims any responsibility for the materials
contained in any third party website referenced in this work.

For Paolo

PREFACE

My work on *Topics* VI began when I was Lecturer at the Queen's College, Oxford, and came to conclusion in Geneva with the generous support of the Fond National Suisse. During this time, I benefitted from seminars, workshops, and informal discussions with many colleagues and friends. I express my gratitude to all of them. In particular, I thank Lindsay Judson, whose kind and punctual comments helped me to improve on my raw material. I am grateful to Paolo Crivelli for the endless discussions on Aristotle's philosophy and logic. Written correspondence with Jonathan Barnes fostered my understanding of the text and its arguments.

In Oxford, I received valuable aid from Lesley Brown, David Charles, Gail Fine, Michael Frede, Terence Irwin, Thomas Johansen, Benjamin Morison, Michael Peramatzis, Christopher Shields, and Tim Williamson. My work profited from conversations with visiting scholars, and I thank Lucas Angioni, David Bronstein, Walter Cavini, Oliver Primavesi, and Christof Rapp. An invitation to the Department of Philosophy of the University of São Paulo, Brazil, offered me the opportunity to discuss some chapters, and I am indebted to Marco Zingano for organizing my stay. Robin Smith read some chapters and encouraged me to pursue my research. On several occasions I presented papers based on my work and I thank Francesco Ademollo, Dominic Bailey, Luca Castagnoli, Lorenzo Corti, Sten Ebbesen, and Paolo Fait for their helpful suggestions.

In Geneva, I had many profitable exchanges with Alexander Bown, Alvise Lagnerini, Eduardo Saldaña Piovanetti, Fabrice Correia, Katerina Ierodiakonou, Laurent Cesalli, Maria Fiorella Privitera, Marcel Weber, and Christian Wüthrich.

When I had finished the first version of this book, Pieter Sjoerd Hasper invited me to participate in the Tübingen Research Seminar on Aristotle's *Topics*. It was a significant opportunity to examine the Greek text and the philosophical implications stemming from different readings of the MSS. I am grateful to Pieter Sjoerd for this invitation and for the inspiring exchanges with Klaus Corcilius, Coling King, Justin Vlastis, and all the doctoral students.

PREFACE

My first mentor could not see the completed version of my book. I took my first steps in the philosophy of Aristotle under the guidance and supervision of Enrico Berti: my debt to him is unfathomable.

CONTENTS

Abbreviations	xi
Typographical conventions	xii
INTRODUCTION	1
I. The Place of the *Topics* in Aristotle's Corpus	1
II. The Contents of the *Topics*	2
III. The Four Predicables	4
IV. The Classifications of the Predicables	7
V. The Logical Relations among the Predicables	10
VI. The Predicable Definition	11
VII. Types of Definition and their Rules	13
VIII. The Notion of Causality in the *Topics*	16
IX. Some Prominent Themes Concerning Standard Definitions	19
X. Structure and Interpretations of Book VI of the *Topics*	24
TRANSLATION	27
COMMENTARY	57
Chapter 1	57
Chapter 2	72
Chapter 3	85
Chapter 4	101
Chapter 5	128
Chapter 6	147
Chapter 7	191
Chapter 8	200
Chapter 9	234
Chapter 10	257
Chapter 11	279

CONTENTS

Chapter 12	294
Chapter 13	310
Chapter 14	330
Terminological Clarifications	343
Notes on the Text	345
Appendix: The Predicables' Logical Relations	357
Select Bibliography	359
Glossary	
English–Greek	371
Greek–English	373
Index Locorum	377
General Index	382

ABBREVIATIONS

ARISTOTLE

APo.	*Posterior Analytics*
APr.	*Prior Analytics*
Cael.	*De Caelo*
Cat.	*Categories*
De An.	*De Anima*
De Int.	*De Interpretatione*
EN	*Ethica Nicomachea*
GA	*De Generatione Animalium*
GC	*De Generatione et Corruptione*
HA	*Historia Animalium*
MA	*De Motu Animalium*
Metaph.	*Metaphysica*
MM	*Magna Moralia*
Ph.	*Physica*
Pol.	*Politica*
Rh.	*Rhetorica*
SE	*Sophistici Elenchi*
Top.	*Topica*

PLATO

Ap.	*Apologia*
Euthd.	*Euthydemus*
Euthphr.	*Euthyphro*
Grg.	*Gorgias*
Men.	*Meno*
Phd.	*Phaedo*
Phdr.	*Phaedrus*
Phlb.	*Philebus*

ABBREVIATIONS

Plt.   *Politicus*
Prm.   *Parmenides*
Prt.   *Protagoras*
ps.-Platonic *Def.*   pseudo-Platonic *Definitiones*
R.   *Respublica*
Smp.   *Symposium*
Sph.   *Sophista*
Tht.   *Theaetetus*
Ti.   *Timaeus*

Work by other ancient authors

Alex. Aphr.   Alexander of Aphrodisias
  in *Metaph.*   in *Aristotelis Metaphysica Commentaria in Aristotelem Graeca i*, M. Hayduck (ed.) (Berlin: Georg Reimer) 1891.
  in *Top.*   in *Aristotelis Topicorum libros octos commentaria, Commentaria in Aristotelem Graeca ii pars iii*, M. Wallies (ed.) (Berlin: Georg Reimer) 1891.
Hero   Heron of Alexandria
  Deff.   *Definitiones*, F. Hultsch (ed.) (Berlin: Georg Reimer) 1864.
Procl.   Proclus
  in *Euc.*   in *primum Euclidis librum commentarius*, ed. G. Friedlein (Leipzig: Teubner) 1873.

TYPOGRAPHICAL CONVENTIONS IN THE TRANSLATION

Corner brackets <...> signal words added by me for the sake of readability of English. The additions are explained in the commentary.

Square brackets [...] enclose words which translate portion of the Greek text that are to be deleted. The deletions are justified in the commentary and in Notes on the Text.

INTRODUCTION

I. The Place of the *Topics* in Aristotle's Corpus

The *Topics* is a treatise in eight books and belongs to Aristotle's early logical works. In the order of Aristotle's writings, as we find them in the corpus, the *Topics* is included in the *Organon*. It stands after *Categories*, *De Interpretatione*, *Prior Analytics,* and *Posterior Analytics*; it is followed by the *Sophistici Elenchi*, which, according to some ancient and modern commentators, is the ninth book of the *Topics*. Even if it were true that the *Sophistici Elenchis* had been conceived as an addition to the *Topics*, this does not undermine the originality and importance of the treatise, whose subject matter is distinct from the *Topics* although it shares a certain method. The *Topics* seems to be the first work by Aristotle that was handed down in its entirety: the manuscripts are in a good state and they allow us to reconstruct a text which is rather faithful to the intention and to the mind of the author.

The *Topics* was mainly composed when Aristotle was lecturing in Plato's Academy in the early fourth century BC. This work is Aristotle's earliest contribution to the study of logic. For the most part, it was written before Aristotle began to develop the syllogistic theory in his *Analytics*. It is possible to establish the chronology of the eight books of the *Topics*. On the one hand, it is believed that the first and the eighth book are more recent since they were written after the others; for this reason, some commentators call them 'peripheral books'. On the other hand, the second, third, fourth, fifth, and sixth books, and (possibly a part of the) seventh book, belong to an earlier phase of Aristotle's philosophical development; these are often referred to as 'the central books'. It is likely that Aristotle collected the material for the central books and then joined them together. Afterwards, he wrote and added the peripheral books. There is evidence to suggest that, in a more advanced stage of his philosophical production, Aristotle went back to the earliest parts and made some changes. It is worthwhile mentioning that there is a problem concerning the authenticity of the fifth book. In Reinhardt 2000, there is a selection of passages that can be attributed to

Aristotle, whereas other portions of text were probably written by an anonymous *Bearbeiter* (reviser).

II. The Contents of the *Topics*

The dialectical method is the cornerstone of Aristotle's project in the *Topics* and has to be understood in the context of the dialectical debate. The method consists in the ability to form a series of deductions (dialectical syllogisms) having as their starting point premises not dealing with a specific branch of knowledge. In *Top.* I.1, 100^{a}18–21, Aristotle says: 'The goal of this study (*sc.* the *Topics*) is to find a method on the basis of which we shall be able to construct deductions (*sullogizesthai*) from reputable opinions (*endoxa*) concerning any problem that is proposed and—when submitting to argument ourselves—will not say anything contradictory' (trans. Smith 1997, slightly modified). What are a dialectical syllogism and a reputable opinion that is used as its premise? Aristotle defines them in relation to a syllogism *tout court*:

> T1
> A syllogism, then, is an argument in which, certain things having been posited, something different from the things laid down results of necessity through the things laid down. A syllogism is a demonstration if it is from things which are either themselves true and primary, or have attained the starting point of knowledge about themselves through things primary and true. A dialectical syllogism, on the other hand, is one which deduces from reputable opinions (*endoxa*). Those things are true and primary which get their trustworthiness through themselves rather than through other things (for, in the case of scientific principles, one must not ask 'Why?' but each of the principles ought to be trustworthy in and of itself). Reputable opinions are those which are accepted by the majority, or by the wise—i.e. by all, or by the majority, or by the most reputable of them.   (*Top.* I.1, 100^{a}25–100^{b}25)

The dialectical method can be used only in certain contexts, namely in a structured discussion where there are (at least) two speakers, namely the questioner and the answerer. The discussion is structured because it is strictly regulated by some rules that will be discussed throughout the treatise. The role of the questioner consists in refuting the views granted by the answerer. The role of the

INTRODUCTION

answerer consists in avoiding the refutation. According to Aristotle, 'a refutation is a syllogism with the contradictory of the conclusion' (*SE* 1, 165^{a}2–3). The division of the roles between questioner and answerer is extremely important. For the present purposes it suffices to understand the general outline of the exchange. Roughly speaking, the questioner must put questions which can be answered by 'yes' or 'no' (except in a few specified cases). When the answerer says 'yes', he grants some premises to the questioner. Although there is a tendency to look primarily at the questioner (who corresponds to the dialectician), Aristotle does not forget the answerer, whose role is not simply uttering 'yes' or 'no' in a passive way. Set rules concerning the answerer are specified in *Topics* VI.10 and VIII.5.

In the presentation of the dialectical method, Aristotle describes it as a tool for 'constructing deduction from reputable premises *concerning any problem*'. But it is highly unlikely that the dialectician be acquainted with the varieties of views that might be held by the interlocutor. For this reason, Aristotle introduces and discusses a number of *topoi*, namely 'commonplaces' (literally 'locations'). We can think of these commonplaces as sets of general rules whose application enables the dialectician to develop his arguments. Some commonplaces will be useful for refutative arguments, others for constructive arguments. The following is an example of a refutative commonplace, which concerns the lack of clarity in a proposed definition: 'In case what is being defined is said in many ways, see whether he (*sc.* the interlocutor) has spoken without distinguishing them' (*Top.* VI.2, 139^{b}24–5; see commentary *ad loc.*). There are also commonplaces which are more difficult to understand and to unfold into a refutative strategy: 'In the case of the relatives, examine whether he gives an account of the species as relative to a particular case of that relative to which he gives an account of the genus' (*Top.* VI.9, 147^{a}23–4; see commentary *ad loc.*).

The commonplaces are classified according to the so-called predicables, namely *definition*, *genus*, *unique property*, and *accident* (more on this below). The central books of the *Topics* are organized according to the commonplaces proper to each predicable. The second and the third books contain the commonplaces about the predicable accident. The fourth book discusses the commonplaces about the predicable genus. The fifth book is about the commonplaces of unique property. The sixth book and chapters 1–3 of the seventh contain a lengthy analysis of commonplaces about definition. As for the peripheral books, the first presents the aims of the entire treatise and contains an introduction to the theory of predicables, whereas the eighth mainly contains practical hints for questioners and answerers who face each other in a dialectical debate.

III. The Four Predicables

The dialectical method is strongly connected to the logical analysis outlined in the *Topics*. The type of logical analysis used throughout this treatise differs from the well-known theory of syllogism developed in the *Analytics*. The analysis of the predicative relation set forth in the *Topics* is called the 'theory of the predicables'. It says that in any predication the predicate must be in one of four relations with the subject: the predicate must be either *definition* of a subject, or a *genus*, or a *unique property*, or an *accident*. The first step of a dialectician who is about to deploy his argument for refutative or constructive purposes stands in identifying under which of the four predicables the subject falls. Then, he will apply the commonplaces corresponding to the selected predicable. Aristotle introduces the predicables in *Top*. I.4, 101^{b}15-28; this text allows us to find out some important characteristics.

T2
Arguments are made of propositions ... and every proposition, as well as every problem, exhibits either a unique property, or a genus, or an accident (the differentia, since it is genus-like, should be classified together with the genus). But since one sort of unique property signifies *what-it-is-to-be* something and another sort does not, let us divide the unique property into both the parts stated, and let us call the sort that signifies *what-it-is-to-be* something a definition, while the remaining sort may be referred as the unique property. Clearly then, from what has been said, it turns out that according to the present division they are four in all: *definition*, *unique property*, *genus* or *accident*. No one should take them to mean that each one of these, uttered by itself, is a proposition ... but instead that it is out of these that ... propositions arise.[1]

---

[1] Translation by Smith 1997, slightly modified. I write 'propositions' instead of 'premises': since arguments are made of premises and conclusion (which are propositions), it is more adequate to translate *protaseis* with 'proposition'.

Two points immediately capture our attention. First, in this list the differentia is associated with the genus and is not ranked among the predicables. This seems to suggest that the differentia plays only a secondary, or auxiliary, role with respect to the genus. If this is the case, then there is a tension with Aristotle's later theory in his *Metaphysics* where he seems to give priority to the differentia over the genus. Then, the post-Aristotelian and medieval tradition included the differentia in the predicables. There is an extensive treatment of the differentia in the analysis of the commonplaces that relate to the predicable definition, of which the differentia is a component, in *Topics* VI.6. In this chapter, important features of the differentia are discussed—for example, its relation with the genus it divides and with the extension of the species it contributes to form (see below commentary *ad loc.*, and Schiaparelli 2016).

Second, in T2 the unique property is defined in relation to the predicable definition. The unique property is divided into two parts: one expresses the essence, the other does not. Then, the part expressing the essence is the defining part; the part not expressing the essence retains the name 'unique property'. In the *Topics*, however, Aristotle distinguishes two ways of being a unique property. In a narrow sense, A is a unique property of B just in case A is necessarily coextensive with B and A is not the essence of B. In a wide sense, A is a unique property of B just in case A is necessarily coextensive with B, but nothing is said concerning the relation between A and the essence of B: the possibilities are left open that A might or might not be the essence of B (see commentaries to *Top.* VI.1, 139^a24–35; 3, 140^a33–140^b15; 6, 144^a28–144^a11; the commentaries contain a bibliography on this issue). It is a central feature of a unique property that 'it belongs only to it (*sc.* the subject) and it counter-predicates with it'. In other words, the unique property is coextensive with its subject. For instance, capable-of-becoming-literate is a unique property of a human since 'if something is a human, then it is capable-of becoming-literate, and if it is capable-of-becoming-literate it is a human' (*Top.* I.5, 102^a19–22).

In *Top.* I.5, 102^a31–2, Aristotle describes the genus as 'what is predicated in the *what-it-is* of many things that are different in species'. For example, animal is a genus and is predicated of the different species that fall under it, such as human, bird, ox, and horse. We say that a human is an animal, a bird is an animal, an ox is an animal, and a horse is an animal. It is interesting to observe that the genus is 'predicated in the *what-it-is*' but it is not apt fully to express the essence, namely the entire *what-it-is-to-be*. This has an important consequence on the predicative relation between the predicable genus and its subject. The genus does not counter-predicate with the subject, or, in modern jargon, it is not coextensive with it. The entire fourth book of the *Topics* examines the commonplaces pertaining to the predicable genus. A further analysis is carried out in chapter 5 of the sixth book, where the discussion is centred on the genus (not as a predicable in itself but) as a necessary component of the definition. The analysis in chapter 5 presupposes some of the main theses illustrated in the fourth book. Further remarks on the genus can be found in *Top.* VI.6, 144^{a}11–16 and 17–18 (see commentary *ad loc.*).

The predicable accident is defined in two ways. First, Aristotle says: 'An accident is something which is none of these—not a definition, a unique property, a genus—but yet belongs to the subject' (*Top.* I.5, 102^{b}4–5). This begins as a negative definition since it says what the accident is not. The positive characterization is that it belongs to the subject. But, as Aristotle observes in the sequel of the passage, the first definition is not useful if someone does not know what the other predicables are (*Top.* I.5, 102^{b}11–12). The second definition is formulated a few lines after the first and says that an accident is 'what can possibly belong or not belong to one and the same thing, whatever it may be' (*Top.* I.5, 102^{b}6–7). For instance, white can belong and not belong to the same thing at different times. Although the following example does not employ general terms, it helps to illustrate the case at hand: Socrates is white when he spends his time in Athens, but after a week at the beach he is no longer white but tanned. The second seems to be Aristotle's preferred definition of the accident (*Top.* I.5, 102^{b}10). It is worth noting that it is framed in terms of a modal notion, namely possibility. The comparison between the two definitions invites some questions that deserve to be mentioned even though they cannot be developed in the present introduction. To begin with, it is far from clear whether the two definitions coincide; that is to say, it is legitimate to ask whether they pick up the same object. Then, one can also ask whether they are sufficient to give us a complete characterization of the accident. Are they intended to satisfy the needs of the dialectical exchange's participants only? The commonplaces relative to the accident are developed in *Topics* II–III. Then, in VI.1,139^{a}37–139^{b}3 Aristotle explains why the commonplaces relative to the predicable accident are helpful in the discussion of the definition (see commentary *ad loc.*, which contains a bibliography on this issue). The predicable accident does not counter-predicate with the subject.

The concept of definition will be the focus of this volume. It is helpful to look at its description as it appears in the *Topics*' first book: 'A *definition* is a *logos* (account) that signifies *to ti ên einai* (the what-it-is-to-be)', (*Top.* I.5, 101^{b}38). The expression 'the what-it-is-to-be' has been extensively analysed. The literal translation of the Greek *to ti ên einai* is 'the what-it-was-to-be'. The most frequent rendering is 'essence'. A *what-it-is-to-be* is always a *what-it-is-to-be for something*. The definition of Y tells us the *what-it-is-to-be for Y*, or *what-it-is for Y to-be*. For example, to be for a human is to be an animal that is rational. Being an animal that is rational is the essence of a human, and the definition of a human will be 'A human is a rational animal'. The definition counter-predicates with its subject.

IV. The Classifications of the Predicables

Aristotle's way of introducing the predicables in the *Topics*' first book leads to the possibility that they are differently classified. Here is an outline of four possible classifications of the predicables.

The first is based on the relation of counter-predication: the expression 'P counter-predicates with Q' can be rephrased as 'If anything falls under P then it falls under Q, and if anything falls under Q then it falls under P'. The classification according to the relation of counter-predication adopts an extensional approach since it does not employ modal notions. Some predicables counter-predicate with their subjects, whilst others do not. On the one hand, definition and unique property counter-predicate with their subjects. On the other, genus and accident do not counter-predicate with their subjects:

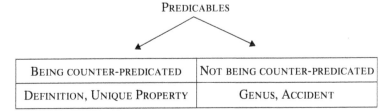

The second classification is based on a modal notion. The predicables are grouped according to whether or not they belong necessarily to their subjects. This way of classifying the predicables offers a different result:

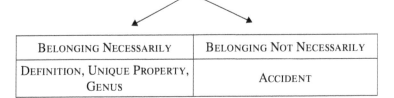

The third classification is based on a different notion. In some passages Aristotle seems to insist that, although it does not express the essence, a unique property is necessary. This introduces a problem for the first and second classifications (which are illustrated in the first two diagrams) because they do not give us any means by which we can distinguish between definition and unique property. For they are both necessary and they counter-predicate with the subject. The third classification, which is based on the notion of essence, tries to avoid this problem:

PREDICABLES

BELONGING TO THE ESSENCE	NOT BELONGING TO THE ESSENCE
DEFINITION, GENUS	UNIQUE PROPERTY, ACCIDENT

INTRODUCTION

The comparison between the second and the third classification (displayed in the last two diagrams) shows that different results are obtained. The difference depends on whether we divide the predicables according to the notion of necessity or according to that of essence. This points to an important distinction that is drawn in modern metaphysics. It goes without saying that it would be interesting to ask what the relation between necessity and essence according to Aristotle is; in other words, one might want to understand which the primitive notion is. The primitive notion should allow us to define the derived one. In this context, however, there are not sufficient elements to find an answer.

The last possibility consists in offering a classification of the predicables which is not exclusively based either on extensional or on other notions (necessity, essence). The fourth classification uses both extensional and other notions, and, for this reason, the fourth classification is characterized as 'mixed'. The division of the predicables comes in two steps. The first is to divide the predicables according to the relation of counter-predication. The second step is to subdivide the predicables that counter-predicate with their subject in those belonging to the essence and those not belonging to the essence. An analogous subdivision must be done in the case of the predicables that do not counter-predicate with their subjects. The following diagrams illustrate the steps of this classifying procedure.

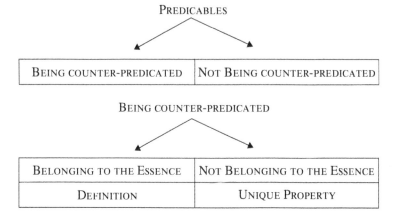

NOT BEING COUNTER-PREDICATED

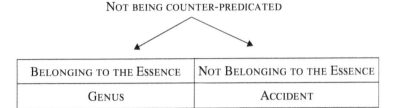

BELONGING TO THE ESSENCE	NOT BELONGING TO THE ESSENCE
GENUS	ACCIDENT

This classification successfully distinguishes between definition (i.e. the predicable that counter-predicates with its subject and belongs to the essence) and unique property (i.e. the predicable that counter-predicates with its subject *but does not belong* to the essence). For this reason, one might be tempted to prefer it over the previous three classifications. But something remains to be said against it. It makes no room for the relation of belonging not necessarily. Perhaps, none of the four classifications taken on their own are apt to reconstruct a complete picture of the complex relation holding between each predicable and its subject.

V. The Logical Relations among the Predicables

The classifications of the predicables and the relations they hold with their subjects raise a question. What is the general idea that stands at the basis of Aristotle's individuation of exactly four predicables? Very likely, the four predicables allow him to cover all the *positive* extensional relations holding between two classes. An extensional relation is *positive* just in case there is at least one thing that falls under the two classes. For any two classes A and B, there are four possible positive relations: (1) A is *included* in B, but not vice versa; (2) B is *included* in A, but not vice versa; (3) A is *coextensive* with B; (4) A *overlaps* with B.

The four predicables and their subjects are general terms. Then, (1) the relation of *inclusion* of A by B can be said to hold between the species to be defined and its genus; that is to say, the species to be defined A is included in its genus B, but the genus does not include it. This is because, as Aristotle often says, the genus has a wider extension than its species. (2) The relation of A *including* B can be said to hold between the genus and its species. That is to say, the genus A includes the species to be defined B. (3) The relation of *coextension* can be said to hold between the thing to be defined and its definition. The same relation holds in the case of a species and its unique properties. (4) The relation of *overlap* holds between the species and its accidents.[2] Since we start from the assumption that a class is not empty, there is no instance of the relation of total exclusion.

Can this interpretation be accepted? It is an interesting attempt to interpret Aristotle's theory of predicables because it highlights some ideas that Aristotle might have had. In particular, his ideas foreshadow the modern logical relation among classes. This interpretation, however, must be handled with care. If it is pushed too far, it runs the risk of introducing misleading concepts. Aristotle's general terms are not classes. The criterion of identity for classes is extensional; classes are collections of individuals (i.e. their members). But the criterion of identity for Aristotle's general term is intensional: they are universals. Consider the following example: 'All animals with kidneys' and 'All animal with hearts'. In an extensional interpretation, the two classes are the same because they have the same extension. But in an intensional reading, they are different: the classes will not be identified with their members. Thus, the interpretation of general terms as classes might lead to a misunderstanding of Aristotle's ontology.

VI. The Predicable Definition

The predicable definition occupies a central place in the *Topics* as is made clear in I.6, $102^b 27$–33:

T3
We should not forget that *the things relating* (*ta pros*) to the unique property, the genus, and the accident are also appropriate to use in connection with definitions. For if we have shown that something fails to belong uniquely to what falls under the definition (as we do in the case of a unique property), or that what is given as such in the definition is not the genus, or that something stated in the account does not belong (as might also be said in the case of an accident), then we shall have refuted the definition.

---

[2] The Appendix contains a simple proof for a reader who is not an expert logician and wishes to know how the four positive relations are derived from the principle: $X \cap \neg Y = \neg \emptyset \rightarrow X \subseteq Y$.

Here '*the things relating* to the unique property, the genus, and the accident' are the discussions about these predicables and, in particular, the analysis of their commonplaces. They are useful for two purposes. On the one hand, they are useful in relation to each predicable. That is to say, they allow the dialectician to establish whether or not the answerer has individuated the correct predicable of a given subject. Following Aristotle's instructions, the dialectician will be able to deploy constructive or refutative arguments concerning each predicable. On the other hand, the discussions about unique property, genus, and accident are helpful in the analysis of the predicable definition. In particular, the refutative arguments concerning the first three predicables can be used to criticize and reject an unsuccessful definition proposed by the answerer. It is not surprising, then, that, in the order of central books of the *Topics,* the study of definition is preceded by the analysis of the other predicables. At first, the dialectician becomes familiar with the constructive and refutative commonplaces concerning unique property, genus, and accident. Then he will be able to use the refutative arguments to criticize and reject an unsuccessful definition.

Further evidence concerning the prominent place occupied by the predicable definition in the *Topics* comes from the first chapter of book VI, which contains an extensive treatment of definition. At $139^{a}24$–35, Aristotle says:

T4
The study of definitions has five parts. For we must show either that it is not true at all to attribute also the account to that to which the name is truly attributed (for the definition of human must be true of every human), or that, although there is a genus, he has not placed it in the genus or has not placed it in the appropriate genus (for having placed it in the genus the person who defines must add the differentiae; for among the things in the definition the genus seems most of all to indicate the essence of what is being defined), or that the account is not proper (for the definition must be proper, as we also said previously), or see whether, although he has done all the things mentioned, he has neither defined nor expressed the what-it-is-to-be of what is being defined. It remains, besides the foregoing, to see whether he has defined but has not defined well.

The details of the arguments in this passage are analysed in the commentary *ad loc*. For the purposes of this introduction, it suffices to observe that T4 contains a list of different types of failure that can occur in a proposed definition. If the dialectician meets one of them, then he must apply the appropriate refutative strategy to reject the proposed account. Some of these strategies are not new: they are the result of the analyses of the commonplaces concerning the other predicables (in particular, genus and unique property). In certain cases, the dialectician must use the commonplaces pertaining to the other predicables in order to carry out a refutation of an unsuccessful definition.

The centrality of the predicable definition in the project of the *Topics* invites some general remarks. As is well known, the search for a definition is the leading theme of Socrates' philosophy. Plato's dialogues, especially the earlier ones, are the witnesses of the Socratic method. Socrates aims to test the knowledge of would-be experts in certain subjects, for example piety or virtue. The test consists in asking the interlocutor who professes knowledge about, say, piety to offer a definition of it. And much time is spent on the refutation of the interlocutor's attempts to come up with a successful definition. Although the methods and the settings of the Socratic dialogues are diffcrent from those described in the *Topics*, the centrality of definition remains the same. In the *Topics*, among the accounts that are analysed, criticized, and very often rejected, there are proposed definitions of certain ethical concepts discussed in some Platonic dialogues (e.g. courage, virtue, justice). But the dialectical exchange concerning definitions that is described in the *Topics* is structured and regimented by sets of precise rules. As a result, Aristotle's thorough examination of definitions discovers and theorizes about the necessary requirements that a successful definition must satisfy. Furthermore, it hints at the possibility that there be more than one type of successful definition (see chapter 13 of book VI) and that certain things cannot be defined according to the standard criteria (e.g. the things that are simultaneous by nature: see *Top.* VI.4, 142^{b}7–10, and commentary *ad loc.*).

VII. Types of Definition and their Rules

As previously seen, book I of the *Topics* contains a description of the predicable definition exactly as it does in the case of the other predicables. It is useful to remember that in chapter 5, 101^{b}37–102^{a}2, Aristotle says:

T5
A definition is an account that signifies the what-it-is-to-be. It is given either as an account in place of a word or as an account in place of an account (for it is possible to define something signified by an account).

These few lines have attracted the interest of many ancient and modern commentators, and they continue to do so. They offer us a fundamental insight into the nature of the definitions Aristotle is concerned with. His inquiry is about definitions revealing the essence of the thing to be defined (see commentary on *Topics* VI.1).[3] But the description in T5 is hardly sufficient to show the complexity of the rules concerning successful definitions. Book VI contains a discussion of these rules. For the most part, namely from chapter 1 to 12, book VI deals with standard Aristotelian definitions, namely definitions that are characterized by the presence, in the defining part, of the genus and differentia (one or more) of the thing to be defined. A standard Aristotelian definition is composed of a term indicating the thing to be defined, followed by the copula (the verb *einai* in one of its forms, which in ancient Greek could be understood), followed by the phrase (namely the defining expression) whose components signify the genus and one or more differentiae. By contrast, chapter 13 of book VI analyses commonplaces that point to an alternative understanding of the relation between the thing to be defined and its defining elements: the thing to be defined is conceived of as a whole and the defining elements are its parts. This leads Aristotle to explore certain aspects of the relation between parts and whole. One could label these definitions 'mereological'. Since the main part of book VI contains a discussion of standard definitions, in what follows I shall consider the most important results of this discussion. A detailed analysis of mereological definitions can be found in the commentary on chapter 13.

In the context of standard definitions, it is important to see what Aristotle's preferred method to obtain them is. His approach is grounded in division and classification: the defining

---

[3] Definitions revealing the essence of the thing to be defined are often called 'real definitions'. They are distinguished from, on the one hand, 'nominal definitions', which indicate what a term means and are non-committal about essences, and, on the other hand, 'factual definitions', which state true facts about the thing to be defined (the secondary literature on this is vast; see, e.g., LeBlond 1979; Robinson 1953; Modrack 2010; Charles 2000; Charles 2010; Karasmanis 2006).

part must indicate the position of the thing to be defined within a classification. For this reason, Aristotelian standard definitions could be labelled 'class definitions'. A method of division is theorized and used by Plato in several of his dialogues. Although it is generally believed that Aristotle rejects the Platonic method of division, the details of Aristotle's position are complex and often problematic. They can be reconstructed by analysing some passages of the *Topics* as well as some texts belonging to the *Prior* and *Posterior Analytics*. In the *Topics*, Aristotle conducts the first and fundamental revision of the method of division. The introduction of the concept of differentia makes a significant change in the method for accomplishing the division of the genus into its species. It also results in a modification of the way in which definitions are expressed. The criticism of Plato's method of division is particularly prominent in chapter 6 of *Topics* VI (the chapter entirely devoted to the analysis of the differentia). There Aristotle forbids the 'division of the genus by negation' when the genus is conceived of as a Platonic Idea. He says that if the genus is divided into species by two determinations, one of which is the negation of the other, some absurd consequences will follow with regard to the definitions thus obtained. In particular, it becomes difficult to understand whether the differentia has the same extension as the species it contributes to form. But what happens if the genus is conceived of (not as a Platonic Idea but) as an Aristotelian universal? The textual evidence is not sufficient to offer an exhaustive answer to this question (*Top.* VI.6, 143^{b}11–32; see commentary *ad loc.*).

Another issue emerging from Aristotle's discussion of the division of the genera concerns the way in which the genera are subordinated. In *Topics* VI.6, Aristotle formulates the rule that it is not possible for the same thing to be in two genera not containing one another. Similarly, in *Top.* IV.2, 121^{b}29–31, he states that 'when one species is under two genera, one is subordinate to the other'. The idea is that for any species there is only one upward chain of genera and this presupposes, among other things, that there is only one way to classify reality. We can see that in the background of Aristotle's rule for the subordination of the genera there is a very strong metaphysical assumption, which some might not want to share. For example, at the beginning of the *Politicus*, Plato explicitly acknowledges that the kind art can be divided in different ways so that the same species can fall under two different genera that are not subordinate (*Plt.* 258B7–21).

Furthermore, even though the introduction of the concept of differentia marks an important change in the method of division, it is difficult to understand what the ontological status of the differentia is. In some cases, according to Aristotle, 'every differentia seems to indicate a certain qualification' (*Top.* VI.6, 144^{a}22). But in the case where the items involved are relatives, the differentiae are relatives and not qualities (*Top.* VI.6, 145^{a}15). This creates a tension in the text, a tension that is important to explore and explain.

At the very beginning of *Prior Analytics* I.31, Aristotle claims that the division by genera is a weak deduction: 'what is to be proved is postulated, while what is deduced is always something higher up. First of all, then, this very point was overlooked by all those who used division'(46^{a}32–5). In other words, Aristotle is here criticizing the method of division by genera used by Plato as it is not able to demonstrate a definition. But is there really a method that allows us to demonstrate a definition? In the *Prior Analytics*, Aristotle admits that there cannot be demonstrations of definitions. Perhaps the method of division, as it is modified in the *Topics*, constitutes the best means we have in order to establish or analyse definitions.

VIII. The Notion of Causality in the *Topics*

Scholars often insist on a crucial difference between the account of definition offered in the *Topics* and that developed in the *Analytics*: their main concern is the notion of causality. They observe that, on the one hand, in the *Topics* Aristotle's search for an account does not explicitly appeal to causal notions. In *Top.* VI.4, 141^{a}24–31, Aristotle sets out the most fundamental criteria for a successful definition and says:

T6
Whether or not he has defined and expressed the what-it-is-to-be, however, we must consider from what follows. First, we must consider whether he has not made the definition through prior and more familiar things. For, since the definition is given for the sake of one's becoming familiar with what is said, and we become familiar not on the basis of just any things but on the basis of things that are prior and more familiar, as in demonstrations (for it is so in

every case of teaching and learning), it is evident that the person who does not define through such things has failed to define.

Thus, for a definition to be successful, its defining part must contain elements that are ontologically and epistemologically prior to what is to be defined.[4] On the other hand, in *Posterior Analytics* II, the search for definitions is closely connected to the search for causes. In *APo*. II.10, 93^{b}38–9, Aristotle discusses different types of definition and says that 'another definition is an account which shows *why* something exists'. Let us call it 'causal definition'. One of Aristotle's favourite examples of causal definition is to be found in *APo*. II.8, 93^{b}7–12:

T7
What is thunder? Extinction of fire in the clouds. Why does it thunder? Because the fire in the cloud is extinguished. Cloud C, thunder A, extinction of fire B. B holds of C, the clouds (the fire is extinguished in it), and A, noise, holds of B – and B is indeed the account of A, the first extreme.

This passage has received a lot of attention, and there is no need to spell out the intricate details.[5] For our purposes, it suffices to say that, according to Aristotle, a certain combination of the terms A ('thunder)', B ('extinction of fire'), and C ('clouds') allows us to read off the definition of thunder, namely noise of the extinction of fire in the clouds. Moreover, this definition tells us the cause of thunder: there is thunder because there is noise of the extinction of fire in the clouds.

The comparison between the definition's characteristics described in the *Topics* and those theorized in the *Analytics* has been the source of several interpretations. Let me summarize the most widespread options. First, it is possible to reconcile the views expressed in the two treatises. In the *Topics*, the concept of cause, as we find it in the *Analytics*, is simply understood. A definition that is successful according to the criteria of the *Topics* is a causal definition exactly like that in the *Analytics*.

---

[4] A detailed analysis of this passage can be found in the commentary *ad loc.*, where it will be shown that in this passage 'prior' and 'more familiar' introduce the concepts of ontological and epistemological priority.

[5] See, among others, Barnes 1993, *ad loc.*; Charles 2000, pp. 179–204; Charles 2010, pp. 286–328.

Although in the *Topics* the concept of cause is not explicitly expressed, it can be imported from the *Analytics*. Second, it is possible to reconcile the two treatises' views in a different way. The discussion of the definition in the *Topics* is preliminary to the causal model favoured in the *Analytics*. Third, it is not possible to reconcile the claims of the two treatises. Aristotle's project in the *Topics* is *purely* logical or dialectical, and the notion of causality is alien to it. A scientific and a metaphysical discourse must employ a conceptual apparatus which evokes the concept of cause. Some advocates of this interpretative option maintain that a work that deals with logic and dialectic *only* is less interesting than any treatise engaged in a causal project.

None of the three interpretative options is without difficulties. The first is speculative and lacks adequate textual support. Although in *Topics* I it is possible to find some terminology that is germane to the doctrine of the *Analytics* (e.g. the definition of syllogism in I.1, 100^{a}25–7 and that of demonstration in the immediately following lines, i.e. 27–9), in the central books there is no mention of the concept of cause and of a causal project. The second option has an advantage over the first as it avoids its main difficulty. It does not rely on an understood concept that is not textually supported. It opens up an attractive reading that tries to square two different standpoints in the Aristotelian treatment of definition. Nevertheless, it is unsatisfactory because it fails to outline the details of how exactly the discussion in the *Topics* is preliminary to the one in the *Analytics*. One might be tempted to identify the definition in the *Topics* with the nominal or shallow definition that is the starting point of a search for the essence and its causes. This exegetical move is, however, unsuccessful since the definition in the *Topics* aims at revealing the essence of the thing to be defined and, therefore, is not merely nominal. The third option outlines some promising suggestions that can be improved, but it has to be modified. In particular, if we want to make the third option a feasible interpretation, we must refrain from any negative assessment about logic and dialectic. It is true to say that the *Topics* is a treatise about logic and dialectic. For it is the place where Aristotle formulates his theory of the four predicables and individuates the logical relations holding between each of them and their subjects. Moreover, Aristotle's discussion is grounded on a dialectical exchange between a questioner and an answerer. Of course, there is much more. In the *Topics* we also find refined ontological analyses, for example arguments about priority and simultaneity (VI.4), the classification of opposites, and the discussion about relatives (VI.8 and 9). All of this is closely reminiscent of some ontological theses presented in the *Categories*. Still, the sort of ontology presupposed in the dialectical exchange cannot be overloaded, or else the answerer will not be able to accept it. In other words, the ontology of the *Topics* is loaded just to the point that can be accepted by the interlocutor.

Consider what happens with modern logic. It is an independent discipline that has reached an advanced and sophisticated level of development. It deals with ontological theses (e.g. the ontology of set theory) in a very moderate way. This, however, is not a good reason to criticize it. Modern logic has a degree of generality and flexibility that gives it the advantage of a wide application in many fields. I am not trying to say that the *Topics* should be considered on an equal footing with modern logic. But just as it would be unreasonable to criticize modern logic because it does not take a stand on many ontological questions, so also, analogously, it would be unreasonable to criticize the *Topics* on the grounds that it does not contain a discussion of metaphysical or scientific concepts.

IX. Some Prominent Themes Concerning Standard Definitions

By looking at the analysis of the commonplaces concerning standard (or class) definitions, it is easy to find some themes that Aristotle regards as especially important. These themes are often discussed more than once in chapters 1–12 of book VI. Three of them deserve to be mentioned: (1) ambiguity, (2) coordinates, and (3) relatives.

(1) AMBIGUITY

There is a passage in book VIII of the *Topics* which summarizes nicely the reasons why a dialectician must learn how to deal with ambiguities and other forms of unclear expressions such as metaphors.[6]

T8
(i) Among definitions, the hardest of all to deal with are those in which words have been used such that, first of all, it is unclear whether they are said simply or in many ways, and on the top of that one cannot even tell whether they have been used by the definer literally or metaphorically ... (158^b8–12)
(ii) In general, you should assume that when a problem is hard to deal with, either it requires a definition, or something is said in many ways or metaphorically, or it is not far from the starting points ... (158^b16–17)

In T8 (i), the focus is on definitions that are difficult to overthrow because they contain an ambiguity or a metaphor. There is a discussion of homonymy (i.e. of what is said in many ways) in *Top.* I.15, where Aristotle sketches possible strategies to deal with it in a dialectical and in a definitory context (see, in particular, lines 107^b6–7: 'But frequently, in definitions themselves, the homonym escapes notice; for this reason, you should also examine definitions'). In *Top.* VI.2, Aristotle puts forward the view that homonymy is strictly connected with the problem of lack of clarity in proposed definitions. Homonymies as well as metaphors make the accounts unclear. According to the view presented in VI.2, homonymies can be found in the defining part or in what is to be defined, whereas the examples of metaphors concern their presence in the defining part only. Aristotle introduces here a further element that undermines the proposed definitions' lack of clarity. He insists that the dialectician must look for the presence of something that is responsible for the account's obscurity, but it is neither a homonymy nor a metaphor (Aristotle does not specify what it is—for a detailed discussion of these points, see commentary on *Top.* VI.2). The last commonplace of *Top.* VI.6 contains an analysis of the ambiguity occurring in the expression 'deathless now' (*aphtharton nun*). Aristotle's discussion is extremely intricate and his argumentative steps are difficult to unfold. In certain cases, there is a complex combination of modal and temporal concepts, and the scope of the adverb 'now' (*aphtharton*) is unclear (see commentary on *Top.* VI.6, 145^b21–33).

---

[6] The division of the passage into two parts is mine: it helps to single out the points connected to present discussion.

Another discussion of homonymy can be found in *Top.* VI.10, 148^{a}23–148^{b}32 (see commentary *ad loc.*). In this case, Aristotle examines the effect of the presence not only of a homonymy but also of a synonymy in the proposed definitions. Aristotle's remarks in *Top.* VI.10 are in line with his well-known description of synonymy and homonymy at the beginning of the *Categories* (1.1^{a}1–2 and 1.1^{a}6–7). In the discussion of homonymy belonging to *Top.* VI.10, Aristotle does not distinguish between homonyms which are a matter of chance (*apo tuchês*) and those which are not, as he does in *EN* I.6, 1096^{b}26–7. Furthermore, one might wonder whether, in the context of things that are said in many ways, Aristotle hints at the discussion of cases of 'focal meaning' (aka 'core dependent association'; see in particular *Metaph.* IV.2, 1003^{a}33–^{b}15). There is no evidence, however, to support the idea that the concept of 'focal meaning' is at work in *Topics* VI. The discussion of ambiguity in the *Topics* is very different from that in the *Sophistici Elenchi*. On the one hand, in the *Topics*, Aristotle alerts the questioner and the answerer to the possibility that ambiguous expressions occur in some of their theses. He is especially interested in showing how an ambiguity can affect the dialectical exchange. There is no attempt to study more closely the cases of ambiguity. On the other hand, the project behind the *Sophistici Elenchi* is a classification of the fallacies that are used in eristic arguments to give the impression that the interlocutor is refuted. But a refutation obtained through a fallacy is only apparent. In this context, Aristotle studies more closely the cases of ambiguity and distinguishes between lexical and syntactic ambiguity.

In T8 (ii), Aristotle restates the difficulties arising from the use of ambiguous or metaphorical expressions. But another interesting point is made. Good and clear definitions are fundamental for the application of a successful refutative strategy. In other words, definitions play a central role as they are needed for the refutation of any type of problems, namely problems concerning not only the predicable definitions but also genus, unique property, and accident. This brings further support to the view (stated above) that the predicable definition occupies a central place in the *Topics*. As for the idea that it is difficult to argue when the thesis granted by the interlocutor 'is not far from the starting points', it does not seem to occur in book VI.

(2) COORDINATES

The Greek word for coordinates is *sustoicha*. They can be characterized as coordinate elements that are grouped together in virtue of the fact that they possess a common linguistic root. They are introduced in *Top.* II.9: according to Aristotle, 'just things and the just (*sc.* are coordinate) with justice, and courageous things and the courageous (*sc.* are coordinate) with courage' ($114^a 27$–9). There is an analysis of the commonplaces that are based on coordinates in *Top.* VI.9, $147^a 12$–22. The patterns of argument based on coordinates are important since they can be applied not only to definitions but also to the other predicables (unique property, genus, and accident). In the case of the predicable definition, Aristotle's view is that sometimes the proposed definition of coordinate$_1$ contains elements that are useful to define coordinate$_2$. Consider courage (which is our coordinate$_1$) and courageous (which is our coordinate$_2$). The idea is that in the definition of courage (coordinate$_1$) it is possible to find elements that enter into the definition of the courageous (coordinate$_2$). A more detailed discussion can be found in the Introduction to *Top.* VI.9, and in the commentary *ad loc*. In the *Topics*, coordinates are closely related to *ptôseis*. Literally, *ptôseis* means 'cases' and indicates grammatical cases. But Aristotle uses *ptôseis* also to refer to grammatical modifications of nouns or adjectives; for example, the adverb 'justly' is a grammatical modification derived from the adjective 'just'. Similarly, the adverb 'courageously' is a grammatical modification derived from the noun 'courage'. The analysis of a commonplace based on grammatical modifications can be found in *Top.* VI.10, $148^a 10$–13 (see Introduction to *Top.* VI.10, and commentary *ad loc*). The refutative strategies associated with the commonplaces based on coordinates and grammatical modifications are difficult to understand. The examples that are meant to clarify the strategies are problematic too. The discussion of the refutative strategies and the attempts to grasp the examples open up several questions. For example, does Aristotle use 'coordinates' to indicate cognate linguistic expressions or to refer to things whose names are cognate linguistic expressions? If he has in mind things and not names, what is the ontological relation between the things whose names are cognate linguistic expressions?

(3) RELATIVES

Relatives are the subject of discussion in several passages of *Topics* VI. Aristotle's analysis of the behaviour of relatives in a definitional context is complex and raises many interpretative difficulties. Perhaps some of these difficulties are due to Platonic antecedents. Here are the four examples representative of Aristotle's treatments of relatives in the *Topics*. They will highlight some important questions concerning this intricate subject.

The first example belongs to chapter 4 where Aristotle introduces and examines a fundamental requirement for successful definitions. This is the priority requirement and says that the defining expression must mention things that are prior to and more familiar than what is to be defined. But relatives represent a challenge for the priority requirement. At 142^{a}26–33, Aristotle's view is that there is no ontological priority between a relative and its correlative. Since ontological priority is likely to be the ground of epistemological priority (see *Top.*VI.4, 141^{b}28–34), it is not possible to say which (if any) is epistemologically prior. This suggests that either relatives are not definable at all or they are not definable in the standard way, namely in the way that respects the priority principle (see commentary *ad loc.*).

The second example is to be found in chapter 5 where there is a discussion of the commonplaces about the genus (not as a predicable on its own, but) as a component of a definition. At 142^{b}30–143^{a}11, Aristotle analyses the cases of relatives that are said in relation to several correlatives. He instructs the dialectician to 'consider whether, although what is being defined is said in relation to several things, he (*sc.* the interlocutor) has not given an account in relation to all' (142^{b}30–1). The context, the examples, and a parallel passage (*Top.*VI.8, 146^{a}33–146^{b}12; more on this passage below) indicate that here Aristotle is expressing himself in a very succinct way. Properly speaking, what is said in relation to several correlatives is the genus of what is being defined. This introduces a complication in the criteria that a successful definition ought to fulfil.

The third example is in chapter 8, 146^{a}33–146^{b}12 (see commentary *ad loc.*). For the most part, the commonplaces discussed in this chapter criticize proposed definitions of things with a relative genus. Aristotle analyses the particular case in which 'what is being defined is a relative either with respect to itself or with respect to the genus'. He instructs the dialectician to 'examine whether the (proposed) definition does not mention that in relation to which it (*sc.* what is being defined) is said, either itself or with respect to the genus'. As in chapter 5, the basis of the criticism consists in the fact that the proposed definition does not mention the appropriate correlatives. But, in chapter 8, Aristotle explicitly holds that if a correlative is left out, then the proposed definition will be incomplete, and hence unacceptable. A proposed definition is incomplete if an essential specification is left out. This suggests that a correlative (of the thing to be defined or of its genus) plays a role in the individuation of the essence. One, then, wonders whether in a definitional context the correlative has to be classified alongside the genus (as a part of it) or it plays the role of the differentia. Both these interpretative lines present problems and it remains unclear what the function of the correlative is in a definition.

The fourth example comes from the second part of chapter 9, which contains an analysis of commonplaces concerning opposites. In the background of this discussion, there is the Aristotelian classification of opposites (that is illustrated in the introduction to chapter 9). Aristotle holds that the relation between a relative and its correlative is a special case of opposition. Commonplaces about relatives occupy lines 147^a23–8: they are not easy to understand because of the syntactic intricacies of the Greek text (see commentary *ad loc.*). Even if we could find a solution for the syntactic difficulties, an interpretative problem remains. Aristotle does not seem to put forward a rule that allows the reconstruction of a valid refutative strategy. His proposed refutation is effective against a restricted number of cases, namely in the case of mathematical notions.

X. Structure and Interpretations of Book VI of the *Topics*

Book VI is entirely devoted to the study of commonplaces concerning definitions. It consists of 14 chapters and, in a way, is structured as a complete book. It begins with an introduction, namely chapter 1, where Aristotle outlines problems concerning the dialectical examination of proposed definitions. Some of these problems relate to the other predicables discussed in earlier books. In chapters 2–13, Aristotle analyses a large number of commonplaces that, for the most part, are refutative (the few exceptions are indicated in the commentary). Chapter 14 can be considered as the conclusion of the entire book, and its final line reads: 'Let this much, then, be said about definitions' ($151^{b}24$). For these reasons, one might be tempted to regard book VI as an independent and separate treatise. Some of its features, however, make it deeply connected with a specific context, namely with the theory of the predicables expounded in books II–V. Moreover, book VI contains several explicit references to arguments in earlier books. Aristotle often mentions commonplaces concerning accident, genus, and unique property; he then explains how they can be used or adapted in the analysis of proposed definitions. In other words, book VI can hardly be regarded as a self-contained treatise since it presupposes the theory of predicables, their relations to their subjects (e.g. coextensivity or inclusion), and some of their commonplaces. Here are some examples. At the beginning of chapter 1, Aristotle says: 'We must show ... that, although there is a genus, he (*sc.* the interlocutor) has not placed it in the genus or has not placed it in the appropriate genus ... or that the account is not proper (for the definition must be proper, as we also said previously)' ($139^{a}24$–8 and 31–2; see commentary *ad loc.*). These lines refer to the treatment of the genus and the unique property as we find them in books IV and V respectively. Then, in chapter 5, Aristotle puts forward an account of the genus as an element that must be mentioned in the defining part: in the background of this discussion, there is the study of the predicable genus carried out in book IV. In particular, at 143a12–3, Aristotle instructs the dialectician thus: 'Again, on the basis of the rule concerning the genera, consider whether what is being spoken about is not placed in the appropriate genus'. The connection between books IV and VI is confirmed in IV.1, $120^{a}12$-15: 'Next, we must go on to examine questions relating to genus and property. These are elements in the questions that relate to definitions, but dialecticians seldom address their inquiries to these by themselves.'

When we think about the long and elaborate discussions of the predicable definition, we cannot fail to ask whether Aristotle's aim is *theoretical*, i.e. providing the dialectician with the *theory* that lies behind any strategy aimed at refuting unsuccessful accounts, or *practical*, i.e. illustrating the *practice* of dialectic with a series of examples showing how to demolish the opponent's granted definitions. It is not always easy to distinguish between theory and practice. Nevertheless, the examination of book VI shows that, for the most part, it contains theoretical discussions individuating the crucial requirements for a successful definition, and it outlines strategies to be used in case these requirements are not met. Throughout this book, the formulations of the general commonplace rule precede a group of examples that illustrate it. Even though Aristotle does not always expand or fully elaborate on these examples, their function is to specify what should be done to avoid strategic mistakes. The practical advices are strictly dependent on the theory. The place to look for practical ways of conducting a dialectical exchange is book VIII.

Some authors interpret Aristotle's dialectic, as it is found in the *Topics* and in the *Sophistici Elenchi*, by adopting an approach that has some similarity with the modern pragmatic framework.[7] According to this reading, the most fundamental concept is that of common ground, namely 'a body of information that is presumed to be shared by the parties to a discourse'.[8] This type of approach has some advantages. By stressing the role of the context of an exchange, it seems to rely on a theory that is not philosophically loaded. It is an advantage for Aristotle's dialectic if the questioner can obtain the answerer's agreement without forcing upon him a specific view of how things are. This approach, however, also has limits: it cannot offer a complete and satisfactory interpretative model that replaces entirely the logical, semantic, and ontological theses which constitute the basis of other more 'traditional' interpretations. These perspectives are intrinsically tied to the way Aristotle develops his ideas. Although this approach cannot be applied in isolation, its use in tandem with a more logically and ontologically loaded perspective has an important benefit in that it promises to bridge the gap between the purely theoretical and the downward practical styles of interpretations mentioned above.

---

[7] King 2021: '*Via* the theory of sophistical refutations Aristotle recognizes something like common ground as a constitutive element of dialectical procedures of deduction. One way to approach the common ground of dialectical argumentation is through the theory of argument schemes, as it is done in the *Topics*' (p. 8).

[8] Stalnaker 2014, p. 2.

TRANSLATION[1]

CHAPTER 1

The study of definitions has five parts. For we must show either 139^{a}25 that it is not true at all to attribute also the account to that to which the name is truly attributed (for the definition of human must be true of every human), or that, although there is a genus, he has not placed it in the genus or has not placed it in the appropriate genus (for having placed it in the genus the person who defines must add the differentiae; for among the things in the 30 definition the genus seems most of all to indicate the essence of what is being defined), or that the account is not proper (for the definition must be proper, as we also said previously), or see whether, although he has done all the things mentioned, he has neither defined nor expressed the what-it-is-to-be of what is being defined. It remains, besides the foregoing, to see whether he has defined but has not defined well. 35

Whether, then, the account also is not true of that of which the name is true, we must examine on the basis of the commonplaces relative to the accident; for even there all of the examination turns on whether it is true or not true. For when we argue that the 139^{b}1 accident belongs, we mean that it is true; but when we argue that it does not belong, we mean that it is not true. Whether he has not placed it in the appropriate genus, or whether the given account is not proper, must be examined on the basis of the commonplaces we have spoken about relative to the genus and the unique 5 property.

It remains to say how we should proceed in case he has not defined or he has not defined well. First, then, it must be examined whether he has not defined well; for it is easier to do anything whatsoever than to do it well. It is, then, clear that the mistake about this is more frequent since it is a more difficult task. So that 10 the attack against this is easier than that against the other.

---

[1] Unless otherwise stated, the translation is based on the text of Brunschwig 2007.

There are two parts of the failure to define well. One consists in using an unclear expression (for the person who defines must use the clearest possible expression since the definition is given for the sake of becoming familiar), the second is whether the account he formulated goes beyond what is required; for every addition in the definition is superfluous. Again, each of the points mentioned is divided into several parts.

CHAPTER 2

One commonplace of the lack of clarity is to see whether what is mentioned is homonymous with something; for example, that coming to be is a passage to being and health is a balance between the hot and the cold. For passage is homonymous, and balance too. It is unclear, then, which of the two things indicated by the thing which is said in many ways he wants to say. Similarly also in case what is being defined is said in many ways, see whether he has spoken without distinguishing them. For it is unclear of which of the two things he has given the definition, and it is possible to argue captiously as if the account were not to apply to all the things of which he has given a definition. It is most of all possible to do this sort of thing if the homonymy escapes notice. But it is also possible to produce a deduction by distinguishing oneself in how many ways what is given in the definition is said. For if it is adequately formulated with respect to none of the ways in which it is said, it is clear that he would not have defined appropriately.

Another commonplace: see whether he has spoken metaphorically. For example, see whether <he has said that> knowledge is immovable or that the earth is a nurse or that temperance is consonance. For everything that is said metaphorically is unclear. But it is also possible to argue captiously against the person who has uttered a metaphor as if he had spoken properly. For the formulated definition will not be adequate, as in the case of temperance; for all consonance is in sounds. Furthermore, if consonance is the genus of temperance, the same thing will be in two genera not containing one another; for consonance does not contain virtue, nor does virtue contain consonance.

Furthermore, see whether he employs non-usual terms. For example, Plato called the eye 'eyebrow-shaded' or the widow spider 'kill-sting' or the marrow 'bone-generated'. For everything that is not customary is unclear.

But some things are said neither homonymously nor metaphorically [nor properly]; for example, the law is a measure or image of what is by nature just. Things of this sort are worse than the metaphor. For the metaphor makes what is indicated somehow familiar by virtue of a similarity (for all those who use metaphors use them according to a certain similarity), whereas a thing of this sort does not make it familiar. For there is no likeness in respect of which the law is a measure or image and it is not customary to call it so properly. Thus, if he says that properly the law is a measure or image, he speaks falsely (for an image is a thing whose coming about is through imitation; but this does not belong to the law). If it is not said properly, it is evident that he has spoken unclearly and worse than any of the things that are said metaphorically.

Furthermore, see whether the account of the contrary is not evident on the basis of what has been said; for the accounts that have been given well indicate in addition the contrary accounts too. Or see whether, being said by itself, it would not be evident of which thing it is the definition, but just as the works of the ancient painters, if nobody put an inscription on them, it was not recognized what each was.

CHAPTER 3

If, then, it is not formulated clearly, it is on the basis of things of this sort that we must conduct our examination. If, on the other hand, the definition he formulated goes beyond <what is needed>, first examine whether he has employed something that belongs to everything, either to beings in general or to the things falling under the same genus as what is being defined; for, necessarily, expressing this goes beyond <what is needed>. For the genus must separate it from the other things, whereas the differentia must separate it from the things in the same genus. But then what belongs to everything separates it from absolutely nothing, and what belongs to all the things falling under the same genus does not separate it from the things in the same genus, so that an addition of this sort is superfluous.

Or see whether, though what is added is proper, if it is removed, the remaining account also is proper and makes clear the essence. For example, in the account of human the addition of 'capable of knowledge' is superfluous; for, if this is removed, the remaining account also is proper and makes clear the essence. Generally speaking, everything is superfluous after whose removal the remainder makes clear what is being defined. Of this sort is also the definition of the soul if it is a 'number which moves itself'; for what moves itself also is the soul, just as Plato defined it. Or what is said is proper but does not make clear the essence, if 'number' is removed. Thus, in which of the two ways things are it is difficult to show clearly. But in all cases of this sort, we must use it to our advantage. For example, suppose that the definition of phlegm is 'the first fluid coming from food that is undigested'. For what is first is one, not many, so that the addition of 'undigested' is superfluous. For even when this has been removed, the remaining account will be proper, since it is not possible that both this and something else be the first thing coming from food. Or phlegm is not simply the first thing coming from food, but the first of the undigested ones, so that we must add 'undigested'; for if it is formulated in that way the account is not true, if indeed it is not the first of all.

Furthermore, see whether one of the things in the account does not belong to all the things falling under the same species; for an account of this sort has given a worse definition than those that use what belongs to all beings. For, in that way, if the remaining account is proper, the entire account also will be proper. For, in general, by adding something true to what is proper, the whole account comes to be proper. But if one of the things in the account does not belong to all the things falling under the same species, it is impossible for the whole account to be proper; for it will not counter-predicate with the thing. For example: two-footed terrestrial animal six feet high; for an account of this sort does not counter-predicate with the thing because six feet high does not belong to all the things falling under the same species.

Again, see whether he has mentioned the same thing several times; for example, by saying that appetite is desire for the pleasant. For every appetite is for the pleasant, so that what is the same as appetite also will be for the pleasant. Thus, the desire for the pleasant comes to be for the pleasant.[2] For there is no difference in saying appetite or desire for the pleasant, so that both of them will be for the pleasant. Or this is by no means absurd. For human is also two-footed, so that what is the same as human also will be two-footed. But two-footed terrestrial animal is the same as human, so that two-footed terrestrial animal is two-footed; but it is not the case that by virtue of this something 35 absurd results. For two-footed is not predicated of terrestrial animal (for if it were so, two-footed would be predicated twice of the same thing), but two-footed is said of two-footed terrestrial 141ª1 animal; so that two-footed is predicated only once. Similarly also in the case of appetite; for being for the pleasant is not predicated of desire but of the whole, so that there, too, the predication occurs once. It is not uttering the same name twice that is one 5 of the absurdities, but predicating the same thing of something several times, as Xenocrates says that prudence is definitory and contemplative of beings. For being definitory is a form of being contemplative, so that he says the same thing twice by adding again 'and contemplative'. Similarly also for all those who say 10 that cooling is a privation of natural heat; for every privation concerns what belongs naturally, so that the addition of 'natural' is superfluous, but it was sufficient to say that it is privation of heat since privation on its own makes it familiar that it is said of what is naturally.

Again see whether, although the universal has been mentioned, 15 he has added the particular as well. For example, if he <has defined> equity <as> a diminution of what is advantageous and just; for the just is something advantageous: so that having mentioned the universal,[3] he has added the particular. Also see whether he has said that medicine is knowledge of things that are healthy for an animal and a human, or that law is an image of 20 things that are fine and just by nature. For the just is something fine, so that he says the same thing several times.

---

[2] Following Brunschwig 2007, I accept the deletion of ὅρος τῆς ἐπιθυμίας at 140ᵇ29–30: see 'Notes on the Text' ad loc.

[3] Following Bekker 1831, Waitz 1846, and Strache and Wallies 1923, at 141ª18 I omit the γὰρ printed by Ross 1958 and Brunschwig 2007: see 'Notes on the Text' ad loc.

CHAPTER 4

Whether, then, a person has defined well or not, we must consider on the basis of these and similar points. Whether or not he has defined and expressed the what-it-is-to-be, however, we must consider from what follows.

First, we must consider whether he has not made the definition through prior and more familiar things. For, since the definition is given for the sake of one's becoming familiar with what is said, and we become familiar not on the basis of just any things but on the basis of things that are prior and more familiar, as in demonstrations (for it is so in every case of teaching and learning), it is evident that the person who does not define through such things has failed to define. Or else there will be several definitions of the same thing. For it is clear that the person who defines through prior and more familiar things has also defined, and in a better way, so that both will be definitions of the same thing. But this kind of thing does not seem to be the case; for each of the things that are has one being-just-what-it-is. So that, if there will be several definitions of the same thing, the being of the thing defined will be the same as just what is indicated in each of the two definitions. But these are not the same, since the definitions are different. It is clear, then, that the person who has not defined through prior and more familiar things has failed to define.

The claim that the definition is not formulated through more familiar things may be taken in two ways: either if it is from things that are unqualifiedly more unfamiliar or from things that are more unfamiliar to us; for both ways are possible. What is prior is unqualifiedly more familiar than what is posterior, as for example a point than a line, a line than a plane, and a plane than a solid, just as also a unit than a number, since it is prior to and a principle of every number; similarly also a letter than a syllable. But sometimes things work out with us in the reverse: for the solid most of all falls under perception, the plane more than the line, a line more than a point. For the majority becomes familiar with such things first: for they can be grasped by any ordinary intelligence, the others by an accurate and extraordinary one.

In an unqualified way then it is better to try to become familiar with posterior things through prior ones, for this is more scientific. For those who are not able to become familiar through things of this sort, however, it is perhaps necessary that the account be made through things that are familiar to them. Among such definitions are that of the point and that of the line and that of plane; for they all indicate prior things through posterior ones. For they say that the first is the limit of the line, the second of the plane, the last of the solid. It should not escape notice that those who define in this way cannot indicate the what-it-is-to-be of the thing defined, unless the same thing happens to be both more familiar to us and more familiar unqualifiedly, since the person who defines well must define through the genus and the differentiae and these are among the things unqualifiedly more familiar than and prior to the species. For the genus and the differentia carry the species to destruction with them, so that these are prior to the species. They are also more familiar: for when the species becomes familiar necessarily the genus and the differentia also become familiar (for the person who becomes familiar with human becomes also familiar with animal and terrestrial), but when the genus or the differentia becomes familiar it is not necessary that the species should also become familiar, so that the species is more unfamiliar. Furthermore, those who state that definitions of this sort, namely those made from things familiar to each person, are in accordance with the truth will find themselves saying that there are many definitions of the same thing. For different things happen to be more familiar to different people and not the same for all, so that a different definition would have to be given with respect to each person, since the definition must be made from things that are more familiar to each person. Furthermore, different things are more familiar to the same people at different times: at first perceptible things are more familiar, but then when they have become more accurate the reverse happens, so that—according to those who say that the definition must be given through things more familiar to each— not even to the same person must one always give the same definition.

It is clear, then, that we must not define through things of this sort, but through those that are more familiar unqualifiedly; for only in this way will the definition always come to be one and the same. But perhaps what is familiar unqualifiedly is not what is familiar to all but what is familiar to those whose thinking is in a good condition, just as what is healthy unqualifiedly is what is healthy for those whose body is in a good condition. We must, then, make each of the things of this sort precise and use them in our discussions in an advantageous way. But it is possible to destroy the definition in a way that will meet with most agreement if someone happens to have made his account neither from what is more familiar unqualifiedly nor from what is more familiar to us.

One way, then, of failing to give a definition through more familiar things is to indicate prior things through posterior ones, as we said before.[4] Another way is if the account of what is at rest and what is definite is given us through what is indefinite and what is in motion: for what remains still and what is definite are prior to what is indefinite and in motion.

There are three ways of failing to give a definition on the basis of prior things. First, if he has defined the opposite through its opposite, for example good through evil; for opposites are simultaneous by nature. Moreover, some people think that the knowledge of both opposites is one and the same, so that the one is not more familiar than the other. We must not fail to notice that perhaps some things cannot be defined otherwise, for example the double without the half, and all the things that are called relatives in themselves. For all such things to be is the same as to be in a certain relation to something so that it is impossible to become familiar with the one without the other. For this reason, it is necessary that in the account of the one the other also be included. We must, then, become familiar with all such things and use them as it seems to be advantageous.

Another way of failing to define is if he has used the thing that is being defined: it escapes notice when the name he uses is not the same as that of what is being defined, for example, if he has defined the sun as a star that appears by day. For the person who uses day uses sun. In order for such cases to be detected, you must replace the name with the account, for example by saying that the day is the passage of the sun over the earth. For it is clear that the person who has mentioned the passage of the sun over the earth has mentioned the sun, so that the person who uses day uses sun.

---

[4] Deleting the comma between δηλοῦν and καθάπερ (see 'Notes on the Text' ad loc.).

Again, see whether he has defined one coordinate element of a division by means of the other, for example odd as greater by a unit than even. For the coordinate elements of a division coming from the same genus are by nature simultaneous: and odd and even are coordinate elements of a division—for they are both differentiae of number.

Similarly, also see whether he has defined what is superior through subordinate things, for example even number as that which is divisible into halves or the good as the possession of virtue. For into halves is taken from two, which is an even number, and virtue is a good, so that the former are subordinate to the latter. Furthermore, the person who uses the subordinate necessarily uses this too. For the person who uses *virtue* uses *good*, since virtue is a good; similarly also the person who uses *into halves* uses *even*, since to divide into halves means to divide into two and two is even.

CHAPTER 5

To speak in general, then, one commonplace[5] is not to have made the account on the basis of prior and more familiar things, and the parts of it are those mentioned. A second one is if, although the thing is in a genus, it is not placed in a genus. An error of this sort occurs in all cases in which the what-it-is is not laid down at the forefront of the account, for example the definition of body as that which has three dimensions, or if someone has defined human as that which knows how to count; for he has not mentioned which being has three dimensions or which being knows how to count. But the genus is meant to signify the what-it-is and is put forward as first among the things said in the definition.

Furthermore, consider whether, although what is being defined is said in relation to several things, he has not given its account in relation to all, for example if literacy <is defined as> knowledge of writing what is dictated; for its being of reading is also needed. For the person who gives an account of it as of writing has defined

---

[5] Retaining τόπος with Ross (see 'Notes on the Text' *ad loc.*).

it no more than the one who gives an account of it as of reading,[6] so that neither of them has, but the person who says both these things has, since it is not possible that there be several definitions of the same thing. In some cases, then, things are truly as we have said, but in others they are not, for example in the case of things that are not said in themselves in relation to both things, as medicine is said of the production of health and disease; for of the one it is said in itself, of the other incidentally. For the production of disease is without qualification alien to medicine. So that the person who gives an account in relation to both things has defined no more than the person who gives it in relation to one of the two—but perhaps even worse, since anyone among the rest is also capable of producing disease.

Furthermore, consider whether he has given an account not in relation to the better but to the worse, if there are several things in relation to which what is being defined is said; for every instance of knowledge and every capacity seem to be of the best.

Again, on the basis of the rules concerning the genera, consider whether what is being spoken about is not placed in the appropriate genus, as was mentioned before. Furthermore, consider whether he speaks omitting the genera, for example saying that justice is a state productive of equality or distributive of what is equal; for the person who defines in this way omits virtue. Then, having left out the genus of justice, he does not state the what-it-is-to-be; for the essence of each thing involves the genus. This is the same as failing to put it in the proximate genus; for the person who puts it in the proximate genus has mentioned all the ones above, since all the genera above are predicated of those below. So that he must either put it in the proximate genus or add to the genus above all the differentiae through which the proximate genus is defined; for in this way he would have left out nothing but would have mentioned the genus below with a phrase instead of a name. But the person who has mentioned only the genus above on its own does not mention the genus below as well: for he who has mentioned plant does not mention tree.

---

[6] For a discussion of the textual variants see 'Notes on the Text' *ad loc.*

CHAPTER 6

Again concerning the differentiae, it must be also similarly examined whether he has said the differentiae of the genus. For if he has not defined with the proper differentiae of the thing, or even has mentioned something such that it is totally impossible for it to be the differentia of anything, for example animal or substance, it is clear that he has not defined; for those mentioned are the differentiae of nothing. But it must also be seen whether there is something coordinate with the differentia that is mentioned. For if there is not, it is clear that the one mentioned would not be a differentia of the genus; for every genus is divided by coordinate differentiae, just as animal by footed and winged and aquatic [and two-footed][7]. Or see whether there is a coordinate differentia, but it is not true of the genus. For it is clear that none of them would be a differentia of the genus; for all the coordinate differentiae are true of their appropriate genus. Similarly see also whether it is true of it but adding it to the genus does not make a species. For it is clear that this would not be a [species-making] differentia of the genus. For every [species-making] differentia together with the genus makes a species. But if this is not a differentia, neither is the one that has been mentioned, since it is an element of a division coordinate with this.

Furthermore, see whether he divides the genus by negation, just as those who define line to be a breadthless length; for it indicates nothing else than that it does not have breadth. Then it will follow that the genus partakes of the species; for every length is either breadthless or having breadth, since of everything either the affirmation or the negation is true, so that also the genus of the line, which is length, will be either breadthless or having breadth. Breadthless length, however, is the account of a species; but similarly also length having breadth. For breadthless and having breadth are differentiae; but the account of the species comes from the differentia and the genus, so that the genus would admit the account of the species. Similarly, also it would admit that of the differentia, since one or other of the differentiae mentioned is necessarily predicated of the genus. The commonplace just mentioned is

---

[7] Retaining ἐνύδρῳ and deleting καὶ τῷ δίποδι (see 'Notes on the Text' *ad loc.*).

helpful against those who posit that Ideas exist. For if length itself exists, how will it be predicated of the genus that it has breadth or that it is breadthless? For one of them must be true of every length, if it is going to be true of the genus. But this does not follow; for there are both breadthless lengths and lengths which have breadth. So that the commonplace will be helpful only against those who say that each genus is one in number. Those who posit Ideas do this: for they say that length itself and animal itself are genera.

Perhaps in some cases it is necessary that the person who defines uses a negation, for example in the case of privations. For being blind is not having sight when it is natural to have it. But it makes no difference whether one divides the genus by a negation or by an affirmation which is such that it is necessarily opposed as a coordinate element of a division to a negation; for example if he has defined length as having breadth; for not having breadth, and nothing else, is opposed as a coordinate element of a division to having breadth, so that again the genus is divided by negation.

Again, see whether he has given the species as a differentia, just as those who define insult as insolence with mockery; for mockery is a certain insolence, so that insolence is not a differentia but a species.

Furthermore, see whether he has mentioned the genus as a differentia, for example if he says that virtue is a state that is good or noble. For the good is a genus of virtue. Or rather the good is not a genus but a differentia, if it is true that it is not possible for the same thing to be in two genera which do not contain one another. For the good does not contain state nor does state contain the good; for not every state is a good, and not every good is a state, so that both of them will not be genera. Therefore, if state is a genus of virtue, it is clear that the good is not a genus, but rather a differentia. Furthermore, state indicates what virtue is, but the good indicates not what it is but of what sort it is; the differentia, however, seems to indicate a certain qualification.

See also whether the given differentia indicates not a certain qualification but a this so-and-so; for every differentia seems to indicate a certain qualification.

Examine also whether the differentia belongs to the thing defined incidentally. For no differentia is among the things that belong incidentally, as neither is the genus; for it is not possible that the differentia belongs and does not belong to something.

38

Furthermore, if the differentia or the species or one of the things below the species is predicated of the genus, no definition would have been given. For it is not possible that one of the things mentioned be predicated of the genus, since the genus is said most widely of all. Again, see whether the genus is predicated of the differentia; for the genus seems to be predicated not of the differentia, but of the things of which the differentia is predicated; for example, animal is predicated of human and of ox and of the other footed animals, not of the differentia itself that is said of the species. For if animal was predicated of each of the differentiae, many animals would be predicated of the species; for the differentiae are predicated of the species. Furthermore, if they are animals, all differentiae will be either species or individuals; for each animal is either a species or an individual.

Similarly, it must also be examined whether the species or something subordinate to the species is predicated of the differentia; for this is impossible since the differentia is said more widely than the species. Furthermore, it will follow that the differentia is a species, if one of the species is predicated of it; for if human is predicated of it, it will be clear that human would be the differentia. Again, see whether the differentia is not prior to the species; for the differentia must be posterior to the genus, but prior to the species.

Examine also whether what is mentioned as a differentia is of another genus, which neither is contained in nor contains the other; for the same differentia does not seem to be of two genera which do not contain one another. Otherwise, it will follow that the same species is also in two genera which do not contain one another. For each differentia brings in its appropriate genus, just as footed and two-footed bring animal in with themselves. So that if each of the genera is also <said> of that of which the differentia is <said>, it is clear that the species is in two genera which do not contain one another. Or rather, it is not impossible that the same differentia be of two genera which do not contain one another; but it must be added 'when they are not both under the same thing'. For footed animal and winged animal are genera not containing one another, and two-footed is a differentia of both of them. So that it must be added 'when they are not both under the same thing'; for these are both under animal. But it is also clear that it is not necessary that the differentia brings the appropriate genus every time, since it is possible for the same thing to belong to two genera which do not contain one another, but it is necessary that it brings with itself only one of the two as well as all those above it, just as two-footed brings winged or footed animal in with itself.[8]

See also whether he has given being-in-something as a differentia of a substance; for a substance does not seem to differ from a substance in its being somewhere. Hence to those who divide animal by footed and aquatic they raise the criticism that footed and aquatic indicate somewhere. Or in these cases they do not raise the criticism correctly; for aquatic indicates neither in something nor somewhere, but a certain qualification. For even if it is on dry land it is still aquatic; in like manner concerning the land-animal, even if it is in water, it will be a land-animal, not aquatic. But still, if ever the differentia indicates being-in-something, it is clear that he would have made a mistake.

Again, see whether he has given the affection as a differentia: for every affection when it is increased too much disrupts the substance, whereas the differentia does not do such a thing. For the differentia seems rather to preserve that of which it is a differentia, and it is without qualification impossible for each thing to be without its appropriate differentia; for if it is not footed, it will not be a human. But speaking without qualification, as for the things with respect to which the possessor alters, none of them is its differentia; for all the things of this sort when they are increased too much disrupt the substance. So that if he has given such a thing as a differentia, he has made a mistake: for we do not alter at all with respect to the differentia.

See also whether in the case of one of the relatives he has not given the differentia relatively to another. For the differentiae of relatives are also relatives, just as those of knowledge are too. For they are said to be speculative [and practical] and productive; each of these indicates a relative. For it is speculative of something and productive of something [and practical with respect to something].

Examine also whether the person who defines gives each relative in relation to its natural correlative. For in some cases

---

[8] Retaining all the occurrences of 'animal' (ζῷον) *pace* Brunschwig.

[each relative] they can be used only in relation to a natural correlative, and nothing else, but in other cases also in relation to something else; for example, the eye can be used only in relation to seeing, but a strigil can be used also if one wants to draw liquid. But still if someone has defined it as a tool relative to drawing water, he has made a mistake; for it is not its natural correlative. But a definition of the natural correlative is 'that for which the prudent person [in so far as he is prudent] and the knowledge appropriate to each thing would use it'.

Or see whether he has not given an indication of the first when it happens to be said in relation to several things, for example wisdom as a virtue of human or soul but not of the reasoning faculty. For wisdom is a virtue of the reasoning faculty first; for it is with respect to this that both the soul and a human are said to think.

Furthermore, if that of which the defined thing has been said to be an affection or a disposition or anything else is not able to receive it, he has made a mistake; for every disposition and every affection naturally come to be in that of which it is a disposition or an affection, just as knowledge too in a soul, since it is a disposition of a soul. But sometimes they make mistakes in cases of this sort, for example those who say that sleep is a sense-perception inability, and perplexity is an equality of contrary arguments, and pain is a forced separation of naturally conjoined parts. For sleep does not belong to sense-perception (but it should, if it is a sense-perception inability); similarly, perplexity does not belong to [contrary] arguments nor pain to naturally conjoint parts; for inanimate things will suffer pain, if pain is present in them. Of this sort is also the definition of health, if it is a due proportion of hot and cold things; for it will be necessary that things that are hot and cold are healthy. For the due proportion of each belongs to those things of which it is a due proportion, so that health would belong to them. Furthermore, the result for those who define in this way is that they posit the product for the producing factor or the other way round. For the separation of naturally conjoint parts is not pain but is productive of pain; and the sense-perception inability is not sleep, but one is productive of the other: for either we fall asleep because of the inability or we are unable to perceive because of the sleep. Similarly also, the equality of contrary arguments would seem to be productive of perplexity; for when we give consideration to both arguments, everything appears to us to be alike in accordance with each one, we are perplexed as to which of the two we should do.

Furthermore, with regard to every period of time, consider whether somewhere there is a discrepancy, for example if the immortal has been defined as an animal that is deathless now; for the animal now deathless will be now immortal. Or in a case of this sort the result does not follow: for to be deathless now is ambiguous. For it means either that it has not died now, or that it is not possible that it dies now, or that it is now such as never to die. Thus, when we say that an animal is deathless now, we say this, that now an animal is such that it never dies. This, however, was the same as the immortal, so that it does not follow that now this is immortal. But still, if it follows that what is given according to the account belongs now or previously, whereas what is given according to the name does not belong, it would not be the same thing. We must use, then, this commonplace as it is said.

CHAPTER 7

It must also be examined whether what is defined is said more according to some other account than according to the given one, for example if justice <has been defined as> a capacity that is distributive of what is equal. For the person who chooses to distribute what is equal is more just than the one who has the capacity, so that justice would not be a capacity distributive of what is equal; for then the one who has the capacity to distribute what is equal would be the most just.

Furthermore, examine whether the thing admits of the more, but what is given according to the account does not admit of it, or, conversely, examine whether what is given according to the account admits of it, but the thing does not. For both of them must admit of it or neither, if indeed what is given according to the account is the same as the thing in question. Furthermore, examine whether both admit of the more, but they do not increase at the same time. For example, if love is a desire for intercourse. For the person who loves more does not desire intercourse more, so that they do not become more at the same time; but they must if they were the same.

Furthermore, if two things were put forward, examine whether what is given according to the account is said less of that of which the <defined> thing is said more; for example, if fire is a body with the finest parts. For the flame is more fire than light is, but the flame is less a body with the finest parts than light. But both must have belonged more to the same thing, if they had been the same. Again, examine whether the one belongs equally to both the things put forward, but the other does not belong to both equally but to one of them more.

Furthermore, examine whether in the case of what is relative to two things he gives the definition according to one of them; for example, what is beautiful is that which is pleasant to the eye or to the ear, and a being is what has the capacity of being acted upon or acting; for the same thing will be pleasant and not pleasant at the same time, and similarly it will be a being and not a being. For what is pleasant to the ear will be the same as what is beautiful, so that what is not pleasant to the ear will be the same as what is not beautiful; for the same things are opposed to the same, and what is not beautiful is opposed to what is beautiful, and what is not pleasant to the ear to what is pleasant to the ear. It is clear then that what is not pleasant to the ear is the same as what is not beautiful. If then something is pleasant to the eye but not to the ear, it will be both beautiful and not beautiful; similarly, we will also show that the same thing is both a being and not a being.

Furthermore, examine whether there is some discrepancy when he produces the accounts instead of the names of the genera and differentiae and all the other things given in the definitions.

CHAPTER 8

If what is being defined is a relative either with respect to itself or with respect to the genus, examine whether the definition does not mention that in relation to which it is said, either itself or with respect to the genus; for example, if he has defined knowledge as incontrovertible belief or wish as painless desire. For the substance of each relative is in relation to something else, since for each of the relatives to be was precisely the same as to be in a certain relation to something. Then he ought to have said that knowledge is belief in a knowable and that wish is desire for a good. Similarly also, if he has defined literacy as knowledge of letters; for in a definition he should have given either that in relation to which the thing itself is said or that, whatever it is, in relation to which the genus is said. Or see whether a thing said in relation to something is not defined in relation to the end: in each thing the end is the best or that for the sake of which all other things are. One must therefore mention either the best or what comes last, for example appetite is not for something pleasant but for pleasure, since it is for the sake of this that we choose something pleasant.

Examine also whether that in relation to which he has given the account is a becoming or an activity; since none of the things of this sort is an end. For to have been in activity and to have become are more an end than to become and to be in activity. Or is such a thing not true in all cases? For the majority perhaps wish to feel pleasure rather than to have ceased to feel pleasure, so that they would make the end to be in activity rather than to have been in activity.

Again, in some cases, see whether he has not distinguished the quantity or quality or place or <has not distinguished> according to the other differentiae; for example, an honour-lover is the one who desires honour of a certain quality and in a certain quantity. For all desire honour, so that it is not enough to say that an honour-lover is the one who desires honour, but we must add the differentiae mentioned. Similarly also, a money-lover is the one who desires money in a certain quantity, or an uncontrolled person is the one who is concerned with a pleasure of a certain quality; for it is not the one who is overcome by whatever pleasure that is called an uncontrolled person, but the one who is overcome by a certain one. Or again, see whether they define night as shade of the earth, or earthquake as movement of the earth, or clouds as condensation of the air, or wind as movement of the air; for we must add quantity and quality and place and 'by virtue of what'. Similarly also, in the other cases of this sort; for if he leaves aside any differentia whatsoever, he does not state the what-it-is-to-be. We must always argue against the deficiency. For it is not when the earth is moved in any way whatsoever nor when any quantity whatsoever of it is moved that there is an earthquake; similarly, it is not when the air is moved in any way whatsoever nor when any quantity whatsoever of it is moved that there is wind.

Furthermore, in the case of desires, and in all the other cases where it applies, see whether 'apparent' is not added; for example, <if he says> that wish is desire for a good or appetite is desire for something pleasant, but not for an apparent good or what is apparently pleasant. For often those who desire are not aware of what is good or pleasant, so that it is not necessary for it to be good or pleasant but to be apparently so. Then the given account should also have been of this sort. Even if he gives an account of what has been said, the person who posits that there are Ideas must be led to the Forms. For there are no Ideas of anything apparent, and the Form seems to be said in relation to the Form, for example appetite-itself is for the pleasant-itself and wish-itself is for good-itself. So that it will be neither for an apparent good nor for something apparently pleasant; for it is absurd that there be an apparent good, or pleasant, itself.

CHAPTER 9

Furthermore, if the definition is of a possession, examine the possessor, while if it is of the possessor, examine the possession; similarly also, in other cases of this sort. For example, if the pleasant thing is precisely what is beneficial, then the person who feels pleasure will be benefitted. To speak generally, in definitions of this sort the person who defines happens, in a way, to define more than one thing. For the person who defines knowledge defines, in a way, ignorance too; similarly, he defines also what has knowledge and what lacks knowledge, and to know and to be ignorant. For once the first has become clear, in a way the others also become clear. Then in all cases of this sort we must examine whether there is some incongruity by using as elements the rules derived from contraries and coordinates.

Furthermore, in the case of the relatives, examine whether he gives an account of the species as relative to a particular case of that relative to which he gives an account of the genus. For example, if belief is relative to believable, a particular belief is relative to a particular believable, and if multiple is relative to fraction, a particular multiple is relative to a particular fraction; for if he has not given the account in this way, it is clear that he has made a mistake.

See also whether the account of the opposite is the opposite account, for example the account of the half is the opposite of that of the double; for if double is what exceeds by an equal amount, half is what is exceeded by an equal amount. Likewise also in the case of the contraries; for the contrary account of the contrary will be based on one combination of the contraries. For example, if the beneficial is what produces a good, the harmful will be what produces an evil or what destroys a good; for one of these is necessarily contrary to what was originally specified. Then if neither of them is contrary to what was originally specified, it is clear that neither of those given later would be an account of the contrary, so that the account originally given was not given correctly. Since some of the contraries are said by privation of the other, for example inequality seems to be the privation of equality (for non-equal things are called unequal), it is clear that the contrary said by privation is necessarily defined through the other, whereas the other is not defined through the contrary said by privation; for it would follow that each of the two is known through both. Then in the case of the contraries we must look for this sort of mistake, for example if someone has defined equality as being the contrary of inequality; for he is defining through the contrary which is said by privation. Furthermore, the person who gives a definition in this way necessarily uses the very thing that is being defined. This becomes clear if the account is substituted for the name; for there is no difference between saying inequality or privation of equality. Then equality will be the contrary of privation of equality, so that he would have used the very thing. But if neither of the contraries is said by privation and the account has been given in the same way, for example good as the contrary of evil, it is clear that evil will be the contrary of good; for the account of contraries of this sort must be given in the same way. So that again it follows that he used the very thing that is being defined; for good is contained in the account of evil. So that if good is the contrary of evil and evil is in no way different from the contrary of good, the good will be the contrary of the contrary of the good. It is then clear that he has used the very thing.

Furthermore, see whether in giving the account of what is said by privation he has failed to give that of which it is a privation, for example the possession or the contrary or whatever the privation is of. See also whether he has failed to add that in which it is by nature, either at all or the first thing in which it is by nature. For example, if he says that ignorance is privation but he fails to say 'privation of knowledge', or he has failed to add that in which it is by nature, or, although he has added it, he has not given the first thing in which it is by nature; for example, if he has not said 'in the rational part' but 'in a human' or 'in the soul'. For if he has failed to do any of these things, he has made a mistake. Similarly also, if he fails to say that blindness is privation of sight in the eye; for the person who gives a good account of the what-it-is must also give what the privation is of and what the thing which has suffered privation is.

See also whether, although it is not said by privation, he has defined it by means of privation; for example, even regarding ignorance, a mistake of this sort would seem to occur in the case of those who say ignorance by negation. For it does not seem that what does not possess knowledge is ignorant, but rather what errs; for this reason, we do not say that inanimate beings or children are ignorant. So that ignorance is not said by privation of knowledge.

CHAPTER 10

Furthermore, see whether similar modifications in the account apply to similar modifications in the name; for example, if beneficial <is defined as> productive of health, beneficially <will be defined as> productively of health and he who has been beneficial <will be defined as> he who has produced health.

Examine also whether the definition stated applies to the Idea. For in some cases it does not happen, for example when Plato defines by adding 'mortal' to the definitions of animals; for the Idea, e.g. human-itself, will not be mortal, so that the account will not apply to the Idea. And, in general, in the cases where 'capable of affecting' or 'capable of being-affected' is added, the definition necessarily is at variance with the Idea; for the Ideas seem to be incapable of being affected and are unchangeable. Arguments of this sort are equally helpful beyond such cases.

Furthermore, see whether he has given one common account of all the things that are said by homonymy; for things of which there is one account with respect to the name are synonyms. So that the given definition belongs to none of the things falling under the name if it applies to the same extent to every homonym. This was also the case with Dionysius' definition of life if indeed it is 'a change natural to and present in a food-sustained kind'; for this belongs to animals no more than to plants. Life, however, does not seem to be said with respect to a single form, but one type of life seems to belong to animals, and a different one to plants. It is possible that he has intentionally given the definition in this way, as if life were a synonym and it were said in every case with respect to a single form. But nothing prevents it being the case that, even though he saw the homonymy and wished to give the definition of one of the two, he has inadvertently given, not an account proper to one, but an account common to both. But none the less, whichever of the two he has done, he has made a mistake. Since some of the homonyms escape notice, in setting the question we must use them as synonyms (for the definition of the one will not apply to the other, so that he will not seem to have defined in the ordinary way; for it must apply to every synonym), whereas in answering we must ourselves draw the distinction. Since some answerers say, on the one hand, that the synonym is a homonym when the account given does not apply to everything, and, on the other hand, that the homonym is a synonym if it applies to both, we must agree beforehand on such matters or it must be established by a preliminary deduction that it is a homonym or a synonym, whichever of the two it might be; for they are more prepared to agree when they do not foresee what will result. If in the case where there is no agreement someone says that the synonym is a homonym due to the fact that the account given does not apply also to this, examine whether the account of this applies to the others too; for it is clear that it would be synonymous with the others. Otherwise there will be several definitions of the others; for the two accounts with respect to the name apply to them, both the first that has been given and the second. Again, if someone who has defined one of the things said in many ways denies that it is a homonym although the account does not apply to all, but denies that the name applies to all since neither does the account, we must respond to such a person that we must use traditional and common language and not change things of this sort, even though in certain cases we must not speak like the many.

CHAPTER 11

If a definition of something complex has been given, examine whether, by taking away the account of one or the other of the elements of the complex, the remaining account is also of what remains. For otherwise, it is clear that neither is the whole account of the whole. For example, if he has defined 'finite straight line' as 'limit of a surface having limits whose intermediate point intercepts the view of the limits', and if the account of 'finite line' is 'limit of a surface having limits', the rest, viz. 'whose intermediate point intercepts the view of the limits', must be the account of 'straight'. But the infinite line has neither a middle point nor limits, yet it is straight, so that the remaining account is not of what remains.

Furthermore, if what is being defined is a composite, see whether the account that was given has an equal number of elements as what is being defined. An account is said to be 'having an equal number of elements' when the components are exactly as many as the names and verbs in the account. For necessarily in cases of this sort there is a replacement of the names themselves, either of all or of some, since he has not mentioned more names now than before. But the person who defines must give an account instead of the names, preferably of all, but otherwise of the majority. For in this way, even in the case of simples, the person who substitutes the name, for example cloak in place of mantle, would have defined.

Furthermore, a still greater mistake occurs if he has made the substitution with even more unfamiliar names, for example bright mortal instead of white person; for he has not defined and by being expressed in this way it is less clear.

Examine also, in the substitution of names, whether the meaning is no longer the same, as in the case of the person who says that theoretical knowledge is theoretical supposition. For supposition is not the same as knowledge; but it must be if the whole account also really intends to be the same. For 'theoretical' is common to both accounts, but the rest is different.

Furthermore, see whether, in making the substitution of one of the two names, he has made the replacement not of the differentia, but of the genus, exactly as in the example just mentioned. For 'theoretical' is more unfamiliar than 'knowledge': for one is the genus, the other the differentia, and the genus is the most familiar of all. So that he should have made the substitution not of the genus but of the differentia, since it is more unfamiliar. (Or rather the criticism is ridiculous; for nothing prevents the differentia, but not the genus, being expressed by the most familiar name. When things are this way, it is clear that the substitution on the level of names should be of the genus and not of the differentia.) If he substitutes not a name with a name, but a name with an account, it is clear that he must give the definition of the differentia rather than of the genus, since the definition is given for the sake of becoming more familiar with the thing; for the differentia is less familiar than the genus.

CHAPTER 12

If he has given the definition of the differentia, examine whether the given definition is also common to something else. For example, when he says that the odd number is a number that has a middle [we must further determine in what way it has a middle]. For 'number' is common to both phrases, while the account has been substituted for 'odd'; and both a line and a solid have a middle, although they are not odd. So that this would not be a definition of odd. But if 'having a middle' is said in many ways, we must determine in what way it has a middle. So that there will be a criticism or a deduction showing that he has not defined.

Again, see whether that of which he has given the account is among the things that are, while what falls under the account is not among the things that are. For example, if he has defined white as colour mixed with fire; for it is impossible that the incorporeal be mixed with the corporeal, so that colour mixed with fire is not, but white is.

Furthermore, those who, in the case of relatives, do not pick out that in relation to which it is spoken of, but in their description include it among many things, are wrong either entirely or in some respect; for example, if someone says that medicine is knowledge of a thing that is. For, if medicine is knowledge of none of the things that are, it is clear that he was entirely wrong, whereas if it is knowledge of one of them but not of another, he was wrong in some respect. For it must be knowledge of all if indeed it is said to be of what is[9] in itself and not incidentally, just as it is in the case of the other relatives; for every knowable is so-called in relation to knowledge. Similarly also in the other cases, since all relatives reciprocate. Furthermore, if indeed it is by producing the account not in itself but incidentally that he gives the account correctly, each relative would be spoken of not in relation to one thing, but in relation to many. For nothing prevents the same thing from being a being and white and good, so that in giving an account in relation to any whatsoever of these he would have given the account correctly, if indeed it is in giving the account incidentally that he gives it correctly. Furthermore, it is impossible for an account of this sort to be proper to that of which the account is given; for not only medicine but also most of the other branches of knowledge are so called in relation to a thing that is, so that each will be knowledge of a thing that is. It is, then, clear that an account of this sort will not be a definition of any branch of knowledge; for the definition must be proper and not common.

Sometimes they define not the thing but the thing in a good or perfect state. The definition of the rhetorician or of the thief is of this sort, if indeed a rhetorician is one who has the capacity to see what is persuasive in each argument and to omit nothing, and a thief is one who purloins secretly. For it is clear that if each of them is of this sort, the one will be a good rhetorician, the other a good thief. For it is not the person who purloins secretly but he who wishes to purloin secretly that is a thief.

---

[9] Following Bekker 1831, Waitz 1846, Strache and Wallies 1923, and Ross 1958, at 149^{b}9 I read ὄντος after συμβεβηκὸς (pace Brunschwig 2007): see 'Notes on the Text' *ad loc.*

Again, see whether he has given the account of what is choice-worthy for its own sake as what produces or what achieves or, in whatever way, what is choice-worthy for the sake of something else; for example, by saying that justice is what preserves the laws or wisdom is what produces happiness. For what produces or preserves is among the things which are choice-worthy for the sake of something else. Or nothing prevents what is choice-worthy for its own sake from being also choice-worthy for the sake of something else; yet, the person who has defined what is choice-worthy for its own sake in this way has no less made a mistake. For the best of each thing is above all in the essence, but what is choice-worthy for its own sake is better than what is choice-worthy for the sake of something else, so that the definition should have rather indicated this.

CHAPTER 13

Examine also whether, in giving a definition of something, he has defined it as these things or what is composed of these or this with that. For if he has defined it as these things it will follow that it belongs to both and neither; for example, if he has defined justice as temperance and courage. For if there are two people and each has one of the two, both and neither will be just since both have justice while each of them does not have it. Even if what is said is not exceedingly absurd since this sort of thing happens in other cases too (for nothing prevents that both together have a hundred drachmae although neither has it), nevertheless the fact that contraries belong to them would seem totally absurd. This will happen if one of them had temperance and cowardice, the other courage and intemperance; for both will have justice and injustice. For if justice is temperance and courage, injustice will be cowardice and intemperance. In general, all the reasoning seeking to prove that the parts and the whole are not the same thing are useful for what is said now. For the person who defines in this way seems to claim that the parts are the same as the whole. The arguments are particularly apt in the cases where the combination of the parts is very clear, just as in the case of a house and of other things of this sort. For it is clear that when the parts exist nothing prevents the whole from not existing so that the parts are not the same thing as the whole.

If he has said that what is being defined is not these things but what is composed of these, at first examine whether one thing does not come to be by nature from the things mentioned. For some things are so related to each other that no one thing comes from them, for example a line and a number. Furthermore, see whether, while what has been defined is by nature primarily in one thing, the things of which he has said it is composed are not primarily in one thing but each is in another. For, clearly, that thing would not be composed of these; for it is necessary for the whole to be in the things in which the parts are so that the whole is not primarily in one thing but in several. But if both the parts and the whole are primarily in one thing, consider whether they are not in the same thing, but the whole is in one and the parts in another. Again, see whether the parts are destroyed together with the whole. For the reverse must happen: when the parts are destroyed the whole is destroyed, but when the whole is destroyed it is not necessary that the parts also are destroyed. Or see whether the whole is good or evil whereas the parts are neither, or conversely the parts are good or evil whereas the whole is neither. For it is not possible that a good or an evil comes to be from what is neither, nor that what comes to be from evils or goods is neither. Or see whether one is a good more than the other is an evil, but what is composed of these is not more a good than an evil; for example, if shamelessness is composed of courage and false opinion. For courage is more a good than false opinion is an evil. Then what is composed of these should have followed upon what is more, and have been either a good unqualifiedly or more a good than an evil. Or this is not necessary if each of the two is not a good, or an evil in itself, since many of the productive things are a good not in themselves but when mixed; or, conversely, each of the two is good, but when they are mixed they are evil or neither. What has just been said is particularly evident in the case of things producing health and disease; for some medications are such that each of the two is a good, but if both are given as mixed, they are an evil.

Again, see whether, although it is composed of better and worse, the whole is not worse than the better and better than the worse. Or this is not necessary if the things of which it is composed are not good in themselves, but nothing prevents the whole from being a good, precisely as in the cases just mentioned.

Furthermore, see whether the whole is synonymous with one or the other part. For it must not, just as it is not in the case of the syllables, for the syllable is synonymous with none of the letters of which it is composed.

Furthermore, see whether he has not mentioned the mode of combination; for saying 'composed of these' is not sufficient for understanding it. For the essence of each composite is not being composed of these, but being composed of these in this way, just as in the case of a house; for it is not the case that when these things are combined in any way whatsoever there is a house.

If he has given the account as this with this, first it must be said that this with this is the same as either these things or what is composed of these. For the person who says honey with water says either honey and water or what is composed of honey and water. So that if he agrees that this with this is the same as either of the two cases mentioned, it will be appropriate to say the same things as those mentioned above against each of these cases. Furthermore, having distinguished in how many ways one thing is said <to be> with another, examine whether this is not with this in any way. For example, if one thing is said <to be> with another, either because they are in the same thing apt to receive them, as justice and courage in the soul, or because they are in the same place or at the same time, but if in these cases what is said is not true in any of these ways, it is clear that the given definition would not belong to anything since there is no way in which this is with this. If among the ways that have been distinguished it is true to say that each of the two things exists at the same time, consider whether it is possible that they are not both said in relation to the same thing; for example, if he has defined courage as bravery with correct reasoning. For it is possible to have the bravery of committing a fraud while having the correct reasoning concerning healthy things, but the person who has this with this at the same time is not thereby courageous. Furthermore, see also whether both are said in relation to the same thing, for example in relation to medical matters. For nothing prevents that he has both bravery and correct reasoning in relation to medical matters; but, nevertheless, even this person who has this with this is not courageous. For the two of them must not be said in relation to different things nor in relation to the same chance thing, but in relation to the end of courage; for example, in relation to the dangers of war or whatever is more an end than this.

Some of the accounts given in this way do not fall under the division mentioned in any way; for example, if anger <is defined as> pain with the belief of being under-esteemed. For he wants to indicate this, that it is through a belief of this sort that the pain comes to be. But the fact that this comes to be through this is not the same as this being with this in any of the ways mentioned.

CHAPTER 14

Again, if he has said that the whole is a combination of these things, for example that an animal is a combination of the soul and the body, first examine whether he has not said what sort of combination it is, just as if in defining flesh or bone he said that it is the combination of fire and earth and air. For it does not suffice to say 'combination', but it must also be additionally determined of what sort it is. For it is not when these things are combined in any way whatsoever that flesh comes to be, but when they are combined in such-and-such a way flesh comes to be, and when in such-and-such a way bone. But it does not seem at all that either of the things mentioned is identical to a combination, since for every combination there is a contrary dissolution, whilst nothing is contrary to either of the things mentioned. Furthermore, if it is equally plausible that every composite is a combination or that none is, and if each animal, although it is a composite, is not a combination, then none of the other composites would be a combination either.

Again, if the contraries are equally in something by nature, and if he has defined it through one of the two, it is clear that he has not defined it. Otherwise, it will follow that there is more than one definition of the same thing. For why has the person who defined it through this one given more of an account than the person who defined it through the other, since both are equally in it by nature? Such is the definition of the soul if it is 'substance receptive of knowledge'; for it is equally receptive of ignorance too.

Also, if someone cannot attack a definition as a whole because the whole is not familiar, he must attack one of the parts if it is familiar and if it appears that the account has not been given well; for when a part is destroyed, the entire definition also is destroyed. As for the cases of unclear definitions, once they have been improved and corrected in order to make some points clear and obtain a line of attack, conduct the examination in this way. For it is necessary for the respondent either that he accepts what is assumed by the questioner or that he himself presents clearly whatever the thing indicated by the account is. Furthermore, just as in the assemblies it is customary to introduce a law, and, if the introduced one is better, they abolish the preceding one, in the case of definitions we must proceed in this way too and we must ourselves propose a different definition. For if it appears to be better and to indicate more what is being defined, it is clear that the definition laid down will be destroyed since there is not more than one definition of the same thing.

In countering all definitions, it is not an unimportant principle that one should define for oneself, by making a good shot, the thing set forth, or assume a well-expressed definition. For it is necessary, as if looking towards a model, to observe both what is missing among the things that the definition ought to have and what is superfluously added, so as to have many lines of attack.

Let this much, then, be said about definitions.

COMMENTARY

CHAPTER 1

Introduction: Book VI deals with the predicable definition and is almost entirely refutative. It concerns the analysis of attempted, but unsuccessful, definitions and outlines many commonplaces to refute these attempts. In chapter 1 of book VI there is no introduction to the subject of definitions. Nothing is said about the nature and the aim of a definition. If we want to know something about it, we must look at book I: the predicable definition is presented in a rather detailed way in chapter 5, lines 101^{b}38–102^{a}17. For the purposes of the present discussion, it is sufficient to keep in mind three of this predicable's most important features: (a) 'A definition is an account which signifies the what-it-is-to-be' (*esti d'horos men logos ho to ti ên einai sêmainôn*, 101^{b}38); (b) 'Every definition is an account of a certain kind' (*pas horismos logos tis estin*, 102^{a}4–5); (c) 'In connection with definitions, the better part of our time is taken up with whether things are the same or different' (*peri tous horismous poteron tauton ê heteron hê pleistê ginetai diatribê*, 102^{a}7–9). In other words, according to Aristotle, (a) the definition reveals the essence; (b) in every defining activity, there is a replacement of expressions indicating the kind to be defined with an articulated account of its essence; (c) in analysing definitions, a central role is played by arguments concerning whether certain things (presumably the kind to be defined and what is mentioned in the defining part) are the same or different. It is also possible to find some scattered remarks about definitions in books II–V. For example, at the beginning of book IV, which discusses the predicable genus, Aristotle says: 'These (*sc.* genus and unique property) are elements in questions relating to definitions' (1, 120^{b}12–14). (For my use of 'kind', see '"Genus", "species", and "kind"' in 'Terminological Clarifications'.)

Chapter 1 can be divided in four main parts. (1) 139^{a}24–35 contains an introduction to the five parts of the study of definition. (2) 139^{a}36–139^{b}5 attempts to show that, in arguing against a proposed definition, we must use some of the commonplaces examined in previous books of the *Topics*. (3) 139ᵇ6–11 introduces the distinction between two cases: the failure to define and the failure to define well. (4) 139ᵇ12–18 distinguishes two parts in the mistake of failing to define well.

139ᵃ24–35: The first chapter begins with the claim that the study concerning definitions consists of five parts, which are then outlined in a schematic way. What is a part of the study concerning definitions and why does Aristotle begin with this distinction? Each part corresponds to a possible failure that can occur in the framing of an account. Aristotle offers to the dialectician a first and general classification of starting points that are helpful in searching for instances of unsuccessful definitions. This is a very early stage of the dialectician's inquiry since no refutative strategy is indicated yet. It is as if Aristotle thinks that the dialectician must at first acquire a general map that will allow him to individuate where the mistake can be found. This division in five parts serves a double purpose: it is useful to the dialectician who wishes to retain in his mind a general picture of how the refutative arguments can be organized and it structures the exposition of the commonplaces in the whole of book VI.

At 139ᵃ24, the Greek word *horos* is one of the technical terms employed by Aristotle to indicate a definition. He uses also *horismos* and *logos*. Among commentators, there is a debate concerning whether Aristotle sees a difference between *horos* and *horismos*. According to Colli, there is a small difference between the meaning of *horos*, which indicates the definition as a unity, and *horismos*, which refers to the definition as a discursive expression where the components, especially the genus and the differentia, maintain a certain independence (see Colli 1970, vol. III, pp. 918–19 and 975–6). Smith sees no difference between *horos* and *horismos* but points out that *horismos* is more frequently found outside the *Topics* and that, in the *Analytics*, *horos* is employed in a different technical sense whereby it refers to terms (Smith 1997, p. 58). Brunschwig is more inclined to think that *horos* indicates the complete definitional sentence (e.g. 'A human is a rational animal' is a *horos*), whereas *horismos* indicates the component of the definitional sentence that does the defining (e.g. 'rational animal' is a *horismos*) (Brunschwig 2007, p. 41, n. 1). Chiba provides additional evidence in support of Brunschwig's position (Chiba 2010, p. 206 and n. 3). However, I cannot spot any difference between *horos* and *horismos* in *Topics* VI. In my translation, I render both as 'definition', whilst in the case of *logos* I opt for 'account'.

Lines 139ᵃ25–35 can be divided into five subsections, and each corresponds to a part of the study of definition: (1) 139ᵃ25–7; (2) 139ᵃ27–31; (3) 139ᵃ31–2; (4) 139ᵃ32–4; (5) 139ᵃ34–5. All the subsections are introduced by the particle *ê* ('or') and they contain the description of the sort of failure that the dialectician must search for when he attempts to destroy a proposed definition. There is an increasing degree of complexity in the types of failure listed here. It starts from the simpler cases, which are easier to detect, and it ends with the most difficult instances, which are arduous to address.

(1) 139ᵃ25–7. At 139ᵃ25, English grammar requires that we supply a main verb, e.g. 'We must show', which introduces the four subordinate declarative sentences contained in 139ᵃ25–32. Each declarative sentence begins with an occurrence of *hoti* ('that'): see 139ᵃ25, 27, and 31. Then, at 139ᵃ32, the syntactical construction of the Greek text changes and the subordinate sentence is preceded by *ei* ('if' or 'whether'). For this reason, a different main verb must be supplied, e.g. the imperative form of 'to see' ('see whether ... ').

It is not easy to understand the structure and the meaning of the sentence's Greek formulation at 139ᵃ25–6 (*hoti holôs ouk alêthes eipein, kath'hou tounoma, kai ton logon*). In particular, the clause 'that to which the name' (*kath'hou tounoma*) does not make sense unless it is completed by a verbal form. There are three options. (A) A verbal form derived from one of the verbs indicating the action of saying or attributing, e.g. *legesthai*, can be supplied after 'the name'. In ancient Greek prose, such verbs are often understood. Then, the sentence would be translated as: 'It is not true to attribute also the account to that to which the name *is attributed*'. (B) Two verbal forms of the type described in (A) can be supplied: the first is inserted after 'the account' and the second after 'the name'. The sentence would be translated as: 'It is not true to say that also the account *is attributed* to that to which the name *is attributed*'. (c) A verbal form similar to *alêthes eipein*, e.g. *alêthes legesthai*, is supplied and read after 'the name'. This would result in the following translation: 'It is not true to attribute also the account to that to which the name *is truly attributed'*. Which is the best option? The occurrences of *alêtheuesthai* in the immediately following line, which contains the example illustrating the general case, and of *alêtheuetai* at 139ª35 support option (C). Furthermore, the reading suggested by (C) is plausible from a grammatical viewpoint since the verbal form *alêthes eipein* is construed in common with *tounoma* and *ton logon*. For these reasons, I am inclined to favour option (C).

The type of failure described here concerns the relation of inclusion between the kind to be defined and its defining elements. Here Aristotle proposes to the dialectician that he makes a test to see whether the kind to be defined is included in the defining elements. The dialectician must verify that the defining part can be truly applied to all the cases to which the expression indicating the kind to be defined is truly applied. The parenthetical clause at 139ª26-7 explains this general rule with an easy example: 'rational animal' must be truly applied to all the cases to which 'human' is truly applied. If this does not happen, the proposed definition must be criticized on the basis of the commonplaces that will be illustrated later in book VI. It should be noted that the approach adopted in these lines is simply extensional. Aristotle speaks in terms of something being truly said or attributed to something else. There is neither an alethic modalization, as the concept of necessity is absent, nor an essential one, as the concept of essence is not present in this context.

(2) 139ª27–31. The second type of failure has to do with the genus of the species to be defined. At 139ª27, the clause 'although there is a genus' (*ontos genos*) poses a restriction on the group of proposed definitions where the failure of mentioning the genus amounts to a mistake. Only suggested accounts of entities that fall under a genus are good candidates for the type of analysis recommended here to the dialectician. For example, attempted definitions of *summa genera* are excluded from this examination since, obviously, *summa genera* cannot be placed in a genus. 'He has not placed' is the translation of *ouk hetheken*. In ancient Greek the subject of a verb can be understood, whereas in English it must be expressed. In this case, the subject is 'he' and refers to the dialectician's interlocutor in a dialectical context. In Aristotle's time, the participants of a dialectical debate were men; for this reason, it is appropriate to use the masculine

pronoun 'he'. At 139ᵃ27–8, the sentence 'He has not placed it in the genus or did not place it in the *appropriate* (*oikeion*) genus' contains a disjunction of two cases. (a) In the first, the mistake consists in failing to place the thing to be defined under a genus. This indicates that, although the thing to be defined has a genus, the defining part mentions no genus: for example, if one says that 'human is rational', he fails to mention the genus animal in the defining part. (b) In the second case, the mistake consists in the failure of placing the kind to be defined in its *appropriate* genus. Since Aristotle does not explain here what an *appropriate* genus is, case (b) can cover two different failures. (b*) The failure of placing the thing to be defined in its appropriate genus corresponds to placing it in the *wrong* genus. That is to say, the thing to be defined is placed in a genus that does not belong to it *at all*. Suppose, for example, that whale is placed in the genus fish. But the genus fish does not belong *at all* to whale; for whales are mammals. So, whale is not placed in the appropriate genus, but in the *wrong* genus. (b**) The failure of placing the thing to be defined in its appropriate genus corresponds to placing it not in its proximate genus, but in a genus higher than it. In this case, the appropriate genus coincides with the proximate genus. Consider, for example, the case where someone attempts to define justice and says that it is a state of the soul ('state' translates the Greek *hexis*; see 'The value of *hexis*' in 'Terminological Clarifications'). It is true to say that justice is a state since state is one of the genera belonging to justice. Nevertheless, state is not the proximate genus of justice. Rather, the proximate genus of justice is virtue. According to the view expressed here, a genus higher than the proximate is not apt to be mentioned in the defining part. It is the genus virtue that should be mentioned in the defining part of justice. It is easy to see that, in this instance, the person who is offering a definition has not placed the thing to be defined in the wrong genus. In these introductory remarks, Aristotle gives us a schematic version of the mistakes concerning the failure of mentioning the genus in the defining part. He offers a more complete picture in *Top.* VI.5, i.e. in the chapter containing an analysis of the genus as one of the defining elements, and he suggests to the dialectician several lines of attack (see *Top.* VI.5, 142ᵇ22–30, 143ᵃ12–28, and commentary *ad loc.*).

According to Aristotle, the failure of expressing the genus (or a certain genus) in the defining part invalidates the success of a proposed definition. Why must the genus (or a certain genus) be mentioned in the defining part? An answer is partly provided by the argument contained in the parenthetical clauses at 139^{a}28–31. There we find two sentences and each of them is introduced by *gar* ('for'): (1) '*For* having placed it (*sc.* the thing to be defined) in the genus, the person who defines must add the differentiae'; (2) '*For* among the things in the definition the genus seems most of all to indicate the essence of what is being defined'. This argument is extremely condensed and raises several philosophical problems. A reformulation of this argument might help to clarify Aristotle's idea. It is only after having stated the genus (or a certain genus) of the thing to be defined that the differentiae can be added. And they can be added only after having stated the genus, since the genus is that which reveals the essence of the thing to be defined in the highest degree. It is for these reasons that it is a necessary requirement for the success of a proposed definition that the genus be mentioned in the defining part. But the presuppositions lying behind the premises are neither made explicit nor justified. Still there are some passages in book VI where something more is said. As mentioned above, *Top.* VI.5, 142^{b}22–30 and 143^{a}12–28 shed further light on the role of the genus as one of the defining elements. The relation between genus and differentia is addressed also in *Top.* VI.6, 144^{a}9–22 and 144^{a}28–144^{b}3 (see commentary *ad loc.*). Even though it is not possible to give here the details of the arguments in *Top.* VI.5 and 6, a sketch of Aristotle's main line of thought can be attempted. Aristotle claims that one must first place the kind to be defined in the genus. When one places a kind in its genus, one distinguishes it from the kinds that belong to different genera. Only after this is it possible to add one or more differentiae since the differentiae distinguish the kind to be defined from the other kinds falling under the same genus. Consider the species human and suppose you want to define it. First, the species human must be placed in the genus animal in order to distinguish it from plants or rocks. Second, the differentia rational must be added to the genus animal. The differentia rational distinguishes human from other species that are contained in the genus animal: human is distinguished from, e.g. dog, horse, and ox (for a more detailed discussion see

Schiaparelli 2016). This argument is interesting since it partly explains how Aristotle proceeds when he divides and classifies reality. But it does not seem sufficient to justify the claim that the genus is that which reveals the essence of the kind to be defined in the highest degree. Consider a different approach to this problem, namely an approach that is based on the natural language employed in an exchange between a questioner and an answerer. If someone asks, 'What is *x*?', there is one appropriate initial reply that the answerer ought to give. He should reply by stating the genus of *x*. If he were to answer by stating a differentia, the reply would not be adequate. Suppose, for example, that someone asks, 'What is a human?' If the answerer says that a human is rational, he will not offer an adequate answer: there is something awkward in saying this. But if he says that a human is an animal, he will give an appropriate initial reply. (The idea that one must reply to the question 'What is it?', in Greek *ti esti*, by giving the essence, i.e. the *ousia*, and not something else, e.g. a *pathos*, can be found in Plato's *Euthphr.* 11A7–9. This passage shows that there is a connection between the verb *esti*, as it appears in the formulation of the question, and the etymologically linked noun *ousia*, which is used to refer to the appropriate answer.)

(3) 139^{a}31–2. Very little is said about the third type of failure. The context suggests that the characteristic of being proper (*idion*) belongs not to the entire definition but to what is mentioned in the defining part only. The Greek *idion* can be used as an adjective and can individuate the characteristic of being proper. But there is also the substantive form *idion* that refers to the unique property. In what sense must what is mentioned in the defining part be proper to the kind to be defined, or, in other words, be its unique property? In the *Topics*, Aristotle distinguishes two ways of being a unique property. In a narrow sense, A is a unique property of B just in case A is necessarily coextensive with B and A is not the essence of B. In a wide sense, A is a unique property of B just in case A is necessarily coextensive with B, but nothing is said concerning the relation between A and the essence of B: the possibilities are left open that A might or might not be the essence of B. In the present context, it is in a wide sense that what is mentioned in the defining part ought to indicate a unique property of the kind to be defined. It would be a flat contradiction to say that what is mentioned in the defining part must indicate a

unique property of the kind to be defined and, at the same time, it must not show its essence. For it is one of Aristotle's basic assumptions about definitions that what is mentioned in the defining part must reveal the essence. The analysis of the two ways of being a unique property and the relation between the unique property and the other predicables are discussed in Brunschwig 1967, pp. LXXVI–LXXXIII; 1986 *passim*; 2007, p. 41, n. 4; Verbeke 1968; Barnes 1970; Hadgopoulos 1976; Ebert 1977; Slomkowski 1997, pp. 76–8.

At 139^a32, when Aristotle says *kai proteron eirêtai* ('As we also said previously'), he refers to a passage that should contain some elements that are helpful in understanding the discussion of the third type of failure. In the secondary literature, there is a debate concerning the passage Aristotle has in mind. Some scholars (see, e.g., Pickard-Cambridge 1928; Tricot 1950; Forster 1960) think that the reference is to *Top.* I.4, 101^b19–23. Others (Barnes 1970, pp. 140–2; Brunschwig 2007, p. 41, n. 4) convincingly argue that this cannot be the passage in question since its main focus is on the narrow sense of being a unique property. They suggest that the reference is to *Top.* IV.1, 120^b12 or to I.6, 102^b29–33. It should be noted that the latter of the two passages is particularly relevant to our discussion, for it says:

> We should not forget that all arguments about unique properties, genera, and accidents are also appropriate to use in connection with definitions. For if we have shown that something fails to belong uniquely to what falls under the definition (as we do in the case of the unique property), or that what is given as such in the definition is not the genus, or that something stated in the account does not belong (as might also be said in case of an accident), then we shall have refuted the definition.

(4) 139^a32–4. As anticipated above, the outline of the fourth type of failure is not introduced by *hoti* ('that'), but by *ei* ('if' or 'whether'). So, an occurrence of a verb like 'see' must be supplied. Two points about the translation must be made. (a) In the expressions *panta ta eirêmena* ('all the things mentioned', 139^a32–3) and *mêd'eirêke* (lit. 'nor has he mentioned', 139^a33) different forms of the same verb are used (*eirêmena, eirêke*). But if in translating them we employ the same English verb ('to mention'), we do not succeed in conveying the precise meaning of the entire clause

mêd'eirêke to ti ên einai. For it is not right to say that the what-it-is-to-be (*to ti ên einai*) has to be simply mentioned; rather, it ought to be said that the what-it-is-to-be must be expressed. Thus, I adopt two different renderings for these two occurrences of the same verb. (b) The phrase 'what-it-is-to-be' translates (and is grammatically close to) the Greek *to ti ên einai*. The literal meaning of *to ti ên einai* is 'what-it-was-to-be': this phrase belongs to Aristotle's technical jargon and is used to indicate the essence. It is, in general, followed by a substantive (or by a form indicating a substantive) in the dative. For example, at 139^{a}33-4, we find *tôi horizomenôi*. The entire expression *to ti ên einai tôi horizomenôi* literally means 'what-it-was-to-be for what is being defined'. In similar cases, it is nowadays customary to adopt the translation: 'the what-it-is-to-be of what is being defined', which indicates the essence of the kind to be defined. I am following the customary translation, but, in the commentary, I am using 'what-it-is-to-be' and 'essence' interchangeably.

The thought behind the fourth type of mistake is that, even though the proposed definition contains none of the problems outlined above in (1), (2), and (3), it can still fail to define or express the essence of the thing to be defined. Alexander of Aphrodisias seems to believe that the failure of defining and that of expressing the essence of the thing to be defined are two distinct cases. He says that one fails to define when one offers a general description (*hupographê*) of the kind. And one fails to express the essence of the kind to be defined when its nature is not captured by the 'what is' mentioned in the defining part (*in Top.* 421, 27-9). By contrast, the majority of translators give to the negative particle *mêde* (lit. 'and not') an epexegetic function. In this case, the entire clause would be translated as 'he has not defined, *that is to say*, he has *not* expressed the what-is-to-be of what is being defined'. Although this interpretation has the disadvantage that it does not fully respect the correlation between *mê* and *mêde* (lit. 'neither ... nor'), perhaps it should be preferred. For it is difficult to see what the difference is between offering a general description of a species and failing to express its essence. Lines 139^{a}33-4 have a parallel in *Top.* VI.4, 141^{a}24-5. If we follow Ross's edition (1958), the Greek text reads: *poteron d'hôristai kai eirêke to ti ên einai ê ouchi, ek tônde* ('Whether or not he has defined and expressed the what-it-is-to-be, however, we must consider from what follows'). In his edition, Brunschwig follows the reading of the manuscripts A and B (a reading that is accepted also by Bekker 1831; Waitz 1846, vol.2; and Strache and Wallies 1923), and he prints: *poteron d'eirêke kai hôristai to ti ên einai ê ouchi, ek tônde* (Brunschwig 2007, p. 48, *apparatus*. He translates: 'Si maintenant l'on a véritablement dit et défini l'essentiel de l'essence, ou non, c'est à partir de ceux que voici'). Nothing hinges on the difference between Ross's and Brunschwig's readings. Perhaps lines 139^{a}33–4 anticipate the discussion in chapter 4. But it is also possible that Aristotle here refers to all the commonplaces concerning the failure of putting forward a successful definition as they are discussed in the rest of book VI, i.e. from chapter 4 to chapter 14.

(5) 139^{a}34–5. The last type of failure sketched by Aristotle belongs to a different level from that of the other failures. On the one hand, the outline of (1), (2), (3), and (4) suggests that the examined accounts may fail to contain the elements that are necessary to individuate the essence of the kind to be defined. On the other hand, in the proposed definitions containing the last type of failure the essence is indicated, but the defining part is phrased in an inadequate way. When this happens, the interlocutor is responsible for 'not having defined *well*'. As we shall see below (139^{b}12–18) and in chapters 2 and 3, there are two ways in which one fails to define well: (a) one might use unclear expressions, or (b) one might mention more characteristics than needed (the problem is, of course, not that of using too many words: it makes absolutely no difference if one says 'four-footed' or 'quadrupedal'). On the translation of the Greek adverb *kalôs* see Brunschwig 2007, p. 41, n. 4.

139^{a}36–139^{b}5: Having enumerated the five parts of the study of definition, parts which coincide with types of failure that can occur in a proposed account, Aristotle associates some of these failures with refutative strategies already presented in other books of the *Topics*. Lines 139^{a}36–7 refer back to (1) that is described above at 139^{a}25–7. The phrase 'The account also is not true of that of which the name is true' (139^{a}36–7) restates the claim at 139^{a}25–7, i.e. 'It is not true at all to attribute also the account to that to which the name is truly attributed'. In other words, the dialectician must verify that, in the proposed account, the defining part truly applies to all the cases to which the expression indicating the kind to be defined truly applies. When this does not happen, the dialectician must criticize the proposed account by using the commonplaces described in the discussion of the predicable accident (*sumbebêkos*). In the order of the chapters that is handed down to us, the commonplaces relative to the accident are developed in *Topics* II. Lines 139^{a}37–139^{b}3 explain why the commonplaces relative to the predicable accident are helpful in the case at hand. The explanation comes in two stages, and each stage is introduced by an occurrence of *gar* ('for', lines 139^{a}38 and 139^{b}1). The first stage of the explanation tells us that the inquiry relative to the accident takes the form of the question 'Whether it (*sc.* the accident) is true or not true (of the subject)' (*poteron alêthes ê ouk alethês*, 139^{a}38). In this respect, the inquiry relative to the accident is similar to that concerning the predicable definition. But a question of the form (Q) 'Whether the accident is true or not true of the subject' does not represent the standard way of speaking about the relation between the accident and its subject. Rather, the accident is said 'to belong or not belong' (*huparchein ê mê huparchein*) to the subject; see *Top.* II.1, 109^{a}20–2 and 2, 109^{a}34–5. So, a question of the form (P) 'Whether the accident belongs or does not belong to the subject' would be more faithful to the treatment of the accident in *Top.* II. The second stage of the explanation shows that (Q) and (P) are equivalent. For the relation of '*x* being true or not true of *y*' is equivalent to the relation of '*x* belonging or not belonging to *y*'. That is to say, *x* belongs to *y* if and only if *x* is true of *y*, and *x* does not belong to *y* if and only if *x* is not true of *y*. A passage in *APr.* I.37, 49^{a}6–7 seems to presuppose that *huparchein* construed with the dative is synonymous with *alêtheuesthai* construed with the genitive: see Bonitz 1870, pp. 789A34–5. In *Top.* I.5, there are two definitions of the predicable accident: (D1) 'An accident is something which is none of these—not a definition, a unique property, a genus—but yet belongs to the subjects' (102^{b}4–5); (D2) An accident is 'What can possibly belong or not belong to one and the same thing, whatever it may be' (102^{b}6–7). In the context of *Top.* VI.1, the concept of accident conforms to (D1), which speaks only of the relation of belonging and does not mention any modality. For a detailed discussion of the predicable accident, see Brunschwig 1992; Slomkowski 1997, pp. 69–73, 79–84, 92–4; Smith 1997, pp. 64–6; Ebert 1998.

At 139^{a}38, there is a discrepancy in the punctuation printed by the editors. Bekker 1831, Waitz 1846, vol. 2, and Strache and Wallies 1923 print a comma between *ekei* and *poteron*. In Ross 1958, there is a colon (one might suspect that it is a typo). In Brunschwig 2007, any sign of punctuation disappears.

Lines 139^{b}3–5 refer to (2) and (3) that are introduced above at 139^{a}27–32. At 139^{b}3, Aristotle warns the dialectician that the failure of placing the kind to be defined under the appropriate genus must be addressed by developing the commonplaces that are specific to the predicable genus and that are studied in book IV. It should be noted that here Aristotle only speaks of the appropriate genus, whereas at 139^{a}27–38 he talks about the genus or the appropriate genus. It is possible that at 139^{b}3 Aristotle uses the expression 'the appropriate genus' as an abbreviation of 'the genus or the appropriate genus'. But it is also possible that Aristotle is suggesting that only the commonplaces concerning the appropriate genus are to be found in *Top.* IV. This possibility is supported by the passage in *Top.* VI.5, 143^{a}12–14: 'Again, on the basis of the rules concerning the genera, consider whether what is being spoken about is not placed in the appropriate genus, as was mentioned before'. This is a back-reference to *Top.* IV.

At 139^{b}4–5, the failure of offering an account where what is mentioned in the defining part is *proper* to the kind to be defined (in the sense of *proper* discussed above) is associated with the commonplaces belonging to the unique property (*idion*). The entire book V is devoted to the analysis of these commonplaces.

One should not be surprised by the fact that the study of definition profits from the discussion of the commonplaces relative to the other predicables. For this is not a novelty introduced only at the beginning of book VI. This claim is stated also elsewhere as, for example, in *Top.* I.6, 102^{b}7–9: 'All arguments about unique properties, genera, and accidents are also appropriate to use in connection with definitions'. This suggests that if a dialectician wishes to master the lines of attack against proposed definitions, he ought to become an expert on the commonplaces concerning the other predicables too. This invites a further thought, namely in Aristotle's systematic treatment of the four predicables, definition seems to be the most important, and it gives a unity to the entire project of the classification of the predicables. It is clear that the commonplaces concerning the predicables unique property, genus, and accident are useful not only in relation to the discussion of the corresponding predicable but also in the analysis of a different predicable, namely definition. As a final remark, one might think that whoever was responsible for establishing the order of the books in the *Topics* (as we have it now) was perhaps aware of the fact that the discussion of accident, genus, and unique property (in books III, IV, and V respectively) contributes to the study of the predicable definition (in book VI).

139^{b}6–11: In this stretch of text, Aristotle considers the two remaining parts, namely (4) the failure to define (*mê horistai*), i.e. to express the essence of the thing to be defined, and (5) the failure of defining well (*mê kalôs horistai*). Then, in his analysis, he reverses the order of the presentation and he begins his discussion with (5). His way of proceeding is motivated by a methodological choice stated at 139^{b}8: 'For it is easier to do anything whatsoever than to do it well' (*hrâion gar hotioun poiêsai ê kalôs poiêsai*). Aristotle's idea is that the completion of a task *in a good way* is more difficult than its completion *in some way or other*. He continues to explain (139^{b}8–9) that in the case of a task more difficult to carry out, a greater number of mistakes is likely to be made. If a greater number of mistakes is likely to be made, it becomes easier to launch criticisms. According to Aristotle, it is good practice to begin with the easier case. Defining well, being a more difficult task than defining *tout court*, is likely to involve a greater number of mistakes. So, it is an easier target for criticisms. For this reason, Aristotle begins with the examination of the attempts at defining well. The justification for this methodological choice can be intuitively appealing. Furthermore, it explains the structure of the entire book VI. Chapters 2 and 3 deal with the criticism against the attempts at defining well. Then, from chapter 4 to 14 we find possible objections against the attempts at defining *tout court*. Still, despite Aristotle's reasonable, motivated, and appealing methodological choice, nothing would prevent us from adopting an alternative procedure, namely dealing with more difficult cases at first.

139ᵇ12–18: The last portion of this chapter introduces us to the failure of defining well (*mê kalôs, sc. horistai*, see 139ᵇ6), which consists of two parts. In the proposed definition, one fails to define well if (a) one makes use of unclear expressions, and if (b) one adds superfluous elements to the defining part. Here we find merely a brief description of (a) and (b) and an extremely concise explanation of each. A more detailed analysis is contained in chapters 2 and 3 dealing with (a) and (b) respectively.

At 139ᵇ13–15, the parenthetical clause offers us a first outline of the reason for banning the use of unclear expressions. In the framing of an account, the person who defines ought to favour the use of clear expressions since they are more conducive than unclear ones to an understanding of the kind to be defined. For, according to Aristotle, here the aim of a definition consists in improving the understanding of the thing to be defined, and this requires a clear formulation of the defining part. In this case, Aristotle is emphasizing the epistemological function of a definition. There is a similar line of argument in other places of the *Topics*; see, in particular, *Top*. VI.11, 149ᵃ26–7 (see commentary *ad loc.*). The well-known distinction between 'familiar to us' and 'familiar unqualifiedly' does not belong to this stage of the argument: it is drawn below in chapter 4, where a more sophisticated reasoning on the epistemological function of a definition is presented (see commentary on chapter 4).

At 139ᵇ16–17, the motivation for avoiding redundant expressions is stated in a very succinct way. It is not easy to find a satisfactory literal translation of the phrase *epi pleion* (139ᵇ15) in this context. It can be used as an adverbial form and be equivalent to the English 'more' or 'further'; it can also be followed by an expression in the genitive and it can correspond to 'beyond' (LSJ, *s.v. pleiôn* II.1). In the present context, the idea conveyed by *epi pleion* is that the proposed account contains more elements than what is needed to reveal the essence of the kind to be defined. Modern translators adopted different readings of the clause *epi pleion … ton logon tou deontos*. Here are some examples: 'The account is longer than necessary' (Pickard-Cambridge 1928, followed by Barnes 1984, vol. 1); 'Une expression plus étendue qu'il ne fallait' (Tricot 1950); 'a description which is unnecessary long' (Forster 1960); 'Il discorso definitiorio è più esteso del dovuto' (Colli 1970); 'Die Begriffsbestimmung länger ist, als sie sein muss'

(Wagner and Rapp 2004); 'Une formule qui a plus d'extension qu'il ne faut' (Brunschwig 2007, see also p. 42, n. 6). In my translation, I choose to highlight the grammatical construction of *epi pleion* followed by a genitive. Moreover, I try to give to *epi pleion* a non-technical meaning since here Aristotle is not talking about the extension of a general term or of a universal. The technical meaning of *epi pleion* is found in *Top*. VI.6, 144^{b}6, where Aristotle claims that the differentia's extension is wider than that of the species it contributes to define (*epi pleion hê diaphora tôn eidôn legetai*: 'The differentia is said more widely that the species').

Aristotle justifies the requirement of avoiding to mention characteristics that are not necessary by saying that 'Every addition is superfluous'. But it is not clear why redundancy is unwelcome. There are at least three options. (i) Redundancy clashes against a criterion of logical precision and elegance; for example, mathematicians or logicians prefer proofs containing only the premises that are necessary and sufficient to draw the conclusion). (ii) In a debate, redundancy introduces an antieconomic way of expressing an idea (i.e. Aristotle is working under the assumption that an efficient communication avoids redundancy). (iii) Redundancy is an obstacle in attaining the epistemological aim of a definition, which consists in improving the understanding of the kind to be defined. Option (iii) is the most likely since it is mentioned above in relation with the requirement of avoiding unclear expressions (139^{b}14–15). But nothing rules out that Aristotle might also have (i) and (ii) in mind.

Aristotle's final remark in chapter 1 announces that each of the two ways of defining well is divided into several parts, i.e. subsections. These subsections will be explored in the following two chapters.

CHAPTER 2

Introduction: Chapter 2 discusses some commonplaces concerning the lack of clarity in a proposed definition. It can be divided into six parts. (1) 139^{b}19–31 establishes that a homonymy makes the account unclear and contains an analysis of the presence of a homonymy either in the defining part or in the kind to be defined. (2) 139^{b}32–140^{a}2 discusses and criticizes the use of metaphorical expressions in a definitional context. (3) 140^{a}3–5 finds fault with the choice of employing unusual terms in the defining part of the account. (4) 140^{a}6–17 is about the presence of something that is responsible for the account's obscurity, but it is neither a homonymy nor a metaphor. (5) 140^{a}18–20 deals with the case where the proposed definition is not sufficiently clear and does not allow the formulation of the definition of the contrary. (6) 140^{a}20–2 tells of the situation where the lack of clarity hinders the individuation of the kind to be defined.

It is easy to see that, on the one hand, parts (1), (2), (3), and (4) single out a precise cause of the unclarity in the proposed definition and expand on it; for example, in (2) the metaphor is a cause of the account's obscurity. On the other hand, parts (5) and (6) look at symptoms of the lack of clarity; for example, in (5) the difficulty met in formulating the account of the contrary is a symptom of the proposed definition's obscurity.

139^{a}19–31: The first commonplace concerns the presence of the homonymy in a proposed definition. The homonymy can be found either (A) in the defining part (139^{b}20–3) or (B) in the kind to be defined (139^{b}23–7). In both cases, the homonymy must be detected, and possibly eliminated, as it is responsible for the lack of clarity in the suggested account. There is a lengthy discussion of homonymy (lit. of things said in many ways) in *Top.* I.15, where Aristotle puts forward several rules apt for discovering its presence (for an analysis of these rules see Smith 1997, pp. 92–9). Another discussion of homonymy can be found in *Top.* VI.10, 148^{a}23–148^{b}22 (see commentary *ad loc.*). Shields 1999 and Ward 2008 contain more general discussions of homonymy in Aristotle.

(A) There are two examples of the presence of a homonymy in the defining part. But Aristotle does not illustrate the homonymies; perhaps he assumes that it would not be difficult for a Greek speaker to grasp them. (i) It is hard (or even impossible) to find an adequate English translation that conveys exactly the ambiguity of *agôgê*. I have adopted 'passage' even though it does not correspond closely to the meaning of *agôgê*. The reason for my choice is that in the English 'passage' there is a certain ambiguity. For example, in the sentence 'The *passage* leading from the rose garden to the maze', 'passage' is equivalent to 'walkway'. But if someone says, 'In the passage of the *Topics* we are reading, there are several philological problems', 'passage' is equivalent to 'section of text'. Alexander of Aphrodisias explains that *agôgê* can be used in two different ways (*in Top.* 423, 19–21). It is possible to say, 'The carrying (*agôgê*) of food and wine'. But it is also possible to say, 'The training (*agôgê*) of the character through the habits', and this corresponds to the 'education of the children' (*paidôn agôgê*). According to Düring 1968, p. 228, the definition of becoming as *agôgê eis ousian* has a Platonic background. In particular, Plato speaks of *eis ousian agêi* (*Sph.* 219B) and of *genesin eis ousian* (*Phlb.* 26D). Also, in *Def.* 411A, *genesis* ('becoming') is defined as *kinesis eis ousian* ('movement into being'). This suggests that Aristotle has a Platonic target in mind when he criticizes the obscurity produced by the presence of *agôgê*. Lines 139[b]21–3 can be interpreted in two ways. (1) In the clause *homônumos gar hê agôgê kai hê summetria*, the terms *agôgê* and *summetria* are mentioned. The corresponding translation is: 'For "passage" is homonymous and "balance" too'. In this case, the homonymy applies to linguistic expressions. (2) In the same clause, the terms *agôgê* and *summetria* are (not mentioned but) used. The corresponding translation is: 'For passage is homonymous and balance too'. In this case, the homonymy applies (not to linguistic expressions but) to things. Both (1) and (2) are possible readings and both present interpretative difficulties. In (1), the difficulty consists in the fact that writing *hê agôgê* and *hê summetria* to mention *agôgê* and *summetria* is not the first and most natural reading of the Greek text. Moreover, it is not the standard Aristotelian view about homonymy that it applies to linguistic expressions. Still, in support of (1), it must be said that there are few places in the *corpus* where homonymy applies to linguistic expressions: in Fait 2007, pp. 109–10, there is a reference to two passages in the *Sophistici Elenchi* where homonymy is a characteristic not of things but of words (17, 175[a]36–7; 22,

178ª25–8). In (2), there is a different problem: when Aristotle says that *agôgê* and *summetria* are homonymous, he should mean that *agôgai* are homonymous and that, similarly, *summetriai* are homonymous. This interpretation is favoured by Brunschwig 2007, p. 42, n. 8. Nevertheless, finding these collections of objects behind the singular forms of *agôgê* and *summetria* is certainly not the most intuitive interpretation of the Greek text. In any case, what Aristotle says amounts to the same thesis. Aristotle's view is that the linguistic expression is said in many ways (*pollachôs legomenon*); hence the term is homonymous and the things to which it applies are homonymous too.

(ii) In the case of the translation of *summetria* with 'balance', the original homonymy is not completely captured either. The Greek *summetria* can indicate either 'due proportion', i.e. 'balance', or 'commensurability' (see LSJ, *s.v. summetria*). Clearly, in the proposed account of health, *summetria* has to be taken to mean 'due proportion'. This account occurs also in *Ph.* VII.3, 246ᵇ4–5: 'Health and vigour (*sc.* consists) in a mixing and a balance of the hot and the cold' (*hugieian kai euexian en krasei kai summetriai thermôn kai psuchrôn*). As noted by Brunschwig (2007, p. 43, n. 1), the definition of health as balance (*summetria*) between the hot and the cold is widespread in ancient medicine.

(B) When the homonymy applies to the thing to be defined, the obscurity concerns the subject of a proposed definition and it is problematic to see what the kind to be defined is. At 139ᵇ25–7, there is a brief remark on how to deal with the presence of a homonymy in the thing to be defined. The text sketches an elementary refutative strategy. An important role is played by the Greek verb *sukophantein* that is used three times in the *Topics* (here at 139ᵇ26, at 139ᵇ35, and in VIII.2, 157ª32). Translators adopt different renderings for the two occurrences of *sukophantein* in the present context. On the one hand, Forster 1960 chooses 'to make a quibble objection' (139ᵇ26) and 'to quibble against' (139ᵇ35). On the other hand, Pickard-Cambridge 1928 writes 'to bring a captious objection' (139ᵇ26) and 'to argue sophistically' (139ᵇ35). Similarly, in Barnes 1984, vol. 1, we find 'to bring a captious objection' (139ᵇ26) and 'to argue captiously' (139ᵇ35). The expressions 'to quibble' and 'to argue captiously' are not equivalent, for 'to quibble' need not entail dishonesty or sophistry, which are implied by 'to argue captiously'. In ancient Greek, the verb *sukophantein* was originally employed to indicate the action of accusing falsely and maintained the connotation of dishonesty. For this reason, it is more properly rendered as 'to argue captiously'. One might think that Aristotle is sketching a dishonest line of attack (see, e.g., Brunschwig 1999 and 2007, p. 43, n. 2). This is not, however, the only possible reading of the passage. Aristotle might be saying that if someone proposes an account of the type under scrutiny, then he must be prepared to face a criticism that uses a dishonest strategy. There is no indication of the fact that the dialectician is the person responsible for the *mala fide* attack. Aristotle's idea could be that one reason to avoid accounts where the thing to be defined is homonymous is that they can be the target of an attack put in place by anyone (for example, by a sophist). One might be puzzled by the fact that this alternative interpretation requires Aristotle to switch from the point of view of the questioner to that of the answerer, but this is not unparalleled (see *Top.* VI.10, 148^{a}37–148^{b}4).

Here is a possible reconstruction of the refutative strategy. Consider a case of homonymy: two kinds K^* and K^{**} have the same name but different definitions corresponding to that name. The homonymy, however, remains undetected (139^{b}27–8). In this case, according to Aristotle, it is possible to argue captiously. Suppose that the interlocutor proposes an account that is an adequate definition of the kind K^{**} but has not realized that K^* has the same name and that the proposed definition could, therefore, be taken to concern K^*. The attacker can pick out the kind K^*, which the interlocutor was not thinking of when he gave his definition. The attacker, then, can object that the defining expression does not apply to all the things falling under K^*, which he treats as the kind that must be defined. So, he concludes that the proposed account is inadequate and must be rejected. There are two ways to find the strategy just described in the text (139^{b}26–7). (1) It is possible to give a declarative value to *hôs* followed by the absolute genitive. The attacker argues captiously by pointing out that the proposed definition does not apply to all (*epi panta*) the things which fall under K^*, which is what is being defined. (2) It is possible to give a causal value to *hôs* followed by the absolute genitive. The attacker can argue captiously because the proper definition is not fitting (*ouk epharmottontos*) both to K^* and K^{**}, namely to all the things (*epi panta*) of which the interlocutor is giving a definition. This criticism is not pursued further.

At 139ᵇ28–31, Aristotle puts forward another refutative line. This is different from the case illustrated in the immediately preceding portion of text since it is not based on the possibility that someone could come up with a captious objection. This suggested strategy seems more suited to a dialectician whose opponent concedes an account where the thing to be defined is homonymous. Aristotle's idea is that, after hearing the account, the dialectician himself should distinguish the ways in which the thing to be defined is said (*dielomenon auton posachôs legetai to en tôi horismôi apodothen*, 139ᵇ28–9) and produce a deduction (*sullogismon poiêsai*, 139ᵇ30). This is helpful because the dialectician can then check whether the proposed defining expression corresponds to any of the ways in which the thing to be defined is said. This is a way of reconstructing the argument:

> Premise (1) K^* or K^{**} have the same name but different definitions corresponding to that name.
> Premise (2) The proposed definition is not fitting to K^*.
> Premise (3) The proposed definition is not fitting to K^{**}.
> Conclusion (4) The proposed definition is not adequate.

In this way, the dialectician shows that, at the beginning of the exchange, the interlocutor did not offer an appropriate account.

139ᵇ32–140ᵃ2: The second commonplace addresses the use of metaphors in proposed definitions. Aristotle also discusses metaphorical expressions elsewhere in the corpus (see especially the *Rhetoric*, in particular book III, chapters 2–6 and 10–11, and the *Poetics*, chapter 21). It is impossible to offer here a detailed reconstruction of his view; the secondary literature is extremely vast. Aristotle speaks of metaphors as a source of obscurity in *Top*. IV.3, 123ᵃ33–7, in *SE* 17, 176ᵇ14–25, and in *APo*. II.13, 97ᵇ37–9. At 139ᵇ32–3, I added 'he has said': see 'The translation of *hoion ei*', in 'Terminological Clarifications'.

In this portion of text, there are three examples of accounts containing a metaphor. In all these cases, a metaphor is present in the proposed defining expression and is responsible for the lack of clarity of the account. The examples share two common features.

The first is that all the defining expressions mention one element only. This is strange because, according to Aristotle, the defining expression must mention at least two elements, namely genus and differentia. Does Aristotle think that if the proposed definition contains a metaphor, the defining expression must mention one element only? Or is Aristotle offering an account that has an abbreviated form? In this case, the defining expression would mention only the element that is responsible for the metaphor. The second option seems the most likely: at 139^{b}38, in his second criticism of 'Temperance is consonance', Aristotle speaks of consonance as the genus of temperance. This suggests that he is working with the standard concept of a definition, which is composed of genus and differentia. The second common features of these examples is that they all have a Platonic background. The idea that the epistemic state dealing with the non-perceptible world is immovable can be found in *Ti.* 29B7: 'So accounts of what is stable and fixed and transparent to understanding are themselves stable and unshifting'. In ps.-Platonic *Def.* 414B10, knowledge (*epistêmê*) is said to be 'An apprehension of the soul that cannot be changed by reason' (*hupolepsis psuchês ametaptôtos hupo logou*). The image of the earth as a nurse goes back to *Ti.* 40B8, albeit with a small change in the terminology: 'The earth he devised to be our nurse (*trophon*)'. In *Ti.* 88D6, *trophon* appears to be equivalent to *tithênên* ('nurse'), which is etymologically linked to *tithênêtikon* and has the same meaning. *Tithênên* occurs also in *Ti.* 49A6 and 52D5. (As for *tithênêtikon* and *tithênên*, see 'Notes on the Text' *ad loc.*). The source of the thought that temperance is consonance can be found in Plato's dialogues. In *R.* IV, 431D8, Plato says that 'Temperance is a kind of harmony' (*harmoniai tini hê sophrôsunê hômoiotai*), and, as we learn from *Smp.* 187B4, 'Harmony is consonance' (*hê harmonia sumphônia esti*); hence, according to Plato, temperance is a kind of consonance. This is not the only time Aristotle criticizes the use of metaphors in relation to Plato's philosophy; see, for example, *Metaph.* I.9, 991^{a}20–2: 'And to say that they (*sc.* the Forms) are patterns and the other things share them is to use empty words and poetical metaphors (*kenologein esti kai metaphoras legein poiêtikas*)'.

At 139^{b}35–140^{a}2, there are two criticisms of the use of a metaphor in a proposed defining expression, and both are very succinct. (a) At 139^{b}35–8, the first criticism concerns the possibility of understanding properly (or lit. *kuriôs*) what is expressed by a metaphor. Suppose that a metaphor occurs in a definitional context: someone can put forward a captious argument based on the fact that he understands the metaphorical expression in its literal sense. How does the objection unfold? Aristotle expounds only on the account 'Temperance is consonance'. If 'consonance' is taken literally, the resulting definition will not be adequate since every instance of consonance inheres in sounds and not, for example, in ethical virtues or in parts of the soul. (The example of a metaphorical use of 'consonance' in the account of temperance is present also in *Top.* IV.3, 123^{a}33–7.) A similar case can be made for 'The earth is a nurse': it is possible to argue that the earth is not a person trained to take care of sick or weak people. So, this account is not appropriate to describe the nature of the earth. What does it mean to say that 'Knowledge is immovable (*ametaptôton*)'? There are two ways to understand this claim. (1) Knowledge cannot change truth-value; that is to say, it cannot change its value from true to false. The suggestion is that what is known is necessary as knowledge is of what cannot be otherwise (see *APo.* I.2, 71^{b}14–16). (2) Knowledge cannot be lost. The idea is that knowledge is a mental state that can hardly be removed (see *Cat.* 8, 8^{b}27–30: 'A state differs from a condition in being more stable and lasting longer. Such are the instances of knowledge and the virtues. For knowledge seems to be something permanent and hard to change'). Aristotle's point is that, in this context, the adjective *ametaptôton* (which derives from privative *alpha* and a form of the verb *meta-piptô*) is used in a metaphorical way. In its literal sense, *metapiptô* indicates the action of undergoing a change in place. In particular, the meaning of the verb *piptô* is 'I fall'. Clearly, this cannot be attributed to knowledge. So, the account 'Knowledge is immovable' must be criticized and rejected.

As a final remark, it must be observed that this line of criticism shares a common feature with the objection raised above at 139^{b}25–7: in both cases, we find the verb *sukophantein*. In this instance too, Aristotle need not be saying that the dialectician is entitled to use a captious refutative strategy. He might simply be warning us that if we speak through metaphors, anyone can argue captiously against us.

(b) At 139ᵇ38–140ᵃ2, the second criticism of the use of a metaphor in a definitional context is based on a different idea. According to Aristotle, it is not possible for the same species to fall under two genera, neither of which contains the other. This rule is introduced in *Top.* IV.2, 121ᵇ29–31 and is explained in a more detailed way in *Top.* VI.6, 144ᵃ12–20 (see commentary *ad loc.*; in that passage the rule's ontological implications are discussed). Aristotle applies the second criticism only to 'Temperance is consonance'. It is possible to expand on Aristotle's suggestion in the following way. In this proposed definition, consonance is the genus of temperance. But temperance is also a virtue. Then, temperance will fall under virtue and under consonance. These two genera, however, are not contained in one another: consonance does not fall under virtue and virtue does not fall under consonance. For this reason, the initial account must be rejected. Can a similar criticism be applied to the other accounts? In 'The earth is a nurse', earth falls under nurse. But, one could object, the earth is a planet. So, it would fall under nurse and under planet. Nurse and planet, however, are not genera containing one another. Hence, this account cannot be accepted. In the case of 'Knowledge is immovable', it is more difficult to see how this refutative line can be applied since it is not clear what the genus is. By indicating a quality, 'immovable' seems more apt to express a differentia than a genus. One possibility is that account 'Knowledge is immovable' cannot be criticized on these grounds. But there is another possibility that emerges from a consideration about some basic ontological tenets. According to Aristotle, the things that can undergo a change in place are substances. So, when 'Knowledge is immovable' is taken literally, it can be elliptical for 'Knowledge is an immovable substance'. But, in the *Topics* and in the *Categories*, it is often claimed that knowledge is a relative (see, e.g., *Top.* VI.8, 146ᵃ36–146ᵇ6, where the account of knowledge as 'A belief that is incontrovertible' is criticized). Hence, knowledge would be a substance and a relative. But this is not possible: substances do not contain relatives and relatives do not contain substances. If this is the correct reconstruction, one might wonder whether the strategy is effective. It seems to me that it is effective when it is used to refute an interlocutor who shares certain basic assumptions of the Aristotelian philosophy.

But it might be more difficult to persuade someone with a different ontological background.

140ᵃ3–5: The third commonplace concerns 'non-usual terms'. An alternative translation of the Greek clause *mê keimenois onomasi* (140ᵃ3) is 'non-established terms': see LSJ, *s.v. keimai*, IV.5. Translators adopt different renderings (see, e.g., Pickard-Cambridge 1928, 'terms that are unfamiliar'; Tricot 1950, 'termes inusités'; Forster 1960, 'terms of which the use is not well established'; Colli 1970, 'termini non comunemente accettati'; Barnes 1984, vol. 1, 'terms that are not in current use'; Wagner and Rapp 2004, 'unübliche Ausdrücke'; Brunschwig 2007, 'termes qui ne sont pas usuels'). The description of this commonplace is compressed, but the context helps us to understand when it can be applied. Aristotle is telling the dialectician that he should look out for the presence of unusual terms in a proposed definition. Aristotle warns us against the choice of an expression that is not customary (*mê eiôthos*) since it is responsible for the lack of clarity in the account (140ᵃ5). As he argued in chapter 1, 139ᵇ14–15, the lack of clarity prevents the account from reaching its epistemological aim, which consists in the improvement of the understanding of the kind to be defined. Aristotle does not explain what non-usual or non-customary terms are but offers some examples of composite expressions that he attributes to Plato. As noted by the majority of commentators, none of these examples can be found in the extant work of Plato (the philosopher); they might belong to an early and lost work of his or to unwritten lectures or to discussions in the Academy. Alternatively, this might be a reference to Plato Comicus, an Athenian comic-poet contemporary of Aristophanes. The three examples are difficult to translate as there is no English expression that corresponds exactly to the Greek formulation offered by Aristotle and that conveys the sense of unfamiliarity perceived by the speaker. Presumably, the idea is to single out some expressions that are not part of the ordinary speaker's lexicon. Is it a justified requirement that this type of expression should not be employed in the framing of an account? In this chapter Aristotle does not add anything else to the claim that 'Everything that is not customary is unclear' (140ᵃ5). One might think that this requirement introduces a tension as it pulls in different directions. On the one hand, it is a basic condition for a fair dialectical exchange that the terminology adopted be familiar to the speaker (it is a requirement inherited from, e.g., Plato's *Meno*, 75B–E). On the other hand, in a linguistic community, it is very difficult to prevent the formation of new ways of expressing certain ideas. For example, this would clash against any conception of a scientific discovery which promotes a certain revision of some linguistic uses. Aristotle modifies his stance in *Top*. VI.10. He is ready to adopt a more flexible approach to the problem of employing non-usual terms. At 148^b16–22, Aristotle speaks in favour of respecting the traditional rules of the natural language as well as the linguistic use established by the speakers. But he leaves open the possibility that, in certain cases, new ways of using existing terms should be accepted (see commentary on *Top*. VI.10, 148^b10–22).

140^a6–17: The commonplace analysed in these lines is characterized only negatively. According to Aristotle, there are cases that fall neither under homonymy nor under metaphor as they are described above at 139^b19–31 and 139^b32–140^a2 respectively. These new cases are responsible for the obscurity of the proposed definition. (As for the expression *oute kuriôs*, see 'Notes on the Text' *ad loc.*). At 140^a7–8, there is an example illustrating the type of expression Aristotle is criticizing: 'The law is a measure or an image of things that are just by nature'. It is not clear who formulated this description of the law (see Düring 1968, p. 226, and Brunschwig 2007, p. 44, n. 4). Also, it is not clear whether (a) there is one account that takes the form of a disjunctive definition, or (b) there are two distinct definitions. As for (a), disjunctive definitions do not conform to the standard model of Aristotelian definitions, so this is not a very likely option. In case (b), the example at 140^a7–8 should be cashed out as 'The law is measure (*sc.* of things that are just by nature)' and 'The law is image of things that are just by nature'. Aristotle does not explain why this example cannot be a case of homonymy. He goes on to add, however, a justification for the view that if someone says that the law is a measure and that it is an image, he is not using a metaphor, but something worse than it. At 140^a8–11, there is a very succinct argument in favour of a certain cognitive value possessed by metaphors but not present in the type of expressions under scrutiny: this lack of cognitive value makes certain expressions worse than metaphors. Metaphors acquire their cognitive value by virtue of a relation of similarity, and, for this reason, people use them. In other words, if x is a metaphor of y, then x bears a relation of similarity with y: this similarity relation allows a certain understanding of y. Since there is no similarity between law and measure, or between law and image, the proposed defining expression does not improve the understanding of the thing to be defined. If we follow Brunschwig's text (2007), where a first occurrence of *kuriôs* ('properly') is retained at the beginning of line 140^{a}13, Aristotle continues with the following thought: the suggestions that the law is a measure and that it is an image cannot be taken literally as this way of speaking is not present in the traditional use of the language ('It is not customary to call it so properly'). For alternative readings of the Greek text, see 'Notes on the Text' *ad loc.*

At 140^{a}13–17, Aristotle puts forward some reasons to reject the accounts of the law proposed in this section. Two possibilities are examined: (a) the interlocutor is speaking literally (140^{a}13–15), (b) the interlocutor is not speaking literally (140^{a}16–17). In both cases, the proposed accounts do not stand up to scrutiny. But, as it is found in the text, the analysis of (a) and (b) is deficient and convoluted, and in order to obtain a complete argument some assumptions must be supplied. Consider (a): if the interlocutor is speaking literally when he says that the law is a measure and that it is an image, then his assertions will be false. Aristotle's explanation focuses only on the case of the law being an image. He claims that, by definition, an image is something resulting from the process of imitation. It must be observed that this is a 'causal' definition of image: an image is not only what has a certain similarity with something but also what is produced by the action of imitating. But the law is not the product of such an action. So, the law is not an image. Nothing is said about the case of the law being a measure. Perhaps Aristotle considered this an easier or less interesting case. He might have thought that one could be able to develop it by oneself along the following lines. Suppose that a measure corresponds to an indication of quantity. It would be absurd to say that this description can be literally applied to the law. Consider, now, (b): the interlocutor is not speaking literally when he says that the law is a measure and that it is an image. The interlocutor is expressing himself in a non-metaphorical and obscure way. This is even worse than the use of metaphors since a metaphor still retains a certain cognitive value, which is not present in the case under examination.

140ᵃ18–22: The last two commonplaces, sketched in 140ᵃ18–20 and in 140ᵃ20–2, differ from those analysed so far since they do not concern the cause of the proposed definition's obscurity. Rather, they deal with certain signs of the lack of clarity in the interlocutor's account. No refutative strategy is outlined in either of these commonplaces. At 140ᵃ18, a first sign of unclarity is that 'The account of the contrary is not evident on the basis of what has been said'. The idea is that the dialectician must analyse the given account to see whether it is sufficiently clear to allow the formulation of the contrary (if there is any) of the kind to be defined. This commonplace is grounded on the view that 'The accounts that have been given well indicate in addition the contrary accounts too' (140ᵃ19–20). No example is offered. Suppose that the interlocutor grants that the definition of courage is 'The state (*hexis*) which cleaves to the law' (see ps.-Platonic *Def.* 412B; in the *Topics*, many instances of ps.-Platonic definitions are criticized and rejected). For the translation of *hexis*, see 'The value of *hexis*' in 'Terminological Clarifications'. Taking this definition of courage as a starting point, it is not evident what the definition of the contrary of courage, i.e. cowardice, would be. The only possible candidate for the definition of cowardice that could be obtained from the aforementioned account of courage is 'The state which does not cleave to the law'. But this is not a good definition of cowardice. A person who is in a state which does not cleave to the law is not thereby described as a coward (for example, he could be a thief). The general thought is that there are different ways in which the defining expression lacks clarity. One of them is about the case where the definition concerns one of a pair of contraries and the proposed defining expression does not allow us to find the definition of the other contrary. According to Aristotle, contraries (*enantia*) are a specific kind of opposites (*antikeimena*) and they are discussed in *Top.* II.8 (see Smith 1997, pp. 165–7). The commonplaces based on opposition are dealt with in a more detailed and technical way in *Top.* VI.9. A discussion of the importance of the relation of contrariety in a definitional context can be found in the introduction of *Top.* VI.9 and in the commentary on 147ᵃ12–22.

A second sign of unclarity is that 'Being said by itself, it would not be evident of which thing it is the definition' (140ᵃ20–2). That is to say, if by looking at the proposed defining expression in isolation (i.e. not combined with the name of the kind to be defined), it is not evident what the kind to be defined is, then the given account is inadequate. Aristotle says nothing except for a concise comparison between this type of obscurity in the proposed defining expression (taken in isolation) and certain works of ancient painters. If those painters did not add an inscription that describes what the painted subject is, then it is difficult to grasp what it is. Suppose one is looking at a painting hanging on a wall and has reasons for thinking that it is a portrait of a family member. By looking at a painting, however, one is unable to identify the family member depicted. One would need an inscription to carry out the identification. Aristotle's example presupposes that there is an analogy between, on the one hand, the relationship of the kind to be defined to the defining expression and, on the other, the relationship of the depicted individual to its portrait. It is not clear, however, how far one can push this analogy.

CHAPTER 3

Introduction: At 140^a23-4, a remark on the proposed definition's lack of clarity, which is discussed in the preceding chapter, is followed by a concise presentation of the general theme of chapter 3, namely the problem of redundant definitions (140^a24). There are five commonplaces concerning the presence of an element that is responsible for the redundancy of the proposed account. Their discussion occupies the rest of this chapter. These five commonplaces can be gathered in two groups.

On the one hand, the first three commonplaces are concerned with the relation between the extension of what is mentioned in the defining part of the account and that of the thing to be defined. (It must be noted that in talking about extension, I am using a modern notion, whereas Aristotle adopts a different terminology that expresses his own conceptual *apparatus*. In the secondary literature it is customary to employ the modern notion to speak about Aristotle's view, but in my commentary, when it is possible, I try to follow more closely Aristotle's terminology.) (1) 140^a24-32 analyses the first commonplace: it concerns the cases where the defining expression mentions an element that is unnecessary since it belongs either to all beings or to all the things falling under the same genus as that of what is defined. (2) 140^a33-140^b15 examines the second commonplace: the defining expression mentions an element that is superfluous even though it belongs to all and only the objects falling under the thing to be defined. (3) 140^b16-26 presents the third commonplace, which criticizes definitions in which the added element is superfluous because it does not belong to all the things falling under the same species.

On the other hand, the fourth and the fifth commonplaces examine whether a proposed definition contains a repetition or a double predication of the same element to a subject. (4) 140^b27-141^a14 develops the fourth commonplace and explains when a proposed definition that contains a repetition of an element ought to be criticized: Aristotle's idea is that the dialectician must look for the cases where there is a double predication, which introduces a pernicious redundancy in the account. (5) 141^a15-22 contains the fifth and last commonplace of the chapter: the unnecessary element can be either a general kind or a particular species when they are both mentioned in the defining expression. No clear solution for the fifth commonplace is offered.

140^{a}23–4: The beginning of the chapter contains a brief remark on the lack of clarity, which is the subject of the discussion in chapter 2. Nothing new is added. It is a connecting clause that serves the purpose of moving on to a new subject.

140^{a}24–32: This introduces the theme of the chapter's discussion, which concerns the problem of redundancy in a proposed definition. Establishing whether the interlocutor offers a redundant definition coincides with the second part of 'the failure of defining well' (*mê kalôs hôristhai*) that was set forth in chapter 1, 139^{b}15–18. The present section (140^{a}24–32) also develops the first commonplace of chapter 3. This commonplace, which has two parts (see below), deals with the unwelcome cases where the added element in the defining expression belongs to all, i.e. either to all beings or to all the things falling under the same genus as what is defined. The expression *epi pleion* (140^{a}24, 26) occurs for the first time with the same meaning in chapter 1, 139^{b}15, where the complete form is *epi pleion tou deontos*. It conveys the idea that the proposed account contains more elements than what is needed to reveal the essence of the kind to be defined (on the value of the expression *epi pleion tou deontos* see commentary on the last portion of chapter 1). In my translation of VI.3, 140^{a}24 and 26, I have supplied *tou deontos* after *epi pleion* as we find it in chapter 1.

At 140^{a}24–6, Aristotle invites the dialectician to see whether, in the proposed account, the interlocutor has included 'Something that belongs to everything' (*tini ho pasin huparchei*, 140^{a}25). If the interlocutor has included it, then he has failed to define well, since the account contains a redundancy, i.e. a superfluous element. An element is superfluous when it does not help us in attaining the aim of a definition; that is to say, it does not contribute to revealing the essence of the kind to be defined. The disjunctive clause 'either to beings in general or to the things falling under the same genus' (*ê holôs tois ousin ê tois hupo tauto genos tôi horizomenôi*, 140^{a}25–6) specifies the range of the unrestricted quantifier 'everything' (*pasin*). At 140^{a}27–9, the two parts of the first commonplace are introduced: one concerns the genus and the other the differentia. By considering the role of what is mentioned in the defining expression, i.e. genus and differentia, Aristotle explains what makes a definition redundant. On the one hand, the role of the genus G consists in distinguishing the kind to be defined K from many other kinds; for example, the genus animal distinguishes the kind human from many other kinds, e.g. from vegetable, mineral, etc. Alternatively, G distinguishes the members of K from those of many other kinds; for example, the genus animal distinguishes humans from whatever is not an animal, e.g. from rocks, vegetables, etc. On the other hand, the role of the differentia D consists in distinguishing the species to be defined S from many other species $S_1, \ldots, S_n$ contained in the same kind; for example, the differentia rational distinguishes the species human from the species horse, dog, ..., all of which are contained in the kind animal. Alternatively, D distinguishes the members of S from those of the other species $S_1, \ldots, S_n$; for example, the differentia rational distinguishes humans from horses, dogs, ..., all of which are contained in the kind animal. Similar remarks on the role of the genus and the differentia are present in *Top.* VI.1, 139^{a}28–9: 'Having placed it (*sc.* the thing to be defined) in the genus the person who defines must add the differentiae' (see commentary *ad loc.*). At 140^{a}29–32, the unwelcome consequences of including superfluous elements in the proposed definition are presented. Suppose that, in framing his definition, the interlocutor mentions something that belongs absolutely to everything and, therefore, does not separate the kind to be defined from anything: such a trait does not perform the role of the genus (nor, of course, that of the differentia). If, instead, the interlocutor includes in his proposed account something that does not separate a species from the others in the same kind, then such a trait does not perform the role of the differentia. In either case, what is mentioned in superfluous.

140^{a}33–140^{b}15: The second commonplace is introduced here. In this case, the superfluous element mentioned in the defining expression belongs to all and only the objects falling under the same species. This is the characteristic of the predicable *idion* ('unique property'). It is often said that there is coextensivity between the subject to be defined and a unique property; this coextensivity is stated several times in the *Topics* (see, e.g., I.5, 102ª18–26). Note that, in the Aristotelian technical jargon, the concept of coextensivity can be expressed by the verb 'to counter-predicate': the unique property counter-predicates (*antikatêgoreitai*) with the thing to be defined. It must be observed that here the unique property must be understood in a wide way; that is to say, A is a unique property of B just in case A is necessarily coextensive with B, and the possibility is left open that A might or might not be the essence of B (see commentary on *Top*. VI.1, 139ª31–2, where the narrow and the wide way of being a unique property are discussed).

At 140ª35–7, there is an illustration of this commonplace: it is based on a standard Aristotelian example of a human's unique property, namely 'capable of knowledge' (*epistêmês dektikon*). It is likely that the definition envisaged here is something like 'A human is a two-footed terrestrial animal capable of knowledge'. (Other occurrences of the property 'capable of knowledge' can be found in I.7, 103ª28; II.5, 112ª19; II.6, 113ᵇ4; V.1, 128ᵇ36; V.2, 130ᵇ8; V.5, 132ª20; V.5, 132ᵇ1; V.5, 133ª20–2; V.5, 134ª15–17; VI.14, 151ᵇ1. In Brunschwig 2007, p. 45, n. 2, the two proposed definitions of human as 'two-footed terrestrial animal' and as 'two-footed terrestrial animal capable of knowledge' are compared.) If the definition of human is successful, the removal of the property of being capable of knowledge does not prevent the other remaining elements mentioned in the defining expression (i.e. 'two-footed terrestrial animal') from revealing the essence of human and from being coextensive with it. It is for this reason that, in the account of human, the presence of the unique property just mentioned is superfluous. This remark on the removal of one of the elements mentioned in the granted defining expression might have led Aristotle to suggest a general test for detecting the presence of something superfluous in the proposed account: 'Everything is superfluous after whose removal the remaining account makes what is being defined clear' (140ª37–140ᵇ1). But it is strange to find this remark here since in the immediately following lines Aristotle introduces two dubious cases where the general test does not seem to produce a clear result. These cases are analysed at (1) 140ᵇ2–7 and at (2) 140ᵇ7–15.

(1) Aristotle begins by examining Xenocrates' definition of the soul as 'Number which moves itself (*arithmos autos hauton kinôn*,

140ᵇ2–3). This definition is reported in Isnardi Parente 1982, frs 165–87 (= fr. 60 Heinze). Isnardi Parente observes that while this quotation speaks in favour of the authenticity of the definition, it is not helpful for a faithful reconstruction of Xenocrates' doctrine since it is mentioned in a dialectical context where the aim is the refutation of the opponent's account (Isnardi Parente 1982, pp. 382–5). On Aristotle's general attitude towards Xenocrates in the *Topics*, see Brunschwig 2007, pp. XLVII–XLVIII, and p. 45, n. 6. At 140ᵇ3–4, Aristotle compares Xenocrates' account with Plato's definition of the soul as 'What moves itself' (*to auto hauto kinoun*, 140ᵇ3); see *Phdr*. 245E. *Prima facie*, the comparison suggests that 'number' is the superfluous element of the proposed defining expression: if 'What moves itself' is the defining expression of the soul, as Plato said, then there is no need to add 'number'. At 140ᵇ4, the particle *ê* ('or'; on the value of *ê* more is said below) introduces a criticism to this line of thought. Perhaps the proposed defining expression (i.e. 'What moves itself') indicates something that is coextensive with the thing to be defined (i.e. the soul) but does not reveal its essence after the removal of 'number'. It is interesting to observe that, in the context of this criticism, *idion* (140ᵇ4) is used in a narrow way; namely, A is an *idion* of B just in case A is necessarily coextensive with B and A is not the essence of B. If the unique property 'What moves itself' does not reveal the essence, there is nothing superfluous in the definition proposed by Xenocrates. Aristotle does not seem to be totally persuaded by this line of criticism: he does not seem to have a solution for this problem and leaves the two options open ('Thus, in which of the two ways things are it is difficult to show clearly', 140ᵇ5–6). At 140ᵇ6–7, the sentence 'But in all cases of this sort, we must use it (*sc.* the commonplace) to our advantage' marks a transition to the example of the subsequent lines. There is more than one way to understand the clause 'We must use it (*sc.* the commonplace) to our advantage'. An uncharitable interpretation would say that Aristotle recommends exploiting the opponent's weaknesses in order to gain victory. A more charitable interpretation would deny that the only goal of the discussion is the victory at all costs. Rather, it would suggest that the choice of a specific line of attack depends on a variety of factors, such as the proposed account's characteristics, the opponent's background, his intellectual skills, and his capacity for granting or rejecting certain premises of the argument.

Note that one might be tempted to translate the particle *ê* (at 140ᵇ4) not with 'or' but with 'or rather' because Aristotle seems to introduce an objection that marks a complete change of direction in the argument. From a grammatical viewpoint, this would be unproblematic as *ê* can have the force of 'or' as well as that of 'or rather'. Since the sequel of the passage seems to indicate that Aristotle is not completely happy with the criticism (so that he leaves the options open), it is better to give to *ê* the value of 'or' (see 'Note on the value of *ê*' in 'Terminological Clarifications' and Brunschwig 2007, p. 45, n. 6.)

In the *Topics*, there are other arguments concerning the view that the soul is a number and they are all refutative. In III.6, 120ᵇ3–6, Aristotle says: 'Likewise, also, you can show that the soul is not a number, by dividing all numbers into either odd or even; for if the soul is neither odd nor even, clearly it is not a number'. In book IV, there are two further arguments. The first says: 'If no differentia belonging to the genus is predicated of the given species, neither the genus will be predicated of it, e.g. of the soul neither odd nor even is predicated; neither therefore is number' (IV.2, 123ᵃ11–14). And, in the second argument, Aristotle instructs the dialectician to see 'Whether the species shares in any character which is utterly impossible for any member of the genus to have. Thus, e.g. if the soul has a share in life, while it is impossible for any number to have, then the soul will not be a species of number' (IV.3, 123ᵃ23–6).

(2) The analysis of the second case is not easy to unfold. Aristotle begins by offering an example of a proposed definition containing a superfluous element: in the account of phlegm as 'The first fluid, coming from food, that is undigested' (*hugron prôton apo trophês apepton*, 140ᵇ8), the addition of 'undigested' (*apepton*) is not needed. This example belongs to the field of physiology. According to the tradition of ancient medicine, phlegm is one of the four humours in the human body together with blood, yellow bile, and black bile. In *HA* I.1, 487ᵃ5–6, phlegm is classified as a substance that is 'composed of parts uniform with themselves' and moist. In *GA* I.18, 725ᵃ14–16, there is a description of phlegm similar to the one offered in the present passage of the *Topics*: 'Of the nutriment in the first stage the residue is phlegm and the like'.

Lines 140^{b}8–11 contain an argument in support of the redundancy of this definition of phlegm. It must be noted that the scope of 'first' (*prôton*) is unclear since it can be interpreted as being narrow or wide. (a) On the narrow-scope reading, the range of 'first' comprises only some of the other elements mentioned in the proposed defining expression, namely 'coming from food', whereas 'undigested' is a further element and does not fall within the scope of 'first'. In other words, only one of the two characteristics attributed to fluid is governed by 'first', and it is possible to rephrase the proposed defining expression as follows: 'The fluid which is the first to have the characteristic of coming from food and which has also the characteristic of being undigested'. (b) On the wide-scope reading, the range of 'first' comprises all the other elements mentioned in the proposed defining expression (except fluid). In this case, the proposed defining expression can be paraphrased as: 'The fluid which is the first to have the following two characteristics: to come from food and to be undigested'. Aristotle's argument is directed against (a), i.e. the reading where 'first' has a narrow scope. It comes in three stages (each stage is introduced by an occurrence of *gar*, 'for' or 'since': 140^{b}8, 9, and 10). (i) The presence of 'undigested' is superfluous because there is only one thing and not many to be so-and-so (e.g. coming from food). So, the phrase 'The first to be so-and-so (e.g. coming from food)' suffices to distinguish the thing in question from anything else, and any characteristic that one may add to the description plays no role in the identification of the essence. (ii) 'Undigested' is superfluous because its removal will not affect the coextensivity between what is mentioned in the defining expression and the thing to be defined. (iii) The coextensivity will not be affected since it is impossible for two things to be both 'The first fluid coming from food'. At 140^{b}12–15, Aristotle raises an objection to this criticism. This objection is introduced by *ê* ('or'). Aristotle considers reading (b), where 'first' has a wide scope, and argues in favour of it. If 'first' refers to the first of the fluids that are undigested and that come from food, then 'undigested' is not superfluous and must be added in the defining expression. The reason is that the account will not be true if we say 'The first thing coming from food' and if phlegm is not the first thing coming from food.

140ᵇ16–26: These lines contain the discussion of the third commonplace. It concerns a case that is related to those developed in the first and second commonplaces. While in the first commonplace the added element belongs to all, i.e. either to all beings or to all the things falling under the same genus as that of what is defined (140ᵃ24–5), and in the second commonplace the superfluous component belongs to all and only the objects falling under the species to be defined, in the third commonplace the added element does not belong to all the things falling under the same species (140ᵇ16–17). At 140ᵇ17, the expression 'under the same species' (*hupo tauto eidos*) can be taken in two ways: (i) it is elliptical for 'under the same species as what is being defined (*tôi horizomenôi*)', where 'as what is being defined' can be supplied from a very similar formulation occurring at the beginning of the chapter (140ᵃ26); (ii) it is a generalizing expression and it means 'to every member of any natural kind'. Since option (i) refers to something that is quite far in the text, option (ii) might be preferred.

At 140ᵇ17–18, Aristotle explains why the dialectician must investigate this type of account: the reason is that they are worse than the cases examined in the first commonplace where the added element belongs to all. Why are they worse? The answer is at 140ᵇ18–21. Consider the type of account of the first commonplace and remove from the proposed defining expression the added element that belongs to all. If what remains is coextensive, then the entire account (i.e. the account resulting from adding something true, see 140ᵇ20) will be coextensive too. A general rule explains why this happens: usually, if you add something true to what is coextensive, then the entire account remains coextensive. It goes without saying that the added element must be universally true. For if it is not universally true, then there are things to which it does not belong, and the original problem will resurface. The idea is that the failure involved in the account of the third commonplace is worse than that occurring in the account of the first because the coextensivity of the entire definition is undermined. Since the coextensivity is a necessary, although not sufficient, requirement for a successful definition, the mistake involved in the third commonplace should be classified not as a failure of defining well, but as a failure of defining *tout court* (see *Top.* VI.1, 139ᵃ31–2: a type of failure of defining *tout court* consists in granting a defining expression that mentions something that is not proper to, or coextensive with, the kind to be defined).

At 140^{b}21–3, Aristotle goes back to the initial formulation of the third commonplace; he repeats it *verbatim*, and adopts a technical jargon to explain why in the entire account, i.e. in the account containing the element that does not belong to all the things falling under the same species, there is no coextensivity between what is mentioned in the defining expression and the thing to be defined. There is no coextensivity because what is mentioned in the defining expression does not *counter-predicate* with *the thing* to be defined (*ou gar antikatêgorêsthêsetai tou pragmatou*). At 140^{b}23–6, an example illustrates the mistake under scrutiny. Suppose that the defining expression is 'Two-footed terrestrial animal six feet high'. But for every kind, the characteristic 'six feet high' does not belong to everything falling under it. In particular, one might add, 'six feet high' does not belong to every human. For this reason, the counter-predication fails and the proposed defining expression must be rejected since what it mentions is not coextensive with the species to be defined. It is interesting to observe that Aristotle does not tell us to look for an element that does not belong to all the members of the species we are defining. Rather, his suggestion is that we should search for an element that does not belong to all the members of any natural kind. This is a more general and surely more effective strategy to find out inadequate characteristics. Aristotle's example is well chosen.

140^{b}27–141^{a}14: This text contains an analysis of the fourth commonplace. The discussion differs from what has been said so far since the focus is no longer on the relation between the extension of what is mentioned in the defining expression and that of the thing to be defined (see first, second, and third commonplace), but on another way in which the proposed definition can be redundant, namely if it contains a repetition of the same item (140^{b}27). The passage can be divided into three parts: (A) 140^{b}27–31 contains a first example of an account with a repetition of the same item; (B) 140^{b}31–141^{a}4 introduces an objection to the idea that in example just proposed the repetition leads to an absurdity;

(C) 141ᵃ4–14 restates the commonplace in a more precise way and illustrates it with two adequate examples.

(A) The first example is: 'Appetite is desire for the pleasant' (*tên epithumian orexis hêdeos*, 140ᵇ27–8). At 140ᵇ28–31, there is an argument that shows where the repetition occurs. It must be observed that at 140ᵇ29–30 my translation follows the text proposed in Brunschwig 2007, namely *ginetai oun hê orexis hêdeos hêdeos* ('Thus the desire for the pleasant comes to be for the pleasant': see 'Notes on the Text' *ad loc.*). The basic structure of the argument can be reconstructed as follows:

(*p*) Appetite is for the pleasant (140ᵇ28 and 31).
(*q*) What is identical to appetite is for the pleasant (140ᵇ28–9).
(*r*) Desire for the pleasant is identical to appetite (140ᵇ30–1).
(*s*) Desire for the pleasant is for the pleasant (140ᵇ29–30 and 31).

This is an acceptable argument based on the principle of the indiscernibility of identicals (Aristotle's own formulation of (*p*) contains an unnecessary universal quantifier: 'Every appetite is for the pleasant', 140ᵇ28). The idea that a definition expresses a sort of identity recurs elsewhere in the *Topics* and can be found in, e.g., book I, chapter 7. Nevertheless, one might have the impression that there is something wrong in the conclusion of the argument, namely in (*s*), because saying that desire for the pleasant is for the pleasant is not an ordinary way of speaking. As we shall presently see, Aristotle goes on to point out that contrary to appearances this formulation is acceptable. (The proposed definition of appetite as 'Desire for the pleasant' is discussed also in *Top.* VI.8, 146ᵇ36–147ᵃ11: see commentary *ad loc.*)

(B) The particle *ê* ('or', see 140ᵇ4 and 12) marks a change of direction. Aristotle raises some doubts as to whether conclusion (*s*), 'Desire for the pleasant is for the pleasant', is absurd. He continues by defending the idea that the conclusion is not absurd (140ᵇ35), and he offers another example that he develops in the argument at 140ᵇ31–141ᵃ2. The argument proceeds in this way:

(*f*) Human is two-footed (140ᵇ32).
(*g*) What is identical to human is two-footed (140ᵇ31–2).
(*h*) Two-footed terrestrial animal is identical to human (140ᵇ32–3).
(*i*) Two-footed terrestrial animal is two-footed (140ᵇ34).

As in (A) above, this is an acceptable argument based on the principle of indiscernibility of identicals and on the thought that a definition expresses a sort of identity. If one wants to claim that conclusion (*i*) is absurd, one must reject one of the argument's premises. But this is difficult since premise (*f*) contains an obvious truth, (*g*) gives us an instance of a logical principle, and (*h*) offers a standard definition of human, a definition that can hardly be rejected. So, one is left with the only option of saying that (*i*) is not absurd.

At 140^{b}35–141^{a}2, Aristotle argues in favour of the claim that conclusion (*i*), 'Two-footed terrestrial animal is two-footed', is not absurd. Consider the definition 'A human is a two-footed terrestrial animal'. In the defining part, which is 'two-footed terrestrial animal', two-footed is not predicated of terrestrial animal. If in the defining part two-footed were predicated of terrestrial animal, then in the complete sentence 'Two-footed terrestrial animal is two-footed' two-footed would be predicated twice. Note that this view is a particular instance of a general thesis discussed in *Metaph.* VII.12, 1037^{b}18–20: there Aristotle says that the differentiae are not predicated of the genus they contribute to specify.

The third commonplace is based on the general claim according to which predicating twice the same attribute to the same subject is wrong. One wonders where exactly the mistake is. The sentence (1) 'Terrestrial animal is two-footed is two-footed' can be wrong in two ways. The first is syntactic: sentence (1) is absurd since it is syntactically wrong; in other words, it is not a well-formed sentence. The problem of uttering a sentence that is not well formed is reminiscent of a discussion present in Aristotle's *Sophistici Elenchi*, chapter 13. It is possible to give an apparent refutation of the opponent by inducing him to babble (*poiêsai adoleschein*, 173^{a}32): see discussion in, e.g., Dorion 1995, pp. 310–12, and Fait 2007, pp. 166–7. The second way in which sentence (1) can be wrong is semantic: sentence (1) can be rephrased as (1*) 'Terrestrial animal is two-footed *and* is two-footed'. Sentence (1*) is well formed. In this case, the absurdity stands in the fact that the same piece of information is repeated. This repetition is superfluous and makes the sentence redundant. Since in the present context Aristotle is discussing a commonplace that concerns redundancy in a proposed definition, the semantic analysis is preferable. Moreover, Aristotle's examination of other examples in the sequel of the text goes in the direction of a semantic treatment (more on this below).

At 141^{a}2–4, Aristotle goes back to the example of the account 'Appetite is desire for the pleasant' (see above at 140^{b}27–8). In the proposed defining expression of appetite, which is 'Desire for the pleasant', for-the-pleasant is not predicated of desire. If it were, the complete sentence 'Desire for the pleasant is for the pleasant' would contain two predications of for-the-pleasant. And this would be absurd. According to the argumentative line sketched here, in the complete sentence 'Desire for the pleasant is for the pleasant' the predication of for-the-pleasant occurs only once. In particular, it is predicated of the whole complex (*tou sumpantos*, 141^{a}3–4) 'Desire for the pleasant'.

(c) On the basis of the elements discussed above, Aristotle can now draw the distinction between uttering the same term twice and predicating the same attribute of a given subject several times. This helps to specify the commonplace under scrutiny: the account must be criticized if its analysis shows that it contains a repeated predication of the same attribute to the subject. There are two examples of accounts with a repeated predication, and each is followed by a short argument explaining where the repetition occurs.

(i) At 141^{a}6–9, the first account is attributed to Xenocrates, who said that 'Prudence is definitory and contemplative of beings' (*tên phronêsin horistikên kai theorêtikên tôn ontôn*, 141^{a}7). See Isnardi Parente 1982, fr. 84 (= fr. 7 Heinze) and her commentary on pp. 313–14. Here 'definitory' is equivalent to 'apt to produce definitions'; one might expand on this by saying that 'Prudence is a form of knowledge that is apt to give definitions and is contemplative of beings' (see Brunschwig's translation in his 2007). In this account, contemplative is predicated twice of prudence (141^{a}8–9). How is the double predication obtained? It must be assumed that when Aristotle says that 'Being definitory is a form of being contemplative' (paraphrase of *hê horistikê theorêtikê tis esti*, 141^{a}8), he means that the definition of definitory mentions the contemplative. In other words, the contemplative is an intensional part of, i.e. is intensionally contained in, what is definitory (when I speak of 'intensional part', I am using 'part' in the fifth and last of the uses of 'part' distinguished in

Metaph. V.25, 1023^{b}24, where the genus is called a 'part' of its subordinate species because it is mentioned in their definitions). If, in the proposed defining expression of prudence, the definitory is replaced by its definition, the result is that 'Prudence is contemplative... and contemplative' (the dots stand for the remaining part of the definition of definitory that Aristotle does not specify). This substitution shows that there is a double predication of the same attribute to prudence. It is easy to see that the problem in Xenocrates' proposed definition is not syntactic (as the sentence is well formed), but semantic. This confirms the choice of the semantic reading mentioned above in (B). It is worth noticing that there is a moment of carelessness in the way Aristotle expresses himself when he analyses Xenocrates' account. In his introductory remarks at 141^{a}4-6, Aristotle states that the absurdity consists not in uttering the same thing twice, but in predicating the same attribute of the subject more than once. At 141^{a}8-9, however, he seems to forget his own distinction: he affirms that the mistake under scrutiny consists in saying twice the same thing. The same happens below in the final part of the second example's discussion at 141^{a}21-2.

(ii) At 141^{a}9-10, the second account containing a double predication is 'Cooling is a privation of natural heat' (*tên katapsuxin stêresin tou kata phusin thermou*). Aristotle uses the concept of cooling (*katapsuxis*) in several treatises dealing with different areas (see Bonitz 1870, p. 376B). How is the double predication obtained here? At 141^{a}11-12, the explanation is based on the standard Aristotelian notion of privation as it is expounded in *Cat.* 10 and *Top.* II.8: privation is connected with possession, and they constitute one of the four ways in which things can be opposed (a discussion of privation in the context of framing definitions can be found in *Top.* VI.9, 147^{b}17-148^{a}9: see commentary *ad loc.*). Aristotle's point here is that privation of *x* is equivalent to absence of *x* which belongs naturally. Let us replace *x* with 'Heat which belongs naturally'. It follows that privation of heat which belongs naturally is equivalent to absence of heat which belongs naturally, which belongs naturally. Clearly, one of the occurrences of 'which belongs naturally' is superfluous and makes the proposed definition redundant. The unnecessary presence of one of the occurrences of 'which belongs naturally' in the proposed definition of cooling is also justified with an epistemological remark: the concept of privation brings with it the idea that 'It is said of what belongs naturally'. As in the other cases, the problem affecting redundant definitions is not that they come out as syntactically not well formed, but that there is a surplus of information.

It must be noted that in the first example the subject of the double predication is the thing to be defined, namely prudence. This differs from the situation of the second example, where the subject of the double predication is an element mentioned in the defining expression. This is interesting since it shows that any item in the definition can be the subject of the double predication.

141ª15–22: It is difficult to find a good translation for these lines as they contain a number of intricate textual problems. At 141ª17–19, I partly translate the text proposed in Brunschwig 2007, but I follow Bekker 1831, Waitz 1846, vol. 2, and Strache and Wallies 1923, who do not print *gar* ('for') at 141ª18. The result is: *to gar dikaion sumpheron ti, hôste katholou eipas epi merous prosethêken* ('for the just is something advantageous, so that having mentioned the universal, he has added the particular'); see 'Notes on the Text' *ad loc.*

Line 141ª15 gives us a general formulation of the fifth and last commonplace: 'Although the universal has been mentioned, he has added the particular as well' (*ei tou katholou eirêmenou prostheiê kai epi merous*). But this is hardly sufficient to understand where the mistake is: it is only at the end of the passage that some hints can be found (more on this below). How is 'particular' (*epi merous*) used in this context? The sequel of the text makes it clear that 'particular' is used not to indicate an individual but to point at a specific case. A specific case is still a universal, but it is a more specific one. It is a species whose definition mentions its kind; in other words, the kind is intensionally contained in the particular species. The commonplace's general formulation is followed by three examples: (i) 141ª16–19, (ii) 141ª19–20, and (iii) 141a20–22. Whilst examples (i) and (iii) are accompanied by a short explanation, nothing is said about (ii). It is interesting to note that these examples seem to have something in common with Xenocrates' proposed definition at 141ª6–9. If this is so, then the analysis of the problems involved in Xenocrates' definition could have suggested the formulation of the fifth commonplace.

(i) The first example of a proposed definition containing the mistake under examination is 'Equity is a diminution of what is advantageous and just' (*tên epieikeian elattôsin tôn sumpherontôn kai dikaiôn*, 141^{a}16–17). For the addition of 'defined as' at 141^{a}16, see 'The translation of *hoion ei*' in 'Terminological Clarifications'. The same example occurs in a slightly different phrasing in ps.-Platonic *Def.* 412B: *epieikeian dikaiôn kai sumpherontôn elattôsin*. In *Nicomachean Ethics* book V, there are (at least) two descriptions of the equitable person where the concept of diminution occurs: 'The equitable person tends to take less than his share (*ho gar epieikês elattôtikos esti*) (9, 1136^{b}20–1); 'It is evident from this who the equitable person (*ho epieikês*) is: the person who chooses and does such actions, and is no stickler for justice in a bad sense but tends to take less than his share (*all' elattôtikos*)' (10, 1137^{b}34–1138^{a}1). The concept of equity in Plato and Aristotle is discussed at length in Brunschwig 1996. At 141^{a}17, Aristotle explains that what is just is a particular case of the advantageous. This amounts to the claim that the definition of the just mentions the advantageous. That is to say, the advantageous, i.e. the universal, is intensionally contained in what is just, i.e. in the particular case. (ii) The second example says that 'Medicine is knowledge of things that are healthy for an animal and for a human' (*tên iatrikên epistêmên tôn hugieinôn zôiôi kai anthrôpôi*, 141^{a}19–20). This case looks very intuitive and it is probably for this reason that Aristotle does not expand on it. As is well known, the universal animal is intensionally contained in the particular species human (as the definition of human mentions animal). (iii) The third example puts forward a definition of the law as 'An image of things that are fine and just by nature' (*ton nomon eikona tôn phusei kalôn kai dikaiôn*, 141^{a}20–1; a similar example is discussed in chapter 2, 140^{a}6–17). Then Aristotle adds two comments. In the first, he explains the relation between just and fine by telling us that 'The just is something fine' (141^{a}21). Adopting the terminology introduced above, we can rephrase Aristotle's thought by saying that the fine, which corresponds to the universal, is intensionally contained in the just, which is the particular species. In the second comment, Aristotle draws the unwelcome consequence that stems from the type of accounts mentioned here. In a proposed definition where the particular is also added even though the universal is present, the interlocutor 'says the same thing several times' (141^a21–2). Why? No suggestion is offered and the chapter concludes here. Very likely, one of the background assumptions of Aristotle's argument is something along the following lines: what one says by using a name *n* is exactly the same as what one says by using the definition of the thing of which *n* is the name. For instance, what one says by using 'just' is exactly the same as what one says by using the definition of justice, and one of the things that one says by using the definition of justice is the advantageous. So, if in the proposed defining expression the interlocutor mentions the just and the advantageous, he will mention the advantageous twice. Something similar happens in the other examples. In (ii), animal will be mentioned twice, and, in (iii), the fine will be said more than once. The nature of the mistake behind the fifth commonplace becomes now clearer: there is a superfluous repetition of the same element, and this is responsible for the definition's redundancy. Obviously, if the interlocutor wants to 'define well' (*Top.* VI.1, 139^b6–9, and 12) by giving a definition that 'does not go beyond what is needed' (*Top.* VI.1, 139^b15, and 3, 140^a124), he should avoid offering a defining expression that mentions both the universal and the particular case (in the sense discussed at the beginning of this section). But which is the superfluous element? Is it the universal or the particular case containing the universal? The text does not offer an answer. A possible way to shed light on this problem consists in having a look back at the formulation of the second commonplace in this chapter. At 140^a33–6, Aristotle shows that there is a problem with the *added* element: it is the qualification contained in the *addition* that is superfluous. In the fifth commonplace too, Aristotle speaks of an *added* element (141^a15). This might suggest that the *added* element, which in this context is the particular case, is the superfluous one. But the evidence is not decisive. It is more plausible to think that, in the fifth commonplace, Aristotle leaves open the question whether the superfluous element is the particular case or the universal. The question is left open since it is the case-by-case analysis that tells us which of the two must be removed in order to obtain a successful and non-redundant definition.

CHAPTER 4

Introduction: The discussion about the predicable definition carries over from the previous chapters, where poor definitions were analysed. Definitions, in so far as they are definitions, indicate the essence. Poor definitions still qualify as definitions: they are, however, poor because they are formulated in an unclear or redundant way (*Top.* VI.2, 139^{b}12–18). In order to be good definitions, they must indicate the essence clearly and non-redundantly. For example, 'Coming to be is a passage (*agôgê*) into being' is a poor definition because it contains a homonymous term (*Top.* VI.2, 139^{b}20—see commentary *ad loc.*): the Greek *agôgê* can mean (i) passage, movement, and (ii) education, training (see, e.g., *EN* X.9, 1179^{b}31). At 141^{a}24–5 the problem is stated that will be discussed in this chapter, where the main objective is to provide techniques mainly for refuting proposed definitions because they fail to express the essence of the thing to be defined. This discussion leaves room for an analysis of important philosophical notions such as priority and knowledge.

This chapter is concerned with a fundamental requirement of definitions: the things signified by the defining expression must be prior to and more familiar than what is to be defined. When a proposed definition does not meet this requirement, then the answerer's position may be attacked. In other words, whether the defining expression mentions things that are prior to and more familiar than what is to be defined is a commonplace, namely a point where the answerer's position may be examined for criticism (see Smith 1997, pp. xxiv–xxx). At the beginning of chapter 5 (142^{b}20–2), we read that there is a single commonplace regarding the failure to give an account in terms that are prior and more familiar, and this commonplace consists of several parts (*merê*). These are presented as ways (*tropoi*) to refute a proposed definition and they are discussed throughout chapter 4. The chapter is structured as follows: the first *tropos* (or *meros*) extends over 141^{a}26–142^{a}16. Lines 142^{a}17–18 briefly refer to the previous discussion. Lines 142^{a}19–21 deal with a second *tropos* (or *meros*) within the main commonplace, and three further *tropoi* (or *merê*) are presented at 142^{a}22–33, 142^{a}34–142^{b}6, and 142^{b}7–19. Some of these last ways involve concepts (e.g. opposites and relatives) which are employed also in the discussion of other predicables.

141ᵃ23–141ᵇ2: At 141ᵃ23–4 there is a reference to the problems discussed in chapters 2 and 3, where proposed definitions that are unclear or redundant are analysed. At 141ᵃ24, *kai* could be epexegetic: 'Whether he has defined, i.e. expressed the what-it-is-to-be or not, we must consider from what follows'. At 141ᵃ25, the phrase 'what-it-is-to-be' translates (and is grammatically close to) the Greek *to ti en einai*; it is equivalent to 'essence' (*ousia*). In my commentary, I shall use 'what-it-is-to-be' and 'essence' interchangeably. Although in other parts of the text I translated *eirêke* with 'he has mentioned' (and similarly for its cognate forms), in this context (141ᵃ24) it is more apt to say 'he has expressed'.

At 141ᵃ26, 'first' (*prôton*) marks the beginning of the discussion of this chapter's commonplace. The expected 'second' (*deuteros*) occurs at the beginning of chapter 5 (142ᵇ22). Aristotle offers a line of attack in order to refute a definition proposed by the interlocutor. A proposed definition must be analysed to see whether certain conditions are met. If they are not, the proposed definition must be rejected, because it does not qualify as definition (see the distinction between poor and good definitions in this chapter's Introduction). According to Aristotle, we give definitions in order to enable an audience to become familiar with what is said, i.e. with what one means when one uses a certain expression. This goal is achieved when the defining expression mentions things that are prior to and more familiar (*gnôrimôtera*) than what is to be defined. The meaning of 'prior and more familiar' is not clear, and it raises some problems (hardly any help comes from passages in the corpus where similar terminology occurs, e.g. *APr.* II.16, 64ᵇ30–3; *APo.* I.2, 71ᵇ33–72ᵃ5). First, at this stage of the argument it is difficult to determine what sort of priority is intended; there are two plausible candidates, namely epistemological and ontological priority ('to be prior in knowledge' and 'to be prior in being' are among the several senses of 'prior' distinguished in other works; *Cat.* 12, 14ᵃ26–ᵇ9 and *Metaph.* V.11). For the most part of this chapter, Aristotle seems to have epistemological priority in mind. At 141ᵇ28–30, however, he seems to imply something different; he discusses the case of a definition, which is given through genus and differentiae, and he suggests that genus and differentiae are ontologically prior to the species to be defined. Ontological priority is explained by appealing to the notion of co-destruction (*sunairesis*): whenever the destruction of *a* involves the destruction of *b*, *a* is prior to *b*, but *a*'s priority over *b* requires also that the destruction of *b* should not involve the destruction of *a* (more on this in the commentary on 141^{b}28–34).

Second, 'prior and more familiar' might mean 'prior, i.e. more familiar', where the conjunction has an epexegetic value, so that being prior would be explained in terms of being more familiar: this would be easily accepted by an interlocutor, for it does not commit one to a specific ontology where some items are ontologically prior to others. Alternatively, 'prior and more familiar' might express a conjunction of two distinct concepts: in this case, as I have already noted, 'prior' could mean 'prior in knowledge' or 'prior in being'. There is a difficulty with 'prior in knowledge': it is unclear what the difference between the concept of prior in knowledge and that of more familiar could be, and the context does not provide any indication. There seems to be some reasons in favour of 'prior in being' as it fits well with the suggestion that we find later in the chapter, where ontological priority seems to be the ground on which the epistemological one is based. It could be the case that Aristotle mentions ontological priority without having in mind how it is connected with the notion of greater familiarity (he plans to fill out the theory later). Another possibility is that he has already worked out an account of their relation and he plans to expound it later (see commentary on 141^{b}28–34).

Third, the expression 'more familiar' (*gnôrimôtera*) needs more explanation: there are (A) linguistic and (B) philosophical problems. (A) It is difficult to find a satisfactory rendering for *gnôrimôtera* (141^{a}26), and this difficulty has been discussed at length (see, e.g., Barnes 1993; Mansion 1979). The rendering that is etymologically closer to the Greek is 'more known', but it sounds harsh in English. An attractive option is 'better known', but *gnôrimôteron* (more familiar) is the comparative form of *gnôrimon* (familiar), and strictly speaking it has nothing that corresponds to 'better'. The sense of what Aristotle is trying to convey is better expressed by 'more familiar', and this rendering is accepted by recent scholarship (Barnes 1993; Smith 1997). In my translation, I adopt 'more familiar', although at times this expression misses some of the linguistic and conceptual nuances of Aristotle's argument. Similarly, I have translated the verb *gnôrizein* (141ª27) as 'to become familiar with'. Perhaps the meaning of *gnôrizein* is better captured by 'to acquire knowledge' or 'to come to know', because these expressions explicitly show the link with the notion of knowledge. However, 'to become familiar with' (*gnôrizein*) is etymologically closer to the adjective 'familiar' (*gnôrimos*) and its comparative form that occur many times in this chapter. (B) It is unclear how we must understand the condition of being more familiar at 141ª26. This notion is discussed at a later stage in this chapter, where the distinction between 'more familiar unqualifiedly' and 'more familiar to us' is drawn (141ᵇ4–5). For present purposes, it will suffice to say that 'more familiar unqualifiedly' corresponds to what is conceptually simpler and more basic, whereas 'more familiar to us' corresponds to what is closer to sense-perception and may be more easily grasped by an untutored mind (more on this in the commentary on 141ᵇ3–14). The most intuitive way to read this passage is to understand 'things that are prior and more familiar' as 'things that are prior and more familiar to the audience': the logical subject of 'becoming familiar with' (*gnôrisai*) is the audience and this is transferred to 'more familiar' (*gnôrimôteron*). In other words, the sentence 'The definition is given for the sake of becoming familiar with what is said' means that the definition is given for the sake of the audience becoming familiar with what is said. This is the way in which the interlocutor would grant this assumption: it is in the nature of a dialectical argument that the premises must be granted by the interlocutor. This reading is further supported by the fact that in their previous occurrences 'familiar' and 'more familiar' (*Top.* II.2, 110ª6; II.4, 111ª8–10) indicate what is more familiar to the audience, and by the fact that at this stage of the argument the distinction between 'more familiar for us' and 'more familiar unqualifiedly' has not been drawn.

When in the next sentence (141ª28–9) Aristotle says that 'We become familiar not on the basis of just any things but on the basis of things that are prior and more familiar', he is expanding on the assumption that a definition is given for the sake of the audience becoming familiar with what is said. At 141ᵃ30 the clause 'As in demonstrations (for it is so in every case of teaching and learning)' refers to the general view that Aristotle expresses also at the beginning of his *Posterior Analytics*: all learning requires pre-existing knowledge (*APo*. I.1, 71ᵃ1; Barnes 1993, pp. 81–2; Bronstein 2010 and 2016, ch. 1). The claim that this is the procedure followed in process of teaching and learning suggests that a teacher should always adopt a method of teaching that is based upon demonstration; accordingly, a student should always learn in this way. However, this plainly contradicts the claim at 141ᵇ12, namely that the majority at first comes to know what is more familiar to us, and secondly what is more familiar unqualifiedly. It is possible to explain the tension between these two claims if one thinks that the process of teaching and learning mentioned in connection with demonstration refers (not to an introductory or preliminary stage, but) to an intermediate level: when the students have gone through the preliminary stage of their career, teaching and learning should follow the demonstrative procedure.

This is possibly Aristotle's earliest exploration of the relation between definitions and demonstrations. He suggests that there is a similarity in the way knowledge is obtained in definitions and demonstrations. In demonstrations, the premises must be true and primary or have attained the *status* of starting points of knowledge through some primary and true premises (*Top*. I.1, 100ᵃ27–9). In definitions, knowledge of what is to be defined is obtained through the defining expression that mentions things that are prior to and more familiar than what is to be defined. A more extensive treatment of how definitions and demonstrations are related can be found in *APo*. II.8–10, where Aristotle's view is that the definition of something is variously connected with an appropriate demonstrative syllogism. The details of Aristotle's discussion are obscure: for some analysis see, e.g., Ackrill 1981; Barnes 1993; Charles 2000. There is a feature that differentiates the discussion in the *Analytics* from that in the *Topics*. In the *Analytics*, a real definition is an account that shows *why* something is and the role of cause (or explanatory factor) is extensively considered. In the *Topics*, a real definition is an account that signifies the what-it-is-to-be (I.5, 102ᵃ1; VI.4, 141ᵃ25) and the notion of cause does not have a prominent place (see also *Top.* VI.13, 151ª16–19, and commentary *ad loc.*).

At 141ª32, Aristotle wants to show that an expression describing something through things that are posterior and less familiar is not a definition. He offers an indirect proof: if an expression describing something through things that are posterior and less familiar is a definition, then there will be several definitions of the same thing, i.e. the definition from things that are prior and more familiar and the one from things that are posterior and less familiar. We know that a successful definition expresses the essence. If there are several definitions, then there will be several essences: given that the definitions are different, the essences will also be different. But this does not seem to be the case: each thing has only one essence. Therefore, there are not several definitions of the same thing. However, one could think that Aristotle's argument begs the question: the opponent might not agree that there is a definition from what is prior as well as a definition from what is posterior. An opponent might have some reasons to think that there is only one definition and that this is given though posterior and less familiar things. For example, he might think that the definition of the geometrical point (which is a primitive notion) should be given through posterior and less familiar things.

The view that prior things are more familiar than posterior ones is already present in Aristotle's *Protrepticus*; there are also examples that are similar to those introduced at 141ᵇ6–8 (Iambl., *Protrepticus*, VI, 38, 3–14 = fragment B 33 Düring): see discussion in Berti 1962, pp. 477–83. Following the traditional translations, I have rendered *dokei* (141ª34) as 'It seems'. Here, the meaning of '*dokei*' is not 'It seems as opposed to reality' but 'It is an established opinion'. In this case, it is an established opinion that is held by Aristotle and (most likely) by others. For an analysis of the meaning of *dokei* in the *Topics* see Brunschwig 2007, pp. XXXVI–XL.

141ᵇ3–14: What is the point of saying 'The claim that the definition is not formulated through more familiar things can be taken in two ways'? This is to be understood as a criticism of a proposed definition (141ª26–9): the distinction between two ways in which the notion of familiarity can be used has a practical purpose in the dialectical debate since it helps the critic to find a way to refute the proposed definition. But the distinction serves also a theoretical purpose: it provides us with an analysis of 'more familiar' and leads us to its refinement. Aristotle offers an analysis of the notion of familiarity because he is confronted with a philosophical problem: despite its being appealing, the notion of familiarity as it was introduced in previous passages cannot be a sufficient requirement for a definition. For different things seem to be more familiar to different people; furthermore, at different times different things seem to be more familiar to the same person. Thus, this notion of familiarity seems to allow for the possibility that the same thing has more than one definition. But Aristotle cannot admit of a plurality of definitions, where each is framed in terms that are familiar to a different speaker. The definition must indicate the essence: the definition is one because the essence is one. Aristotle's move to preserve the oneness of the definition consists in the distinction between 'more familiar for us' and 'more familiar unqualifiedly' and in the claim that the defining expression must mention things that are 'more familiar unqualifiedly' than the thing to be defined. This problem in the notion of familiarity was already present in the case described in Plato's *Meno* 75B–C: Socrates defines 'shape' as 'The only thing which always accompanies colour', but Meno criticizes this definition and objects that if one does not know what colour is, one cannot come to know what shape is. From this point of view, Socrates' definition is not successful. It is possible that the example in the *Meno* influenced Aristotle's search for the definition's requirements. Moreover, Aristotle's distinction between two senses of 'being more familiar' could have been prompted by thinking about the so-called paradox of inquiry in *Meno* 80D–E.

This is perhaps the earliest text where the distinction between 'more familiar for us' and 'more familiar unqualifiedly' is drawn, and then it becomes customary in Aristotle's approach to some of his epistemological discussions. The distinction between 'familiar (or more familiar) for us' and 'familiar (or more familiar) unqualifiedly' can also be found elsewhere in this work (*Top.* VI.4, 141^{b}36–142^{a}11; VIII.1, 156^{a}4–7) and in other places in the corpus (see, e.g., *APr.* II.23, 68^{b}35–7; *APo.* I.2, 72^{a}1–5, I.3, 72^{b}26–30; *Ph.* I.1, 184^{a}16–26, I.5, 188^{b}30–2, I.6, 189^{a}4–7; *De An.* II.1, 413^{a}11–16; *Metaph.* VII.3, 1029^{b}3–12; *EN* I.4, 1095^{b}2–3;

on the stylistic variants of 'unqualifiedly' see below). A number of problematic issues are involved in this distinction: they are discussed in Mansion 1979 and in the main commentaries on those texts (see, e.g., Barnes 1993; Mignucci 1975; Ross 1949; Smith 1997). Although the distinction plays an important role in this chapter, it is not carefully explained. We are left with the difficult task of reconstructing a more precise characterization of these notions. We can single out four ways in which Aristotle presents them, but these ways lead us into too many different directions: (1) Aristotle's examples concern mainly the geometrical notions of solids, planes, lines, and points (141^b6–8): he claims that the earlier items on the list are more familiar to us, whereas the later are more familiar unqualifiedly. What is more familiar to us is what is closer to the data coming from sense-perception (141^b10–11): this suggests that it can comprise individuals as well as properties that are easily detected by our sense-perception. This further suggests that what is more familiar unqualifiedly can be not so close to the data coming from sense-perception and it is to be found at a more abstract level. The examples indicate that what is more familiar unqualifiedly corresponds to what is conceptually simpler. (2) What is more familiar to us is what the majority grasps first: an ordinary intelligence starts its epistemic journey from things that are more familiar to us, whereas a precise and extraordinary mind starts its epistemic journey from things that are more familiar unqualifiedly (141^b12–14). (3) The following rule is introduced: if the person who is familiar with *a* is familiar also with *b* (but it is not the case that the person who is familiar with *b* is familiar also with *a*), then *b* is more familiar unqualifiedly than *a* (141^b29–34). (4) What is familiar unqualifiedly is (not what is familiar to anyone but) what is familiar to people in a good mental condition (*tois eu diakeimenois tên dianoian*), just as what is unqualifiedly healthy is what is healthy for those in a good physical condition (142^a9–11). Cases (1) and (2) belong to this section of the text and will be examined below. Discussion of (3) and (4) will be found in the commentaries on the relevant lines. What is the origin of the terminology employed for this epistemological distinction? Aristotle does not explain it. We can see that '(more) familiar to us' corresponds to the most natural use of '(more) familiar': for when we say that something is (more) familiar, we understand that something is (more) familiar *to someone*. Then, perhaps by contrast with this natural use, the expression '(more) familiar unqualifiedly' was introduced. Sometimes in Aristotle's corpus there are stylistic variants where 'unqualifiedly' is replaced with other expressions such as 'in itself' or 'by nature'. This last variation in terminology could be due to the fact that the notion is difficult and each expression attempts to bring out a different aspect.

At 141^{b}5–9, Aristotle briefly expands on case (1). There are four geometrical examples; then two further instances (a unit and a letter) are said to bear a certain similarity to the geometrical ones. A unit and a letter are said to be (not only prior to, but also) a principle of numbers and syllables correspondingly. Aristotle is extremely concise here. None of the examples is fully explained, and the successful definitions that they intend to represent are not expressed. The conciseness could be explained by the fact that Aristotle's audience was already familiar with these cases. It is likely that in the background of Aristotle's geometrical examples there are some pre-Euclidean definitions. Euclid's *floruit* can be placed around 300 BC, and the date of the *Topics*' composition is placed around 350 BC (Brunschwig 1967, p. XC). There is evidence to claim that although Aristotle did not give original contributions to the development of mathematics, he mastered the mathematics of his time, namely the mathematics that was discussed in Plato's Academy and that was systematized in Euclid's *Elements* (Heath 1949; Apostle 1952).

These examples are meant to illustrate an epistemological thesis, namely the distinction between two ways of being more familiar. So, when Aristotle says talks about priority (141^{b}6 and 8), one is inclined to think that he is talking about epistemological priority. But in the sequel of the passage, some evidence suggests that he is talking about an ontological priority (see commentary on 141^{b}28–34). In any case, the examples discussed in this section will work also if they are intended to illustrate a case of ontological priority (more on this below).

It has been argued that in Aristotle's conception of geometrical entities there is an ambiguity. For it is unclear whether geometry studies objects or properties. The first view is present in *Metaph.* XIII. 3 (Annas 1976, p. 30); the latter seems supported in the *Categories* (Ackrill 1963, p. 91). In *Cat.* 6, 4^{b}20–5, lines, planes, and solids are characterized as belonging to the category of quantity. Here in the *Topics* Aristotle does not seem to commit himself to any specific view about the *status* of points, lines, planes, and solids, but he focuses on some epistemological claim.

At 141^{b}6 we find the Greek term *stigmê* instead of the Platonic (and Euclidean) *sêmeion*. In the apparatus of Ross's edition (1958) we find that only one MS(C: *Parisinus Coislinianus* 330, *saec*. XI) reads *sêmeion*. According to Aristotle, a point is not the constitutive element but the limit of a line: points cannot make up anything continuous like a line (*Ph.* IV.8, 215^{b}9, VI.1, 231^{a}24, VI.10, 241^{a}3; *GC* I.2, 317^{a}10). A point may be the extremity of the line, beginning or division of a line, but it is not a part of it (*Ph.* IV.11, 220^{a}1–21; VI.1, 231^{b}6 ff.; *Cael.* III.1, 300^{a}7–10). Aristotle defines a point as 'Unit having position' (*De An.* I.4, 409^{a}9). Although his definition is almost identical with the Pythagorean one (see Procl. *in Euc.* 95.26), Aristotle does not accept the Pythagorean view that the principles of things are points or numbers. Nor does he accept their view that points, lines, planes are substances contained in bodies (*Metaph.* III.5, 1002^{a}4–14; VII.2, 1028^{b}15–22). There is evidence to claim that the notion of a point was discussed in the Academy, where apparently a different conception of a point was held. In *Metaph.* I.9, 992^{a}19, we read that Plato seemed to have rejected the notion of point and regarded it as 'geometrical dogma'. However, it is uncertain whether Plato himself held this view; the reasons for this rejection are also unclear (Ross 1924, pp. 204–7). The epistemological priority of a point over a line does not seem difficult to justify, and it can be found also in Aristotle's *Physics* (IV.11, 220^{a}10–11; 13, 222^{a}15). As is common practice in geometry, if we want to refer to a line, we must refer to some points that limit it (Hussey 1983, pp. 153–9). The ontological priority of the point over the line is justified in *Metaph.* III.5, 1002^{a}5–8 as follows: a line cannot exist without a point, but a point can exist without a line. For a line to be, it must be limited by some points.

The epistemological priority of a line over a plane and of a plane over a solid can be justified in a way that is analogous to the previous case. A plane figure is limited by lines (its sides), and we measure its area using the length of its sides. A solid is limited by surfaces and we measure its volume using the areas of its faces. The ontological priority of a line over a plane and of a plane over a solid can be explained by referring to the notion of limit: there is a plane only if there are lines that limit it. Similarly, there is a solid only if there are planes that limit it.

An alternative explanation for the ontological priority of all the previous cases might be the following: the point is prior to the line because it is indivisible (*Metaph.* XIII.7, 1082^{a}25). That is to say, the point is the simplest geometrical entity. It is a standard Aristotelian view that, in the order of things, indivisible and simple entities precede divisible and complex ones. Then, the line is the simplest of other divisible geometrical entities (e.g. plane and solid). Thus, the line is posterior to the point but prior to the plane and to the solid, and similarly the plane is prior to the solid but posterior to the line. However, one could doubt this interpretation because the view (which most likely has a Platonic background) that indivisible and simple entities precede divisible and complex ones is not always maintained by Aristotle: in other works, he seems to prefer a more holistic approach where the whole comes before the parts. According to Aristotle, parts and wholes are said in many ways: see discussion in the commentary on chapter 13 where a species is conceived of as a whole and the defining elements are its parts.

In Aristotle's conception, numbers are pluralities of units (*Metaph.* V.13, 1020^{a}13; VII.13, 1039^{a}12; X.1, 1053^{a}30). Numbers are something like aggregates of units: Aristotle holds that a unit is not a number and that the first number is 2 (*Ph.* IV.11, 220^{a}27–32; *Metaph.* X.6, 1056^{b}25; XIII.9, 1085^{b}10). The fact that a number is an aggregate of units guarantees both the epistemological priority of a unit over the number (because elements can be regarded as unqualifiedly prior in knowledge to what they constitute) and the ontological priority of the unit over the number (because elements are ontologically prior to what they constitute). A more extensive presentation of Aristotle's philosophy of mathematics can be found in (e.g.) Apostle 1952; Annas 1976, pp. 26–41; and Cleary 1995, chs 3 and 7.

The view that a letter is prior in knowledge to a syllable is present in *Cat.* 12, 14^{a}38–14^{b}1: 'In a demonstrative science there is a prior and posterior in order, for the elements are prior in order to the diagrams (and in grammar the letters—*stoicheia*—are prior to the syllables)'. It could be plausibly argued that the understanding of the syllables is not possible if we do not recognize their elements, i.e. their letters. Perhaps Aristotle is making an implicit reference to (the teaching of) Plato's *Tht.* 202E–206B: the context is that of Socrates' dream where it is argued that elements (and letters) possess a 'much clearer knowledge' (202B7–8) than compounds (and syllables). The sense in which letters are principles of syllable needs some further explanation. In *Metaph.* V.24, 1023^{a}34, letters are described as that out of which syllables are constituted, and this guarantees their ontological priority. An alternative explanation (for saying that a unit and a letter are principles) can be found in the Aristotelian view expressed in *Metaph.* III.3, 999^{a}1–6, whereby what is undivided is one and is more in the nature of a principle. A unit is undivided and a letter (being an element) is undivided too. Hence, they are both in the nature of principles.

At 141^{b}12–14 Aristotle offers his second characterization of the distinction between 'more familiar to us' and 'more familiar unqualifiedly', and he draws a contrast between an ordinary mind and an extraordinary one. An ordinary mind comes to know first what is more familiar to us (i.e. what is closer to sense-perception), whereas a precise and extraordinary mind comes to know first items more familiar unqualifiedly (i.e. what is conceptually simpler). It is unclear what an ordinary intelligence and what an 'accurate and extraordinary' mind are. Since at 142^{a}2–4 Aristotle writes that 'at first, perceptible things are more familiar', then 'when they become more accurate (*akrisbesterois de genomenois*) the reverse happens', one could think that an ordinary mind refers to people who have begun but not yet completed their education. By contrast, an 'accurate and extraordinary' mind could refer to people who have made good progress in their intellectual training or have already completed it. However, this reading does not fit well with the fact that the definitions criticized in this context are: 'The point is the limit of the line', 'The line is the limit of the plane', and 'The plane is the limit of the solid'. It is unlikely that they were given by people at an early stage of their education (or by people that trust the data coming from sense-perception in order to form their arguments). For these definitions bear similarity with those discussed in Plato's *Meno* 76A–B, and this strongly suggests that they were held in the Academy, where expert geometers were admitted. An alternative option is that an ordinary mind refers to someone who is not new to the discipline and has a certain intellectual training; however, he does not have the proper intellectual training as Aristotle conceived of it: a proper intellectual training is what guarantees that the terms which are more familiar to us (namely those that are grasped first) coincide with those that are more familiar unqualifiedly (namely those that are more abstract).

At 141ᵇ12, we find *prognôrizousin*: it is composed of the prefix *pro* ('first') and the verb *gnôrizein* ('to become familiar'; see commentary on 141ᵃ26–141ᵇ2). The prefix might induce an ambiguity in the meaning of *prognôrizousin*: it could indicate that, for the majority, the order of discovery begins with items closer to sense-perception; but it could also indicate that the majority are better acquainted with what is closer to sense-perception (without making any claim about the chronological order of discovery). Compare the discussion of *pro* within *proairesis* ('deliberation' or, more properly, 'the choice of one thing before another', *EN* III.3, 1112ᵃ15–17) in, e.g., Irwin 1999, p. 206.

141ᵇ15–19: The general thesis is expressed that coming to know what is posterior through what is prior provides us with a better understanding. This way of acquiring knowledge should therefore be favoured and applied to definitions (the function of a definition is to make something known, 141ᵇ29–30). 'Prior' and 'posterior' display parallel ambiguities. A first possibility is that they mean 'prior/posterior in knowledge'—i.e. that Aristotle simply uses them in place of 'more/less familiar unqualifiedly' (a solution which might be favoured by the circumstance that the argument is about knowledge). A second possibility is that 'prior' and 'posterior' mean 'prior in being' and 'posterior in being'. On the ambiguity of 'prior' see commentary on 141ᵃ23–141ᵇ2.

At 141ᵇ16, it is difficult to find an accurate translation for the Greek *epistêmonikôteron*, whose literal meaning is 'more scientific'. It indicates that the procedure of coming to know the posterior through the prior provides us with a better understanding. In other words, the suggestion is that a procedure of the type described here is 'more precise'. One could choose to translate it with 'more precise', as this would make a better English translation. Something, however, would be lost, as the etymology would not be taken into account. Grammatically, *epistêmonikôteron*, which seems to be a *hapax* in the corpus, is the comparative form of the adjective *epistêmonikon*. It is a cognate of *epistêmê* ('understanding', 'science'), which in Aristotle captures the notion of scientific knowledge; this is characterized by the demonstrative procedure as presented in the first book of the *Posterior Analytics* (on the meaning of *epistêmê* see Barnes 1993, pp. 82, 91). By rendering *epistêmonikôteron* with 'more scientific', I am not suggesting that when he was writing this chapter of the *Topics*, Aristotle had already in mind the full-fledged concept of scientific knowledge as we find it in his *Posterior Analytics*.

At 141^{b}17–19, Aristotle considers the case of people that are not capable of framing definitions through prior things. He does not say why they lack this capability. It is possible that Aristotle is considering the case of people who lack a proper intellectual training, as suggested in *Metaph.* VII 3, 1029^{b}3–12 and *EN* I.4, 1095^{b}4 (see Burnyeat 1981). The remark that in the case of some people an account should be offered by means of things that are familiar to them presupposes that for these people 'what is prior' does not coincide with 'what is familiar to them'. This remark may be taken in two ways. (1) There is just one type of definition. Nevertheless, in some cases, a true account that does not respect the order of priority is admitted as a useful approach, provided that we come to realize what the correct procedure is. The process of coming to know something from things which are more familiar to the interlocutor is merely preliminary and will not establish a successful definition. (2) There are two types of definition: the first is framed by means of things that are familiar to the interlocutor and the second is given in terms that are prior. The first type is directed to people that are not properly educated, the second is directed to sharp and educated minds (Brunschwig 2007, p. xxv). However, given Aristotle's insistence on the claim that there is just one successful definition (because there is just one essence), it is difficult to accept (2) as a real option.

141^{b}19–28: There are three examples of attempted definitions: 'The point is the limit of the line', 'The line is the limit of the plane', and 'The plane is the limit of the solid'. These are true accounts, but they do not qualify as definitions, for they are framed in terms of what is more familiar to us (and that is different from what is more familiar unqualifiedly). As we know, in general what is more familiar to us refers to what is closer to sense-perception and does not have an adequate degree of abstraction to pick up items that would enter in a successful definition. The geometrical examples are introduced above at 141^{b}5–9 (see above commentary *ad loc.*). It is uncertain who originally framed those accounts. The (already noted) similarity with the definition offered by Socrates in Plato's *Meno* 76A, namely a shape is the limit of a solid, strongly suggests that they were held in the Academy. According to Aristotle, the account 'The point is the limit of the line' does not qualify as a definition because the line (mentioned in the defining expression) is less abstract and closer to sense-perception than the point. But this might not suffice to convince those who thought that this was the correct way to define it. For example, some might think that this is the way to define a primitive term, since there is nothing prior to it. Moreover, it could be the case that the account of the point as the limit of the line is especially effective (e.g. from the point of view of the interaction of concepts) in the construction of geometry as a deductive science. So, something else is needed to reinforce Aristotle's argument, but no indication is found in the text.

In this chapter, the successful definitions of point, line, and solid are not formulated. The closest we can get to the Aristotelian definitions of line, plane, and solid is a passage in *Metaph.* V.13, 1020^{a}11–12, where we read that line is a limited length, and length is a magnitude continuous in one dimension. Similarly, plane is a limited breadth, and breadth is a magnitude continuous in two dimensions. Then, solid is a limited depth, and depth is a magnitude continuous in three dimensions. But if in the *Topics* Aristotle is saying that (since the point is prior to the line) it must be mentioned in the definition of line (and similarly for the other cases too), then the definitions in the *Metaphysics* do not seem to respect the criteria set in the *Topics*. For the definition of line does mention a point (and similarly with the other cases). There are (at least) three possible explanations: (i) in the *Metaphysics* there are true accounts but not successful definitions; (ii) the accounts in the *Metaphysics* can be further analysed and somehow rephrased in successful definitions; (iii) in the *Topics* Aristotle says that the point is prior to and more familiar than the line (and similarly for the other cases), but he does not mean that the point must be mentioned in the definition of line (and similarly for the other cases). For there could be other things that are prior to what is to be defined, and the defining expression must mention them. The most likely explanation seems to be (iii). For the *Topics* is not a treatise on geometry: Aristotle could be using some geometrical examples without being committed to a specific geometrical theory. This last remark could help to explain a further philosophical problem: Aristotle says that a successful definition indicates the essence. But it is not clear whether points, lines, planes, solids, units, and letters (see above, 141^{b}5–9) have an essence. This is particularly the case if they are conceived of as magnitudes. It seems that these examples are not satisfying all the requirements of a successful definition. They can be viewed, however, as a way to illustrate the relation of priority without any commitment to a specific metaphysical view about geometrical entities. Aristotle seems to suggest that geometrical definitions offer a model of a certain type of definition (namely scientific definitions). These definitions are a model for a certain type of knowledge, namely scientific knowledge. It has been argued that Aristotle may be offering a model of *a priori* knowledge that is based on the practices of Greek geometry (Hintikka 1974). But this view has a problematic implication: it suggests that successful Aristotelian definitions are *a priori*. This could hardly be the case, especially if we read some chapters of *Posterior Analytics* where it is clear that there are definitions only of existing things and that to discover the essence of a natural kind requires empirical investigation.

The sentence 'Unless the same thing happens to be both more familiar to us and more familiar unqualifiedly' (141^{b}24–5) possibly refers to the situation mentioned at 141^{b}13–14 above: for some people with sharp minds (and who may be properly trained in their studies) there is no difference between what is more familiar to them and more familiar unqualifiedly. Alternatively, it could be a step in the *reductio ad absurdum*, being equivalent to 'Because otherwise the absurdity would follow that the same thing is both more familiar to us and more familiar unqualifiedly'.

141^{b}28–34: We find Aristotle's discussion of a definition of a species that is given through genus and differentia (see also *Top*. I.8, 103^{b}15). The example at 141^{b}31–2 of the species human that is defined through its genus (animal) and differentia (terrestrial) is often used in the *Topics*; see, e.g., I.7, 103^{a}27; II.1, 109^{a}15–16;

IV.6, 128ª25–8; V.3, 132ª1–4. At 141ᵇ28, 'The genus and the differentia carry the species to destruction with them' means that if the genus and differentia are destroyed, the species are destroyed too. Although Aristotle's argument is extremely compressed, it seems that he wants to establish that genera and differentiae are (A) ontologically prior to the species and (B) more familiar unqualifiedly than the species. In order to show (A) he employs the notion of *sunairesis*, namely co-destruction or co-suppression (141ᵇ28). This notion can be spelled out as establishing the rule that whenever the destruction of a involves the destruction of b, a is prior to b. The rule stated in the text implies that for every a, a is prior to a. Moreover, it allows the possibility that a is prior to b and b is also prior to a. Surely, this is not what Aristotle wants to say. Both problems are solved if an asymmetry condition is added: a's priority over b requires also that the destruction of b should not involve the destruction of a. However, the asymmetry condition is notoriously problematic in some cases, e.g. in the case of substance and accident. The notion of *sunairesis* (co-destruction or co-suppression) can be found also in *Top.* IV.2, 123ª14–19:

> Moreover, see whether the species is naturally prior and carries the genus to destruction with itself (*sunanairei*); for the contrary seems to be the case. Moreover, if it is possible for the genus stated or for its differentia to be absent, e.g. for movement to be absent from the soul or truth and falsehood from opinion, then neither of the things stated can be its genus or its differentia; for it seems that the genus and the differentia accompany the species, as long as it exists.

See also *Metaph.* XI.1, 1059ᵇ38–1060ª2: 'But in as much as the species are destroyed together with (*sunanaireitai*) the genera, the genera are more like principles; for, that which carries another to destruction with itself (*to sunanairoun*) is a principle of it'. The application of this rule to the case at hand will tell us that since the destruction of the genus or differentiae involves the destruction of the species, genus and differentiae are ontologically prior to the species. The reason why the destruction of the genus brings with it the destruction of the species is that existence for a kind is equivalent to being instantiated: if the genus becomes non-instantiated, then the species also becomes non-instantiated, whereas the converse fails. This follows from the claim that the genus has a wider extension than the species (see *Cat.* 11, 14ª8–10; more on the genus is said in the commentary on *Topics* VI.5). The argument in support of (B) tells us that knowledge of the species follows from knowledge of its genus and differentia, but the converse does not hold. The text seems to presuppose a definition of, or a rule for, 'unqualifiedly more familiar than': whenever knowing *a* involves knowing *b* (but not the converse), then *b* is more familiar than *a*. It is presupposed that (at least whenever *a* is definable) to know *a* is to grasp the definition of *a* (such a presupposition is widespread in Plato's dialogues, e.g. *Men.* 80D5–7). Note that this rule fits well with all the theses that both the genus and the differentia are unqualifiedly more familiar than the species and that the genus is unqualifiedly more familiar than the species (if you define terrestrial, you must mention animal).

This is the only passage in the chapter where ontological and epistemological priorities are associated. The ontological case precedes the epistemological, and the latter is introduced by 'But it is also' (*esti de kai*, 141ᵇ29), and this suggests that ontological priority is the fundamental case on which the relation of being more familiar unqualifiedly is based. This does not mean, however, that the epistemological case could be reduced completely to the ontological one: the first brings in the concept of knowledge, which is not present in the second (for example, the concept of epistemological priority presupposes a knower, who is not at all required by ontological priority). If at 141ᵇ3–4 Aristotle was introducing a genuine conjunction of the concepts of ontological priority and greater familiarity (see commentary on 141ª26–141ᵇ2), this is where he says something more about it.

The concept of ontological priority is discussed in several passages in the corpus (e.g. *Cat.* 12, 14ª29–35; *Ph.* VIII.7, 260ᵇ17–18; *Metaph.* V.11). The concept of priority 'in nature and substance' is attributed to Plato (*Metaph.* V.11, 1019ª2–4). If it is true to say that the *Topics* summarizes the content of Aristotle's lectures in the Academy, then his listeners might have been familiar with the concept of ontological priority, and hence they may have found convincing the argument that relies upon this concept (on Aristotle's philosophical activity in the Academy see, e.g., Berti 1977, pp. 37–8).

141ᵇ34–142ᵃ16: Aristotle strengthens the importance of the notion of 'more familiar unqualifiedly' and points at the difficulty involved in the view of those who do not accept it. There are two related cases: (A) different things are more familiar to different people so that there are different definitions of the same thing (141ᵇ35–142ᵃ2); (B) different things are more familiar to the same person at different times (e.g. at a different stage of their education), so that one must be offered different definitions of the same thing (142ᵃ2–6). There is an unwelcome consequence in both cases, namely the possibility that there are several definitions of the same thing. But this raises an ontological problem (as discussed at 141ᵃ34): if the same thing has several definitions, then it will have several essences; but this is impossible. The definition is one and the same because it indicates the essence and there is only one essence. Here Aristotle seems more interested in the ontological problem; he does not make clear that there is also an epistemological one, which can be expressed by saying that if there are different definitions of the same thing, then the stability needed in a scientific inquiry is lost. For a scientific inquiry into x is an inquiry into the unique essence of x (that is captured by a definition, which must also be unique).

At 142ᵃ9–10, there is a characterization of 'more familiar unqualifiedly' (see above commentary on 141ᵇ3-14): what is familiar unqualifiedly corresponds to what is familiar to those with a mental faculty in good condition. However, having a mental faculty in good condition seems to introduce a trivial requirement; for a standard of familiarity cannot be fixed in terms of what is familiar to someone whose mental faculty is merely sound. So perhaps we need to add that what is familiar unqualifiedly is what is familiar to those who have a mind that is *well disposed* to grasp more abstract notions as a result of a certain intellectual training (namely the intellectual training indicated by Aristotle), and the mind that is well disposed to grasp more abstract notions could be that of a well-trained scholar. This suggests a way to understand the analogy: healthy unqualifiedly is healthy for those whose body is in a normal condition as a result of an appropriate amount of exercise. What is *more* familiar unqualifiedly is what is familiar to those whose mind is in a *better* condition: they correspond to those who have a body in a better condition thanks to a greater amount of exercise, namely the athletes. But we would not say that what is healthy unqualifiedly is what is healthy for these highly trained people: here the analogy breaks down. At 142ª10, 'thinking' (*dianoia*) does not seem to be used in a technical sense, for it is not opposed to 'understanding' (*nous*). The example of the healthy body has a Platonic background (see Plato's *Grg.* 464A). There is a passage in the *Ethics* where Aristotle defines what is truly healthy as what is healthy to those people who are in a good bodily condition (*EN* III.4, 1113ª26-9). Moreover, when Aristotle is debating cases of epistemological relativism, he often appeals to the good (healthy) or poor (sick) condition of the body (*Metaph.* IV.5, 1010ᵇ3-9).

The key to understanding 142ª13-16 is in the expression 'In a way that will meet most agreement' (*malista d'omologoumenôs*): it will be agreed by most people, including those (mentioned at 141ᵇ34-5) who claim that 'Definitions of this sort (*sc.* those that come from things familiar to each) are in conformity with the truth'. Even these people will agree that a certain definition should be discarded if the defining expression mentions things that are neither more familiar unqualifiedly nor more familiar to us.

142ª17-21: At 142ª17-18, there is a brief reference to the previous part of the chapter, i.e. the investigation as to whether the defining part mentions things that are prior to and more familiar than what is to be defined. This is a clause of transition between the long discussion of the first *tropos* (141ª26-142ª16) and the others (for the structure of this chapter see the Introduction, above). At 142ª19-21, another way in which one can fail to give a definition is briefly described; this is centred on the distinction between being at rest and definite on the one hand, and being in motion and indefinite on the other. The brevity of the passage and the lack of examples make it difficult to understand what Aristotle has in mind. He says that 'What remains still and what is definite are prior to what is indefinite and in motion' (142ª19-20), and he does not offer a justification for this view. It may be just a generic reference to Plato's ontology where Forms are motionless, but perceptible items (ontologically dependent on Forms) are in constant flux. However, Aristotle's claim is phrased in a general way, so that it could also be explained by ideas about motion that lie behind different philosophical doctrines (see Düring 1968, pp. 207–8, and Brunschwig 2007, p. 52, n. 2). In particular, the idea that motion is associated with what is indefinite can be explained by reference to different metaphysical backgrounds. When in *Ph.* III.2 Aristotle discusses other thinkers' views about motion, he says: 'Motion is thought to be something indefinite, and the principles in the second column (*sc.* of correlated opposites) are indefinite because they are privative' (201^{b}24; Hussey 1983, translation slightly modified). Here Aristotle refers to the Pythagorean list of opposites arranged in two columns (*Metaph.* I.5, 986^{a}23–6). We know that some intuitions behind this list influenced Plato. Aristotle himself retained some of these intuitions and integrated them in his metaphysics of potentiality and actuality. He held that motion is incomplete in itself because it points forward to its completion. Motion is a potentiality that can be understood only by referring to the corresponding actuality (the end-state of this motion) and is ontologically dependent on it. Although at 142^{a}17–21 Aristotle does not commit himself to any specific view about motion, it is likely that he had already formed some of his opinions, since *Ph.* III.1–3 was probably composed early, i.e. soon after the *Topics* (for a discussion about Aristotle's concept of motion and a commentary on the passage from the *Physics* quoted above see Hussey 1983). At a later stage, namely in *Metaph.* IX.8, potentiality is explicitly associated with every principle of motion, and actuality is said to be prior (to potentiality) both in formula (or definition) and in substance. It could be noted that motion can be easily associated with the concept of potentiality, but rest seems to be a less happy match for actuality, for it is not clear that every case of rest can be described as one of actuality. But this does not undermine Aristotle's argument because here the connection between rest and determinacy does not need a mediation of the concept of actuality.

It is difficult to illustrate this case without making reference to a specific conceptual *apparatus*, and this may be the reason why Aristotle does not give us an example. If we adopt the Aristotelian framework (as it was probably developed at this stage of his philosophical speculation), we can illustrate this case by expanding on a suggestion offered by Pacius 1597, p. 432. Suppose knowledge is defined as a disposition acquired through a long period of study. Here the defining part (i.e. 'Disposition acquired through a long period of study') is framed in terms of motion, namely in terms of something incomplete that points forward to its completion. Since the completion is the state of knowledge, i.e. the thing to be defined, it follows that the defining expression signifies something that is not prior to the thing to be defined, but that is dependent on it.

142^{a}22–33: This is the first of three further ways to detect that proposed definitions are unsuccessful because the priority requirement is not respected. Aristotle deals with the accounts of opposites and relatives. He offers a more extensive and technical discussion of this issue later in this book. Accounts of relatives are further explored in *Top.* VI.8, 146^{a}33–146^{b}12 and 9, 147^{a}22^{b}35 (see commentaries *ad loc.*). Some Academics listed opposites among relatives: this might be behind Aristotle's treating them in tandem here and elsewhere. Opposites are exemplified by the case of good and evil. Aristotle's idea seems to be that one fails to offer a definition in terms of prior items if one opposite is defined through the other. The reason for this seems to lie in the fact that 'Opposites are simultaneous by nature', and this means that neither of the two opposites is ontologically prior to the other. If it is correct to say that epistemological priority is based on ontological priority (see commentary on 141^{b}28–34), it follows that neither of the two opposites is epistemologically prior to the other. The claim that knowledge of opposites is the same was presented as an *endoxon* in *Top.* I.1, 104^{a}15–16, and here Aristotle uses an implication of this claim to strengthen his (or the interlocutor's) position. The notion of 'simultaneous by nature' is discussed in *Cat.* 7, 7^{b}15 and 13, 14^{b}27–33, where the important point is made that, in the case of things that are simultaneous by nature, neither is the cause of the other's existence. It is also said that (not only opposites but also) relatives are 'simultaneous by nature'. Further difficulties involved in the definition of good and evil will be discussed in *Top.* VI.9, 147^{b}20 (see commentary *ad loc.*). Note that there are some general questions about the possibility of defining good. As Aristotle often repeats, good does not belong to any of the categories (see, e.g., *EN* I.6, 1096^{a}25–8). Thus, it seems difficult to offer a definition of good that matches the criteria set in the

Topics, namely a definition that is framed in terms of genus and differentia of the thing to be defined.

Relatives are introduced at 142^{a}26. The text is extremely concise, and the notion of relative is not fully explained. Examples of relatives are double and half. Aristotle's view on relatives is notoriously very complex; some of his difficulties in this area might be due to Academic antecedents. For our present purposes, it will suffice to make the following points. There are two ways to read the expression 'Things that are called relatives in themselves': (i) we can take 'in themselves' as modifying 'relatives'; or (ii) we can take 'in themselves' as modifying 'are called'. Option (i) seems to be adopted by (e.g.) Forster 1960; he translates: 'Things which are described as in themselves relatives'. This suggests that among all relatives there is a subgroup formed by relatives in themselves. If this is the case, then Aristotle is using the expression 'relatives in themselves' in a technical sense; but, to the best of my knowledge, this reading is not supported by other passages in the corpus. Option (ii) suggests a reading that is supported by the discussion of relatives in *Cat.* 7: at the very beginning of this chapter (6^{a}36–7) Aristotle explains what a relative is, and he uses the expression *haper* ('precisely what') that qualifies the complement of *legetai* ('are said') to describe the features that a relative possesses when it is called a relative. It has to be noted that for Aristotle *haper* ('precisely what') has the same value of *kath'auta* ('in themselves'); see Bonitz 1870, pp. 33B36–8. Moreover, at 7^{b}10 Aristotle says: 'One must give as a correlative whatever is properly spoken of in relation to'. In other words, double is called the relative of half (and half is called its correlative); similarly, slave is called the relative of master (and master is its correlative). That is to say, the correlative of a relative will reciprocate only if it is properly expressed. For, although master is human and two-footed, human and two-footed are not called the correlative of slave. At 7^{b}10, the adverb 'properly' (*oikeiôs*) does a similar job to 'in themselves' (*kath'auta*) at 142^{a}28; namely it qualifies 'is called' (*legetai*).

If we compare this discussion of relatives with the one in *Cat.* 7, we see that in the *Topics* Aristotle emphasizes a restriction in the criterion for being a relative. The restriction is expressed at 142^{a}29: 'It is impossible to become familiar with the one without the other'. Aristotle's emphasis on the restriction can be understood in (at least) two ways. First, it may be intended to warn us about the problematic case presented in the *Categories*, namely to avoid parts such as hands and heads being described as relatives. For it is true to say that a head is called someone's head, but it is not true to say that a head is a relative. For it is possible to know the head without knowing that in relation to which it is spoken of (see discussion in Ackrill 1963, pp. 101–3); by contrast, in the case of double and half, you cannot know the one without knowing the other. Second, it is possible that Aristotle emphasizes the restriction because he is interested in the possibility of defining relatives and he wants to suggest that this is a problematic case because one is not prior to the other.

To sum up, Aristotle's suggestion is that the cases of opposites and relatives present a feature that is different from the cases considered so far (particularly the geometrical ones). Since there is no ontological priority between opposites and between a relative and its correlative, it does not seem possible to say which (if any) is epistemologically prior (epistemological priority seems to be based on ontological priority; see 141^{b}28–34). Thus, we are left with the problem of whether it is possible to define them. There are three alternatives. (i) A first alternative seems to be implied at 142^{a}21, when Aristotle says that he is discussing cases of 'failing to give a definition'. This suggests that for some things there is no definition. That is to say, opposites and relatives are not definable in the standard way, hence they are indefinable. But this is a very demanding consequence indeed since it prevents many things from having a definition. (ii) A second alternative is that they can be defined but not through one another. (iii) A third alternative seems to be envisaged at 142^{a}26–7: 'Perhaps some things cannot be defined otherwise', and at 142^{a}31–2: 'It is necessary that in the account of the one the other also be included'. In other words, some opposites and relatives are not definable in the standard way, but they are still definable, for they can be interdefined. However, this third alternative also has a problematic consequence that is not easy to accommodate. For we need to drop the criterion that the defining expression must mention things that are prior to the kind to be defined. We know that this is a fundamental requirement (Aristotle said that if one fails to meet it, one fails to offer a successful definition). Unfortunately, at this stage in the text there seems to be no satisfactory solution of this problem, but we are simply alerted to it. A further discussion of relatives and opposites can be found in *Metaph.* V.15.

142ª34–142ᵇ6: This is the second of three ways (introduced at 142ª22) to detect that definitions are unsuccessful because the priority requirement (namely that the defining expression must mention things that are prior to and more familiar than what is to be defined) is not respected. In other words, Aristotle's idea is that if the interlocutor phrases the defining expression in a way that it mentions things present in the kind to be defined, then he is not offering a definition through prior and more familiar items. Rather, he is trying to define something through itself, and this leads to circularity in the proposed definition. As his example shows, Aristotle is not interested in straightforward cases where the same item is explicitly named in both parts of the definition. His example says that the definition of sun cannot be 'It (*sc.* the sun) is a star that appears by day' since the definition of day is 'It (*sc.* day) is the passage of the sun over the earth'; thus, the definition of sun would be 'It (*sc.* the sun) is a star that appears during the passage of the sun over the earth' (the example reproduces a definition that occurs also in ps.-Platonic *Def.* 411B; this is the second reference to Platonic definitions in this chapter). Two points can be made. The first is epistemological: if we assume that the function of a definition is to make what is to be defined known through the defining expression, and if we accept that we come to know through what is (unqualifiedly) more familiar, then a definition of this kind cannot be accepted, for something cannot be (unqualifiedly) more familiar than itself. The second point is ontological: if we accept that what is (unqualifiedly) more familiar corresponds to what is ontologically prior, then the above definition cannot be accepted because something cannot be ontologically prior to itself. If we adopt a conceptual *apparatus* that Aristotle develops later (and particularly) in the *Posterior Analytics*, we could say that the sun is prior to and more familiar than the day since it is its cause (Aristotle's position in *APo.* II.8–10 is that the definition indicates the essence and in the essence you find the cause; see above commentary on 141ª26–141ᵇ2).

One can understand 142ᵇ2 as being about names ('For, when he uses "sun" he uses "day"'), or about things ('For, when he uses sun he uses day'). Since Aristotle is interested in real definitions (and not in definitions that give the meaning of a term), it is more likely that he is talking at a level of things.

142^b7–19: This is the third of three ways (introduced at 142^a22) to detect proposed definitions that are unsuccessful because the priority requirement is not respected. According to Aristotle, there are two cases that are similar because they concern the relation between two differentiae or two species that are involved in same stage of the division of a genus.

The first case (142^b7–10) concerns the relation of two coordinate elements into which the same genus is divided. The account of an odd number as a number which is greater by one than an even number does not qualify as a definition: odd and even are coordinate elements, and if you try to define one coordinate element through the other, you will not offer a definition through what is prior. For coordinate elements are called in at the same stage in the division of the same genus, and hence neither is ontologically prior to the other (i.e. they are simultaneous by nature). Since at 141^b28–34 Aristotle seems to suggest that ontological priority is the primary case on which the relation of being more familiar unqualifiedly is based, it follows that one coordinate element cannot be epistemologically prior to the other. When Aristotle talks about coordinate elements that are called in at the same stage of the division of a genus, he simply states his view without any justification. This may be explained by the fact that he considers it intuitively plausible, or he may think that (with their Academic background) his listeners are accustomed to the issues concerning the division of a genus. Alternatively, since he is very concise, he may be planning to come back to this point elsewhere in the treatise. The example at 142^b12 makes it clear that here coordinate elements are the differentiae: odd is described as greater by a unit than even, where odd and even are the differentiae of number. This discussion is very brief but interesting because it raises the general question of whether it is possible to define differentiae. If 'the genus is *always* divided by differentiae that are coordinate members of a division' (*Top.* VI. 6, 143^a35), then there are three possibilities: (i) differentiae cannot be defined at all; (ii) differentiae can be defined but not through one another; (iii) differentiae can be defined, but their definitions constitute an exception to the general criterion that a definition must be framed through what is prior. These alternatives remind us of the discussion about the definition of opposites and relatives. Also in that case we were left with the problem of whether it is possible to define them, and the three envisaged possibilities were similar to (i), (ii), and (iii) here (see the last part of the commentary on 142^{a}21–33). However, here in the case of differentiae there is no textual support to favour either of the alternatives. Still the following can be argued with some plausibility: Aristotle is talking about the possibility of pointing out a mistake in an unsuccessful definition, and he seems to assume that a successful definition can be given. In other words, in this passage there is an implicature that differentiae *can* be defined (against (i)), but it remains unclear whether they are definable in the way indicated by (ii) or (iii).

The second case (142^{b}11–19) concerns the relation between two species with a superior and a subordinate position in the division of the same genus (for the translation of *hexin* with 'possession' at 142^{b}12, see 'The value of *hexis*' in 'Terminological Clarifications'). If you try to define the superior through the subordinate, you violate the fundamental requirement for a successful definition: you do not define through what is prior. For 'The person who uses the subordinate necessarily uses this (*sc.* the superior)' (142^{b}15). In other words, if you try to define the superior through the subordinate, you will get a circular account: the definition of even number cannot be expressed as number that is divisible by two, for 'The person who uses *into halves* uses *even*, since to divide into halves means to divide into two and two is even' (142^{b}17–19). The italics (*virtue*, *good*, *into halves*, and *even*) indicate that Aristotle is talking at a level of things, or concepts, rather than that of names. Aristotle offers a more extensive discussion of these questions in chapter 6, where some of the previous examples are discussed in detail.

CHAPTER 5

Introduction: The beginning of chapter 5 refers to the discussion in the preceding chapter, where Aristotle argued that the defining expression must mention things that are prior to and unqualifiedly more familiar than what is to be defined (*Top.* VI.4, 141^{a}28–9). This is the first commonplace regarding the failure of offering a successful definition, namely the first point where the answerer's proposed definition may be examined and criticized. This commonplace is divided into several parts that are discussed throughout chapter 4. The second commonplace concerns the role of the genus in a definition and is introduced in what immediately follows. In the *Topics* the discussion of the genus takes two standpoints: the genus is analysed both as a predicable on its own and as an element of the definition. More precisely, the genus is one of the four predicables together with definition, unique property, and accident (*Top.* I.4, 101^{b}25). The genus as a predicable is discussed throughout book IV of the *Topics*. The role played by the genus in definitions is presented at the beginning of book VI (1, 139^{a}27–31; see commentary *ad loc.*) and is resumed in this chapter. Here the discussion is extremely compressed, and as it stands it would not be an adequate presentation of the role of the genus in the definition. Many of the claims that we find in this chapter are to be understood on the basis of previous discussions of the genus, in particular on the basis of the commonplaces concerning the genus that were analysed in book IV. The discussion of possible mistakes regarding the genus within a definition is the main focus of this chapter and refers back to *Top.* VI.1, 139^{a}27–31. In general, the second commonplace regarding the definition is described as the failure of giving an account that mentions the genus of the thing to be defined as the first element in the defining expression. This failure can take a number of forms, but Aristotle's way of indicating them is unclear. We can single out three cases: (1) omitting the genus entirely, (2) placing the thing to be defined in the wrong genus, and (3) leaving out some correlatives (when the genus is a relative). Case (2) can be further divided into (2a) placing the thing to be defined in a genus to which it does not belong at all (e.g. if human is placed in quantity and not in substance), and (2b) placing the thing to be defined not in its proximate genus but in a higher one (e.g. if raven is placed not in the genus bird but in animal). The chapter is structured as follows: the examples at 142^{b}24 and 142^{b}25–6 refer to (1); the cases discussed at 142^{b}30–143^{a}11 illustrate (3); the remark at 143a12–4 could cover (2a) and (2b) (see commentary *ad loc.*); the examples in the last portion of the chapter (142a15–8) illustrate (2b).

142^{b}20–9: At 142^{b}22 the proviso that the thing to be defined (*pragma*) is in a genus is designed to exclude from this commonplace the case in which what is to be defined is a *summum genus* and so, of course, cannot be placed in a genus. There is a list of eight philosophically important uses of 'to be in' in *Ph.* IV.3, 210^{a}14–24 (see Hussey 1983, pp. 107–8; Morison 2002, pp. 71–6). The sense of 'to be in' at 142^{b}22 corresponds to the third of the list in the *Physics*, namely 'As human is in animal and, generally, species in genus' (210a17–8). Adopting a modern terminology, we say that it expresses the notion of being extensionally contained; that is to say, it indicates that the thing to be defined is extensionally contained in its genus (for example, the species human is extensionally contained in the genus animal). Despite its conciseness, the remark is important: it sheds light on the relation between what is to be defined and its genus. It tells us that the genus has a wider extension than the thing to be defined, or, to use technical jargon, it does not counter-predicate with it. This feature distinguishes the genus from the definition; for they both indicate the essence of what is to be defined, but only the definition counter-predicates with it (on the relations between the predicables see Barnes 1970; Brunschwig 1986).

In LSJ, *s.v. prokeimai*, the suggested translation for the phrase *prokeitai tou logou* (142^{b}24) is 'is first stated in the account', but I feel unhappy about this proposal. For, strictly speaking, in this expression there is nothing that corresponds to 'first'. In the verb *prokeimai* the suffix *pro* means 'before', 'at the front of', or 'at the forefront of'; for this reason, I suggest the rendering 'is laid down at the forefront of the account'. In this way it is possible to show the difference between *prokeitai tou logou* and *prôton upotithetai* (142^{b}28), which I have rendered as 'to be put forward as first': here the word 'first' has something explicitly corresponding to it in the Greek.

At 142^{b}23–4, Aristotle claims that the genus must be the first element in the defining part: as we know, the defining expression mentions two elements, namely genus and one or more differentiae (*Top.* VI.4, 141^{b}25–7). Why must the genus be put forward as the first element? The primacy of the genus is justified by saying that it indicates the what-it-is of the thing to be defined (142^{b}24). One might find puzzling the claim that the genus indicates the what-it-is, since it seems that it is the role of the definition as a whole to do so (see *Top.* I.5, 101^{b}38). Perhaps a distinction could be drawn between higher genera, which are predicated in the what-it-is, and the proximate genus (namely the one that must be expressed in a definition), which is linked with the 'what-it-is-to-be' (see commentary on 143a15–9). In *Top.* VI.1, 139^{a}29–31, we read that 'Among the things in a definition the genus seems *most of all* to indicate the essence of what is being defined' (see commentary *ad loc.*). That is to say, according to Aristotle the genus is more appropriately mentioned in answering the 'What is it?' question. In giving the appropriate answer to the 'What is it?' question (*Top.* I.5, 102^{a}33–4), the genus 'must separate it (*sc.* the thing to be defined) from the other things, whereas the differentia must separate it from any of the things in the same genus' (*Top.* VI.3, 140^{a}27–9; see commentary *ad loc.*). Again, in *Top.* I.5, 102^{a}31–2 we read that the genus is predicated in the what-it-is of the thing to be defined, whereas in *Top.* VI.6, 144^{a}20–2 we are told that the differentia reveals what sort of thing what is to be defined is (see commentary *ad loc.*). This suggests that one must first posit the genus, as it provides us with a first insight into how things can be divided. There are some tensions in Aristotle's writings on this point; elsewhere he seems to think that the differentia indicated the essence, see *Metaph.* VII.12, 1038^{a}19–20: 'If then this is so, clearly the last differentia will be the substance of the thing and its definition'. The view in the *Metaphysics* is discussed in, e.g., Burnyeat 1979, pp. 99–105; Frede and Patzig 1988, pp. 233–40; Bostock 1994, pp. 176–84. The tensions between these texts are addressed in, e.g., Granger 1984. In the *Topics*, Aristotle does not offer a systematic and complete justification of the primacy of the genus as well as of the procedure of dividing the genus into its species; this may be due to the fact that his Academic audience was well acquainted with Plato's view in this area (see discussion in Berti 1977, pp. 192–4). In *Top.* VI.11, 149^{a}17–20, the remarks that 'The genus is most familiar of all' and that 'It (*sc.* the differentia) is more unfamiliar (*sc.* than the genus)' suggest another way to understand why the genus has to be the first element of the definition. From the discussion of the meaning of 'more familiar' in the previous chapter (*Top.* VI.4, 141^{b}2–14) it follows that when Aristotle says that the genus is 'more familiar' he means that the genus is 'more familiar unqualifiedly' (see commentary *ad loc.*). Moreover, in *Top.* VI.4, 141^{b}28–9 he suggests that the relation of epistemological priority is based upon that of ontological priority. In other words, it can be argued that the genus is epistemologically prior to the differentiae because it is ontologically prior to them (in the sense of 'prior' discussed in *Cat.* 13, 15^a 4–7). It could also be the case that, were one to give an account of a differentia, one should mention the genus it contributes to divide.

If the rule that the genus must be stated as first in the account is taken in a strictly formal sense (namely that in a definition the word order is such that the genus is the first element of the defining expression), it works in ancient Greek but not in English. For example, in the definition of conviction (*pistis*) the Greek formulation of the defining part is *upolêpsis sfodra* (*Top.* IV.5, 126^{b}18); in English this is rendered as 'strong belief' and not as 'belief strong'. The word order is important for Aristotle because it can help to avoid the mistake of confusing the genus with the differentia (see his discussion in *Top.* IV.5, 126^{b}13–19).

In the expressions 'If someone has defined ... ' (142^{b}25), 'He has not mentioned ... ' (142^{b}26), and 'He has not given its account ... ' (142^{b}31), there is a question about who is being envisaged as giving the definitions. These are examples of definitions, and they are given by the opponent in a dialectical context: Aristotle's aim is to provide us with means to criticize these accounts according to the commonplace regarding the genus.

In general, in this chapter Aristotle does not say whether he is talking for constructive or destructive purposes. However, the fact that he is discussing possible mistakes concerning the genus suggests that he is concerned with destructive purposes (namely, one can destroy the opponent's definition by pointing out that it does not meet the requirements concerning the genus). This is in line with the fact that book VI is 'refutative' (Brunschwig 2007, p. 205). As Aristotle says, 'It is more difficult to construct than to destroy a definition', since it is hard to get a good grasp of the constituents of a definition (*Top.* VII.5, 154^a23–8).

142^b30–143^a11: The illustration of the failure of leaving out from the definition some correlatives (when the genus is a relative) begins here and comes in two stages. First, a general rule for criticizing a proposed definition is stated and illustrated by an example (142^b30–5). Second, this general rule is qualified on the basis of a different example (142^b35–143^a8). At 142^b30–5, Aristotle wants to discuss the case where the kind to be defined is said in relation to several things. He suggests that the speaker's proposed definition must be analysed according to the general rule that if the kind to be defined is said in relation to several things, the definition must mention all of them. But this way of presenting the problem does not make it clear why this case is discussed in the commonplace dealing with the failure to place the thing to be defined in its genus (142^b22–3). One way of shedding some light on this point is by reading *Top.* VI.8, 146^b7–9: 'In the definition he should have given either that in relation to which the thing itself is said or that, whatever it is, *in relation to which the genus is said*'. This suggests that when Aristotle says that what is to be defined is said in relation to several things, he is expressing himself succinctly: properly speaking, what is said in relation to many things is the genus of what is to be defined in so far as it is its genus. For example, knowledge is related to reading and writing what is dictated in so far as it is the genus of literacy; but it is related to (e.g.) playing an instrument and singing in so far as it is the genus of music. If one fails to mention some of the things in relation to which the genus is said (in so far as it is the genus of the thing to be defined), one does not properly locate the thing to be defined within its genus. One does mention the genus, but a mistake is made in giving the position of the thing to be defined within it. An alternative interpretation might be attempted: one could retain the suggestion that the relativity concerns primarily the genus of the thing to be defined (*Top.* VI.8, 146^b6), and one could propose that knowledge-of-reading-and-writing-from-dictation is the genus of literacy. Suppose that someone is attempting to place literacy in one of its genera, and suppose that they try to do this by saying that literacy is knowledge-of-writing-from-dictation. Such an account may be criticized by pointing out that knowledge-of-writing-from-dictation is not a genus of literacy: the genus of literacy is knowledge-of-reading-and-writing-from-dictation. So, the person in question has failed to place literacy into one of its genera.

There is a difficulty with the first interpretation: the refutative strategy does not amount to failing to place the thing to be defined into its genus. The mistake to which Aristotle draws our attention is very much like that of mentioning the wrong differentia. But perhaps this is a special case that concerns the mistake of placing the thing to be defined (not in any genus whatsoever but) in a genus that is a relative. There is also a difficulty with the second interpretation: 'Knowledge of reading and writing what is dictated' seems to be the entire defining expression of literacy rather than mentioning its genus only. However, this difficulty can perhaps be overcome by insisting that despite appearances 'Knowledge of reading and writing what is dictated' is not the entire defining expression of literacy; the entire defining expression would, rather, be something like 'Knowledge of reading and writing what is dictated according to the rules of a correct pronunciation' (where 'according to the rules of a correct pronunciation' expresses the differentia). If this is right, one could suggest that in these lines Aristotle is focusing on the role of the genus, and when he says that 'The person who says both these things has (*sc.* defined)' (142^b34), he means that the proposed definition is successful because the genus has been adequately expressed.

For the addition of 'is defined as' at 142^b31–2, see 'The translation of *hoion ei*' in 'Terminological Clarifications'. At 142^b31, Aristotle uses *apodedôken*. In a definitional context, this verb has the technical meaning of 'to give an account'. In the *Topics* it is very often used in this technical sense (see 'The verb *apodidonai* and its forms' in 'Terminological Clarifications').

The first example is an attempt to define *grammatikê,* which I have translated with 'literacy'. Here and in other contexts, most scholars and translators render *grammatikê* as 'grammar' (see, e.g., Ackrill 1963, Forster 1960, and Barnes 1984, vol. 1; Tricot 1950 and Brunschwig 2007 adopt the French '*grammaire*', but in his notes Brunschwig explains his unhappiness with this translation [see p. 54, n. 2]). Although it is etymologically close to the Greek, this translation is not accurate: the concept of grammar generally refers to a set of rules for forming words and combining them into sentences, whereas the concept of literacy refers to the capacity of reading and writing, and Aristotle has the latter in mind (this translation is adopted by Smith 1997; Barnes 1993 translates *grammatikos*, a cognate of *grammatikê*, with 'literate'). As for the translation of *epistêmê* (142^b31), it must be noted that in philosophical contexts (and especially in the *Posterior Analytics*) *epistêmê* refers to the notion of scientific knowledge and is usually rendered with 'science' or 'understanding' (Barnes 1993, Burnyeat 1981). However, here the meaning of *epistêmê* is not technical, and the expression is best translated with 'knowledge'. In English, 'knowledge of writing', and in general 'knowledge of φ-ing', is rather vague and unspecific. In this vagueness it matches the Greek expression it translates. But the context clearly indicates that what Aristotle has in mind by 'knowledge of writing' (and in general by 'knowledge of φ-ing') would be more precisely expressed by 'knowledge of how to write' (and in general 'knowledge of how to φ').

It is Aristotle's view that the genus of literacy is knowledge, and knowledge is a relative (*Cat.* 8, 11^a24–6); for knowledge is always knowledge of something (*Cat.* 7, 6^b5). It is also his view that literacy is not a relative, but 'It is in virtue of the genus that it is so spoken in relation to something' (*Cat.* 8, 11^a29). In *Top.* IV.4, 124^b20, Aristotle maintains that knowledge is a relative, but literacy is not. This view raises a categorial problem: literacy belongs to the category of quality and its genus, i.e. knowledge, belongs to a different category, i.e. relative. Moreover, it clashes with what is claimed in other passages in the *Topics* where we read that genus and species must fall under the same category (see, e.g., IV 1, 120^b36–121^a8). To ease this tension, it has been suggested that literacy is not a proper species of knowledge (Ackrill 1963, pp. 108–9).

At 142^b33–4 the text is compressed and can be paraphrased as 'The person who gives an account of literacy as "knowledge of writing what is dictated" has defined it no more than the person who gives an account of it as "knowledge of reading", so that neither of them has defined it, but the person who says both these things has'. Aristotle is here offering a concise argument. The first premise is that the person who gives an account of literacy as 'Knowledge of writing what is dictated' has defined it no more than the person who gives an account of it as 'Knowledge of reading'. The second premise is that literacy does not have two definitions: we know that a definition expresses the essence, and the definition is one because the essence is one (see *Top.* VI.4, 141^{a}34–141^{b}1, and commentary *ad loc.*). Suppose that the person who has given an account of literacy as 'Knowledge of writing what is dictated' had defined it. Then (by the first premise) the person who has given an account of it as 'Knowledge of reading' would also have defined it. Then literacy would have two definitions contrary to the second premise. Hence the person who has given an account of literacy as 'Knowledge of writing what is dictated' has not defined it. A parallel argument will establish the result that the person who has given an account of literacy as 'Knowledge of reading' has not defined it (the first premise must be modified into the assumption that the person who gives an account of literacy as 'Knowledge of reading' has defined it no more than the person who gives an account of it as 'Knowledge of writing what is dictated'). Hence neither person has defined literacy. Aristotle's view is that in similar cases the definition of literacy must contain both aspects.

At 143^{a}1–8, a second example is introduced. The point of the example is to draw a distinction between two cases, namely when the thing to be defined is said *in itself* (*kath'auto*; lit. 'in virtue of itself') in relation to something, and when it is said *incidentally* in relation to something. (I have rendered *kata sumbebêkos* as 'incidentally'. *Sumbebêkos* is traditionally rendered as 'accident'; others translate it as 'incidental'—see, e.g., Barnes 1993, p. 89. Some problems regarding the concept of *sumbebêkos* in the *Topics* are discussed in Slomkowski 1997, pp. 69–94, and Smith 1997, pp. 64–6.) This distinction leads to a qualification of the general rule mentioned above (i.e. the rule that if what is to be defined is said in relation to several things, then the definition must mention all of them). The speaker's proposed definition must be analysed according to the qualified rule that if what is to be defined is said *in itself* in relation to some things, then the proposed definition must mention all of them. If what is to be defined is said *incidentally* in relation to some things, then the proposed definition must ignore them. However, the argument is difficult to unfold: it is not clearly presented and relies on a number of implicit assumptions. Aristotle talks about what is to be defined being said in itself or incidentally in relation to something, but he does not explain that this happens when its genus is a relative: this explanation should be given since the main focus of this text is the discussion of a genus that is a relative. At 143^a1-2, 'Medicine is said of the production of disease and health' could be understood as an elliptical account of medicine that will be examined and criticized according to the commonplace discussed in this chapter. The full account is: 'Medicine is the knowledge of how to produce disease and health'. Although it is omitted here, the genus of medicine, that is knowledge (*epistêmê*), is easily carried over from the discussion of the definition of literacy in the immediately preceding lines (this is confirmed by *Top.* II.3, 110^b18, and VI.12, 149^b7, where we explicitly read that the genus of medicine is knowledge; see also *SE* 31, 181^b34-5[1]). The notions 'to be said in itself' and 'to be said incidentally' play a fundamental role in the argument, but they are not sufficiently explained. This pair will become part of Aristotle's technical jargon; it will be used on a number of different occasions with different philosophical meanings (see, e.g., *APo.* I.4 and *Metaph.* V.18). In the example of medicine, the contrast between 'in itself' and 'incidentally' suggests a distinction between essential and non-essential features. Since the definition expresses the essence, it must contain only essential features; other features must be excluded from the definition. Aristotle seems to explain the introduction of the notions 'in itself' and 'incidentally' by adding: 'For the production of disease is without qualification alien to medicine' (143^a4-5). What is the meaning of this clause? Most plausibly, this is a stylistic variant of 'not to belong to the essence of medicine'. If one were to say that medicine is knowledge of how to produce disease, one would not give a good answer to the question 'What is medicine?'; in this sense, knowledge of how to produce disease is no part of medicine's essence (what is a part of the essence of x can be mentioned in an answer to the question 'What is x?'). Alternatively, one could say that the production of disease is not the function of medicine: if it is exercised to produce disease, medicine is not used in its proper function, but in a

---

[1] I thank Pieter Sjoerd Hasper for drawing my attention to this passage of the *Sophistici Elenchi*.

function that is alien to it. Similarly, you could use a screwdriver to open a bottle of wine, but this is not its proper function, and it would be wrong to include in the definition of screwdriver that it is a tool to open a bottle of wine. Although it is not employed by Aristotle in this context, the notion of function is one of his conceptual tools used in the analysis of the notion of essence (*EN* I.7). But there is something more to say. The connection between medicine and the production of disease seems tighter than the one between a screwdriver and opening a bottle of wine (adopting modern terminology, one could be tempted to say that there is a conceptual connection between medicine and the production of disease). It might also seem that this connection is so tight that one may want to consider the production of disease as part of medicine's essence. This would fit well with Aristotle's claim that knowledge of contraries is the same (see, e.g., *Top.* I.10, 104^{a}16, and II.3, 110^{b}17–20; this view was also held by Plato, see *R.* I, 334A): this claim might suggest that since doctors know how to produce health, they also know how to produce disease (and vice versa). So, one could object that the tight connection puts some pressure on Aristotle's manoeuvre of excluding the production of disease from the definition of medicine. But it is possible to discard this line of objection and accept Aristotle's argument. One could allow that there is a tight connection between medicine and the production of disease, but deny that the latter is part of medicine's essence; for there are some characteristics that are necessary but not essential (e.g. having the sum of the angles equal to two right angles is a necessary characteristic of a triangle, but it is not included in its definition; see *APo.* I, 4). Moreover, *Top.* II.3, 110^{b}19–21, suggests that the same knowledge is of both contraries when they are both ends; this is surely not the case with medicine, the production of health, and the production of disease (the production of health is one of the ends of medicine, whereas the production of disease is not). So, the production of disease and the production of health are not proper instances of the claim that the knowledge of contraries is the same: the claim that the doctor knows how to produce disease would not follow from the claim that she knows how to produce health. One can also suggest that in this context 'incidentally' means something like 'in an improper sense'. Aristotle would be saying that the production of disease is said of medicine 'in an improper sense', because the end of medicine is to produce not disease but health, or, in other words, the end of a doctor is to produce health and not disease in the patient. According to some, Aristotle does use 'incidentally' to mean 'in an improper sense' in other works: see, e.g., *Cat.* 6, 5^a38–5^b10 and *Ph.* II.3, 195^b3–4 (for a full list of references see Crivelli 2004, p. 107, n. 29).

At 143^a4–6, Aristotle's point may be rephrased as follows: the person who has given an account of medicine as knowledge of how to produce health and disease has given a definition no more than (i.e. as much as or less than) the person who has given an account of it as knowledge of how to produce one of the two (i.e. health). At 143^a5, the expression *ouden mallon* must be taken in its literal meaning of 'no more', which is equivalent to 'as much or less'. Then, at 143^a6–7, the expression *all'isos kai cheiron* ('but also even worse') corrects and strengthens 'no more' (equivalent to 'as much or less') into 'worse' (equivalent to 'less'). The account of medicine as knowledge of how to produce health and disease is worse because it mentions the production of disease that is not an essential aspect of medicine. The previous occurrence of *ouden mallon* ('no more') at 142^b32 must be taken in this literal meaning too (the use of comparatives in Aristotle is discussed in Casari 1984). At 143^a7, 'anyone among the rest' can be rephrased as 'anyone among the people that are not experts in medicine'.

At 143^a9–11, knowledge (*epistêmê*) and capacity (*dunamis*) could be two different genera. Alternatively, this could be one of the passages where Aristotle uses interchangeably 'knowledge' and 'capacity' (Bonitz 1870, p. 207B5–7), and in this case 'and' (*kai*) would have an epexegetic value. The view that 'Every instance of knowledge and every capacity seem to be for the best' can be explained in the light of *Top.* IV.5, 126^a36, where we read that 'A capacity is always a desirable thing ... So then capacity can never be the genus of anything blameworthy. Otherwise, the result will be that some blameworthy thing is desirable; for there will be a capacity that is blameworthy.' The point made here ('Every instance of knowledge and every capacity seem to be for the best') is meant to support the view that the definition of medicine has to refer to the production of health because it is a good result.

143ª12–14: 'What is being spoken about (*sc.* the thing to be defined) is not placed in the appropriate genus' is unclear because it is not specified what an appropriate (*oikeion*) genus is. The clause could be saying either of the following: (i) the thing to be defined is placed in a genus to which it does not belong (e.g. human is placed in the genus vegetative creature, or white is placed in the genus animal—the latter categorial mistake being an extreme case), or (ii) the thing to be defined is not placed in its proximate genus but in a higher one (e.g. raven is not placed in the genus bird but in animal). According to De Pater 1965, p. 217, Aristotle has (i) in mind here, but no decisive evidence is provided. If one takes this view, one would understand 'furthermore' (*eti*) at 143ª15 as introducing an argument that is new with respect to what is mentioned at 143ª12–14, and this new argument illustrates (ii). But one can also think that Aristotle has (ii) in mind here: on this reading, 'furthermore' at 143ª15 would not introduce a new argument but would indicate further ways of failing to place the thing to be defined in the proximate genus, further with respect to those that can be gathered by examining the elements of the genera. There are arguments in favour of both options. Option (i) is supported by the fact that it would be difficult to think that Aristotle ignores such an obvious case as that of a thing to be defined that is placed in a genus to which it does not belong. Moreover, option (i) provides a natural reading of the back-reference at 143ª13–14: it refers to *Topics* IV.1, 120ᵇ17–19, where Aristotle is illustrating the case of placing the thing to be defined in something that is not its genus. In favour of option (ii) counts the beginning of *Topics* VI.1, where Aristotle introduces the discussion of the predicable definition and presents us with a summary of the issues to be dealt with in the rest of the book. He says: 'Although there is a genus, he has not placed it (*sc.* the thing to be defined) in the genus or has not placed it in the appropriate genus' (VI.1, 139ª27–8). These lines can be taken as an anticipation of the content of VI.5. In particular, the first disjunct ('He has not placed it in the genus') refers to the first part of chapter 5, whereas the second disjunct ('He has not placed it in the appropriate genus') refers to its last part. The last part of the chapter covers an extensive portion of the text (143ª15–28), where the discussion of the proximate genus occupies a prominent place; this suggests that the occurrence of 'appropriate genus' in VI.1 may refer to the discussion of the proximate genus. Since there is no decisive support to choose between those two options, one can suggest that 'appropriate genus' covers both the case described in (i) and that in (ii). This suggestion is further supported by looking again at VI.1, 139^{a}27-8 (quoted above): these lines give us the structure of chapter 5 that concerns the second commonplace about definition and can be easily divided into two parts. The first is introduced by the clause 'Although the thing is in a genus, it is not placed in a genus' (*en genei tou pragmatos ontos mê keitai en genei*, 142^{b}22-3); this clause has a linguistic correspondence to the first disjunct in VI.1, 139^{a}27, namely 'Although there is a genus, he has not placed it in a genus' (*ontos genous ouk ethêken eis to genos*). The first part of chapter 5 discusses the case where the thing to be defined is not placed in any genus even if there is a genus to which it belongs, and it deals with the case of a thing to be defined whose genus is a relative. Then the second part of chapter 5 begins at 143^{a}12 and is introduced by the clause 'Again, on the basis of the rules concerning the genera, consider whether what is being spoken about (*sc.* the thing to be defined) is not placed in the appropriate genus' (*palin ei mê keitai en tôi oikeiôi genei to lechthen skopein ek tôn peri ta genê stoicheiôn*). Note that this is the only argument in chapter 5 that starts with 'again', whereas the other sub-arguments start with 'furthermore'. The clause just mentioned corresponds to the second disjunct in VI.1, 139^{a}28, namely 'He has not placed it in the appropriate genus' (*ouk eis to oikeion genos ethêken*). This second part concerns the case where the thing to be defined is not placed in the appropriate genus, and this covers the case where the thing to be defined is placed in something that is not its genus and the case where the thing to be defined is not placed in its proximate genus. One could doubt the appropriateness of the parallel between VI.1 and VI.5, because at 139^{a}27 there is 'the genus' (*to genos*), with the article, and at 142^{b}23 there is 'in <a> genus' (*en genei*), without the article. But the article in VI.1, 139^{a}27, may be regarded as a generic article, whereby it is equivalent to the quantifier 'any' (Smyth 1956, p. 288). The word *stoicheia,* which I have translated with 'rules', can also be rendered as 'elements', 'elementary rules', or 'fundamental principles'. It occurs (at least) four times in book IV of the *Topics* with a similar meaning: IV.1, 120^{b}12;

IV.1, 121ᵇ11–14; IV.3, 123ᵃ27; IV.6, 128ᵃ20–9. In the *Topics*, the meaning of *stoicheion* can be very close to that of *topos* ('commonplace' or 'commonplace rule'; see LSJ, *s.v. stoicheion* II.3).

143ᵃ15–19: When he speaks of someone who 'omits the genera', Aristotle has in mind a speaker who is trying to offer a definition and puts forward an account that fails to mention one or more of the genera of the species whose definition is being attempted. As we shall see, Aristotle seems to have an argument for the claim that one omits at least one of the genera if and only if one omits the proximate genus (see commentary on 143ᵃ19–28, below). For this reason, Aristotle concentrates on the case where the proximate genus is omitted.

It is interesting to note that Aristotle distinguishes the function of higher genera from the one of the proximate genus. For higher genera are predicated in the what-it-is (*Top.* IV.2, 122ᵃ5), like all genera (*Top.* I.5, 102ᵃ32), whereas the proximate genus is linked with the what-it-is-to-be (143ᵃ17–18). This distinction is not further explored by Aristotle, and it raises a number of philosophical questions. For example, (a) it is unclear whether predication in the what-it-is is the same as essential predication (predication in the what-it-is is defined in *Top.* I.5, 102ᵃ32–5: 'Let us say that those sorts of things are "predicated in the what-it-is" which it would be appropriate to give as an answer when asked what the thing in question is, as it is appropriate in the case of a human, when asked what it is, to say that it is an animal'); (b) it remains unexplained whether there is a difference between the what-it-is and the what-it-is-to-be. One could suggest that the what-it-is can indicate a trait of the essence but fail to characterize it fully, whereas the what-it-is-to-be expresses the whole of the essence.

The claim that 'Having left out the genus of justice he does not state the what-it-is-to-be; for the essence of each thing involves the genus' (143ᵃ17–18) calls for clarification. It could mean that the proximate genus alone coincides with the what-it-is-to-be; this is, however, unlikely because it would be unclear what the specific differentia (*eidopoios diafora*; *Top.* VI.6, 143ᵇ8) could add by being mentioned in the defining part (literally, *eidopoios* means 'species-making'; on the textual problems concerning the expression *eidopoios diafora* see commentary *ad loc.*). It is more likely that the claim in question means something weaker, namely that the proximate genus is required (but does not suffice) for the what-it-is-to-be: in this case, the differentia can add something by being mentioned in the defining part (it adds the quality of the thing to be defined, *Top.* IV.2, 122^{b}17). Then we can explain the difference between the higher and proximate genera on the basis of a passage in the *Categories*: 'If one is to say of the primary substance what it is, it will be more informative and apt to give the species than the genus' (2^{b}8–12). If we take this line of thought to the next level, namely to the level of species and proximate and higher genera, it follows that if one is to say of the species what it is, it is more informative and apt to give the proximate genus than one of the higher genera.

There is an attempt to define justice as 'A state productive of equality or distributive of what is equal' (143^{a}15–16). (For the translation of *hexis* with 'state' see 'The value of *hexis*' in 'Terminological Clarifications'.) But this definition cannot be accepted: the proximate genus of justice is not state (*hexis*) but virtue (*aretê*). It is not wrong to say that justice is a state, but this account will not express the essence of justice, since, as Aristotle explains below, the essence is expressed not by any genus but by the proximate genus. It is unclear whether there are two proposed accounts of justice ('A virtue productive of equality' and 'A virtue distributive of what is equal'), or one that takes the form of a disjunction ('A virtue productive of equality or distributive of what is equal'). Since this example bears a similarity with some views expressed in *EN* V, it is likely that Aristotle is talking about two accounts of justice indicating two so-called forms of particular justice. In *EN* V.2, Aristotle distinguishes between general (or universal) justice, which is manifested in obedience to the law, and some forms of particular justice, namely justice in distribution and justice in rectification. Justice in distribution deals with the equality of the shares of the good distributed according to the worth of the recipients (*EN* V.3). Justice in rectification deals with the equality between the position of the parties before a transaction and after the proper rectification (*EN* V.4). The Greek word *ison* ('equal') can express the concept of equality but also that of fairness; we can relate the two forms of particular justice to the concept of fairness in the outcome. In particular, the fair outcome of a distribution is one that treats the recipients in proportion to their worth, and the fair outcome of a rectification is one that treats both parties equally, namely irrespective of their worth (on the notion of justice in the *Nicomachean Ethics* see, e.g., Hardie 1980, pp. 182–211). In the *Topics*, Aristotle is not interested in a technical discussion about justice: his example helps to make a philosophical point about the role played by the genus in a definition. It has been debated whether in the *Nicomachean Ethics* Aristotle individuates two or more forms of particular justice (see discussion in Irwin 1988, pp. 424–38; Judson 1997). This text can hardly support either view because its conciseness leaves open the possibility that there may be other forms of particular justice.

143ª19–28: The claim that 'The person who puts it (*sc.* the thing to be defined) into the proximate genus has mentioned all the ones above, since all the genera above are predicated of those below' (143ª20–2) is based upon the assumption that it is possible to arrange the genera of the thing to be defined in a descending order. The structure of the arrangement can be described as an ordered sequence of genera from the ones above (*epanô*) to those below (*hupokatô*): <G_n, G_{n-1}, ..., G_2, G_1>, where G_n, G_{n-1}, ..., G_2 are the higher genera and G_1 is the proximate genus of the species S. The proximate genus might be defined as follows: x is the proximate genus of y if and only if x is a genus of y and there is no intermediate genus between x and y (i.e. it is not the case that there is a z distinct from both x and y and such that x is a genus of z and z is a genus of y). Although it is better to translate *eggutaton* with 'nearest' (it is grammatically closer to the Greek adjective, which is in the superlative form), I adopt 'proximate' since in the context of definitions it is customary to talk about proximate genera and specific differentiae.

At 143ª21–2, the relation between genera in the descending order is described by the remark that 'All the genera above are predicated of those below'. As it stands, however, this remark is incomplete and it should be added that the converse does not hold, namely the genera below are not predicated of those above (this is made explicit in, e.g., *Top.* I. 15, 107ª22–9). It is helpful to remember that there is flexibility in the terminology employed by Aristotle in talking about genera and species. For, in general, he says that a genus is divided into its species, but if the division of the genus has not reached its last stage, then the species can be taken as a genus and divided further. The relation between genera and species is analysed at length in *Top.* IV.1 and 2. For example, in IV.1, 121ª10–20 Aristotle says that a species partakes (*metechei*) of its genus when it admits the definition of that which it partakes of; the species admits the account of the genus, but the genus does not admit that of the species. In *Top.* IV.2, 122ª3, the relation between genera in a descending order is illustrated by saying that 'The genus above does not partake (*metechein*) of any of the lower'.

The idea that higher genera are predicated of those below can be explained by the fact that higher genera are intensionally contained in the lower ones, but the converse does not hold (see *Ph.* IV.3, 210ª18–19; *Metaph.* V.25, 1023ᵇ24–5). For example, animal is predicated of bird because the former is intensionally contained in the latter, but not vice versa. The remark that 'All the genera above are predicated of those below' raises the question of the number of genera involved in the chain of predication. Elsewhere in his writings, Aristotle argues that the chain of predication cannot be infinite: in *Metaph.* I.2, he presents an argument against infinite explanatory chains, and in *APo.* I. 19–23, he has a longer argument against predicational chains of infinite length (see Barnes 1993, pp. 169–83; Lear 1980, pp. 15–33). In the *Topics,* this question does not seem to be explicitly addressed. Were one to take the view that the 'genera of predication' (*ta genê tôn katêgoriôn*) discussed in *Top.* I.9 are the highest genera, one could then suggest that they constitute the upper limit of our chains of predication (see discussions in Ackrill 1963, pp. 79–80; Smith 1997, pp. 74–6; Crivelli 2004, pp. 96–7 and n. 58).

At 143ª19–22 there is a compressed argument. At 143ª19, 'this' (*touto*) refers to the omission of one of the genera (i.e. it refers back to 143ª15: 'Consider whether he speaks omitting the genera'). Then, the claim is that one omits one of the genera if and only if one omits the proximate genus. Trivially, if one omits the proximate genus, then one omits one of the genera. Vice versa, suppose that one does not omit the proximate genus. One mentions the proximate genus, so that one mentions all the higher genera: for 'All the higher genera are predicated of those below' (143ª22), and therefore of the proximate genus. By mentioning the proximate genus and the higher genera one mentions all the genera. One then omits none of the genera. So if one does not omit the proximate genus, then one omits none of the genera. Hence, by contraposition, if one omits one of the genera, then one omits the proximate genus. The argument (as I have reconstructed it) relies on the assumption that if a genus K is predicated of a genus G, and one mentions G, then one mentions K. For example, if the genus animal is predicated of the genus bird, and one mentions bird, then one mentions animal. However, this assumption is problematic and might not be granted. One can accept that higher genera are predicated of lower genera, since the former are intensionally contained in the latter. But one can object to the view that mentioning a species or a lower genus always involves mentioning its higher genera: on many occasions, one mentions a genus without having present in one's mind its higher genera (namely those constituting its essence). Thus, there is a gap in Aristotle's argument. It is perhaps possible to help his argument in the following way: one could claim that mentioning does not involve having present in one's mind. For example, one can mention whale, and hence mammal, having in mind whale but not mammal. But even this does not seem sufficient to warrant the move from the claim that if a genus K is predicated of a genus G, and one mentions G, then one mentions K. There might be possible ways to fill this gap, but no suggestion is present in the text.

At 143^a23, we read that the proximate genus can be replaced by a higher genus combined with all the differentiae: this is the rule that, in a definition, the proximate genus can be substituted by its definition (see *Top.* IV.1, 121^a13–14 and *Cat.* 5, 3^a33–3^b10). To give an example, consider the definition of human as rational animal. Then, consider the definition of animal as living being. According to the rule, we can rephrase the definition of human as rational living being. Perhaps when Aristotle says 'all the differentiae' he considers the possibility of replacing a genus with a definition of it that starts with a higher genus that is not proximate.

At 143^a25, the clause 'He would have mentioned the genus below with a phrase instead of a name' draws attention to the formal difference between the two expressions 'A human is a rational animal' and 'A human is a rational living being'. This suggests a possibility that is new to this book, namely that the definition of (say) human can be phrased in more than one way.

However, since it is impossible for something to have more than one definition, it will not be appropriate to talk about two definitions of it. Thus, one must admit that two formally different expressions can be the same definition. One must then explain that the two formally different expressions are the same definition because they signify the same essence. Aristotle's remark rules out the possibility that a definition is merely a linguistic entity. One could be tempted to say that a definition is an equivalence class of complex linguistic expressions that signify the same essence.

CHAPTER 6

Introduction: Chapter 6 is long, interesting, and very complex. It comes after the discussion of the commonplaces regarding the genus, which is one of the elements mentioned in the defining part, and is concerned with the other element, namely the differentia. The main aim of the chapter is to offer a large number of commonplaces regarding the differentia. That is to say, the chapter contains refutative strategies against those definitions that are flawed because the differentia is not correctly identified. These refutative strategies are based on an analysis of several mistakes that the interlocutor can make when he grants or puts forward a definition; often they are expressed in a very compressed way. This discussion is primarily oriented to help the dialectician who has the task of criticizing the interlocutor's proposed definition; but it also addresses important questions concerning the role of the differentia in a definition, its relation with the genus it differentiates, and with the species it forms. This chapter contains what is possibly Aristotle's longest surviving discussion of the differentia. There are other passages in the *Organon* where Aristotle discusses the differentia: see, e.g., *Top.* I.9 and IV; *Cat.* 3, $1^{b}17$–24, and 5, $3^{a}33$–$3^{b}9$. It is on these texts that the scholars' debate has been mainly focused so far: see, e.g, Frede 1981; Morrison 1993; Mann 2000; Gambra 2003; Malink 2007. Some of the claims in *Topics* VI have remained underexplored.

The chapter is structured as follows. (1) $143^{a}9$–$143^{b}10$ contains some tests to verify whether the differentia is expressed correctly. (2) $143^{b}11$–32 discusses the problem of the division of the genus into species by two determinations, one of which is the negation of the other. There are two subparts: (2a) $143^{b}11$–23 aims at showing that a negative determination cannot be the differentia of the genus, and (2b) $143^{b}23$–32 observes that the argument just sketched can be used only in the case where genera are conceived of as Platonic Ideas. (3) $143^{b}33$–5 contains a brief remark about proposed definitions with privative terms: contrary to what he has established in part (2), Aristotle admits that there are cases where the presence of negative determinations in certain definitions is allowed. (4) $143^{b}35$–$144^{a}4$ completes the discussion of the commonplace outlined in part (2). (5) $144^{a}4$–27 examines refutative strategies applying to the cases where (i) the role of the differentia is attributed to a species, (ii) the role of a differentia is attributed to a genus, (iii) the differentia is not a qualification, (iv) the differentia belongs incidentally to the species. (6) 144^{a}29–144^{b}11 develops possible lines of criticism emerging from an analysis of the relation of predication in a definition. (7) 144^{b}12–30 continues the discussion of part (6) but focuses more on the criticisms arising from an examination of the relation between the proposed differentia and the genus (or genera) that it divides; in particular, the question is asked whether the same differentia can divide two non-subordinate genera. (8) 144^{b}31–145^{a}2 examines the rule that the differentiae of a substance must not indicate a location. (9) 145^{a}3–12 deals with the mistake of giving to an affection (*pathos*) the role of a differentia. (10) 145^{a}13–32 discusses several difficulties that can arise when a proposed definition mentions the differentiae of relatives. (11) 145^{a}33–145^{b}20 deals with the mistake of describing the thing to be defined as an affection or a disposition of something that cannot receive it. For example, if the interlocutor says that sleep is inability of sense-perception, he attributes sleep to sense-perception, but this is absurd. For 'of sense-perception' cannot express the differentia. (12) 145^{b}21–33 introduces the last commonplace of chapter 6 and instructs the dialectician to see whether a temporal qualification that is attached at the differentia (that occurs in the defining part) is mentioned also in the expression that indicates the thing to be defined.

143^{a}29–143^{b}10: The chapter begins with a brief discussion of four different ways to test whether in the proposed definition the differentia is expressed correctly. These tests are of increasing complexity. If the proposed definition fails these tests, thereby containing at least one of the following mistakes, then it must be rejected.

(1) The defining expression does not mention the differentiae of the genus; 143^{a}29–30. (In my translation of line 143^{a}30, I render *eipe* as 'he has said' and not 'he has mentioned', to mark the difference between *eipe* and *eireken*, which occurs at 143^{b}1–2 and *passim*.) This divides into two sub-cases. (1a) In the proposed definition what occupies the position of the differentia *is* a differentia, but it does not pertain to the thing to be defined (143^{a}30–1).

No examples are given. Probably Aristotle has in mind a situation where, e.g., winged is given as a differentia of triangle. Although winged is a differentia of bird and divides the genus animal, it is not a differentia of triangle and does not divide the genus of triangle, i.e. figure. (1b) In the proposed definition, what occupies the position of the differentia *is not* a differentia (143^a31–4). Aristotle considers animal (a genus) and substance (*ousia*): they cannot be differentiae of anything since they are not differentiae at all. Thus, if the proposed definition is framed in such a way that things like animal or substance occupy the position of the differentia, it cannot be accepted. At 143^a29, 'similarly' (*homoiôs*) is probably intended to indicate a link between chapters 5 and 6. Aristotle might be expressing a general similarity between the failure of individuating the genus of the thing to be defined and that of individuating the differentia. But he might also be expressing a more specific similarity between the failure of placing the thing to be defined in its appropriate genus (*Top*. VI.5, 142^b23–9) and the failure of giving the appropriate differentia (143^a29–143^b10).

(2) No element that is coordinate with the given differentia can be found (143^a34–143^b2). This has to be understood in the context of the division of the genus into species by the differentiae. In general, there are different stages in the division of the same genus. Aristotle employs the technical term *antidiêiremena* ('coordinate elements of a division') to refer to the things that are called in at the *same* stage of the division of the same genus (see Bonitz 1870, p. 63B). Since every genus is divided into species by coordinate differentiae, one must check whether what is given as a differentia is coordinate with other differentiae. If this is not the case, then the proposed definition must be rejected. In *Top*. VI.4, 142^b7–10, Aristotle applies *antidiêiremena* to coordinate differentiae, while in *Cat*. 13, 14^b35–15^a4 he uses it to refer to coordinate species.

There is no example illustrating the case where something *is not* coordinate with an element of the division. Aristotle illustrates only the case of differentiae that *are* coordinate elements of the division. It is not easy to offer a precise reconstruction of Aristotle's example because at 143^b2 there are several textual problems (see 'Notes on the Text' *ad loc.*).

(3) In the defining expression, what is given as a differentia *is* coordinate with an element of the division, but the latter is not

true of (*alêtheuetai kata*) the genus. The underlying assumption is that 'All the coordinate differentiae are true of the appropriate genus' (143^b4–5). What is the meaning of 'to be true of x' at 143^b3, 5, and 6? It cannot be intended in its common use, namely 'to be truly predicated of x', since a differentia cannot be truly predicated of a genus. For example, two-footed cannot be truly predicated of animal because not every animal is two-footed. Thus, 'to be true of x' indicates a relation that is different from 'to be truly predicated of x'. The relation of 'to be true of x' could be expressed as 'pertaining to' or 'applying to': to say that two-footed is true of animal is equivalent to saying that it pertains or applies to animal. The case described in this section can be exemplified by considering having-four-angles, which is a differentia dividing plane figure and coordinate with having-three-angles. Since the differentia having-four-angles does not pertain to the genus animal, having-three-angles will not pertain to animal too. So, if the interlocutor gives having-three-angles as a differentia of animal, his definition cannot be accepted. It is important to note that 'pertaining to' or 'applying to' indicates a complex relation that holds between a differentia and the genus it divides. (This is a knotty problem that cannot be fully addressed in the space of a commentary.)

(4) What is given as a differentia is true of (i.e. pertains to) the genus, but it fails to constitute a species when it is added to the genus. No example is offered here, but we can follow a suggestion that is developed later in this chapter, i.e. at 144^b22–5 (see commentary *ad loc.*). Consider the differentia two-footed: it pertains to the genus, but it does not constitute a species since two-footed is a differentia of both footed and winged animals. What are the reasons for the view that footed and winged take priority over two-footed? They are not easy to find. Here is a sketch of four options. (i) The reasons might be merely classificatory; that is to say, Aristotle is seeking to offer a good and complete classification of some species of animals. He might think that a division where footed and winged come before two-footed is better suited to meet the requirements of a good classification. After all, two-footed is a particular case of footed, and a classificatory arrangement that proceeds from the general to the particular has a certain attractiveness. In this case, the division could be arbitrary, and it need not have an ontological basis.

(ii) Aristotle might think that it is a brute fact of nature that, in the division of the genus animal, footed and winged animals come before two-footed (or four-footed) animals. One, however, could find options (i) and (ii) philosophically unsatisfactory. There are other possibilities. (iii) A reason for the priority of footed and winged over two-footed might stem from the following consideration. Suppose that, in the division of the genus animal, two-footed takes priority over footed and winged. Consider the class containing all and only two-footed animals: it will contain, e.g., humans, ducks, crows, penguins, some primates, etc. This class might strike us as heterogeneous; for humans and penguins do not seem to share any basic feature other than being two-footed. Hence one might argue that it is highly counterintuitive to state that the division into footed and winged does not take priority over two-footed. This line of argument could suffice if it is employed in a dialectical exchange, for it offers a plausible line of attack that is based on certain intuitions. These intuitions might well be shared by the people in the audience who are acquainted with the discussion in Plato's *Politicus* 264D–E:

> VISITOR: ... of the rearing of herd animals, some has to do with creatures living in water (*enudroi*), some also with creatures that live on dry land (*xērobatikoi*).
> YOUNG SOCRATES: It does.
> VISITOR: Do you agree, then, that we must split the expert knowledge of collective rearing into this two, allocating one of its parts to each of these, calling one aquatic rearing, the other dry-land rearing?
> YOUNG SOCRATES: I do....
> VISITOR: Everybody would divide the dry-land rearing sort of herd-rearing.
> YOUNG SOCRATES: How?
> VISITOR: By separating it by reference to the winged (*ptenoi*) and what goes on foot (*pezoi*).
> YOUNG SOCRATES: Very true.

(iv) The fourth option is speculative. It is based on considerations about Aristotle's interest in animals' locomotion, interest that emerges from his works. In *De An.* III.9, 432^{a}15–17, Aristotle claims that one of the basic faculties of an animal's soul is that which originates local movement; the discussion of the origin of locomotion in an animal's soul occupies the entire chapter. This suggests that, in Aristotle's view, the animal's capacity of moving enjoys a certain priority. This is supported by the fact that Aristotle wrote an entire work concerning the movement of animals (*De Motu Animalium*). Given its importance, animals' locomotion can work as a criterion to establish whether some characteristics are more fundamental than others. Since some animals use their feet to move on dry land, while some others use their wings to move in the air, the division between footed and winged takes priority over that which is based on a number of feet (e.g. two-footed, four-footed, six-footed).

At 143^{b}7 I understand 'this' (*hautê*) as referring to what the interlocutor puts forward as a differentia. At 143^{b}7–8 there is a textual problem that concerns the two occurrences of *eidopoios*, which I translate as 'species-making' to maintain the etymological link with the Greek. I follow the text established by Brunschwig 2007 (see discussion in 'Notes on the Text' *ad loc.*).

143^{b}11–32: This passage is highly problematic: it has received attention from many commentators; see, e.g., Alex. Aphr. *in Top.* 218, 37–219, 30; Pacius 1597, p. 435; Waitz 1846, vol. 2; Tricot 1950; Colli 1970; Zadro 1974; Wagner and Rapp 2004; Brunschwig 2007. Aristotle's main target is the division of the genus by negation. Here 'division by negation' refers to the case of a genus that is divided into species by two determinations, one of which is the negation of the other. Aristotle's discussion can be divided into two parts. (A) At 143^{b}11–23 he presents an argument aiming to prove that a genus cannot be divided into species by two determinations, one of which is the negation of the other: the negative determination cannot be the differentia of that genus. (B) At 143^{b}23–32 he warns us that the argument sketched in the immediately preceding lines is an effective commonplace only against those who believe that genera are Ideas. If genera are conceived as something like Platonic Ideas (or Forms), then each of them will be an entity of the intelligible world and one in number. The Platonic Idea of *F*-ness is a perfect and supreme example of something that is *F*, serves as a model for particular *F*s, and is separate in the sense that its existence does not depend on that of any *F*-particulars. This way of conceiving genera is different from the Aristotelian thesis that genera are not numerically one and not separated from the sensible world. As we shall see, Aristotle claims that Ideas cannot be divided into species by two contrary determinations.

Analysis of (A). Aristotle considers the case where the interlocutor has divided the genus into species by two determinations, one of which is the negation of the other and has given to the negative determination the role of a differentia in the defining part. As an example, consider the proposed definition: 'A line is a breadthless length'. In this case, the proposed defining part, i.e. 'breadthless length', is the result of adding the negative determination, i.e. 'breadthless', to the expression indicating the genus, i.e. 'length' ('breadthless' is equivalent to 'not having breadth'; $143^{b}11-12$). Note that this is one of several examples of geometrical definitions that we find in *Topics* VI (see, in particular, VI.4, $141^{b}5-7$ and 19–22; see commentary *ad loc.*). It is the second attempted definition of line that Aristotle criticizes (the other is: 'The line is the limit of a solid'; $141^{b}7$ and 21–2). The definition of a line as breadthless length occurs *verbatim* in Euclid's *Elements* (vol. 1, def. 2.1). This definition may be attributed to the Platonic school, perhaps even to Plato himself (see Heath 1956, vol.1, p. 158).

The argument at $143^{b}13-23$ is a *reductio ad absurdum*. If the genus is divided into species by two determinations, one of which is the negation of the other, two absurd consequences will follow with regard to the definitions thus obtained: the genus will partake of the species and the differentiae will be predicated of the genus. Thus, the proposed definitions must be rejected. This argument is intended to justify the rule forbidding the division of the genus by negation. The reasons why the genus cannot partake of its species and the differentiae are not predicated of the genus are discussed in *Top.* IV.1, $121^{a}12-14$; $121^{b}3-4$; $121^{b}11-14$; 2, $122^{b}7-24$. The relation between genus, species, and differentiae will be further explored later in this chapter. The argument can be reconstructed as follows (in order to give a better flow to the argument I have slightly altered the order in which the premises occur in the text).

(1) Of everything either the negation or the affirmation is true (143b15 16).
(2) Every length is either breadthless or having breadth (143b14–15).

(3) The genus of line is (a) length (143b16: *mêkos on*).
(4) The genus of line will be either breadthless or having breadth (143b16–17).
(5) Breadthless and having breadth are differentiae (143b18–19).
(6) The account of the species is made by the genus and the differentia (143b19–20).
(7) Breadthless length is the account of a species (143b17–18).
(8) Length having breadth is also the account of a species (143b18).
(9) The genus will admit the account of the species (143b20–1).
(10) One of the two mentioned differentiae is necessarily said of the genus (143b22–3).
(11) The genus will admit the account of the differentiae (143b21–2).

This is not a good argument: sentences (9), (10), and (11) do not follow from the premises. Hence the *reductio* fails. A way of showing where the problem lies is to introduce an interpretative conceptual tool that is based on the distinction between definitional and ordinary predication. Definitional predication occurs when the predicate is either the whole defining expression (e.g. 'A human is a rational animal') or a part of it (e.g. 'A human is an animal'; 'A human is rational') or a name of the kind to be defined itself (e.g. 'A human is a human'). Ordinary predication occurs when the *denotatum* of the subject instantiates the characteristic expressed by the predicate (e.g. 'Human is a species' or 'Socrates is a human'). One might be inclined to draw a parallel between the distinction just mentioned and the one outlined in the *Categories*. In *Cat*.2, 1ª20–5, Aristotle introduces the distinction between the relations of 'being in' and 'being said of'. However, the interpretation of these two relations raises many difficulties and, most probably, it does not help the understanding of this commonplace (see Crivelli 2017). For our purposes, it is important to note that the failure to distinguish between definitional and ordinary predication makes this argument and the next one (143b23–32) fallacious. This distinction would be helpful in the context where Platonic Forms are discussed since only Forms admit self-predication (i.e. the Form of F-ness is said to be F). But it is not clear whether Aristotle was aware of the distinction. On the one hand, in the passage under discussion (143b11–32), Aristotle takes a naïve stance on the sort of predicates that could be applied to Platonic Forms. For example, he seems to endorse an unsophisticated view on self-predication when he allows length to be applied to length-itself. On the other hand, there are at least two other texts in the *Topics* which show that Aristotle was able to deploy more sophisticated conceptual means to deal with similar cases. In V.7, 137^{b}2–8, there is a distinction between properties belonging to Forms in so far as they are Forms and properties belonging to individuals; Aristotle says that 'In as much as being motionless does not belong to human-itself *qua* human but *qua* Idea, it could not be a property of a human to be motionless'. Similarly, in VI.10, 148^{a}14–18, he says: 'Examine also whether the definition applies to the Idea. For in some cases it does not happen, for example when Plato defines by adding "mortal" to the definitions of animals; for the Idea, e.g. human-itself, will not be mortal, so that the account will not apply to the Idea' (see commentary *ad loc.*). It follows that if Aristotle has some awareness of the distinction between definitional and ordinary predication, then the entire argument at 143^{b}11–32 is sophistic (see Alex. Aphr. *in Top.* 219, 6). But if he has no awareness of it, then he is outlining a poor line of attack. Scholars hold different views. According to Cherniss 1962, pp. 3–5, what Aristotle says in VI.10, 148^{a}14–18 proves that in VI.6, 143^{b}13–23 he plays a 'dialectical trick'. But Huby 1962, p. 79, disagrees: she thinks that the fact that Aristotle employs a dialectical trick elsewhere does not constitute enough evidence to claim that he is also using the same trick here.

The steps of the argument must be analysed. Sentence (1) is a premise and it is nothing else than one of Aristotle's formulations of the Principle of Excluded Middle (PEM); here 'of everything' (*kata pantos*) expresses an unrestricted universal quantification, and 'affirmation' and 'negation' indicate affirmative and negative predicative expressions. PEM holds only in the context of ordinary predication. Sentence (2) is inferred from (1) as an application of PEM. If it is read as containing an instance of ordinary predication, then sentence (2) is true. But if it is read as containing an instance of definitional predication, it is false: neither 'having breadth' nor 'breadthless' occurs in the defining part of length. For sentence (3) to be a true premise, on the other hand, it must express a definitional predication: the predicate 'a length' is a name of the kind to be defined itself. Sentence (4) is inferred from (2) and (3). However, sentence (4) raises a problem: for it to be true, it must express an ordinary predication. Otherwise it is false; for the defining part of the genus of line mentions neither 'breadthless' nor 'having breadth'. This will undermine later steps of the argument that are based on sentence (4). Sentences (5) and (6) are true premises; (6) states some fundamental features of Aristotle's definitions. Sentence (7) follows from (3), (5), and (6). Similarly, sentence (8) follows from (3), (5), and (6). Sentence (9) is a first conclusion; it is presented as following from (3), (4), (7), and (8). But this step is problematic: if (4) is taken as expressing an ordinary predication, then it will not support (9), which says that there is a definitional predication. If (4) is taken as expressing a definitional predication, then it will be false, and so again it will not support (9). Sentence (10) is presented as following from (3) and (4). Once more, there is a difficulty with sentence (4): it supports (10) only if it is taken as expressing a definitional predication. But when it is taken in this way, (4) is false. Sentence (11) is a further conclusion that should follow from (3), (4), and (10). However, the difficulties encountered so far with sentence (4) are at work in this step too. Moreover, sentence (10) should support (11), but it is false.

Analysis of (B). The argument at 143^b23–32 can be reconstructed in the following way (the order in which the premises occur in the text is slightly altered in this case too):

(12) The genus is an Idea, i.e. it is numerically one (143^b24 and 30).
(13) One of the two differentiae is true of the genus (143^b27–8).
(14) One of the two differentiae is true of every length (143^b26–7).
(15) There are breadthless lengths (143^b28).
(16) There are lengths having breadth (143^b29).
(17) It is not the case that one of the two differentiae is true of every length (143^b28; *touto d'ou sumbainei*. Here *touto* refers to 143^b26–7: 'One of the two differentiae is true of every length').
(18) It is not the case that either one or the other differentia is true of the genus (implicit conclusion).

This is not a good argument either, and the *reductio ad absurdum* of (13) and (14) fails. Sentence (12) is an assumption; its role is to show that the commonplace presented at 143^b11–23 can be used only in the case where the genus is an Idea, i.e. it is numerically one. Sentence (13) states a result obtained in the immediately preceding argument and expressed in sentence (10) above. In that context, however, (10) was presented as following from (3) and (4), but the inference is invalid since (4) is false. The falsity of (13) undermines the rest of the argument. For if (13) were true, the sentence (14) would also be true because it would follow from (13). Sentences (15) and (16) show that (14) is false, and this is expressed by (17). Thus, sentence (13) would be false too. Sentence (18), by stating the falsity of (13), would express the result of the *reductio*. Different reconstructions of the arguments at 143^{b}11–32 are offered by Owen 1968b, pp. 115–16; Colli 1970, vol. 3, pp. 977–9; and Brunschwig 2007, p. 57, n. 1.

143^{b}33–5: This is a very compressed interlude concerning the cases of definitions containing a privative term. One could argue that in proposing a definition that contains a privation (e.g. blindness), the interlocutor might fall into the mistake of using a negation (e.g. not having sight). Hence his attempted definition might be attacked because it falls under the case where a negative determination, which follows from the division of the genus by negation, is included in the proposed definition (see the immediately preceding passage). But Aristotle does not agree with this line of argument: he seems to think that, in definitions concerning privations, negative determinations must be used. His justification is extremely succinct and it can be expanded by looking at other texts. In *Top.* VI.3, 141^{a}11, he says: 'Every privation concerns what belongs naturally' (see commentary *ad loc.*). Aristotle's point, as we read also in *Cat.* 10 (especially 13^{b}22–4), is that a privation is not like an ordinary negation but a special one; for it is a negation of a property that would be possessed by nature. For this reason, sentences expressing privation and possession do not behave like ordinary negative and affirmative sentences. In particular, while the PEM holds in the context of a pair of ordinary negative and affirmative sentences (e.g. 'Socrates is not white' and 'Socrates is white'), it does not apply to a pair of sentences expressing privation and possession (e.g. 'Socrates is blind' and 'Socrates has sight'). A further discussion of the concept of privation can be found in *Metaph.* V.22 (especially 1023^{a}27–31).

From Aristotle's analysis of privation, it follows that the previous commonplace's line of argument, which relied on an application of PEM, cannot be used in the present case.

143^{b}35–144^{a}4: These lines refer back to the commonplace at 143^{b}11–32 and complete its discussion. As we saw, Aristotle's main claim was that the genus cannot be divided into species by two determinations, one of which is the negation of the other: such determinations cannot be the differentiae of the genus. He chose the example of the genus length that was divided into having breadth (*platos echon*) and not having breadth (*mê platos echon,* which is equivalent to breadthless, *aplates*; 143^{b}11–12). Then Aristotle examined the case where the defining part mentions the negative determination, namely not having breadth. Now he considers the case where the defining part mentions the affirmative determination, namely having breadth. He concludes that since the coordinate determination of having breadth is not having breadth, the suggested definition 'Length having breadth' suffers from the same problems as 'Length not having breadth'. Aristotle's argument, however, has a problem; for it cannot be extended to all cases of affirmative differentiae. It depends on a specific feature of the chosen example: the coordinate determination of having breadth is not having breadth and nothing else (144^{a}3). The differentia two-footed will not generate similar difficulties: two-footed is coordinate with, e.g. four-footed.

144^{a}5–27: Further lines of attack come from considering whether in the proposed definition (i) the role of the differentia is attributed to a species (144^{a}5–8); (ii) the role of the differentia is attributed to a genus (144^{a}9–19); (iii) the differentia does not indicate a qualification (144^{a}20–2); (iv) the differentia belongs incidentally to the species (144^{a}23–7).

(i) The role of the differentia is given to a species (144^{a}5–8). The attempted definition of insult as 'insolence with mockery' is unproblematic: this example illustrates a case when the role of a differentia is played by a species. This brief example, however, does not give us any reason why the role of a differentia cannot be played by a species. More will be said at the end of section (ii).

(ii) The role of the differentia is attributed to a genus (144^{a}9–19). This mistake is exemplified by the accounts 'Virtue is a state that is good' or '(*sc.* virtue is) a state that is noble'; the order in which the accounts occur and the fact that Aristotle analyses only the first could suggest that he considers the second merely as a variant of the first (for the translation of *hexis* see 'The value of *hexis*' in 'Terminological Clarifications'). The clause that immediately follows the examples ('For good is a genus of virtue',

144ᵃ10–11) should explain the reason why the proposed account cannot be accepted. This claim, however, gives us only a partial explanation and must be understood in the context of at least two other (tacit) assumptions about definitions: the defining part must mention genus and differentia of the species to be defined (see, e.g., VI.4, 141ᵇ25–7; VI.5, 142ᵇ22–9; VI.6, 143ᵃ29–ᵇ10) and it must mention them in that order. The word order is important for Aristotle because it can help to avoid the mistake of confusing the genus with the differentia (see, e.g., VI.1, 139ᵃ29–30; VI.5, 142ᵇ28–9, and commentary *ad loc.*). Although the interlocutor may well agree with these assumptions, he might still wonder why he should grant that good is the genus of virtue. No reason is given here. There is another passage in *Topics* VI where Aristotle says that good is a genus of virtue (VI.4, 142ᵇ14); unfortunately, in this case too Aristotle does not explain or justify his claim. Perhaps when he says that good is a genus of virtue, he has a Platonic thesis in mind: the claim that good is a genus of virtue expresses an Academic view and can be traced back to Plato's *Meno* 87D2 (it is in the second hypothesis of the second argument to which both Socrates and Meno give their consent). Furthermore, since in this chapter Aristotle has explicitly mentioned some Platonic views (143ᵇ29–32), he might think that it is not necessary to repeat the reference here.

At line 144ᵃ11 the sentence 'Or rather good is not a genus but a differentia' marks an abrupt change in the argument, which can be explained in at least two ways. (1) Aristotle might be reacting in a particularly strong way to the claim that good is a genus of virtue. A claim that Aristotle makes in the corpus is that good is not a genus, that is to say it does not follow under one category: the term 'good' is said in many ways, and it can be applied to, e.g., substances, qualities, and quantities. (See, e.g., *Top.* I.15, 107ᵃ3–17, and the commentary in Smith 1997, p. 97. See also *EN* I.6, 1096ᵃ23–9; on the relation between the passages in the *Topics* and in the *Nicomachean Ethics* see Shields 1999, pp. 198–216). (2) Aristotle might be offering a strategy to defend the initially proposed account, namely virtue is a state that is good: the strategy consists in finding faults with the line of attack based on the claim that good is a genus of virtue. If the interlocutor wants to defend the account that virtue is a state that is good, he could employ the line of reasoning outlined at 144ᵃ11–19: he would argue that good is a differentia and challenge the claim that good is the genus of virtue with two arguments. The second option fits better with the dialectical context of the *Topics*. Perhaps Aristotle is inclined to endorse the position of the interlocutor who is arguing against the claim that the good is a genus of virtue.

At 144^{a}11–16 and 144^{a}17–19 there are two arguments challenging the claim that good is the genus of virtue. In the first, Aristotle assumes that state is the genus of virtue, then he applies the rule that 'It is not possible for the same thing to be in two genera which do not contain one another', and he concludes that state and good cannot both be genera of virtue. Some support for the assumption that state is the genus of virtue will be offered in the second argument (see below); this claim is not new to the *Topics* (see, e.g., VI.5, 143^{a}15–20). The rule regarding the subordination of genera (or 'Rule of Subordination' for short) is introduced in book IV: 'When one species is under two genera, one is subordinate to the other' (IV.2, 121^{b}29–31). According to Aristotle's Rule of Subordination, for any species there is one upward chain of genera which are arranged in a linear order. This means that if we consider the genera to which a species S is subordinate, we see that the relation of subordination is *connected* on the set of the genera. A relation is *connected* if and only if, for any distinct elements x and y, either x bears the ordering relation to y or y to x. Whilst the divisional tree is pre-ordered by the relation of subordination, every branch has a linear order. The idea that for any species there is only one upward chain of genera, which are arranged in a linear order, presupposes (among other things) that there is only one way to classify reality; this means that the classification of reality obtained by applying Aristotle's rule is rigid and leaves no room for flexibility. In the background of Aristotle's Rule of Subordination there is a very strong metaphysical assumption, which some might not want to share. For example, at the beginning of the *Politicus*, Plato explicitly acknowledges that the kind art can be divided in different ways so that the same species can fall under two different genera which are not subordinate (*Plt.* 258B7–12). A full-fledged discussion of this metaphysical assumption is far beyond the scope of our present purposes. At 144^{a}13–14, Aristotle examines the extension of state and good; he applies the Rule of Subordination and concludes that they cannot both be genera of virtue. He then argues that if state is the genus of virtue, as it was granted in the initial assumption, then good is not. But Aristotle's argument takes a further step: its conclusion is that good is *not a genus, but rather* a differentia of virtue. This conclusion is not warranted by anything that is explicitly said in the passage, and an extra premise must be added. In the case described here state and good are mentioned in the defining part of the account of virtue: this means that they can play only two roles, either that of the genus or that of the differentia; since good is not a genus of virtue, it must be a differentia. Perhaps Aristotle was aware of the first argument's deficiencies: despite the fact that it is introduced by *eti* ('furthermore', which usually indicates the beginning of a further argument), his second argument might not be an independent piece of reasoning but might bring support to some of the previous arguments' unwarranted claims.

The second argument runs through 144^{a}17–19. This is an elliptical argument, and its stated premises are:

(1) State indicates what it is (144^{a}17).
(2) Good does not indicate what it is (144^{a}17–18).
(3) Good indicates a certain qualification (144^{a}18).
(4) The differentia indicates a certain qualification (144^{a}18–19).

The conclusion is not explicitly stated, and a likely possibility is:

(5) Good is a differentia.

This could be suggested by the fact that (5) is mentioned above at 144^{a}11–12, and it was part of the first argument's conclusion. If we want to have an argument that validly concludes with (5), something has to be added. The argument can have two further tacit premises:

(6) The genus indicates what it is.
(7) Good is either a genus or a differentia.

Premise (6) is understood as:

(6*) Whatever is a genus indicates what it is.

This is one of the fundamental tenets of Aristotle's discussion in the *Topics* (I.5, 102^{a}31–5); it constitutes one of the main theses of Aristotle's concept of definition. Premise (7) is based on the fact that here state and good are mentioned in the definition of virtue and hence they must be either the genus or the differentia.

From (2) and (6*), it follows that:

(8) Good is not a genus.

Then, from (7) and (8) it is possible to draw the conclusion, i.e. (5) 'Good is a differentia'.

This reconstruction brings in two tacit premises, but they are plausible and grounded in Aristotle's text. One may wonder what the role of premises (3) and (4) would be (for they are not appealed to in the reconstruction). I regard them as bringing independent (but weak) confirmation to (5). Premise (4) is read as:

(4*) Whatever is a differentia indicates a certain qualification.

Then, premises (3) and (4*) confirm (5) 'Good is a differentia', because they show that good satisfies a necessary condition for being a differentia. Finally, (1) and (6*) give us some reason to hold:

(9) State is a genus.

For they show that state satisfies a necessary condition for being a genus. This argument does not prove (9), but it still makes an important point because it backs up one of the claims of the previous argument. The criterion used here to distinguish a genus from a differentia is based on an analysis of what they indicate (either the what-it-is or a certain qualification). (4) The differentia does not indicate a qualification (144^a20–2). This is an important criterion for Aristotle since, in the immediately following lines (144^a21–2), he reformulates it as a separate rule: 'See also whether the given differentia indicates not a certain qualification but a this so-and-so; for every differentia seems to point to a certain qualification'. In the reformulation (144^a21–2) there are some terminological variations: the expression 'a this so-and-so' (*tode ti*, 144^a20) replaces what-it-is (*ti esti*, 144^a18), and the universal quantification over differentiae is explicit (at 144^a21 Aristotle says *pasa diafora*: 'every differentia'). It must also be noted, however, that in both cases the claim that a differentia indicates a certain qualification is *doxastic*: 'A differentia, however, *seems* (*dokei*) to indicate a certain qualification' (144^a18–19), and 'Every differentia *seems* (*dokei*) to point to a certain qualification'

(144^a21-2). The verbs *sêmainein* and *dêloun* ('to indicate' and 'to point to') are stylistic variants. The *doxastic* nature of Aristotle's claim invites at least two comments: Aristotle might not have formed a clear view on a differentia's status yet, or he is aware of some cases where this claim has to be reviewed and further analysed. The view that whatever is a differentia indicates a certain qualification is confirmed by other passages in the *Topics*: see, for example, *Top.* IV.2, 122^b16-17; *Top.* IV.6, 128^a20-8. This view, however, seems to clash with *Top.* VI.6, 145^a14-15, where Aristotle says that 'The differentiae of relatives are relatives' (see commentary *ad loc.*).

(iv) The differentia belongs incidentally to the species (144^a23-7). Aristotle's terminology is not precise: properly speaking, at 144^a23 'differentia' indicates 'What occupies the position of the differentia in the defining part' or 'What is given as a differentia'. The following rule is understood here: if in a proposed definition what is given as a differentia belongs incidentally to the species to be defined, then the definition contains a mistake and cannot be accepted. The choice of translating *kata sumbebêkos* with 'incidentally' is explained in the commentary on *Top.* VI.4, $142^b30-143^a11$. The justification of the above mentioned rule comes in two compressed stages: (1) at 144^a24-5, Aristotle states that differentia and genus are not predicated incidentally. This is in line with his view that the definition expresses the essence, and hence it must contain only essential features. (2) At 144^a26-7, he adds that 'It is not possible that the differentia belongs and does not belong to something'. This amounts to saying that it is necessary for the differentia to belong to the species; it fits well with the idea that genus and differentiae are ontologically prior to the species (see *Top.* VI.4, 141^b28-34, and the commentary *ad loc.*). It is very likely that in the background of 144^a26-7 there is the predicables' classification and their definitions drawn in *Top.* I.5; in particular, there is the characterization of *sumbebêkos* ('accident') as 'What can possibly belong and do not belong to one and the same thing.... For instance, it is possible for being seated to belong and not belong to the same thing' (I.5, 102^b6-8).

$144^a28-144^b11$: The refutative strategies considered here are based upon the analysis of the relation between genus, differentia, and species. The relation under scrutiny is that of essential predication or predication in a definition. There is a parallel passage in *Top.* IV, where Aristotle introduces a rule (*stoicheion*) regarding the predicative relation between the genus, species, and differentia; he says that 'The genus is said more widely than the species and its differentia, for the differentia too is said less widely than the genus' (*Top.* IV.1, 121^{b}11–14). The relation between genus and differentia will be further discussed in the immediately following section, i.e. 144^{b}11–30. In the background of many of these arguments there are ontological assumptions that are expressed in *Cat.* 5.

At 144^{a}28–9, 'The differentia or the species or one of the things below the species' indicates what the interlocutor, in the proposed definition, incorrectly takes to be the differentia or the species or something that falls under it. Since they are predicated of the genus, properly speaking they *are not* differentia or species or something that falls under it. At 144^{a}29–30, Aristotle says that 'It is not possible that one of the things mentioned be predicated of the genus': here 'the things mentioned' refer to differentia or species or something falling under it. But now Aristotle has in mind things that *are* differentia or species or something that falls under it since they cannot be predicated of the genus. At 144^{a}29, the expression 'One of the things below the species' can indicate an indivisible species or an individual. At the end of this paragraph, i.e. 144^{b}1–3, there is a distinction between a species (*eidos*), i.e. a universal) and an individual (*atomon*), and this can support the view that the expression at 144^{a}29 indicates individuals. One might object that talking of individuals in the context of definitions might suggest that individuals have definitions. Here, however, it is simply said that individuals are among the things falling under the species, and it need not imply that individuals are definable.

The entire passage at 144^{a}28–144^{b}11 makes three claims that are useful for the dialectician that is criticizing a proposed definition: (i) a differentia or a species or what falls under the species cannot be predicated of the genus (144^{a}29–31); (ii) the genus is predicated not of the differentia but of the species, of which the differentia is predicated (144^{a}31–144^{b}3); (iii) neither the species nor any of the things falling under it are predicated of the differentia (144^{b}4–11).

Claim (i) is justified by the fact that the genus has a wider extension than the other things mentioned. This is unproblematic: it is also held by Aristotle elsewhere in the *Topics* (see, e.g., IV.1, 121^{b}11–14). At 144^{a}29, following the majority of manuscripts, Waitz 1846, vol. 2, and Ross 1958 read *hôrismenos* ('He would not have defined'), whereas Brunschwig 2007 reads *hôrismenon* (*lit.* 'It would not have been defined', where 'it' stands for the species that the interlocutor attempts to define). Ross's reading might have the advantage that it is in line with the general style of many clauses introducing passages where Aristotle often puts forward a direct attack on an opponent (see, e.g., 143^{a}29, 143^{b}11, 144^{a}9) or suggests a move that someone might make (143^{b}34).

Claim (ii) is at first put forward only in a tentative way ('The genus seems': *to genos dokei*; 144^{a}33). Then it is illustrated with three examples and proved by two compressed arguments that take the form of a *reductio ad absurdum*. In the list of examples where the genus is predicated of the species, we read that animal is predicated of the other footed animals, but this might sound unclear. The expression 'the other footed animals' stands for all the species of footed animals that are different from those already mentioned; thus, the list can be rephrased as 'Human is animal, ox is animal, and the other species of footed animals, e.g. horse, dog, sheep, goat, etc., are animals'.

The first argument, at 144^{a}36–144^{b}1, has received attention from scholars and has been interpreted in several ways: see, e.g., Alex. Aphr. *in Top.* 452, 6–11; Waitz 1846, vol. 2, p. 500; Madigan 1999, pp. 73–5; Shields 1999, pp. 252–4; Wilson 2000, pp. 136–40; Brunschwig 2007, p. 60, n. 1. A survey with an assessment of the main interpretative lines can be found in Berti 2003, pp. 103–25, and 2009, pp. 121–6. The argument is closely connected to an *aporia* discussed in *Metaph.* III.3, 998^{b}17–28 (i.e. *aporia* 7). There Aristotle argues against the Platonic view that Being and One are genera of the things that are. Once it is admitted that One and Being are predicated of their differentiae (since a differentia *is* and is *one*), Aristotle puts forward two claims in support of the denial that Being and One are genera: (i) it is impossible for the species to be predicated of their differentiae; (ii) it is impossible for a genus to be predicated of its differentiae. In the *Metaphysics*, however, these claims are not justified. It is the argument in the *Topics* that might contribute to explain the second claim, namely why a genus cannot be predicated of its differentiae. It can be reconstructed thus: suppose that the genus animal is predicated of any of its differentiae. Since the genus is predicated of any of its differentiae it follows that a human is an animal that is a footed animal, a two-footed animal, a featherless animal, and a rational animal. So, there would be many animals in the definition of human. But this is absurd; for it is impossible that a human be many humans.

The second argument, at 144^{b}1–3, can be reconstructed as follows. Suppose that a genus, e.g. animal, is predicated of one of the differentiae that divide it, e.g. footed. Each animal is either a species, e.g. human, or an individual, e.g. Socrates. So, since it is an animal, footed would be either a species or an individual. But this is absurd; hence, the genus is not predicated of any of the differentiae that divide it. In this portion of text, no justification is offered of the reason why it is absurd that footed is either a species or an individual. Perhaps Aristotle thinks that his audience would find a part of this claim immediately clear: a differentia cannot be an individual since a differentia is a universal. But what about the absurdity of the first half of the claim, namely 'A differentia is not a species'? One might think that Aristotle is referring to the commonplace discussed above at 144^{a}5–8; but this does not suffice since no explanation was offered there either. One might then look at 144^{a}17–22, where Aristotle suggests that the differentia is given as an answer to the question *poîon* ('Of what sort?'), and hence it indicates *poión ti* (a certain qualification). As we know, a species does not answer the 'Of what sort?' question, but it is appropriately given as an answer to a question that asks what it is. For this reason, it is not possible for a differentia to be a species.

Claim (iii) is justified by two arguments (144^{b}5–6; 144^{b}6–9), and the thought expressed at 144^{b}9–11 adds further support to this claim. Note that at 144^{b}5 'the differentia' refers to what the interlocutor gives as a differentia when he suggests a definition (see also, e.g., 144^{a}28–9, and 144^{b}12–14). The first argument is based upon the view that the differentia's extension is wider than the extension of the species it contributes to define. This view is problematic (see discussion below). The second argument is a very concise *reductio* and several important steps remain implicit. The following is a possible reconstruction: consider the definition of human as animal that is footed and rational. Suppose that the species can be predicated of any of the differentiae, for example of footed: footed is a human. What can be a human? We can think of only two possibilities: either an individual human (e.g. Socrates or Coriscus) is a human, or a species of human (e.g. Ethiopian or Greek) is a human (see 144^{b}1–3). The first alternative is ruled out because the differentia is clearly not an individual. It follows that the differentia is one of the species. But according to Aristotle this is also absurd. Thus, neither a species nor any of the things falling under it can be predicated of the differentia. There is a problem in the last stage of the *reductio*: Aristotle takes for granted that for the interlocutor it is absurd to claim that the differentia is a species. Probably the explanation outlined above could be applied here too: a species and a differentia are given as answers to different questions, namely 'What is it?' and 'Of what sort?' respectively. Hence a differentia is not a species (see commentary on 144^{b}1–3). At 144^{b}9–11, Aristotle states the priority of the differentia over the species: the differentia divides the genus and hence it is posterior to it; but the differentia is one of the species' constitutive elements and hence it is prior to the species. Probably, one of the reasons why this argument is extremely compressed is that this question had already been discussed in *Top*. VI.4, 141^{b}28–34 (see commentary *ad loc.*).

The claim that the differentia's extension is wider than that of the species it contributes to define gives rise to some difficulties; for this does not seem to be what Aristotle consistently maintains in the corpus. In two passages, i.e. in *Top.*, I.4, 101^{b}17–23 and in *APo.*, II.13, 96^{a}20–35, Aristotle says or implies that the differentia has a wider extension than the species. In *Top*. I.4, 101^{b}17–23 Aristotle suggests a division of the unique property (*idion*) into two parts: one expresses the essence, the other does not. He says that the part expressing the essence is the defining part; the part not expressing the essence retains the name 'unique property' (*idion*). In this division, the differentia, which is mentioned in the defining part, is placed alongside the genus: as we know, the genus has a wider extension than the species. The differentia is also contrasted with the unique property, which, as we know, has the same extension as the species. So according to this passage, the differentia has a wider extension than the species. In *APo*. II.13, 96^{a}20–35, Aristotle is inquiring into the procedure for establishing a definition. He states that each of the components mentioned in the defining part, namely genus and differentia, extend further, i.e. are said more widely, than the species; see, in particular, 96^{a}32–5: 'Well, such things must be taken up to the first point at which so many are taken that each (*sc.* of the components mentioned in the defining part) will belong further, but all <of them together> will not <belong> further; for necessarily this will be the essence of the object.' Hence, in this passage too, the differentia has a wider extension of the species. In *Top.* IV.2 122^{b}39–123^{a}1, however, Aristotle's position is slightly modified: he clearly allows the possibility that the differentia has an equal as well as a wider extension than the species ('But the differentia is always said equally or more widely than the species'). The discussion of the differentia's extension carries over to the immediately following portion of text.

144^{b}12–30: The examination of a proposed account in relation to the mistakes concerning the differentia continues in these lines. The primary aim of this investigation is to devise a refutative line against the interlocutor's proposed account on the basis of what he has given as a differentia: in particular, it concerns the relation between the suggested differentia and the genus (or genera) that it divides. At 144^{b}12–14, the clause 'Examine also whether what is mentioned as differentia is of another genus, which neither is contained in nor contains the other' indicates to the dialectician the following strategy: he should consider what the interlocutor gives as differentia in his proposed definition, and he should examine whether it also divides another genus, which is not contained in nor does contain the one mentioned in the defining part of the proposed definition. This investigation gives to Aristotle the opportunity to touch upon an interesting philosophical question: can the same differentia divide two non-subordinate genera? The entire passage can be divided into two parts. At 144^{b}13–20, there is an attempt to argue for the view that the same differentia *does not* divide two non-subordinate genera, a view which is put forward only tentatively (see 'It seems', *dokei*, 144^{b}13). At 144^{b}20–30, this view is modified: the same differentia *does* divide two non-subordinate genera *only if* the genera fall under the same higher genus. There are textual and philosophical difficulties throughout these lines.

At 144^{b}18–19, the literal translation of the Greek would result in an unclear English clause (i.e. 'If each of the genera is also of that of which the differentia is'); for this reason, two occurrences of 'said' should be understood (i.e. 'If each of the genera is also <said> of that of which the differentia is <said>'). At 144^{b}20–3 and 24, the translation conveys the stylistic carelessness of the Greek. Properly speaking it is not the case that the expression 'When they are not both under the same thing (i.e. the same genus)' must be added to the immediately preceding clause: 'It *is not* impossible that the same differentia be of two genera not containing one another'. Rather, 'When they are not both under the same thing' expresses the condition under which it *is* impossible for the same differentia to pertain to two genera not containing one another. It has to be noted that the negation *mêde* (lit. 'but not'; 144^{b}20 and 24) has a wide scope; hence the clause 'When they are *not* both are under the same thing' is equivalent to 'When *it is not the case that* they are both under the same thing'. There is perhaps a better way to express the sense of 144^{b}20–3; namely, 'It is not impossible for the same differentia to pertain to two genera not containing one another, *provided that* both fall under the same genus'. In order to give a better sense to the Greek text, one might delete the occurrence of 'not' at 144^{b}20 or that at 144^{b}22; this emendation, however, is not easy to make as it is not attested in any manuscript. Brunschwig suggests that reinforcing the punctuation after 'one another' (*allêla*; 144^{b}22) would reduce the tension between the two clauses. Alternatively, we could understand the conjunction 'but' (*alla*; 144^{b}22) with a strong adversative sense such that it interrupts the previous train of thought: it would thus introduce a clause that need not be syntactically dependent on the preceding one. At 144^{b}24, the conjunction *hoti* has the function of introducing a quotation (see LSJ *s.v. hoti*, II).

The occurrences of *zôion* ('animal') at 144^{b}22 and 30 are discussed in the 'Notes on the Text' *ad loc.*

At 144^{b}26, if we want to make good sense of the text which keeps the definite article 'the' (*to*) before 'appropriate' (*oikeion*), we should understand *pan* (lit. 'every') adverbially and translate it as 'every time'. This reading has the advantage that it clearly expresses the contrast between the case where the differentia introduces its appropriate genus and the case where it introduces a higher genus. The example at 144^{b}22–4 strongly suggests that 'appropriate' indicates the proximate genus (on the relation between proximate and higher genera see commentary on *Top.* VI.5, 142^{b}20–9 and 142^{b}30–143^{a}11). Hence, this reading is to be preferred to the alternative suggested by Ross and adopted by several translators, where the occurrence of the article is deleted and the entire clause is rendered as 'It is not necessary that the differentia brings every appropriate genus'. In this case, every genus of a differentia would be an appropriate genus, but this would fail to distinguish between the proximate and those above it, i.e. higher genera, as Aristotle did at the end of the previous chapter (142^{a}20–1). A further possibility is to read *pantôs* ('entirely') instead of *pan to*; one can then translate the clause as 'The differentia brings (*sc.* with it) an appropriate genus entirely'. In this case, one would have to understand that an appropriate genus is a collection of all the genera brought in by the differentia. This line of thought, however, does not seem to be explored in the book of the *Topics* containing the discussion of the genus.

In this entire passage Aristotle says nothing to clarify the relation between the general claim at 144^{b}13–14 (the same differentia *does not* seem to divide two non-subordinate genera) and the modified view expressed at 144^{b}20–3 (the same differentia *can* divide two non-subordinate genera *provided that* they fall under the same higher genus). A sudden change of perspective, marked by 'or' (*ê*, 144^{b}20), introduces the modified view. The change could be explained in different ways: (i) Aristotle wants to correct his initial position because he understands that it is not accurate; (ii) Aristotle wants to give to a dialectician a way to prevent a possible objection from the interlocutor; (iii) Aristotle is answering an objection coming from his audience.

The general claim (144^{b}13–14) can be seen as a broad classificatory rule. It is strange that Aristotle attempts to support it with a sound argument in the form of a *reductio*, but then modifies it without giving us any reason. This *reductio* can be reconstructed as follows. There are five premises:

(1) The same differentia *does* belong to two genera not containing one another (144^{b}14; *ei de mê*, *i.e.* 'otherwise', refers to the negation of the sentence at 144^{b}13–14).

(2) Each differentia introduces its appropriate genus ($144^{b}16$–17).
(3) Both of the differentia's genera are said of whatever the differentia is said of ($144^{b}18$–19).
(4) The differentia is said of the species (tacit assumption).
(5) Both of the differentia's genera are said of that species (tacit, from (3) and (4)).

It follows that:

(6) The same species is in two genera not containing one another ($144^{b}14$–16).

But since (6) is absurd, the conclusion is:

(7) The same differentia does *not* belong to two genera not containing one another ($144^{b}11$–12).

The reason why the claim 'The same species is in two genera not containing one another' cannot be accepted is discussed above at $144^{a}12$–13 (see commentary *ad loc.*); further discussion can be found in *Top.* IV.2. One could think that premise (2) begs the question; for the expression 'to introduce its appropriate genus' could be taken as 'to introduce *only* (i.e. at least and at most) its appropriate genus'. But this is not the correct reading: in this context 'to introduce its appropriate genus' means 'to introduce *at least* its appropriate genus (and possibly others)'.

At $144^{b}17$–18, it is unclear what the point of the example is ('Just as footed and two-footed bring animal in with themselves'). If it is meant to illustrate the claim that 'The same differentia does not seem to belong to two genera not containing one another' ($144^{b}15$–16), then the example is wrong or misplaced (see Brunschwig 2007, p. 61, n. 6.). But if it is meant simply to sketch an instance of differentiae that introduce their appropriate genus ($144^{b}16$–17), then the example can stand. It might be the case that this example prompts Aristotle to give further thought to the relation between genera and differentiae expressed in the immediately following lines.

At $144^{b}20$–3, Aristotle suddenly turns to the modified view. This position can be found in *Cat.* 3, $1^{b}20$–4, where Aristotle says: 'There is nothing to prevent genera that are subordinate one to the other from having the same differentia. For the higher are predicated of the genera below them so that all differentiae of the predicated genus will be differentiae of the subject also.' It is further confirmed by two passages from the *Prior Analytics,* where Aristotle tells us that if the differentiae introduce a higher genus, then they have a wider extension than the species (*APr.* I.1, 24^{a}16–20 and I.2, 25^{a}4–5). Furthermore, as discussed in the commentary on 144^{a}28–144^{b}11, in *Top.* IV.2 122^{b}39–123^{a}1 Aristotle allows for the possibility that the differentia could have an equal as well as a wider extension than the species ('The differentia is always said equally or more widely than the species'). The texts we have considered make it clear that in the early logical writings the differentia has an equal or wider extension than the species it contributes to carve out from the genus. However, it must be added that *Metaph.* VII.12 and VIII.6 are traditionally read as suggesting that since the last differentia implies the genus it divides and, through it, also the higher genera, this differentia is coextensive with the species that is defined.

At 144^{b}29–30, the example ('Just as two-footed brings winged or footed animal in with itself') illustrates the modified view. It gives us a case where the same differentia, i.e. two-footed, divides two non-subordinate genera, i.e. winged animal and footed animal, and contributes to form two further species, i.e. *two-footed footed* animal and two-footed winged animal. Then the two non-subordinate genera, i.e. winged animal and footed animal, are subordinate to a higher and common genus, i.e. animal. Aristotle does not elaborate further on this example, which marks the end of the commonplace's discussion. But the fact that there is no deeper analysis of the example might seem strange. Note that in *HA* I.5, 490^{a}10–12, Aristotle suggests a different classification, where flying animal is divided according to the types of their wings (feathered, leathern, membranous wings). Then winged animals with feathered or leathern wings are divided according to the number of their feet.

Perhaps Aristotle believes that the strategy he outlined in this passage of the *Topics* will be enough to enable the dialectician to develop a criticism of mistaken accounts. As we saw, the strategy is based upon rules which are illustrated by examples. Although it is true to say that these examples are borrowed from the field of zoology, their use does not constitute sufficient evidence to claim that Aristotle was already a zoologist when he wrote the *Topics.* At most, they show that Aristotle did have an interest in zoological classification, but this remains marginal to his project in the *Topics.*

144ᵇ31–145ᵃ2: The differentia of a substance must not indicate a location (*en tini*, 144ᵇ31 and 145ᵃ2). Why does Aristotle specify that he is considering the differentia of a substance? He might think that only differentiae of substances must not express a location; this leaves open the possibility that in cases other than those of substances a differentia could express a location. Or he might not be interested in expressing a view about the other cases; his aim could be simply to find support for the view that footed and aquatic, the differentiae of the substance animal, do not express a location (for example, as we shall see below, 'footed' is equivalent to 'having feet to stand or walk on the ground').

There are different stages in Aristotle's reasoning. At 144ᵇ31–2, Aristotle states the general rule: if in a proposed definition of a substance what occupies the position of the differentia expresses a location (*en tini*, 'being-in-something'), it cannot be accepted. Lines 144ᵇ32–4 describe an attempted criticism of definitions of substances containing the differentiae footed and aquatic. These differentiae are taken to express locations, namely being on land and being in water. Since these differentiae are often used by Aristotle, the criticism might have been directed against his own position. The text, however, does not tell us who is responsible for the criticism. At 144ᵇ34, the particle *ê* ('or') introduces another stage in the argument: lines 144ᵇ34–145ᵃ1 sketch a strategy which should enable the questioner to counter the criticism. The questioner's answer has to be based on the fact that the differentiae footed and aquatic do not describe locations of an animal but other characteristics of it. For example, a horse is a footed animal since it is constituted and equipped in such a way that it can live on dry land; similarly with aquatic animals. At 145ᵇ1–2, Aristotle restates his initial position by ruling out the possibility that a differentia could express a location (see 'Note on the value of *ê*' in 'Terminological Clarifications').

145ᵃ3–12: It is a mistake to give to an affection (*pathos*) the role of a differentia in a definition. What does Aristotle mean by 'affection' here? Although there are no examples of affections in this passage, lines 145ᵃ3–5 indicate that they are properties of the thing to be defined: their characteristic is that they can increase in intensity, and their intensification could disrupt the essential features of the thing to be defined. This suggests that affections are not essential properties of the thing to be defined (as implied in *Top.* IV.5, 126^{b}37–8). At 145^{a}4 and 10, the expression 'It disrupts' translates the Greek verb *existesi*, which literally means 'It displaces' or 'It drives something out of'. According to the literal meaning, the following translation is also possible: 'It (*sc.* the affection) drives something out of its substance'. Perhaps this alternative translation conveys better the sense of what Aristotle is trying to say, but it has the disadvantage that it is more a paraphrase than a translation.

The structure of the reasoning in 145^{a}3–12 is not straightforward: the passage contains two arguments. In the first (145^{a}3–7), Aristotle lays out some premises:

(1) Every affection, if intensified, disrupts the substance of that which is affected (145^{a}3–4).
(2) No differentia, if intensified, disrupts the substance of that which it differentiates (145^{a}4–5).

Premise (2) is supported by two further claims:

(3) Every differentia preserves that of which it is a differentia (145^{a}5–6).
(4) Nothing can be without its differentia (145^{a}6–7).

Then an example is added, namely:

(5) Something that is not footed is not a human (145^{a}7).

This example is an illustration of (4). A justification of (4) is to be found in the view that the differentia is prior to the species (see *Top.* VI.4, 141^{b}28–9, and commentary *ad loc.*). More on premise (3) will be said below. The expected, but not expressed, conclusion is:

(6) No differentia is an affection.

At 145^{a}8–12, the second argument is introduced by the expression 'But speaking without qualification' (*haplôs d'eipein*). It says that:

(7) It is not the case that a differentia of *a* is that with respect to which *a* alters (145^{a}8–9).

This is supported by:

(8) All the things with respect to which *a* alters, if they are increased, disrupt the substance of *a* (145^{a}9–10).

The conclusion is:

(9) If the interlocutor has a given as a differentia of *a* a thing with respect to which *a* alters, he has made a mistake in the definition of *a* (145^a10-11).

There is a final clause:

(10) We do not alter *at all* with respect to the differentia (145^a11-12).

Here the adverb 'at all' makes (10) a strengthened version of (7). The role of (10) is to support the expressed conclusion, i.e. (9).

Premise (3) invites some comments. If its role is to support premise (2), then it has to be understood as:

(3*) Every differentia *if intensified* preserves that of which it is a differentia.

One reading of (3*), however, makes Aristotle's argument implausible. This reading says that a differentia, e.g. aquatic, if intensified preserves the substance of a fish: it interprets 'if intensified' as 'becoming more and more aquatic', then it takes 'becoming more and more aquatic' to mean something like 'living in deeper and deeper water'. Thus, the deeper in water something lives, the more its nature of fish is preserved. But this does not make much sense. A different reading is possible: 'if intensified' could mean something like 'becoming better equipped for living in water'. This need not be an evolutionist thesis, but it can simply express a fact about a natural kind, namely a fish could become better at using the physical structure that allows it to thrive in water. So, Aristotle's claim is that becoming better equipped for living in water, i.e. becoming better at using the physical structure that allows it to thrive in water, preserves the nature of a fish. This reading rescues Aristotle from the charge of introducing a poor premise in the first argument.

What is the relation between the two arguments in this passage? There are two options: the second argument could be either a reformulation or a generalization of the first. It is a reformulation if we understand that 'alteration' (*allôiosis*, from *alloioutai*), which is found in premise (8) of the second argument, expresses a change with respect to an affection (see *Metaph.* XII.2, 1069^b12). 'All the things with respect to which *a* alters', mentioned in premise (8), will coincide with 'every affection' mentioned in premise (1) of the first argument. Hence, (8) does not add anything to (1). Alternatively, the second argument is a generalization of the first if we understand that 'alteration' is not restricted to affections but expresses a change with respect to qualities (see *Cat.* 5, 4^{a}31). Since affections are a type of quality (see *Cat.* 8, 9^{a}28), premise (8) introduces a more general claim than (1), namely 'All the things with respect to which *a* alters include all the affections but extend further than it'. This interpretation further suggests that the second argument introduces a commonplace which differs from that expressed in the first: the second argument's commonplace (145^{a}8–12) tells us that since *no change with respect to a's qualities* is a differentia of *a*, if in the proposed definition of *a* the role of the differentia of *a* is given to one of the things that can change *a* to the point where its substance is disrupted, then the proposed definition is mistaken. The other commonplace (145^{a}3–7) says that since *no affection of a* is a differentia of *a*, if in the proposed definition of *a* the role of the differentia of *a* is given to one of the things that can affect *a* to the point where *a*'s substance is disrupted, then the proposed definition is mistaken. A different reconstruction of the relation between the two arguments can be found in Brunschwig 2007, p. 61, n. 1.

145^{a}13–32. The discussion of the commonplaces used to attack proposed definitions containing relatives can be divided as follows: (1) the general case of definitions containing differentiae of relatives (145^{a}13–18); (2) the specific case where the thing to be defined has one natural correlative; this must be distinguished from the case where the thing to be defined has one natural correlative and also non-natural correlatives (145^{a}19–27); (3) the specific case where the thing to be defined is spoken of in relation to several things since its genus is a relative with many correlatives, and there is a hierarchy among these correlatives: one of them is 'the first correlative' (145^{a}28–32).

(1) Definitions containing differentiae of relatives (145^{a}13–18). There is a textual problem at 145^{a}15–16 and 17–18: see 'Notes on the Text' *ad loc*. At 145^{a}13, what does '(of) one of the relatives' (*tinos tôn pros ti*) refer to? The example at 145^{a}15–18 suggests that it refers to one of the relative genera. This is because theoretical and productive are differentiae that divide knowledge, which is a

relative genus (see *Cat*.8, 11ᵃ23–5). If we apply the principle expressed at 145ᵃ13–14, a dialectician's task is to examine whether the defining part of, e.g. literacy, mentions not only the genus, i.e. knowledge, which is a relative, but also the differentia, i.e. speculative, which must be a relative too. In other words, speculative is one of the differentiae *divisivae* of the genus knowledge. When speculative is mentioned in the defining part of the account of literacy, it is the differentia *constitutiva* of literacy; for literacy could be thought of as knowledge that is speculative of letters. At 145ᵃ14–15, the claim that the differentiae of relatives are always relatives has provoked much debate on the categorial *status* of the differentia: see, in particular, Brunschwig 1986; Morrison 1993; Gambra 2003; Malink 2007. These lines suggest that, at least in the case of relatives, the differentia is always in the same category as that of which it is a differentia. However, this is dissimilar to the case of differentiae of (secondary) substances; for Aristotle says that a differentia of a (secondary) substance expresses a *poión ti*, namely a certain qualification. In an attempt to ease this tension, we can sketch the following interpretative line (a more extensive discussion can be found in Schiaparelli 2016). At 144ᵃ17–19, the text suggests that *poión ti* (a certain qualification) is given as an answer to the question *poîon* ('Of what sort?'). This question is asked in a technical context, namely in the context of definitions. Aristotle's analysis of definitions in the *Topics* tells us that the defining part mentions the genus and one or more differentiae. The genus, which is mentioned in the first position, answers the 'What is *x*?' question. Given that the 'What is *x*?' question has been answered by '*x* is *G*', where *G* is the genus, the differentia (one or more) answers the 'What sort of *G* is *x*?' question. This means that there are some constraints upon the 'Of what sort is *x*?' question: one must first answer the 'What is *x*?' question, i.e. one must first give the genus *G*, before asking 'What sort of *G* is *x*?' and thereby giving a certain qualification. If the genus *G* that is mentioned as the first element of the account's defining part is a (secondary) substance, e.g. animal, then the differentia, which answers the 'What sort of *G* is *x*?' question (*poîon*) might be a quality, e.g. two-footed (*Top*. IV.6, 128ᵃ26–9). If the genus *G* that is mentioned as the first element of the defining part is a relative, e.g. knowledge, then the differentia, which answers the 'What sort of *G* is *x*?' question (*poîon*), will be a relative, e.g. speculative (145ª13–18). This suggests that the expression 'a certain qualification' does not mean 'a certain qualification that is always in the category of quality' but 'a certain qualification that might or might not be in the category of quality'. As a final point, it should be noted that at 145ª20 'The person who defines' means 'The person who puts forward a definition'; for the proposed definition is still under scrutiny and if the attempt is not successful, it will not be correct to call it a definition.

(2) The thing to be defined has one natural correlative and also non-natural correlatives (145ª19–27). At 145ª21, *hekaston tôn pros ti* is to be deleted: it is a dittography generated by repeating the same expression that occurs at 145ª19–20. The rule says that if the proposed definition mentions the non-natural correlative but omits the natural one, then it cannot be accepted. This case is illustrated by comparing the ways in relation to which the eye and a strigil (*stleggis,* see below) can be used. The comparison works if eye is used as 'organ of sight'. We can then say that since the organ of sight has only one natural use, namely seeing, this will be its natural correlative. What is a *stleggis* (145ª23) that I have translated with 'strigil'? Alexander of Aphrodisias (*in Top.* 222, 4–7) tells us that according to some a *stleggis* is a comb (perhaps something like a tiara, i.e. a piece of jewellery like a small crown; see also LSJ *s.v. stleggis*, II), and according to others it is a hollow tool used to wipe off sweat. It has been shown that in this context *stleggis* indicates a strigil, namely the hollow tool, and not a tiara (see Brunschwig 1973, 2007; *pace* Isnardi Parente 1966a, 1966b). This hollow tool can also be used to draw up liquid (Alexander of Aphrodisias notes that *stleggis* occurs in Aristophanes' *Thesmophoriazuae* 556, where it is said that women employed *stleggidas* to draw up wine). When a strigil is used to draw up liquid, it is not employed in its natural use. Hence drawing up liquid is a correlative of a strigil but not the natural one. If the proposed definition of strigil mentions only the non-natural correlative, it cannot be accepted (different interpretations of this argument are discussed in Brunschwig 1973, pp. 33–6). This, however, raises a question: in what way is Aristotle employing the expression '*natural* correlative' when he talks about the strigil? For, as we know, a strigil is an artefact. Perhaps here expression '*natural* correlative' is not intended to introduce a contrast between nature (*physis*) and art

(*technê*). A passage in the *Physics* supports this thought. Aristotle says:

> If a house, for example, had been a thing made by nature, it would have been in the same way as it is now by art: and if things made by nature were made not only by nature but also by art, they would come to be in the same way as by nature. The one, then, is for the sake of the other; and, generally, art in some cases completes what nature cannot bring to a finish, and in others imitates nature. If therefore artificial products are for the sake of an end, so clearly are the natural products. The relation of the later to the earlier items is the same in both. (*Ph*. II.8, 199^{a}12–20)

Aristotle seems to be aware of the problem: at 145^{a}25–7 he suggests that in the case of a strigil the expression 'natural correlative' refers not to any of its uses, but to the use in which strigil can be put by the prudent person. The suggestion seems to be that, in the case of an artefact like strigil, to give a definition is to identify the natural use to which it can be put.

(3) The thing to be defined is spoken of in relation to several things, given that its genus is a relative with many correlatives. There is a hierarchy among these correlatives: one of them is 'the first correlative' (145^{a}28–32). If a proposed definition does not mention the first correlative, it cannot be accepted. To illustrate this commonplace, Aristotle considers wisdom (*phronesis*), which can be defined as virtue in relation to a human, to the soul, and to the reasoning faculty. Lines 145^{a}29–30 can be read as containing examples of proposed definitions: (a) 'Wisdom is a virtue of a human', (b) 'Wisdom is a virtue of the soul', and (c) 'Wisdom is a virtue of the reasoning faculty'. Accounts (a) and (b) cannot be accepted, whereas (c) seems a successful definition. This is one of the very few occasions in *Topics* VI, which is a refutative book, where Aristotle seems to suggest a successful definition. Note that 'Wisdom is a virtue of the reasoning faculty' is used interchangeably with 'Wisdom (*sc*. is a virtue that) is said in relation to the reasoning faculty'. The explanation of this commonplace is not fully developed. There is a compressed and elliptical argument where some of the steps and the conclusion are not expressed. Here is a likely reconstruction: (i) A proposed definition that does not mention the first correlative must not be accepted (premise: paraphrase and expansion of 145^{a}28–9). (ii) A proposed definition of wisdom that does not mention the first correlative is not

successful (non-expressed premise: from (i)). (iii) It is in relation to the reasoning faculty that a human and the soul are said to think (145^a31–2, premise: 'to think' translates *phronein*, a cognate of *phronesis*). (iv) The reasoning faculty is the first thing in relation to which wisdom is said (145^a30–1: from (iii)). (v) Accounts (a) and (b) do not mention the first correlative (non-expressed premise: from the example at 29–30 and (iv)). (vi) Accounts (a) and (b) must not be accepted, namely they are not successful definitions of wisdom (non-expressed conclusion: from (ii), (iv), and (v)).

This argument is not satisfactory. Let me mention at least one problem: very little is said to elucidate the concept of the first correlative, which plays a crucial role in the argument. In premise (iii) it is taken for granted that there is some sort of privileged link between wisdom (*phronesis*), thinking (*phronein*), and reasoning faculty, but this is not further explored: on what grounds should the interlocutor concede this and hence accept (iii)? The lack of convincing support for (iii) might seriously undermine the entire argument; for (iii) leads to (iv), which is a key step towards the conclusion. Two interpretative options can be developed in support of (iii). In the background of Aristotle's argument there is part of the conceptual framework developed in Plato's *Republic*. In particular, there are the claims that the soul has a tripartite structure (i.e. it is a complex of the reasoning—in Greek, *to logistikon*—the desiderative and the spirited part) and that the virtues (i.e. wisdom, temperance, courage, and justice) are to be identified with reference to the soul's parts. This is suggested by the jargon employed by Aristotle at 145^a31–2, when he uses the expression 'virtue of the reasoning faculty' (*aretê tou logistikou*). It is further supported by two other passages. (A) *Top.* I.16, 108^a1–3, where Aristotle deals with the four Platonic virtues and says that 'One should study ... by means of what does justice differ from courage, or wisdom from temperance: all of these are from the same genus (*sc.* virtue)'. (B) *Top.* V.6, 136^b11–14, where wisdom is characterized as a virtue of the reasoning faculty (*logistikou aretê*) and distinguished from temperance, which is a virtue of the desiderative faculty (*epithumêtikou aretê*). Someone who is acquainted with this background will not find it difficult to accept that if we say that a human and the soul think, we mean that they do it by means of the reasoning faculty. Since wisdom is the virtue by which one reasons well, it is easy to infer that wisdom is said primarily in relation to the reasoning faculty. The second interpretative option draws a parallel between this text and other passages in the corpus. Claims (iii), 'It is with respect to this (*sc.* the reasoning faculty) that both the soul and a human are said to think', (145^{a}31–2) and (iv), 'Wisdom is a virtue of the reasoning faculty first', could be reminiscent of the discussion of cases of 'focal meaning' (aka 'core dependent association', see in particular *Metaph.* IV.2, 1003^{a}33–1003^{b}15; there is a vast literature on this, see, e.g., Shields 1999). According to Owen 1960, p. 174, at 145^{a}30–2 Aristotle is very close to giving his views on 'focal meaning'. But there are several reasons why this interpretation is not attractive. A refutative strategy that is based on the concept of focal meaning would be very unlikely to succeed: it is very complex and it involves some conceptual steps that the interlocutor is probably not ready to accept. But the key weakness of this option lies in the fact that it is unclear how the concept of focal meaning could be applied to the case under scrutiny: at most there seems to be a vague association with it.

Aristotle's argument helps us to identify the first correlative. It also implies that, in these cases, it is a necessary condition for a definition to be accepted that it mentions the first correlative; for this seems to coincide with the *last* differentia, i.e. the differentia that must be expressed in the account's defining part. The argument, however, does not say *why* the first correlative should coincide with the last differentia. One might argue that the first correlative and the last differentia identify precisely that feature that distinguishes the species to be defined from the other species in the same genus (e.g. being in relation to the reasoning faculty is the feature which distinguishes wisdom from the other virtues of a human). In other words, the first correlative and the last differentia should coincide because if they are added to the same genus, they single out species that are extensionally equivalent. Alternatively, one might suggest that the first correlative and the last differentia should coincide by virtue of their causal role. For example, the reasoning faculty is the first thing in relation to which wisdom is said and is the cause by which a human thinks. Similarly, being in relation to the reasoning faculty is the last differentia and is the cause of wisdom. This further suggests that the kind of priority that is enjoyed by the first correlative could be the same priority of the last differentia: it could be a causal priority with respect to the species to be defined. Although this second line of argument makes Aristotle's text more interesting, it is not very likely because it is based upon the view that the last differentia is the cause: whilst Aristotle adopts and elaborates this view in the *Analytics*, he never employs it in the *Topics*.

145^{a}33–145^{b}20: This portion of text has the following structure: (1) at 145^{a}33–4 the rule for rejecting a proposed definition is presented; (2) at 145^{a}34–7 the rule is explained and an example is added; (3) at 145^{a}37–145^{b}11 four examples of accounts containing the mistake under discussion are offered and criticized; (4) at 145^{b}11–20 three of the examples are subject to further criticism.

(1) The mistake consists in describing the thing to be defined as an affection (*pathos*) or a disposition (*diathesis*) of something which cannot receive it. 'Affections' or 'dispositions' indicate qualifications or modifications; 'anything else' (*hotioun allo*, 145^{a}34) probably includes other qualifications such as states (*hexeis*). Here Aristotle does not distinguish between affections, dispositions, and states, as he does, for example, in *Cat.* 8, where he says: 'A state (*hexis*) differs from a disposition (*diathesis*) in being more stable and lasting longer' (8^{b}27–8); 'It is what is easily changed and quickly changing that we call dispositions, e.g. hotness and chill, and sickness and health and the like' (8^{b}35–7). In *Top.* VI.6, 145^{a}35–6, knowledge is said to be a disposition, whilst in *Cat.* 8 it is implied that knowledge (being permanent and hard to change when it is acquired) is more like a state.

(2) The justification of the rule relies on the relation of 'to be in'. Here 'to be in' is equivalent to 'to belong to' (*huparchein*; 145^{b}3, 5, 10), and it expresses a general relation of predication. Someone might be tempted to understand that in this passage 'to be in' is used in the technical way that is described in *Cat.* 2, 1^{a}24–5: 'By in a subject I mean what is in something, not as a part, and cannot exist separately from what it is in'. This, however, is not required by this text. Furthermore, an interlocutor could easily object to such a technical use: he could refuse to grant his assent, thereby creating a difficulty for the dialectician's refutative line devised here.

(3) The justification of the rule in terms of the 'to be in' relation provides the dialectician with a general refutative strategy that

can be applied to criticize proposed accounts. Aristotle presents four examples and sketches the arguments against them. The following is a possible reconstruction of the lines of argument and it will help us to assess Aristotle's strategy. It must be kept in mind, though, that most likely these lines of argument must be further developed by the dialectician and they take the form of an exchange composed of questions and answers. (i) Suppose an interlocutor grants that sleep is a sense-perception inability (*adunamia aistheseôs*); then he is attributing sleep to perception, i.e. he is saying that sleep *is in* perception; but this is absurd. Hence the account cannot be accepted. (ii) Suppose an interlocutor concedes that perplexity is equality of contrary arguments ('Perplexity is equality of contrary arguments' is the literal translation of *hê aporia isotês enantiôn logismôn*, 145^{b}1–2; a less literal translation but perhaps a clearer way of phrasing the sentence would be 'Contrary arguments having equal value'). Then the interlocutor is attributing perplexity to arguments, i.e. perplexity *is in* arguments; but this is absurd, for perplexity (if it is in something) *is in* the soul (Aristotle says, at 145^{b}20, *we* are perplexed—*aporoumen*). (iii) Suppose an interlocutor grants that pain is forced separation of naturally conjoint parts; then he is attributing pain to the parts. This further implies that parts, which are soulless, will suffer; but this is absurd since pain *is in* what has a soul. (iv) Suppose an interlocutor concedes that health is a due proportion of hot and cold elements. Then, he is attributing health to hot elements and to cold ones, i.e. health *is in* hot and in cold elements. But, according to the view proposed here this is absurd.

There are some difficulties with Aristotle's suggested strategy: two of them are particularly important. The first difficulty regards how Aristotle's strategy applies to the examples; for his suggested refutative line seems to force upon them a reading which does not seem the most natural one or might not be the one intended by the interlocutor when he grants it. It must be seen what the grounds are for attributing to the proposed examples the reading Aristotle defends. The second, and more general, difficulty arises because it is not clear how the mistake under discussion is related to the main theme of the chapter, which consists in identifying different ways of failing to give the correct differentia. These difficulties are interlinked. The Greek expression corresponding to 'sense-perception inability' is *adunamia aisthesêôs*, where *aisthesêôs* is in the genitive and its literal rendering is 'of sense-perception'. In particular, in a sentence like 'Sleep is a sense-perception inability' (*ho hupnos estin adunamia aisthesêôs*, 145^{b}1), 'of sense-perception' (*aisthesêôs*) is an adnominal genitive, i.e. it is a genitive which limits the meaning of the substantive on which it depends (Smyth 1956, p. 313). If 'of sense-perception' is construed with 'inability', its function will be to restrict it and to identify a certain type of inability. But if 'sense-perception inability' is taken to be the definition of sleep and the expression in the genitive (*aisthesêôs*; lit. 'of sense-perception') plays the role of the differentia, this will create some problems. Since the differentia is predicated of the species it contributes to define (e.g. rational is predicated of human), 'of sense-perception' will be predicated of sleep. But in 'sleep of sense-perception' (*ho hupnos aisthesêôs*) the genitive cannot be understood as adnominal, since it would hardly make any sense at all: sense-perception does not identify a certain type of sleep. So, in this case the link introduced by the genitive must be expressed differently and, according to Aristotle, the most plausible guess is that it is expressed by the relation of to be in, i.e. sleep *is in* sense-perception. But to say that sleep is in sense-perception is absurd; for if it is in anything, sleep is in an organism. Analogous reconstructions can be offered for the three remaining examples. This proves that the proposed accounts cannot be accepted and that the interlocutor has made a mistake. The relation between the mistake under discussion and the main theme of this chapter should be now clearer: at 145^{a}33–145^{b}20 Aristotle shows that if the interlocutor frames his definition of an affection (or of other conditions) in a way that the differentia is expressed in the genitive, then there is a strategy to attack him. This is a subtle strategy that is based on a theoretical and grammatical analysis of the interlocutor's claim.

(4) There is a further criticism of these proposed definitions, namely 'Sleep is a sense-perception inability', 'Perplexity is equality of contrary arguments', 'Pain is forced separation of naturally conjoint parts'. Anyone who grants them makes the mistake of confusing the product (*to poioumenon*, lit. 'the produced') with the producing factor (*to poiêtikon*, lit. 'that which produces'), and vice versa. *To poioumenon* and *to poiêtikon* have been variously translated: see, e.g., Pickard-Cambridge 1928, Barnes 1984, vol. 1, and

Forster 1960 adopt 'the effect' and 'the cause'; similarly, Tricot 1950 adopts 'l'effect' and 'la cause'; Brunschwig 2007 renders them as 'la cause productrice' and 'l'effet produit'. Since 'cause' traditionally translates *aitia* but *aitia* does not appear in this text, I choose to adopt 'the product' and 'the producing factor', which are closer to the Greek. The analysis at 145^{b}12–20 aims to explain the remark at 145^{b}11–12: in the three proposed accounts the thing to be defined points to the producing factor (pain, sleep, perplexity) and the defining part mentions the product (respectively, sense-perception inability, equality of contrary arguments, forced separation of naturally conjoint parts). This leads to the following three claims: (a) the separation of naturally conjoint parts is the product of pain; (b) sense-perception inability is the product of sleep; and (c) equality of contrary argument is the product of perplexity. Claims (a) and (c) are incorrect since the separation of naturally conjoint parts is (not the product of, but) what produces pain; similarly, equality of contrary argument is (not the product of, but) what produces perplexity. Claim (b) is of a different sort: if one says that sense-perception inability is the product of sleep, one does not give a complete account of it. For there could be cases where sense-perception inability is the producing factor of sleep (it induces us to fall asleep): in these cases, claim (b) is incorrect. The purpose of presenting a further line of attack is unclear: it could be a criticism which is alternative to the one outlined in what immediately precedes (145^{a}37–145^{b}1). But it could also be an additional attack that can be launched against the examples involved in this commonplace. Perhaps Aristotle leaves these options open to the dialectician who must judge what the best strategy is in any given situation.

145^{b}21–33: This is the last commonplace in this chapter. The arguments in these lines are difficult to unfold. The text can be divided into three parts: (A) 145^{b}21–3 introduces the commonplace to be discussed and illustrates it with an example; (B) 145^{b}23–30 contains an objection to what is just said; (C) 145^{b}30–3 refers back to part (A) and contains a justification for introducing the commonplace. Note that in this passage there are three occurrences of the verb *sumbainô* (i.e. *sumbainei* at 145^{b}25 and 29, and *sumbainêi* at 145^{b}30). If we want to convey in English the sense of what Aristotle is saying, it is impossible to give the same translation to the three occurrences. In the first two cases, the verb *sumbainô* corresponds to the English 'to follow', whereas in the last case it has the value of 'to happen'.

Part (A). Aristotle instructs the dialectician to analyse the interlocutor's claim according to the following rule:

> (*o*) Concerning every expression of time, you should consider whether somewhere there is a time discrepancy (paraphrase of $145^{b}21$–2).

In sentence (*o*), 'every expression of time' indicates all the temporal qualifications attached to the differentia (or else there would be no reason to discuss this commonplace in the chapter dealing with the differentia). Sentence (*o*) establishes the following rule: the dialectician should examine whether the temporal qualification attached to the differentia introduces a time discrepancy between what is mentioned in the defining part and the thing to be defined. Such a discrepancy would violate a key requirement for a successful definition since it would prevent what is mentioned in the account's defining part and the thing to be defined from being the same (see $145^{b}31$–2, below). Sentence (*o*) is followed by an example:

> (*p*) The immortal is an animal that is deathless now ($145^{b}22$–3).

In sentence (*p*), there is a time discrepancy between the defining part (which contains the temporal qualification 'now') and the thing to be defined (which is not temporally qualified). Thus, (*p*) is not a successful definition of immortal and has to be rejected. The sentence that immediately follows (*p*) is:

> (*q*) The animal deathless now is now immortal ($145^{b}23$).

Sentence (*q*) is a correction of (*p*). In other words, based on what (*o*) says, (*q*) is introduced as an improvement of the proposed and incorrect account expressed by (*p*). This is because in (*q*) there is no discrepancy in the temporal qualification: the adverb 'now' occurs in both parts of the proposed definition. But the role of (*q*) in the argument at $145^{b}21$–3 is unclear. One might be tempted to say that sentence (*q*) is an absurd claim and that its role is to show that (*p*) is unacceptable. Why should (*q*) be absurd? It is possible to argue that 'immortal' is strictly connected with *aidion* (Bonitz 1870, p. 12B) so that it is synonymous with 'eternally alive'

(Aristotle, *Cael.*, II.3, 286ᵃ9) and means 'everlasting'. In this case, it hardly makes sense to qualify it with 'now'. Alternatively, one could say that sentence (*q*) is (not an absurd claim but) a correct modification of (*p*). There are reasons to prefer this second exegesis. One reason is that, contrary to what the first exegetical line assumes, not all that is immortal is eternal. Something can be immortal, but it could have been born at some time. Another (and more important) reason is that if (*q*) is absurd, then it would sit uncomfortably with the rule in (*o*) that requires the presence of temporal qualifications in both parts of the definition. So, I am inclined to think that, at this stage of the argument, sentence (*q*) is a correct result.

Part (B). At 145ᵇ23, the particle *ê* ('or') marks a brisk turn in the reasoning (see 'Note on the value of *ê*' in 'Terminological Clarifications'). A new argument challenges the result obtained in part (A), where it is established that (*q*) is a correct modification of (*p*). The new argument is centred on the ambiguity of the expression 'deathless now' (*aphtharton nun*) and is meant to prove that (*q*) is not, after all, a correct modification of (*p*). At 145ᵇ25–6, a triple disjunction introduces three possible ways to understand the expression 'deathless now':

(1) It has not died now (*ouk ephthartai nun*).
(2) It is not possible that it dies now (*ou dunatai phtharênai nun*).
(3) It is now such as never to die (*toiouton esti nun mêdepote phtharênai*).

The description of the three meanings of 'deathless now' is not easy to understand and raises some difficulties. For example, in certain cases there is a complex combination of modal and temporal concepts (I am working with the standard modern view that there is a difference between these two concepts), and the scope of the temporal adverb 'now' is unclear. But consider *aphtharton* ('deathless'): it is a verbal adjective from *phtheirein* ('to destroy', in the passive form 'to be destroyed' and hence 'to die') with privative *alpha* in the prefix. The word *phtharton* is ambiguous: it can have the force of a perfect passive participle, i.e. 'destroyed' or 'dead', and it can also express a modal determination, namely the possibility of being destroyed, i.e. 'destructible', or the possibility of dying, i.e. 'subject to death'. This ambiguity, however, is not explored by Aristotle and its full analysis goes beyond the limits of the present commentary (a discussion of the ambiguities involved in some temporal and modal notions can be found in, e.g., Prior 1968, and Hintikka 1973). At 145^{b}27–8, Aristotle suggests that 'deathless now' must be understood as in (3), i.e. as 'now such as never to die'. So, the phrase 'An animal that is deathless now' is equivalent to 'An animal that is now such as never to die'. At 145^{b}29, Aristotle claims:

(s) This (*sc.* the animal that is now such as never to die) was the same as the immortal.

What is the role of (*s*)? By establishing that 'now such as never to die' is equivalent to 'immortal', it shows that (*q*) is not a correct modification of (*p*). To sum up briefly, 'deathless now' is ambiguous and can be taken as 'now such as never to die'. But 'now such as never to die' is equivalent to 'immortal'. So, it does not follow that 'deathless now' is equivalent to 'immortal now'. Thus, as said above, (*q*) is not, after all, a correct modification of (*p*). The objection of part (B) concludes here.

Is this objection convincing and well expressed? It does not seem so. Although the argument does not contain any formal difficulty, there is a problem with the premise (*s*). The reasons for granting this premise are not expressed and, at a first reading, one is tempted to reject (*s*). We can try to improve the situation by spelling out some implicit argumentative moves. It must be noted that the Greek formulation of (*s*) uses the imperfect *ên*, i.e. 'was'. This opens up at least three options. First, *ên* corresponds to definitory use of *einai* ('to be'); it is translated with the present 'is' and means 'is by definition'. In this case we are led to accept (*s*) in virtue of the fact that it is true *by definition*. Secondly, *ên* can still be translated with the present 'is', but it indicates that *intuitively* this is what we take to mean 'The animal that is now such as never to die'. In this case, we grant (*s*) because it reflects our intuitions about the meaning of 'The animal that is now such as never to die'. Finally, *ên* can retain the value of the imperfect 'was' and points to the fact that (*s*) was conceded at some point in the dialogue with the interlocutor; the concession remains understood and not reported in the text. To be sure, all the options have something to be said for them. The last, however, seems to me the most plausible, for it is based on the reconstruction of the dialectical account, which is the distinctive method in the *Topics*.

It is interesting to note that, at 145^b22, the expression 'immortal' (*athanaton*) is used as a substantive and takes the place of the thing to be defined. This suggests that the immortal is a kind and that we might look for its definition. The rest of the passage (up to 145^b30) confirms this use of 'immortal' as a substantive. But this is not its only use because 'immortal' can also be taken as an adjective, as it appears in *Top.* IV.2, 122^b12–17:

> Again see whether he has given the differentia as the genus, e.g. immortal as the genus of god. For *immortal is a differentia of animal*, seeing that of all animals some are *mortal* and others *immortal*. Clearly, then, a mistake has been made; for the differentia of a thing is never its genus. And that this is true is clear; for a thing's differentia never indicates what it is, but rather some quality as do walking and two-footed.

This passage shows also that immortal is a standard example of a differentia. Thus, there are good reasons to think that lines 145^b22–3 might well contain an attempt to define the differentia immortal (see also *Cat.* 5, 3^a33–3^b9, where Aristotle speaks more clearly about the possibility of there being definitions for differentiae). This would be further supported by the fact that this chapter deals with the commonplaces concerning the differentia. The view that Aristotle is discussing an attempt to define the differentia immortal has an important consequence: the differentia immortal will bring with it the genus it differentiates, namely animal. This is very close to Aristotle's position in *Metaph.* VII.

A final remark could be added about the way in which this commonplace is presented at 145^b21–3: the initial description of the problem might lead us to think that here we are concerned with an ambiguity concerning the scope of a temporal adverb (as we would call it, adopting a modern terminology). For there are two readings of sentence (p), 'The immortal is an animal that is deathless now'. The first is (p^*), 'The immortal is an animal that is *now* deathless', where 'now' has a narrow scope and ranges only over 'deathless'; this is the incorrect reading of (p). The second can be rephrased as (p^{**}), 'This is *now* the case: the immortal is an animal that is deathless', where 'now' has a wide scope and ranges over both 'immortal' and 'deathless'; this is the correct understanding of (p). The function of rule (o) is to lead us from the incorrect reading (p^*) to the correct reading (p^{**}), which entails (*q*), namely 'The animal *now* deathless is *now* immortal' (145ᵇ23). Aristotle does not explore this line of argument here, but he shows some awareness of these issues in his *Sophistici Elenchi*, in particular in chapters 4 and 20 (see discussions in Schiaparelli 2003, pp. 112–20; Fait 2007, pp. 111–15 and 184–8).

Part (C). 145ᵇ30–3 concludes the discussion of the commonplace contained in the passage under scrutiny. In part (B), Aristotle examines an objection against a difficult example contained in part (A). Now, in (C), he offers a partial and concise justification of the rule established in sentence (*o*). The justification is based on a fundamental requirement for a successful definition: in a successful definition what is mentioned in the defining part ('What is given according to the account', 145ᵇ30–1) must be identical to the thing to be defined ('What is given according to the name', 145ᵇ31–2). In other words, the presence of the same temporal qualification in both parts of the definition is a condition that must be respected.

The long discussion of the commonplaces concerning the differentia ends here.

CHAPTER 7

Introduction: Despite its brevity, chapter 7 contains five commonplaces. For the most part, their description is extremely concise and, in the case where they are illustrated by examples, it is not easy to explain them. The text can be divided as follows. (1) 145^{b}34–146^{a}2 contains the first commonplace. (2) 146^{a}3–12 discusses the second commonplace and can be divided into two subsections: at 146^{a}3–7, there is a presentation of a rule of comparison; at 146^{a}7–12, Aristotle introduces a modification to this rule. (3) 146^{a}13–20 outlines the third commonplace. These commonplaces share a common feature: they are all concerned with certain rules of comparison. Their order shows an increasing degree of complexity in the application of the comparison. They fall under the last group in the large classification of commonplaces. The classification consists of the following three groups (each of them can be applied to every predicable): commonplaces concerning (i) opposites, (ii) coordinates and cases, and (iii) the more and the less and the equal (see Smith 1997, p. xxxi). Then, (4) 146^{a}21–31 illustrates the fourth commonplace, which deals with relatives. (5) 146^{a}33–5 contains the fifth commonplace, which is based on a rule for the substitution of names with accounts.

145^{b}34–146^{a}2: In the first commonplace, the dialectician must consider the account proposed by the interlocutor and see whether there is a different account that expresses the thing to be defined more properly. The rule of comparison suggested for this commonplace is something along the following lines. Suppose we want to define *F*-ness. Let (P) be one account aiming at defining *F*-ness. Let (Q) be another such account. Let *a* be something that satisfies (P), and let *b* be something that satisfies (Q). If *b* is more *F* than *a*, then (P) must be rejected. In the illustration of this case, Aristotle considers first a proposed account of justice; he then observes what happens in the case of a person that is just. This procedure should not surprise us: when in his ethical writings Aristotle tries to establish a definition of a moral concept (e.g. justice or prudence), he often mentions the concept and then ascribes the corresponding property to an agent (e.g. just or prudent; see, e.g., *EN* V.1, 1029^{a}26–1029^{b}1; VI.7, 1140^{a}24–8).

In the specific case of justice and the just person, Aristotle expresses the correlation between the two by saying, 'We see that everyone says that justice is the sort of possession (*hexis*) that makes people do what is just' (*EN* V.1, 1129ᵃ6–7). Here and in the *Ethics*, Aristotle is adopting a dialectical procedure that corresponds to a commonplace put forward in *Top.* VI.9, 147ᵃ12–13: 'If the definition is of a possession (*hexis*), examine the possessor (*skopein epi tou echontos*)'. (For the translation of *hexis* with 'possession', see 'The value of *hexis*' in 'Terminological Clarifications'.)

At 145ᵇ35–146ᵃ2, Aristotle's argument can be reconstructed thus. Consider the following account that is proposed by the interlocutor: (1) Justice is a capacity that is distributive of what is equal. The dialectician is able to obtain from (1) the following: (2) Whoever has the capacity to distribute what is equal is a just person. But whoever chooses to distribute what is equal is more just than whoever has the capacity to distribute what is equal. The rule of comparison introduced above tells us that (1), i.e. the interlocutor's initial account, is unsuccessful. For according to (1), 'The one who has the capacity to distribute what is equal would be the most just'. And this is patently false. It follows that (1) must be rejected: it is not the case that justice is a capacity that is distributive of what is equal. This completes the refutation of the interlocutor's attempted definition. In this example, there is no explicit reference to the 'other account' that is mentioned in the rule (*kath' heteron*, 145ᵇ35). One could suggest that the 'other account' might be 'Justice is the choice of distributing what is equal'. Alternatively, on the basis of what is said in *Top.* VI.5, 143ᵃ15–17, one could suggest that 'the other account' might be (3) 'Justice is the virtue of choosing to distribute what is equal'. (3) might, however, fall under the objection raised against (1). For one can argue that the person who chooses to distribute what is equal is more just than the one who possesses the virtue to do so. A discussion of attempted definitions of justice can be found in *Top.* VI.5, 143ᵃ16–19: see the commentary *ad loc*. For the addition of 'has been defined as' at 145ᵇ35–6, see 'The translation of *hoion ei*', in 'Terminological Clarifications'.

146ᵃ3–12: These lines discuss the second commonplace: the discussion has two parts. (A) At 146ᵃ3–7, Aristotle introduces the commonplace which deals with another rule of comparison.

(B) At 146ª7–12, he adds a modification to the rule governing the refutative strategy sketched in (A). Note that part (B) begins with *eti* ('furthermore', 146ª7), which is generally used to introduce a new commonplace. But the fact that here Aristotle does not put forward an independent rule makes me think that in (B) he does not have in mind a commonplace that is different from that in (A). The discussion of both (A) and (B) is based on the relation of identity between what is mentioned in the defining part and the thing to be defined as it is developed in *Top.* VII.1.

(A) The idea underlying the commonplace can be expressed as follows: let (P) be a proposed account, let *a* be the kind to be defined, and let *b* be that which is mentioned in the defining part of *a*. Since *a* = *b*, *a* admits of an increase if and only if *b* admits of it. If (P) does not respect this condition, then it is not a successful definition. No example is offered. It is possible to expand on a proposal by Pacius (1597, p. 438) and suggest the account, 'The soul is a harmony of the bodily parts'. Following the commonplace outlined here, the dialectician will be able to refute this account; for the harmony of the bodily parts can increase (e.g. there could be more harmony in the interaction of the bodily parts) but the soul cannot.

(B) Aristotle adds a further condition: if *a* and *b* admit of an increase, then they must increase at the same time (*hama*). Here 'at the same time' can mean (i) 'in the same situations' or (ii) 'simultaneously' (i.e. 'at the same instants' or 'over the same periods'). It follows that, according to (i), since *a* = *b*, in any situation *s*, *a* increases in *s* if and only if *b* increases in *s*; then, according to (ii), since *a* = *b*, for any time *t*, *a* increases at *t* if and only if *b* increases at *t*. It is clear that the strictly temporal sense (ii) is not adequate to cover all the instances described by this commonplace. The proposed and unsuccessful definition of love as a desire for intercourse is meant to illustrate this commonplace. Very little, however, is said to explain this case. The same example can be found in *Top.* VII.1, 152ᵇ7–9, but again no explanation is offered. Although there is no decisive evidence to support it, one might perhaps think that in the background of Aristotle's example there could be a discussion of some Academic views about love developed in the discussion of the first part of Plato's *Phaedrus*.

146ª13–20: A different and more complex way of analysing a proposed definition using a test based on a comparison is introduced and an example is offered. At 146ª13–14, the formulation of the rule is not easy to understand. There are two main problems. (1) It is unclear what the 'two things put forward' (*duo tinôn protethentôn*) are (146ª13). A similar expression occurs at 146ª19: 'to both the things put forward' (*amphoterois ... tois protetheisi*). The dialectical context indicates that these things that are put forward are the things that are brought up for discussion in this commonplace. They play an important role in the development of the refutative strategy. (2) It is difficult to translate into good English the clause *kath'hou to pragma mallon legetai to kata ton logon hêtton legetai*. A rendering that is close to the Greek text and shows its syntactic intricacies is 'Of that of which the <defined> thing is said more, what is according to the account is said less'. For the most part, the intricacies stem from the use of the relative pronoun at the beginning of the sentence and from the fact that its referent is unclear. Moreover, it is not easy to understand what the terms involved in the comparison are (it will be made clearer by the example in the immediately following lines). In general, the English translations that I have consulted do not respect the word order and the syntax of the original formulation. My translation also does not completely follow the word order of the Greek text and tries to make for a clearer English than the literal rendering.

It is helpful to look at the example of the refutative strategy devised here. Suppose that the interlocutor has granted the account 'Fire is a body with the finest parts' (here 'fire' means 'fiery body'). Then two things are mentioned, namely flame and light. These are chosen as counterexamples to reject the proposed definition. The dialectician will obtain from his interlocutor claims that will enable the refutation to go through. The following comparisons will be established: (a) The flame is more fire than light; (b) The flame is less a body with the finest parts than light. These comparisons show that the interlocutor's granted account is not correct. The reason is the following: suppose that the definition 'Fire is a body with the finest part' were correct. Then, in comparisons, the thing to be defined, i.e. fire, should behave in the same way as what is mentioned in the defining part, i.e. body with the finest parts. This, however, is not the case because the flame is more fire than light, but it is not the case that the flame is more a body with the finest parts than light: light is more a body with the finest parts than the flame. At 146ᵃ15, I supply 'has been defined as'; see 'The translation of *hoion ei*' in 'Terminological Clarifications'.

The example facilitates the comprehension of the rule, whose technical formulation is as follows. Consider a proposed definition according to which *a* is *b*. Consider two items *c* and *d* such that *a* is said more of *c* than of *d* (so, *a* is said less of *d* than of *c*). If the definition were successful, then, in these comparisons, *b* must behave exactly like *a*. That is to say, if the definition is successful, then it must be the case that *b* is said more of *c* than of *d* (so, *b* is said less of *d* than of *c*). But the dialectician finds out that this is not the case: *b* is said more of *d* than of *c* (so, *b* is said less of *c* than of *d*). Hence the proposed definition is not successful. The formulation of the rule, however, is not complete, for the method for choosing the items *c* and *d* is missing. In this case, as in other places of his writings, Aristotle offers counterexamples without giving us a methodology to find them. Fire, flame, light, and a body with the finest parts are the subjects of a discussion in *Top.* V.5, 134ᵇ28–34, where there is the analysis of a commonplace concerning a unique property (*idion*). The passage aims at showing that 'A body with the finest parts' does not express the unique property of fire. Some arguments in favour of this claim are based on comparison; one of them is that being a body with the finest parts belongs to flame and light in different degrees.

146ᵃ21–32: The initial description of the commonplace discussed in these lines is concise. As the examples show, this commonplace concerns the case where the correct defining expression has to mention the disjunction of two correlatives. The interlocutor makes a mistake because he puts forward instead a defining expression which mentions only one of the two. The passage can be divided into three main parts.

(A) At 146ᵃ21, Aristotle formulates the rule. It can be rephrased thus: consider the case where the correct defining expression should mention both the correlative *e* and the correlative *f*. If the proposed defining expression mentions only one of *e* and *f*, then the definition is not successful.

(B) At 146ᵃ22–3, Aristotle introduces two examples of accounts where the proposed definitions mention the disjunction of two correlatives: (1) 'What is beautiful is what is pleasant to the eye *or* to the ear'; (2) 'Being is what has the capacity of being acted upon *or* acting'. Note that in (1) the expression 'pleasant to the eye' means 'pleasant to sight'; similarly, 'pleasant to the ear' means 'pleasant to hearing'. From (1) and (2) we can obtain four cases of unsuccessful definitions: (1a) 'What is beautiful is what is pleasant to the eye'; (1b) 'What is beautiful is what is pleasant to the ear'; (2a) 'Being is what has the capacity of being acted upon'; (2b) 'Being is what has the capacity of acting'. If the interlocutor grants one of these (unsuccessful) definitions, then a refutative strategy can be applied (see below). The examples discussed in these lines are reminiscent of two definitions that we find in Plato's dialogues (see Tricot 950, p. 262, n. 2; Brunschwig 2007, p. 66, nn. 4 and 5). In *Hippias Major* 298A6–7, Socrates and Hippias agree that the beautiful is what is pleasant through hearing and sight. The formulation of the defining expression as we find it in Plato might seem to be at variance with the Aristotelian one since it mentions (not the disjunction but) the conjunction of the two correlatives. In Greek, however, the conjunctive particle *kai* is sometimes used to express a disjunction (see Bonitz 1870, p. 357B). In *Sph.* 247D8–E4, 248A and 248C5, we find the suggestion that being consists in the capacity of acting or of being acted upon.

(C) At 146ᵃ23–32, Aristotle outlines the strategy that the dialectician could adopt if he wants to refute a granted defining expression that is incorrect because it mentions only one of the two correlatives. The refutative strategy is applied to an incorrect defining expression of what is beautiful and employs arguments that take the form of a *reductio ad absurdum*. From the interlocutor's granted premises the absurd conclusion will follow that (*p*) 'The same thing is pleasant and not pleasant' (146ᵃ23–4). An analogous argument can be applied if an incorrect defining expression of being is proposed. In this case the absurd conclusion will be that (*q*) 'The same thing is a being and is not a being' (146ᵃ24).

How will the dialectician derive the absurd conclusions (*p*) and (*q*)? Suppose that the correct defining expression of what is beautiful mentions what is pleasant to the eye *or* to the ear. Suppose also that the interlocutor grants that the defining expression of what is beautiful mentions what is pleasant to the eye. Consider something (e.g. a piece of music) that is pleasant to the ear but not to the eye, and apply the principle that the same things are opposite to the same (146^{a}26–7). It follows that if what is beautiful is what is pleasant to eye, then what is not beautiful is what is not pleasant to the eye. Since a piece of music is not pleasant to eye, it will not be beautiful. But a piece of music is pleasant to the ear. Then a piece of music is pleasant to the eye *or* to the ear (this follows from an application of the rule for the disjunction's introduction). Thus, a piece of music will be beautiful. Therefore, a piece of music will be beautiful (since it is pleasant to the eye *or* pleasant to the ear) and not beautiful (since it is not pleasant to the eye). The dialectician can now draw the conclusion that (*p*) 'The same thing is beautiful and it is not beautiful'.

Aristotle claims that a similar argument can be employed to derive the conclusion that (*q*) 'The same thing is and is not'. However, he does not specify the argument's details. The similarity between the account discussed here and those in Plato's *Sophist* invites a reconstruction of a refutative argument that takes into account the Platonic context. Since in the *Sophist*'s passages Plato is dealing with the applicability of the account to the Forms, my reconstruction will contain an example concerning them. Suppose that the correct defining expression of being mentions what can be acted upon *or* can act. The interlocutor's proposed defining expression of being mentions what can be acted upon. Consider something (e.g. a Platonic Form) which can act but cannot be acted upon, and apply the principle that the same things are opposite to the same. It follows that if being is what can be acted upon, then not being is what cannot be acted upon. Since a Form cannot be acted upon, a Form is not. But a Form can act. So, a Form can act or can be acted upon (by an application of the rule for the disjunction's introduction). Hence a Form is. Therefore, a Form is (since it can act *or* can be acted upon) and is not (since it cannot be acted upon). In this way, the dialectician can draw the conclusion that (*q*) 'The same thing is and is not'.

146^{a}33–5: The last commonplace of this chapter does not show any connection with the preceding discussion. It seems to be an afterthought which introduces a non-specific rule. The description of this commonplace is extremely concise (it occupies three lines only) and the Greek formulation is convoluted (my translation does not respect the word order of the Greek text). No refutative strategy is discussed. Aristotle simply indicates that the analysis of the proposed definition must aim at seeing whether there is 'some discrepancy when he (*sc.* the interlocutor) produces an account instead of the names' ($146^{a}35$). This suggests that the dialectician must ground his refutative strategy on a replacement; that is to say, he should get the interlocutor to replace the names mentioned in the proposed defining expression with their accounts. If this replacement shows that a discrepancy occurs between what is mentioned in the defining expression and the thing to be defined, then the proposed definition must be rejected. It has to be noted that this is one of the passages where Aristotle hints at the possibility that there are definitions of differentiae. This possibility seems to be envisaged also in *Top.* VI.4, $142^{b}7-19$ (see commentary *ad loc.*). This is not the first time Aristotle invites the dialectician to employ a strategy based on replacement: see, e.g., *Top.* VI.4, $142^{a}34-142^{b}6$; see also the commonplace in *Top.* VI.5, $143^{a}23-5$, which, however, is restricted to the possibility of replacing the proximate genus with its definition (see commentary *ad loc.*).

At $146^{a}33-4$, Aristotle says that the name of 'genera and differentiae and all the other things given in the definitions' must be replaced with the corresponding accounts. But it is difficult to understand what 'all the other things given in the definitions' are. According to Aristotle's standard view (at least as we have met so far in *Topics* VI), a definition is composed of a term indicating the kind to be defined, followed by the copula (the verb *einai* in one of its forms, which in Greek could be understood), followed by the expressions signifying the genus and one or more differentiae (the defining expression). That is to say, according to this view, genus and differentiae (one or more) are sufficient to reveal the essence of the kind and no further addition is required. Even though they do not signify the essence, one might want to include other expressions in the defining part of the account (provided that they are true of the thing to be defined). But a preceding chapter (*Topics* VI.3) tells against redundant definitions, namely definitions that contain more than what is needed to make the essence clear.

It is possible to make sense of the addition of 'all the other things given in the definition' in two ways. (i) The expression 'in the definitions' (in the plural) might suggest the idea that Aristotle is here talking about different types of definitions. In particular, he might have in mind the 'mereological' definitions discussed in *Topics* VI.13. 'Mereological' definitions are not based on genera and differentiae, but they mention other things (see commentary *ad loc.*). (ii) Alternatively, Aristotle might be anticipating the result of a discussion contained at the beginning of the immediately following chapter (namely chapter 8). In the first commonplace of *Topics* VI.8, Aristotle instructs the dialectician thus: 'If what is being defined is a relative either with respect to itself or with respect to the genus, examine whether the definition does not mention that in relation to which it is said, either itself or with respect to the genus' ($146^a36-146^b1$). The analysis of this commonplace suggests that in the case of things that are relatives or that have a relative genus, the defining expression must mention also their correlatives (see commentary *ad loc.*). So, 'all the other things given in the definitions' is likely to indicate (at least) these correlatives that cannot be omitted.

CHAPTER 8

Introduction: This chapter contains a discussion of incomplete definitions: it concerns the cases where the proposed definition is incomplete since an essential specification is left out. This incompleteness makes the proposed definition unacceptable, Aristotle thinks, because it fails to express the essence of the thing to be defined. For the most part, the commonplaces discussed in this chapter criticize proposed definition of relatives or of things whose genus is a relative. In these cases, the incompleteness concerns the failure of giving a successful account of a relative (or of a thing whose genus is a relative) since an essential specification is missing. The discussion has three main parts. (1) The first deals with accounts of different types of relatives (146^a36–146^b19); it is subdivided into three subparts: 146^a36–146^b9; 146^b9–12; 146^b13–19. (2) The second part deals with proposed accounts that are incomplete because they do not specify the quantity or the quality or the place or other determinations of the correlative (146^b20–35); it is formed by three subparts: 146^b20–4; 146^b24–7; 146^b27–35. (3) The third part is concerned with proposed accounts that are not adequate because they fail to add the qualification 'apparent' (146^b36–147^a11). This part contains an argument that aims at showing that the addition of 'apparent' in the definitions is particularly problematic for those who believe in Platonic Ideas. It is a general feature of this chapter that it discusses several examples taken from the fields of ethics; as we shall see, some of the cases analysed here can be found also in the *Nicomachean Ethics*.

146^a36–146^b9: The chapter begins with the formulation of its first commonplace. It instructs the dialectician to see whether, in the proposed account, the interlocutor fails to mention 'That in relation to which it (*sc.* what is being defined) is said, either itself or with respect to the genus'; in other words, he fails to mention the correlatives either of the kind to be defined or of its genus (146^a36–146^b1). The discussion of this commonplace contains a series of textual and philosophical problems, and this complicates the analysis of the passage. For this reason, individual portions of text will be examined first, and then philosophical problems will be addressed.

At 146^{b}1–2, we find two examples of proposed accounts where the interlocutor fails to mention the correlatives of the kinds to be defined: (1) 'Knowledge is incontrovertible (*ametapeiston*) belief'; (2) 'Wish (*boulêsin*) is painless desire (*orexin*)'. Properly speaking, these two examples should be understood as (1) 'Knowledge is belief that is incontrovertible', and (2) 'Wish is desire that is painless'. In this way, the translation would follow the Greek word order and would respect Aristotle's principle that, in the account's defining part, the expression indicating the genus must occur in the first position (*Top*. VI.5, 142^{b}28; for an explanation of this feature see commentary *ad loc.*). Some words are needed to illustrate Aristotle's terminology when he uses *ametapeiston*, *boulêsin*, and *orexin*. The adjective *ametapeistos* is formed by privative *alpha* and *metapeistos* (lit. 'open to persuasion'); it is etymologically linked to the verb *metapeithô*, i.e. 'persuade someone to change their mind'. An accurate translation of *ametapeiston* is 'unalterable by persuasion'. The idea that knowledge is an incontrovertible belief can be found also in *Top*. V.2, 130^{b}15 16 and occurs several times in *Top*. V.4. A link between the epistemic state of knowledge and the characteristic of incontrovertibility appears elsewhere in the corpus: see *APo*. I.2, 72^{b}3–4, and *MM* II.6, 1201^{b}5–6. It should be noted that the concept of persuading someone is central in rhetoric. The term *boulêsis* indicates one of the three species of desire (*orexis*) recognized by Aristotle: 'Wish (*boulêsis*), ... , spirit (*thumos*) and appetite (*epithumia*) are all three forms of desire (*orexis*)' (*MA* 6, 700^{b}22). Wish is to be identified with rational desire, whereas spirit and appetite are forms of non-rational desire and 'are shared with non-rational animals' (*EN* III.2, 1111^{b}12–13); that is to say, spirit (*thumos*) is an expression of the non-rational part of the soul. Aristotle attributes to spirit the self-assertive feelings associated with pride and anger. In the *Topics*, Aristotle discusses wish as well as appetite, and he seems to suggest that they have different objects: wish aims at what is good, or what appears to be so, and appetite seeks what is pleasant, or what appears to be so (see below 146^{b}36–147^{b}11 and commentary *ad loc.*). Although spirit is not explicitly mentioned, the corresponding faculty is discussed in *Top*. IV.5, 126^{a}9–10: 'Pain is found in the appetitive faculty (*en tôi epithumêtikôi*)—for pleasure is found in this too—whereas anger is found in the spirited faculty (*en tôi thumoeidei*)'. When Aristotle talks about the distinction between rational and non-rational faculties and when he states the difference between appetite and spirit, he is using the terminology Plato adopted in speaking of the soul (see *R.* IV, 437C–441C; X, 602E–604E).

There are at least two reasons why accounts (1) and (2) above (i.e. 'Knowledge is incontrovertible belief' and 'Wish is painless desire') cannot be accepted as successful definitions. First, in both cases the things to be defined are relatives, but the proposed definitions do not mention their correlatives. Second, in the Greek formulation of (1) and (2), 'incontrovertible' and 'painless' follow the expressions indicating the genus and occupy the positions belonging to the differentiae of knowledge and wish respectively. It is, however, doubtful whether incontrovertible and painless can be the differentiae; for 'The differentiae of relatives are relatives', as Aristotle says in *Top.* VI.6, 145^{a}14–15, and incontrovertible and painless are not relatives.

The second half of the sentence at 146^{b}3–4 is problematic: see the discussions in Colli 1970, vol. 3, pp. 984–6; Brunschwig 2007, p. 67, n. 4. The main problem concerns the Greek expression *to einai hoper* (lit. 'to be precisely' or 'to be essentially'). On one reading, this expression is taken together because often it constitutes a unity in Aristotle's writing and is part of his technical jargon. For example, in *Top.* VI.4, 141^{a}36–7 *to einai hoper* has to be taken as a unitary expression (see commentary *ad loc.*). This might constitute some support for reading the occurrence of *to einai hoper* at 146^{b}4 in the same way, but it is not conclusive. As Brunschwig remarks, the two passages' syntactical contexts are different and hence they allow for different grammatical constructions. I prefer an alternative reading on which *to einai* ('to be') is taken on its own and occupies the subject position in the clause; *hoper* ('precisely') is grouped with *ên tauton* ('it was the same as') and they are followed by *to pros ti pôs echein* ('to be in a certain relation with something'). In this case, the second clause should be translated as 'For each of the relatives to be was precisely the same as to be in a certain relation with something'. This is not the only place where Aristotle offers this account of relatives. In *Top.* VI.4, 142^{a}28–9, he says: 'For all such things (*sc.* relatives) to be is to be in a certain relation to something'.

These two accounts of relatives in the *Topics* are very close to the one in *Cat.* 7, 8^a39–8^b1: 'They (*sc.* relatives) are those things for which being is the same as being somehow related to something'. The latter account is the result of Aristotle's second and revised attempt to capture the essential features of the relatives. It is worth noting that this replaces a different attempt offered twice in the *Categories*. This second attempt to capture the relatives' essential features consists in the formulation of a 'linguistic test' whose application should enable us to distinguish relatives from non-relatives. In *Cat.* 7, 6^a36–7, we read: 'We *call* relatives all such things as are said to be just what they are of or than other things, or in some other way in relation to something else'. Similarly, at 8, 11^a24–6, Aristotle says: 'For knowledge, a genus, is called just what it is of something else (it is called knowledge of something), but none of the particular cases is called just what it is, of something else'. As Aristotle admits, the linguistic test is not sufficiently reliable, for it can yield unwelcome results (*Cat.* 7, 8^a28–31). According to this test, 'For example, a head is called someone's head and a hand in called someone's hand, and so on; so that these would seem to be relatives' (8^a26–8). The linguistic test leads to the false consequence that a substance can be spoken of as a relative (see Ackrill 1963, pp. 101–3). The relation between the linguistic test and the revised criterion is widely discussed in the secondary literature; it is also the source of many interpretative problems (see, e.g., Duncombe 2015, Frede 1981, Mignucci 1986). For our purposes, it is sufficient to point out that in the *Topics* Aristotle chooses the revised criterion. It is not unlikely that Aristotle's choice might be the result of the discussion in the *Categories* where the linguistic criterion was proved inadequate. Moreover, the linguistic test was present in Plato's *Sph.* 255D. Perhaps, in taking position against the linguistic test, Aristotle also wants to distance himself from the Platonic viewpoint.

At 146^b4, Aristotle uses the past 'was' (*ên*). This can be explained in two ways. (i) The past is used because it refers to a claim that was accepted by the interlocutor at a moment earlier than the present refutation. (ii) The past is to be read as the tense that we often find in Aristotelian definitions. Option (ii) fits better with the context of the present discussion of proposed definitions (see also *Top.* VI.7, 145^b29).

What is the role of the claim concerning the nature of relatives at 146^{b}3–4? Its function is to offer a philosophical ground to the first commonplace of chapter 8, i.e. the rule that if a proposed definition fails to mention the correlatives either of the thing to be defined or of its genus, then it must be criticized and rejected. This claim is also related to what comes at 146^{b}7–8 ('In a definition he should have given either that in relation to which the thing itself is said or that, whatever it is, in relation to which the genus is said'). More on this below in the commentary *ad loc*.

At 146^{b}5–6, the text suggests two examples of accounts that conform to the rule put forward at the beginning of the chapter (146^{a}36–146^{b}1). They are: (1a) 'Knowledge is belief in a knowable', and (2a) 'Wish is desire for a good'. The new examples are based on the cases introduced above, namely (1) 'Knowledge is incontrovertible belief', and (2) 'Wish is painless desire'. They constitute an improved version of (1) and (2) since in both (1a) and (2a) the definitions mention the correlatives as required by the rule. An analysis of the relation between knowledge and knowable can be found in *Cat.* 7, 7^{b}23–35. In particular, in *Cat.* 7, 7^{b}27–31 we read: 'The destruction of the knowable carries knowledge to destruction with it (*sunanairei*), but knowledge does not carry the knowable to destruction with it (*ou sunanairei*). For if there is nothing knowable then there is not knowledge—there will no longer be anything for knowledge to be of—but if there is not knowledge there is nothing to prevent there being a knowable.' This passage establishes the priority of what is knowable (an element mentioned in the defining expression) to knowledge (the thing to be defined). This is an important point because it shows that account (1a) meets one of the fundamental requirements for a successful definition: the defining expression must mention 'things that are prior to and more familiar than' what is to be defined. This requirement is introduced in *Top.* VI.4, 141^{a}26–7 and discussed throughout that chapter. The verb used in the passage of the *Categories* to indicate co-destruction (*sunanairei*) is also employed at 141^{b}28–9: 'For the genus and the differentia carry the species to destruction with them (*sunanairei*), so that these are prior to the species'. The sequel of this passage (i.e. 141^{b}29–34) prompts us to understand '*a* is prior to and more familiar than *b*' as '*a* is ontologically and epistemologically prior to *b*'. This further suggests that in the cases of knowable and knowledge the first is ontologically and epistemologically prior to the second. For a full discussion of these issues see commentary *ad loc.* and Schiaparelli 2011.

At 146^{b}6–9, Aristotle puts forward another account, namely (3) 'Literacy is knowledge of letters', and offers a brief analysis. Here 'literacy' translates the Greek *grammatikê* (see commentary on *Top.* VI.4, 142^{b}30–143^{a}11). For the translation of *apodidosthai* with 'have given' see 'The verb *apodidonai* and its forms' in 'Terminological Clarifications'. Account (3) differs from those mentioned so far because the thing to be defined, i.e. literacy, is not in itself a relative, but its genus, i.e. knowledge, is. The role played by sentence (3) in this context is unclear: is it a proposed account that must be refuted? Or is it a constructive note suggesting a successful definition? The expression 'similarly also' (*homoiôs de kai*, 146^{b}6) does not help us in this respect, for two reasons. First, 'similarly also' is used in introducing a view that must be rejected (see, e.g., *Top.* VI.6, 144^{b}4–6: '*Similarly it must also be examined* whether the species or something subordinate to the species is predicated of the differentia; for this is impossible'). But it is also employed to put forward a view that is correct (see, e.g., *Top.* VI.6, 143^{a}29–33: 'Again concerning the differentiae *it must be also similarly examined* whether he has said the differentiae of the genus. For if he has not defined with the proper differentiae of the thing ... it is clear that he has not defined'). Second, it is unclear whether 'similarly' is to be taken as 'Similarly to what is said in the immediately preceding lines containing a sketch of two promising accounts', or as 'Similarly to the two unsuccessful accounts at 146^{b}1–2'. The analysis of the verb '(*sc.* he) has defined (*hôrisato*)' and its occurrences does not help, however. In *Topics* VI there other seven passages where *hôrisato* is used: VI.4, 142^{b}1; VI.6, 145^{b}22; VI.8, 146^{b}1–2; VI.10, 148^{b}4; VI.12, 149^{a}39–149^{b}1; VI.13, 150^{a}2 and 4; VI.13, 151^{a}3. In all these occurrences the understood subject of *hôrisato* is the opponent. More precisely, in these cases the verb *hôrisato* is employed to introduce accounts proposed by the opponent, and each of these accounts will be criticized as they do not qualify as a successful definition. This indicates that 'Literacy is knowledge of letters' is the opponent's proposal that must be criticized, and hence it does not express a successful definition. This further induces us to think that the adverb 'similarly' introduces a likeness between account (3) and the unsuccessful accounts (1) and (2) at 146^{b}1-2.

Proponents of this interpretative line are Alexander of Aphrodisias and Brunschwig. At *in Top.* 225,47–226,2 Alexander claims that (3) 'Literacy is knowledge of letters' is not a successful definition. He suggests that the proposed defining expression of literacy should mention the correlative of knowledge, which is 'of a knowable' (*epistêtou*, 146^{b}5), instead of 'of letters' (*grammatôn*). Alexander's suggestion, however, cannot be right since 'of a knowable' is too general to capture literacy. Brunschwig also thinks that Aristotle wants to reject 'of letters' and replace it with something else, but he suggests a different substitution: the correlative of knowledge should be 'of reading and writing the letters' (2007, p. 67, n. 5). This proposal has the advantage that it fits well with *Top.* VI.5, 142^{b}30–3, where Aristotle claims: 'Furthermore, consider whether, although what is being defined is said in relation to several things, he has not given its account in relation to all, for example if literacy <is defined as> knowledge of writing what is dictated; for its being of reading is also needed'. But there is an objection to Brunschwig's proposal: the dialectician will not find the appropriate correlative in the immediate context and might not easily remember what was said in a previous discussion.

Note that although in (3) the defining expression mentions the genus of literacy, i.e. knowledge, and, allegedly, *a* correlative, it fails to mention fully *the* correlative. In other words, in 'Literacy is knowledge of letters' the first part of the defining expression is correct since it mentions the genus of literacy, namely knowledge, in the first position (as Aristotle recommends in *Top.* VI.5, 142^{b}27–9). The expression 'of letters', however, does not indicate the genus's appropriate correlative and hence the account cannot be accepted. To be sure, we still do not know what counts as the appropriate correlative in the definition of literacy. Aristotle never tells us this explicitly, but he only hints at some possibilities that could be further developed. This holds also in the case of the correlative proposed in chapter 5, i.e. 'of reading and writing what is dictated'; for nothing guarantees that this is the complete expression capturing the appropriate correlative and that it must be retained as such. Moreover, when he speaks of literacy in *Cat.* 8, 11^{a}29–30, Aristotle says that it is knowledge *of something*, but he does not specify what it is. It is very likely that, in the *Topics* and in the *Categories*, Aristotle does not intend to give us a full correlative of knowledge. In particular, in *Topics* VI his aim is not to provide us with a complete and successful definition of literacy. For this reason, he chooses examples, some of which show necessary but not sufficient requirements that must be met by the definition of a thing whose genus is a relative. In conformity with the refutative purposes of *Topics* VI, it is sufficient for the dialectician to master a strategy to criticize the interlocutor's account.

At 146^{b}7-9, Aristotle adds a general rule aimed at justifying the accounts: (1a) 'Knowledge is belief in a knowable', and (2a) 'Wish is desire for a good'. He says: 'In a definition he (*sc.* the interlocutor) should have given either that in relation to which the thing itself (*sc.* the thing to be defined) is said or that, whatever it is, in relation to which the genus is said'. Accounts (1a) and (2a) are justified since they instantiate the first part of the rule.

Other difficulties emerge from the texts analysed so far. In particular, it should be noted that the relatives to be defined that are introduced at the beginning of the chapter constitute a non-homogeneous group. On the one hand, this group contains things that are relatives *in themselves*. This is the case with knowledge (*epistêmê*); for knowledge is always knowledge *of something*, i.e. *of a knowable* (*epistêtou*, 146^{b}5). Similarly, desire is a relative *in itself*; for desire is always desire *for something*, e.g. *for a good* (*agathou*, 146^{b}6). In general, it is in the nature of a relative to be in relation to something, i.e. its correlative (146^{b}3–4). As we know, a definition expresses the essence of the thing to be defined; that is to say, it tells us its nature. Aristotle takes this to require the definition of a relative to contain its correlative. On the other hand, the relatives Aristotle is interested in defining include things that are not in themselves relative but have relatives as their genera. This is the case with literacy (*grammatikê*); for the genus of literacy is knowledge, namely a relative (146^{b}7). Whereas knowledge is always knowledge of something, literacy is not literacy of something: literacy is a quality (*poiotês*) and not a relative (*pros ti*). Qualities and relatives differ in their nature; for it is not in the nature of a quality to be in relation to something (see the discussion in *Cat.* 8, 11^{a}23–36; Ackrill 1993; Schiaparelli 2016). Nevertheless, according to Aristotle, definitions of species whose genus is a relative must contain certain things to which the genus is related.

Since a brief analysis of proposed definitions of things whose genera are relatives can be found also in *Top.* VI.5, 142^{b}30–143^{a}8, one might expect to gain an insight into this problem by looking at that text. In particular, at 142^{b}30–3, Aristotle argues: 'Consider whether, although what is being defined is said in relation to several things, he has not given its account in relation to all, for example if literacy <is defined as> knowledge of writing what it dictated; for its being of reading is also needed'. When Aristotle says that 'What is being defined is said in relation to several things', he is not expressing himself carefully; for, in his example, it is not true that 'What is being defined is said in relation to several things'. In the case of literacy, what 'is said in relation to many things' is the *genus* of the thing to be defined *in so far as it is its genus*. Consider the relative genus knowledge: it is related to reading and writing from dictation *in so far as it is the genus* of literacy; but it is related to, e.g., playing an instrument and singing *in so far as it is the genus* of music. When this is said in the context of chapter 5 that deals with the genus, the idea is likely to be that if one fails to mention the correlatives of the genus (*in so far as* it is the genus of what is defined), one does not properly locate what is defined within its genus. One mentions the genus but omits to give the position of the thing to be defined within its genus (see commentary on *Top.* VI.5, 142^{b}30–143^{a}11).

If we apply this idea to the case described in chapter 8, we can say that the proposed account is not complete because a part of the genus (that is an essential component of it) is left out. But one could raise an objection; one could think that the failure of omitting the genus's correlative can be classified as that of omitting the differentia. Since it is the function of the differentia to individuate the position of the species within their genera, one can claim that the genus's correlative can be identified with the differentia. This proposal is also not without problems. Suppose that we want to define zoology and propose that 'Zoology is knowledge of animals'. This formulation is in line with the account of music in *Cat.* 8, 11^{a}28–33. What is, properly speaking, the differentia in this definition? One might be tempted to answer that it is the characteristic expressed by 'of animals'. But it would be strange to single out a characteristic on the basis of a grammatical case (e.g. genitive plural). In other words, a characteristic indicated by the genitive plural (e.g. 'of animals') can hardly be different from that indicated by the nominative singular (e.g. 'animal'). The only reasonable option that remains is that the differentia is animal. This, however, cannot be right. For, in *Top.* VI.6, 143^{a}30–4, Aristotle argues that animal cannot be a differentia. More precisely he says: 'If he (*sc.* the interlocutor) has not defined with the proper differentiae of the thing, or even has mentioned *something such that it is totally impossible for it to be the differentia of anything, for example animal* or substance, it is clear that he has not defined; for those mentioned are the differentiae of nothing'. Second, in *Top.* VI.6, 144^{a}37–144^{b}1, Aristotle claims that 'The differentiae are predicated of the species'. But, certainly, animal is not predicated of zoology. Thus, also according to this second text, the correlative cannot be the differentia.

To sum up, the interpretation that classifies the correlative alongside the genus (or as a part of it) and the reading that attributes to the correlative the role of the differentia both present problems. It remains unclear what the function of the correlative in the definition is. According to the standard Aristotelian doctrine, the paradigmatic case of a definition is composed of a term indicating the thing to be defined, followed by the copula (the verb *einai* in one of its forms, which in Greek could be understood), followed by expressions signifying the genus and one or more differentiae (the defining part). If this is the case, there seems to be no further role to fill for the correlative. There is, however, another option to explore: the correlative might be something else, perhaps a further constituent of the defining part. There is evidence to support this option. The last lines of *Topics* VI.7, namely the passage immediately preceding the discussion of proposed definitions of relatives in chapter 8, contain the following remark: 'Examine whether there is some discrepancy when he produces the accounts instead of the names of the genera and of the differentiae and of *all the other things given in the definitions*' (146^{a}33–5). This suggests that in a definition one finds genera, differentiae, but also things that are other than genera and differentiae. It is highly likely that 'all the other things given in the definition' comprise the correlatives discussed in the first part of chapter 8. These are the correlatives of the things to be defined that are relatives *in themselves* and the correlatives of a relative genus (in so far as it is the genus of a certain thing that is being defined). Among the correlatives to be mentioned in the definition there are the ends in relation to which the thing to be defined can be (see the sequel to this text, below). As we shall see later, we must add to this list the correlatives mentioned in the second part of chapter 8 (146^{b}20–35).

146^{b}9–12: The text continues with a brief discussion of a different sort of correlative, namely the end (*telos*) in relation to which the thing to be defined can be. For the translation of *apodidosthai* with '(it) is defined' see 'The verb *apodidonai* and its forms' in 'Terminological Clarifications'. At 146^{b}10, an end is characterized as 'the best or that for the sake of which other things are' (*to beltiston ê hou charin talla*). In his commentary, Pacius (1597, p. 439) links the Aristotelian characterization of an end to *Ph.* II.3, 195^{a}24–5: '(*sc.* There are) causes in the sense of the end or the good of the rest; for what the other things are for tends to be what is best and the end (*to gar hou heneka beltiston kai telos tôn allôn ethelei einai*)'. The presence of a thematic affinity between the two passages seems to be reinforced by the fact that *charin* and *heneka* are synonyms (Bonitz 1870, p. 846A). In this passage from the *Physics* Aristotle is characterizing the so-called 'final cause'; a discussion of the passage can be found in, e.g., Charlton 1970, pp. 101–4. The Aristotelian concept of cause is closer to our modern notion of explanation than that of causation; for this reason, these terms are used interchangeably (the literature on Aristotle's concept of explanation is vast: see, e.g., Matthews/Blackson 1989; Fine 1987). Corcilius (2011, p. 121) adopts a reading that is close to Pacius's interpretative line. Corcilius sees a parallel between the passage of the *Topics* under scrutiny and *APo.* I.24, 85^{b}27–86^{a}2. In particular, at 85^{b}32–8, Aristotle says:

> Proceeding in this way, when it is no longer because of something else or with some other purpose (*mêd'allou heneka*), we say that it is because of this as an end (*hôs telos*) that he came (or that it is or that it came about), and that then we best know why he came. Thus, if the same goes for all explanations and for all reasons why, and if in the case of explanation in terms of purpose (*epi de tôn hosa aitia houtôs hôs hoû heneka*) we know best in this way, then in the other cases too we know best when this no longer holds because something else does.

In brief, Aristotle claims that we know why something is the case (i.e. we know its explanation) when we know its ultimate end; and this is true for the final cause. Analogously, in the case of the other types of explanation we know best why something is the case when we grasp the ultimate element in the explanatory chain. According to Corcilius, this indicates that the requirements for a successful definition set up in *Topics* VI meet the explanatory criteria established in the *Posterior Analytics*; for, in the *Topics*, Aristotle acknowledges the key role of the ultimate end that must figure in the definition of certain relatives. In light of this evidence, should we conclude that the concept of 'final cause' or some of the other explanatory notion is at work in the *Topics*? There are at least three reasons to think that, despite the terminological similarities between the texts quoted above, this is not the case. (i) In the *Topics*, Aristotle is not operating with a theory that distinguishes different types of explanations; to the best of my knowledge, there is no evidence in support of the presence of this piece of doctrine. (ii) Nowhere in the *Topics* does Aristotle say or suggest that the defining expression plays some sort of explanatory role; the approach to definitions that is based on the concept of explanation is a characteristic not of the *Topics* but of the *Analytics*. (iii) A proposed account's refutation that is based on such a specific concept of explanation would not be suitable in this context: it is not adequately introduced and the onus to explain would be on the dialectician. However, if one still favours the idea that Aristotle might be operating with a certain notion of explanation, one could perhaps see a reference to Plato's mention of the so-called teleological cause in, e.g., *Phd.* 97C–D: 'If one wished to know the cause of each thing ... one had to find what is best for it' (*hopêi beltiston autôi estin*).

There is an alternative and more attractive way to read the phrase under scrutiny ('the best or that for the sake of which all other things are', 146^{b}10). Aristotle could simply have in mind the case where what is defined is said in relation to several things and where these correlatives ('all other things', *talla*) are structured in such a way that they lead to an end, which is the best. In this case, the dialectician should examine whether the proposed definition mentions not just any correlative but that which is the end or the best. If it does not, the proposed definition is not successful. This indicates that, if *a* is a relative or a thing whose genus is a relative, a definition that expresses the essence of *a* must mention the end for the sake of which all *a*'s correlatives are; similarly, a complete understanding of what-*a*-is involves a grasp of the end of its correlatives. The following example might help to illustrate this case: if one describes medicine as knowledge of diets or as knowledge of medications, one has not defined medicine. The description of medicine as knowledge of how to produce health is more promising because it mentions 'the best or that for the sake of which all other things are'. Health is the purpose of diets and medications. This idea is not new to this treatise. In *Top.* VI.5, 143^{a}9–11, Aristotle instructs the dialectician to 'Consider whether he has given an account not in relation to the better (*to beltion*) but to the worse, if there are several things in relation to which what is being defined is said; for every instance of knowledge and every capacity seems to be of the best (*to beltiston*)' (see commentary *ad loc.*). At 146^{b}11, the text handed down by the manuscripts contains an exclusive disjunction (*ê ... ê*): on the transmission of the text see Brunschwig 2003, pp. 59–60, and Brunschwig 2007, p. 68, n. 1.

146^{b}13–19: The commonplace in this portion of text is linked to the discussion in the immediately preceding lines (146^{b}9–12). It concerns the case where the correlative of the thing to be defined expresses an end (*telos*). Aristotle states the rule that particular attention should be paid to the proposed correlative of the thing to be defined: if the interlocutor frames his account in such a way that the proposed correlative is a becoming (*genesis*) or an activity (*energeia*), then the account cannot be accepted. The passage has two parts: (1) a general rule is offered and a strategy to refute a proposed definition is outlined (146^{b}13–16); (2) the range of the rule's application is restricted since an exception is found (146^{b}16–19). Note that at 146^{b}14–19 the adverb *mallon* is used three times. In the first occurrence (146^{b}14), it seems to express a genuine comparison, so I translate it with 'more'. In its second and third occurrences (146^{b}17 and 19), *mallon* is governed by an expression of desire. In this case, *mallon* probably indicates (not a comparison but) a disjunction and introduces the preferred alternative. For this reason, I translate it with 'rather'.

(1) The dialectician must consider whether, in the interlocutor's account, the proposed correlative of the thing to be defined is a

becoming or an activity. The brief argument in support of this
rule is based on the view that a becoming and an activity cannot
be ends. This argument can be developed in a full-blown refutative strategy. In order to show that a becoming and an activity are
not ends, Aristotle introduces a distinction between some verbal
forms that are cognates of *energeia* ('activity') and *genesis*
('becoming'). He distinguishes between the perfect infinitives on
the one hand, i.e. *enêrgêkenai* ('to have been in activity') and
gegenêsthai ('to have become'), and the present infinitives on the
other, i.e. *energein* ('to be in activity') and *ginesthai* ('to become').
Aristotle, then, argues that what is expressed by the perfect
infinitives (i.e. 'to have become' and 'to have been in activity') is
more likely to indicate an end than what is expressed by the
present infinitives (i.e. 'to be in activity' and 'to become'). It might
be objected that elsewhere Aristotle says that an activity is complete
at any moment, so, in a sense, it has at any moment accomplished
its end (see *EN* VII.12, 1153^{a}10 and X.4, 1174^{a}14–16). But in
the text of the *Topics* under scrutiny Aristotle perhaps is not
employing the word *energeia* ('activity') in the technical way
that we find in book X of the *Nicomachean Ethics*, where he
draws a distinction between processes and activities. Rather, he
has in mind the ordinary use of this term, which 'refers to movement', as he says in *Metaph.* IX.2, 1046a30–1. However that may
be, it is difficult to understand why a becoming and an activity
cannot *be* ends. No further explanation is given. This argument is
abruptly interrupted and an exception to the rule is introduced.
This might suggest that Aristotle is not satisfied with his previous
argument and tries to improve it.

(2) At 146^{b}16–19, Aristotle introduces the case of pleasure,
which constitutes an exception to the rule mentioned in (1). His
argument employs a distinction between the present infinitive, i.e.
hêdesthai ('to feel pleasure'), and a compound expression containing the perfect infinitive, i.e. *pepausthai hêdomenoi* ('to have
ceased to feel pleasure'). The present infinitive is open-ended and
indicates that the activity is in progress. The force of the perfect
indicates that, at the present time, the action in question has
been completed (Goodwin 1897, pp. 13–14). Thus *enêrgêkenai*
('to have been in activity') implies *pepausthai energein* ('to
have ceased to be in activity'): this explains the *pepausthai hêdomenoi* ('to have ceased to feel pleasure') in Aristotle's example.

213

Aristotle's point is that almost everyone prefers the activity of feeling pleasure to having ceased to feel it. This indicates that many people will set the activity of feeling pleasure as an end. Thus, an activity can be an end. In this instance too, *energeia* must be understood as movement or process exactly as in (1) above (otherwise the case mentioned by Aristotle would not be a counterexample to the immediately preceding rule).

It ought to be mentioned that some of the expressions that play a central role in this text in the *Topics* also occur in other famous passages of the corpus, in particular in the *Nicomachean Ethics*, *Metaphysics*, and *De Anima*. Specifically, in *EN* VII.12, 1153^{a}7–12; X.3, 1173^{a}29–31; X.4, 1174^{a}14–1174^{b}14, Aristotle introduces the distinction between becoming (*genesis*) or process (*kinesis*), on the one hand, and activity (*energeia*) on the other. He claims that pleasure is an activity and not a process. The view that pleasure is a process was held by Plato in the *Philebus*. One of the arguments employed by Aristotle to prove that pleasure is an activity is based on the distinction between present and perfect tense. It is notoriously difficult to reconcile some claims in *EN* VII with others in *EN* X. The analysis of the relation between the claims in *EN* VII and *EN* X goes beyond the limits of the present commentary; they are discussed in, among others, Ackrill 1965; Bostock 1988; Charles 1995. This difficulty, however, does not affect the central point of the distinction between becoming or process and activity. In *Metaph.* IX.6, 1048^{b}18–35, the concept of activity is contrasted to that of *kinesis* (Aristotle is consciously using 'activity' in a way that is different from that of *Metaph.* IX.2 that I quoted earlier). According to some (see, e.g., Ackrill 1965), the general structure of the argument and the choice of the examples might well suggest that the distinction between activity and process drawn in the *Metaphysics* is the same as that in the *Nicomachean Ethics*. By contrast, according to Burnyeat, although the passage in the *Metaphysics* was written by Aristotle, it 'does not fit into the overall programme of *Metaph.* IX.6, it was not written for *Metaph.* IX and should not be printed in the place where we read it today'. Burnyeat argues that the distinction between activity and process in *Metaph.* IX.6 'is unique in the corpus and should not be imported into other Aristotelian contexts such as *EN* X or *De An.* II.5' (Burnyeat 2008, pp. 219–20).

146ᵇ20–35: At 146ᵇ20, the Greek words corresponding to 'quantity' and 'quality' are *posou* and *poiou*; they are the genitive forms of the (indirect) interrogative pronouns *poson* and *poion*. Here I understand them as 'genitives of measure' (Smyth 1956, p. 318, §1325). The literal translation ('He has not distinguished the of how much and of what sort') sounds difficult in English. In my translation of line 146ᵇ21, I supply an occurrence of the verb '(He) has not distinguished': while the Greek syntax allows for a change in the construction of the clauses that follow the main verb, in English this syntactic combination sounds particularly harsh.

The entire passage raises an important question that must be discussed at the outset. The question concerns the three occurrences of the Greek term *diaphora* at 146ᵇ21, 24, and 31. How should we understand the meaning of *diaphora* in these contexts? Consider the stretch of text where we find its first occurrence: 'See whether he has not distinguished the quantity or quality or place or <has not distinguished> according to the other differentiae (*diaphoras*)' (146ᵇ20–1). The expressions 'quantity' (*poson*), 'quality' (*poion*), and 'place' (*pou*) correspond to some of the categories as they are listed in *Top.* I.9, 103ᵇ21–3: 'These are ten in number: what-it-is (*ti esti*), quantity (*poson*), quality (*poion*), ... , place (*pou*), ... '. (For a discussion of the presentation of the categories in *Topics* I see, e.g., Malink 2007.) Suppose that, in this context, the term *diaphora* is used in a technical way and indicates a differentia that is mentioned in the defining expression. Let us call it 'definitory differentia' (it is extensively discussed in *Top.* VI.6). If this is the case, then it is not clear why Aristotle would add definitory differentiae to the list of categories. It is also unclear why he would qualify the differentiae as 'the other(s)'; for no other differentia is mentioned in this context. Of course, one should not yield to the temptation of regarding the categories themselves as differentiae in the technical sense; for the only genus of which they could be differentiae would be being, but Aristotle explicitly says that being is not a kind (*Metaph.* V.7,1017ᵃ22–7; see, e.g., Kirwan 1993, pp. 140–3; Shields 1999, pp. 244–60). The term *diaphora*, however, can be used in another and more generic way: it can refer to a differentiation that need not be the definitory differentia (Bonitz 1870, p. 192B). The more generic use of *diaphora* suggests that the expression 'the other differentiae' can be rephrased as 'the other differentiations'. This opens up two interesting interpretative options. (A) The expression 'the other differentiations' refers to the other differentiations of being, which are the categories. More precisely, it refers to the categories other than those mentioned. (B) The expression 'the other differentiations' indicates a differentiation of something included in the definition, e.g. the correlative. So 'the other differentiae' will be the differentiations of the correlative other than those mentioned (i.e. quantity, quality, and place).

In the second passage where *diaphora* occurs, Aristotle illustrates and briefly explains the commonplace under scrutiny. He says: 'An honour-lover is the one who desires honour of a certain quality (*poias*) and in a certain quantity (*posês*). For all desire honour, so that it is not enough to say that an honour-lover is the one who desires honour, but we must add the differentiae mentioned (*tas eirêmenas diaphoras*)' (146^b21–4). In the most natural reading of the text, the expression 'the differentiae mentioned' refers to the quantity and quality just stated, namely those giving an adequate characterization of honour. But they are not definitory differentiae. They are differentiations of something that is mentioned in the defining expression, which, in the case at hand, is the correlative; in the example under consideration the correlative is honour. A passage in the *Nicomachean Ethics* and the comparison with an example that occurs at the beginning of this chapter will support this reconstruction. In *EN* IV.5, 1125^b7–10, Aristotle examines the virtue concerned with honour. He argues that 'In a *desire for honour* there is the more and less than it is needed...; for we blame the honour-lover for *longing for the honour* more that it is needed'. It is easy to see that the formulation 'desire for honour' (*orexin timês*), where honour is the correlative of desire, is equivalent to 'longing for the honour' (*ephiemenon timês*). This indicates that the role of 'honour' is the same in both cases, namely it functions as a correlative. One, however, might point out that in this passage Aristotle does not explicitly refer to relatives; hence one could find this piece of evidence not completely convincing. The discussion of relatives in the *Metaphysics* offers further and more compelling evidence. In *Metaph.* V.15, 1021^b6–8, Aristotle says that 'There are properties in virtue of which the things that have them are called relatives, e.g. equality is a relative because the equal is, and likeness because the like is'. His point is that the abstract object and the corresponding concrete one are relatives. For instance, consider the pairs equality–equal and likeness–like: the first members of the pairs are abstract objects, whereas the second members are concrete things, and they are all relatives. This warrants the inference that just as desire (*orexis*), which is abstract, is a relative in 'desire of the good' (*orexis agathou*), so also the one who desires (*oregomenos*), which is the concrete thing, is a relative in 'the one who desires honour' (*oregomenos timês*). A comparison between the example occurring at the beginning of *Top.* VI.8 and the case under discussion further confirms this reconstruction. More precisely, at 146^b5–6, Aristotle claims that 'Wish is desire for a good (*orexin agathou*)': here 'desire' (*orexin*) indicates a relative and '(for a) good' (*agathou*) indicates the correlative. This structure is paralleled in the clause at 146^b21–2: 'The one who desires honour of a certain quality and in a certain quantity' (*o poias kai o posês oregomenos timês*). Here the word 'honour' (*timês*) plays the same role as '(for a) good' (*agathou*): they both indicate a correlative. These pieces of evidence prove that 'honour' functions as a correlative and confirm that the characterizations of honour, e.g. its quantity and quality, are to be thought of as its differentiations. This also shows that, in its second occurrence, the term *diaphora* is used generically; that is to say, it can refer to a differentiation that need not be the definitory differentia.

The third occurrence of *diaphora* is at 146^b30–2: 'Similarly also in other cases of this sort; for if he leaves aside any differentia whatsoever (*diaphoran hêntin'oun*), he does not express the what-it-is-to-be'. There are two possibilities. (1) The term *diaphora* refers to the definitory differentia (this position is held by, e.g., Morrison 1993, p. 160, and Deslauriers 2007, p. 200, n. 22). If this is the case, the omission of the definitory differentia is responsible for failing to indicate the essence. One could further suggest that this remark points to the fact that expressing the essence is the proper function of the definitory differentia. This reading might seem attractive because it expresses a view that is close to Aristotle's position in *Metaph.* VII.12, 1038^a18–20 and 27–30: 'The last differentia (*ê teleutaia diaphora*) will be the substance (*ousia*) and the definition of the object ... The definition is the account composed of the differentiae, and—if it is correctly performed— just one of the last differentiae.' But there are reasons to resist this reading. The term *diaphora* would be used in a technical way only in its third and last occurrence of this chapter. Moreover, the thesis that Aristotle expresses in the *Metaphysics* is not attested elsewhere in the *Topics*. Perhaps he has not formed a precise view on the issue yet (some scholars think that in the *Metaphysics* Aristotle abandons the conceptual *apparatus* concerning definitions that is characteristic of the early logical work, in particular the *Topics*: see, e.g., Bostock 1994, p. 184). The difficulties raised by this interpretation make it unpalatable. There is, however, an alternative proposal. (2) The term *diaphora* refers to a differentiation that need not be understood in a technical sense; that is to say, it need not be a definitory differentia. *Diaphora* is used in a generic way just as in the previous two occurrences in this chapter. It indicates a differentiation of something that is mentioned in the defining expression, and this could very well be the correlative of the kind to be defined. But nothing rules out that, in a generic sense, *diaphora* refers to a general differentiation that might include also a differentia understood in the technical sense (i.e. a definitory differentia). This indicates that if one of the general or definitory differentiae is omitted, then the other elements that are mentioned in the defining expression will not be sufficient to individuate the essence.

There are three subparts in the passage under scrutiny (i.e. 146^b20–35): 146^b20–4, 146^b24–7, 146^b27–35. At 146^b20–4, Aristotle introduces his first example to show to the dialectician how he could recognize accounts that are wrong because the definition does not contain the differentiations that are necessary to describe the correlative. It remains to be said that the choice of looking for a definition of honour-lover (*philotimos*) might give rise to some questions. One wonders whether the combination of the species human with the characteristic of loving honour forms a single natural kind. If this is the case, then the search for the definition of honour-lover is justified. But if the combination of the species human with the characteristic of loving honour does not constitute a single natural kind, then honour-lover will be an accidental composite. In the *Metaphysics*, Aristotle denies that accidental composites have essences. He says: 'For the essence is what something is; but when one thing is said of another, that is not what a "this" is, e.g. white human is not what a "this" is since being a "this" belongs only to substances ... Nothing then, which is not a species of a genus will have an essence—only species will have it' (*Metaph.* VII.4, 1030^{a}2–7 and 11–12). If Aristotle is committed to this denial also in the *Topics*, then honour-lover should not have an essence and no definition of honour-lover should be attempted. Perhaps Aristotle's aim is simply to discuss certain types of definition that were debated in the Academy.

At 146^{b}24–7, the text tackles two further proposed definitions of ethical concepts; they are modelled on the account of honour-lover discussed in the immediately preceding lines. First, it warns the dialectician that a successful definition of money-lover must specify that money in a certain quantity (*posôn*) is sought after. As in the case of the definition of honour-lover, the quantity is a differentiation of the correlative, i.e. money. Second, it instructs the dialectician to find the successful account of uncontrolled person (*akrates*). There are notorious difficulties in the translation of the Greek *akrates* and its cognate *akrasia*. It is customary to adopt the renderings 'incontinent' and 'incontinence' respectively (see, e.g., Barnes 1984, vol. 1; Irwin 1999). But 'incontinent' and 'incontinence' do not preserve the important etymological link in the Greek (this link is explicitly brought out by Aristotle below, at 146^{b}26–7). Properly speaking, according to Aristotle, an *akrates* is someone who does not have command over themself and over their passions; similarly, *akrasia* indicates the lack of command over oneself and over one's passions. In our context, *akrates* has the technical meaning of someone who does not have command *over their passions*; similarly, *akrasia* indicates the lack of command *over one's passions*. In my translation, *akrates* is rendered as 'uncontrolled person', whereas in the commentary the transliteration is used. Nowadays, the transliteration has become a technical Aristotelian term.

The problem of *akrasia* is widely discussed by ancient Greek thinkers, and different analyses have been offered by modern scholars (see Bobonich and Destrée 2007). It is helpful to call to mind the main thrust of this problem. In *EN* VII.2, 1145^{b}25–6, Aristotle tells us that Socrates believed there is no such thing as *akrasia*. More precisely, Socrates is reported to hold the view that *akrasia* is impossible since it involves doing the action that one knows to be bad. In other words, according to this view, it is not possible to act badly with the knowledge that the action is bad. So, one does a bad action because one does not know that what one is doing is bad. According to Aristotle's reconstruction, Socrates claimed that knowledge cannot be overcome by passions and cannot be 'dragged about like a slave' (*EN* VII.2, 1145^{b}23). In general terms, Aristotle's report is correct; but the arguments concerning the denial of *akrasia* offered by Socrates in the so-called early and middle Platonic dialogues are more complex. One should distinguish at least three types of arguments as they are found in, e.g., Plato's *Grg.* 466A–472A, *Prt.* 351B–357E, *Men.* 77B–78C, and *R.* IV and IX (the secondary literature on this point is vast; see, e.g., Irwin 1977, pp. 78–82; Irwin 1995, pp. 136–9; Bobonich 2007; Rowe 2007; Shields 2007). As is well known, Aristotle devotes book VII of his *Nicomachean Ethics* to the discussion of *akrasia*, and in his analysis he employs the dialectical method, namely the method presented and used in the *Topics*. He says:

> We must now discuss *akrasia* .... As in the other cases, we must set out the appearances, and first of all go through the puzzles. In this way we must prove the reputable opinions about these ways of being affected—ideally, all the reputable opinions, but if not all, most of them, and the most important. For, if the objections are solved and the reputable opinions are left, it will be an adequate proof.
> (*EN* VII.1, 1145^{a}35–1145^{b}10; translated by Irwin 1999, slightly modified)

Aristotle thinks *akrasia* is possible; he puts forward an analysis of this problem that involves an examination of certain types of knowledge and their interaction with desire and appetites. The Aristotelian approach to *akrasia* opens up several philosophical questions and leads to a variety of interpretations; for a full discussion of Aristotle's analysis of *akrasia* in book VII of his *Nicomachean Ethics* see Natali 2009.

As is said at 146^{b}25–6, it is a necessary requirement for a successful definition of *akrates* that it mentions the sort of pleasure one is concerned with (i.e. in Aristotle's terminology, its quality). It is interesting to note how Aristotle phrases the justification of this claim. He says: 'Not the one who is overcome (*kratoumenos*; lit. controlled, commanded) by whatever (*hoiaspotoun*) pleasure is called an uncontrolled person, but the one who is overcome by a certain one (*hupo tinos*)'. If we take a more literal translation of the participle *kratoumenos*, we shall have a way to spell out the etymological link between *kratoumenos* and *a-krates* in English:

the person who lacks control over his passion is the person who is controlled by a certain type of pleasure. It is also worth marking the contrast between whatever (*hoiaspotoun*) pleasure and a certain one (*tinos*) by which the *akrates* is overcome. This indicates that if the proposed definition contains an unqualified correlative, which in this case is an unqualified pleasure, then it cannot be accepted. The proposed definition cannot fail to mention the feature of the pleasure proper to the *akrates* that differentiates it from the other sorts of pleasure; in other words, it cannot fail to mention the differentiation of the correlative. Although Aristotle does not develop his account of *akrasia* in this passage, his remarks are in line with the theory he offers in *EN* VII.4, 1147^{b}31–4: 'When people go to the excess, against the correct reason in them, in the pursuit of these sources of pleasures, we do not call them simply uncontrolled persons, but add the qualification that they are uncontrolled about money, gain, honour, or spirit, and not simply uncontrolled'. Similarly, in *EN* VII.8, 1151^{a}11–13, Aristotle says that 'The uncontrolled person is the sort to pursue excessive *bodily* pleasure against correct reason'.

At 146^{b}27–35, further proposed accounts are analysed: (1) 'Night is a shade of the earth'; (2) 'Earthquake is a movement of the earth'; (3) 'Cloud is condensation of the air'; and (4) 'Wind is a movement of the air'. These accounts differ from those discussed so far because they concern not ethical concepts but beliefs about natural phenomena. We might draw a parallel between some of these opinions and certain aspect of the speculation of the so-called natural philosophers (see *Metaph.* I.3, 983^{b}6–8 and 18–28). For example, we know that Thales tried to give an explanation of the earthquake that was entirely based on natural phenomena. According to Seneca, *Questiones Naturales*, III. 14,1 (DK 11A15), Thales postulated that the world was floating on water, and the earthquake was due to the earth moving on the water. Furthermore, Anaximenes is reported to be the first to explain the formation of clouds on the basis of condensation of air ('Cloud is produced from air by felting'; DK 13A7, KRS 1983, p. 145). The same explanation of the formation of clouds seems to have been given by Anaxagoras, who was perhaps one of Anaximenes' pupils (see DK 59B16). The view that the wind is movement of the air is present also in

Top. IV.5, 127ᵃ4. Accounts (1)–(4) share an important feature that makes them a proper group in this section of the text and conveys thematic unity to this subpart. These accounts have in common the fact that they can all be characterized as 'pre-scientific definitions'. In other words, they are descriptions of natural phenomena that have not been investigated by science; they reflect some basic ideas about the world, ideas that are captured by expressions of natural language. For this reason, they could also be included among the reputable opinions (*endoxa*) that constitute the starting point of dialectical inquiry in the domain of physics.

Particular attention should be given to the sentence at 146ᵇ30: 'We must add quantity and quality and "by virtue of what"'. This sentence expresses the reason why accounts (1)–(4) are not successful definitions and must be rejected: since key parts of information are left out, these accounts are incomplete. In this context, the expression *hupo tinos* ('by virtue of what') must be handled with care. At first sight, it alludes to what triggers the events mentioned in some of the accounts presented above. I prefer to avoid the term 'cause' because it is philosophically more loaded and should be used only when in the Greek we find *aitia* or *aition* (on the concept of cause in the *Topics* see above the commentary on 146ᵇ9–12). What is the precise role of quantity and quality and 'by virtue of what'? Following the interpretation put forward above (see the analysis of the occurrences of *diaphora*), they indicate differentiations of one of the elements in the proposed definitions (1)–(4). The remark that 'We must always argue against deficiency' (146ᵇ32) explicitly identifies the type of mistake under discussion, i.e. deficiency or incompleteness. It can serve a further purpose: it can suggest the kind of refutative strategy to be employed by the dialectician who could develop his argument on the basis of the examples at 146ᵇ33–5. For instance, the dialectician could produce some counterexamples to the view that any movement of the earth is an earthquake and that any movement of the air is wind: he might say that if one breathes out, there is a movement of the air, but it is not wind, or, analogously, if a group of galloping horses passes by, there is a movement of the earth, but it is not an earthquake.

146ᵇ36–147ᵃ5: This section deals with accounts that are incomplete because the qualification 'apparent' is left out. Two proposed accounts are criticized and a solution to avoid the criticism is put forward. The accounts are: (1) 'Wish is desire for a good' (146^b37–147^a1) and (2) 'Appetite is desire for something pleasant'. The immediate context suggests that (1) and (2) are not complete and must be improved by the addition of 'apparent'; hence they cannot be accepted. But an occurrence of (1) is also present at 146^b5–6 above: it is mentioned in relation to the rule saying that if the proposed account fails to include the correlative either of the thing to be defined or of its genus, then it must be rejected (the rule is stated at 146^a36–146^b1). More precisely, (1) 'Wish is desire for a good' was originally chosen as an example of an account not containing the mistake described in the rule; for the defining expression, i.e. 'desire for a good', mentions the genus' correlative, i.e. a good. This indicates that, in its first occurrence, account (1) can be accepted by the dialectician. If this is the correct reading, then it would be the source of tension within the same chapter; for the first occurrence of the account might be accepted, whilst the second has to be rejected. There is, however, a way to avoid this tension. In the first part, Aristotle is likely to have something else in mind; perhaps he is talking about all the cases where people desire a non-apparent, and hence genuine, good. Alternatively, he could simply be ignoring a defect in the proposed definition that is not germane to the refutative line under consideration in that context. In the final part of the chapter, however, Aristotle is making a different point. He believes that some people might choose a good that is not genuine or objective but apparent (more on the concept of apparent good will be said below). If this happens, (1) is no longer appropriate to define their wish. Aristotle's strategy is that the account must be modified in such a way that good, i.e. the correlative, be qualified as apparent. The same line of argument can be applied to account (2); in other words, 'Appetite is desire for something pleasant' is not correct in the case where the correlative of appetite is what is apparently pleasant. In ancient Greek, 'pleasant' (*hêdus*) primarily indicates what is pleasant to the taste, but its range of application can be extended to other bodily pleasures. *Hêdeos* is a neuter genitive that in this passage is used as a substantive and corresponds to the noun *hêdonê* ('pleasure'). Note that the definition of appetite as desire for something pleasant contravenes the requirement of 146^b11–12, where we had been told that appetite is (not for something pleasant but) for pleasure. In Aristotle, the best-known, but also highly problematic, discussion of good and pleasure can be found in the *Nicomachean Ethics* (especially books VII and X). Although there is no evidence to suggest that in the *Topics* Aristotle has in mind the views expressed in the *Nicomachean Ethics*, it cannot be ruled out that the commonplaces of chapter 8 might contain some basic ideas that he developed on another occasion.

The qualification 'apparent' plays a key role in this commonplace. The corresponding Greek word is *phainomenon*, i.e. the middle passive participial form of *phainô*. In the active *phainô* means 'bring to light', whereas the middle passive *phainomai* means 'come to light' or 'appear'. The middle passive form *phainomenon* ('apparent') and its cognates can be used in several ways. According to some commentators, we can distinguish two uses of 'to appear' (for example, in his 1987, pp. 113–14, Irwin talks about a first use that he calls 'veridical' and contrasts it with a use 'with no implication that the appearance is true'). In the first case, speaking of something as an apparent F implies that the appearance is true so that the thing that appears to be F is F. This happens in all the occurrences where 'an apparent F' is equivalent to 'a clear F' or 'an obvious F' (Bonitz 1870, p. 809A, and LSJ, *s.v. phainô*, II). An example of this factive use can be found in Aristotle's definition of a perfect syllogism in *APr.* I.1, 24^{b}23–4. In the second case, speaking of something as an apparent F leaves it open whether the thing is or is not F. In other words, the qualification 'apparent' implies neither truth not falsehood; for this reason, an adequate rendering of the verb in its neutral use is 'seem' or 'look'. Is there also a 'contrafactual' use of *phainomai* (the use of *phainomai* is contrafactual when the state of affairs to which the verb is applied is required not to be the case)? In this instance, speaking of something that is an apparent F would imply that the appearance is false and that the thing that appears to be F is not F. At first glance, this seems to match with our ordinary linguistic intuitions and it would be highly tempting to introduce the contrafactual use; nevertheless it is difficult to find unequivocal evidence to support it. There is no need to take sides on this issue, however, since there is an alternative explanation concerning the use of *phainomai* worth considering. It suffices to suppose that this verb has a broad semantic spectrum that can nonetheless be suitably restricted by the context. Consider, for example, *SE* 1, 164^{a}20–1: '(We shall speak about) apparent refutations, which are fallacies but not refutations' (*phainomenôn men elenchôn, ontôn de paralogismôn all'ouk elenchôn*). The relative clause seems to require that the use of 'apparent' is the neutral one (otherwise the relative clause would be pointless: the description of certain arguments as 'apparent refutations' would already imply that the arguments in question are not refutations). But the relative clause, by restricting apparent refutations to those which are not refutations, may be plausibly taken to introduce a contextual restriction in the extension of the phrases of the form 'an apparent *F*'. This contextual restriction brings it about that if anywhere in the *Sophistici Elenchi* something is called 'an apparent *F*', it is supposed to be regarded as something that appears *F* without being *F*. The initial position of the restriction of apparent refutations makes it particularly apt to be the first move of a contextual restriction that governs the whole treatise. A further point must be raised concerning the meaning of 'apparent': it would be strange to suggest that in the context of this passage 'apparent' should be taken as 'perceptually apparent'. In the discussion of the apparent good, there is certainly more at stake than a mere perceptual appearance of what is good. A promising alternative comes from the passage in *EN* VII.1, 1145^{b}2–5: 'We must, as in the other cases, set out the appearances (*tithentas ta phainomena*) and first go through the puzzles. In that way we must prove, ideally, the truths of all the reputable opinions ... , or, if not all, of most of them and the most important'. Most scholars agree that the appearances mentioned above coincide with reputable opinions (*endoxa*, also translated with 'common beliefs'); that is to say, the appearances can be what is believed to be the case (see, e.g., Owen 1968b, p. 118; Irwin 1987, pp. 109–11 and *passim*). So, when Aristotle talks about the apparent good, he may be referring to what appears to our senses or to what we believe.

The phrase 'apparent good' occurs in several Aristotelian texts: it refers to a fundamental concept in the discussion of central issues concerning his ethics, psychology, and philosophy of action (Moss 2012, p. xi). It suffices to mention two occurrences: the first is *De An.*, III.10, 433^{a}27–9: 'The object of desire always moves, but this is the good or the apparent good'. The second occurrence belongs to *EN* III.4, 1113ᵃ23–5: 'Without qualification and in truth, the object of wish is the good, but for each person it is the apparent good'. Scholars agree that the concept of apparent good is different from that of unqualified good and they hold that the unqualified good is identical to the genuine good, but they offer (at least) two interpretations of the concept of apparent good. According to the first, the things we desire are in fact good and apparent to us, i.e. somehow present in our awareness. This means that, even though the apparent good is in fact good, it does not necessarily appear as good: for example, it could appear as pleasant (Irwin 1990, pp. 331–2). The use employed here does not occur in our passage. For, at 147ᵃ2–4, Aristotle says: 'For often those who desire are not aware of what is good or pleasant so that it is not necessary for it (*sc.* the object of the desire) to be good or pleasant, but only to appear to be so'. In other words, the apparent good that is desired could fail to be good. According to the second interpretation, the apparent good *seems* or *looks* good to a particular agent, but this appearance may be false (Moss 2012, p. 7). This reading uses 'apparent' in a neutral way: it leaves open the possibility that the agent could be wrong.

How is 'apparent' used when it is part of the expression 'apparent good' at 146ᵇ36–147ᵃ5? If in this context Aristotle were using 'apparent' in a factive way, he would be speaking of what is genuinely good. This would, however, sit uncomfortably with the claim that some agents who feel desire 'are not aware of what is good ... so that it is not necessary for it (*sc.* the object of their desire) to be good' (147ᵃ2–3). In other words, the fact that we desire something is not sufficient to guarantee that it is good: it is not the case that everything desired is also good. Hence, the factive use is not a likely option. Second, as argued above, 'apparent' has either a contrafactual use or can be contextually restricted with an effect equivalent to that of a contrafactual use. But, in the passage under scrutiny, 'apparent' could hardly be employed in any of these ways; for the apparent good would be what seems good without being so. Obviously, saying that a wish is a desire for what—as a matter of fact—is not good would not be a helpful definition because one can wish for something that— as a matter of fact—is good. The third is the best interpretative option: it tells us that 'apparent' is used in a neutral way. In other terms, when Aristotle speaks of the apparent good here, he leaves it open whether what appears to be good is good or not so that people who wish for the apparent good might, but need not, go wrong on what counts as good.

147ᵃ5–11: Aristotle aims at showing that the solution just envisaged, namely the addition of 'apparent' in the definition, is problematic for those who believe in Platonic Ideas and are committed to certain theses about them. In these lines, Aristotle openly confronts some Platonic theses (the relation between Aristotle's thought and the type of Platonic doctrine he addresses is discussed above in the commentary on VI.6, 143ᵇ11–32). This passage received a lot of attention and different interpretations have been put forward. In particular, discussions can be found in Cherniss 1962, vol. I, pp. 11–19; De Vogel 1968, pp. 93, 95–6; Düring 1968, pp. 203–16; Owen 1968b, pp. 118–25; Verdenius 1968, pp. 37–8; Brunschwig 2007, p. 241 (I reconstruct and evaluate the different exegeses in Schiaparelli 2017). According to Aristotle, for the refutative argument to be developed, two conditions must be met: (a) in proposing a definition the opponent must mention the qualification 'apparent' (147ᵃ5); (b) the opponent must be committed to the theory of Ideas (147ᵃ5–6). If these two conditions are satisfied, the opponent should be led to reason about the Ideas (*epi ta eidê akteon*). In particular, he must be led to admit that his definition has an Idea as its object (and any believer in Ideas would be easily led to admit this). Moreover, the refutative argument is based on two ontological assumptions about the Ideas: (1) 'There cannot be Ideas of anything apparent' (147ᵃ6–7), and (2) 'The Idea seems to be spoken of relatively to the Idea' (147ᵃ7). Due to its succinctness, the last sentence is unclear and must be explained. The verbal form *dokei* ('It seems') alerts us to the fact that Aristotle is discussing someone else's opinion without committing himself to endorse it (see Brunschwig 2007, pp. xxxvi–xxxviii). Most probably, the expression '*a* is spoken of relatively to *b*' in (2) is a contraction of '*a* is said to be what it is relatively to *b*'. In the context of this commonplace, saying that an Idea is said to be what it is relatively to an Idea means that the correlatives of Ideas of relative properties, for example pleasant and good, are Ideas. Evidence to support this reading can be found in *Cat.* 7. In particular, at 6ᵇ6–7, Aristotle says: (*a*) 'Relatives, then, are all those things which are called precisely what they are of something else' (*pros ti oun estin hosa auta haper estin heterôn legetai*). It is interesting to note that the Greek pronoun *hoper* (singular of *haper*) is often used to introduce the genus (Bonitz 1870, p. 533B). This suggests that (α) can be rephrased as: (β) 'Some relatives receive the predication *of their own name* with respect to something else, while other relatives receive the predication *of the name of their genus* with respect to something else'. For example, knowledge receives the predication of its own name, viz. knowledge, with respect to something else (knowledge is always knowledge of a knowable); literacy receives the predication of the name of its genus, viz. knowledge, with respect to something else (literacy is always knowledge of letters). Both cases are covered by *hoper*. This fits well with the main theme of the chapter, namely the discussion of the definition of a relative either with respect to itself or with respect to the genus (146^a36–7). It must be observed that the use of *heterôn* (6^b7) does not imply distinctness and could be read loosely as we find it in treatment of relatives before Aristotle (for example, in *Phlb.* 51C–D, Plato uses interchangeably *pros ti*, 'relatively to something', and *pros heteron*, 'relatively to something different'). At *Cat.* 7, 6^b28, sentence (α) is restated using a condensed formulation in the context of the following remark: 'All relatives are spoken of in relation to correlatives that reciprocate' (*panta de ta pros ti pros antistrefonta legetai*). For example, 'The slave is called slave of a master and the master is called master of a slave (*ho doulos despotou legetai doulos kai ho despotês doulou despotês legetai*, 6^b29–30): here the second occurrence of 'slave' (*doulos*) as well as that of 'master' (*despotês*) express the *hoper* mentioned in sentence (α)—though in (α) we read *haper*, i.e. the plural of *hoper*. The condensed formulation is repeated at 7^a22–3: 'All relatives then are spoken of in relation to correlatives that reciprocate' (*panta oun ta pros ti ... pros antistrephonta legetai*).

When assumptions (1) and (2) are introduced, they are not justified. Before looking at their plausibility, it is helpful to show their place in the argument. Its structure can be translated in the following way:

(1) There cannot be Ideas of anything apparent (first assumption, 147^a6–7).
(2) An Idea is spoken of relatively to an Idea (second assumption, 147^a7).

(3) The Idea of appetite is a desire for the Idea of the apparent pleasant (from (2) in the case where appetite is for the apparently pleasant; 146^{b}37–147^{a}2 and 147^{a}5).
(4) There cannot be an Idea of apparent pleasure (from (1)).
(5) The Idea of appetite will not be a desire for the apparently pleasant.

Sentence (3) depends on (2) since it is an application of the general claim that an Idea is spoken of relatively to an Idea to the particular case where the Idea of appetite (e.g. appetite-itself) is for the Idea of the apparently pleasant. Sentences (3) and (4) are inconsistent since (3) introduces the Idea of apparently pleasant, an Idea whose existence is denied by (4). We should remember that sentence (3) is the result of leading the opponent to Ideas, namely leading him to frame his definition in such a way that it is explicitly speaking of Ideas. Given the inconsistency resulting from (3) and (4), Aristotle rejects (3) and concludes (5). If we replace 'appetite' and 'apparently pleasant' by 'wish' and 'apparently good' in (3), (4), and (5), we obtain a perfectly analogous argument.

Is the refutation effective? The answer requires the distinction of two cases. Case (A): assumptions (1) and (2) express basic features of Ideas and are accepted by the interlocutor (most likely a member of the Academy). If this happens, the refutation is effective. The interlocutor has to accept that, in a Platonic framework, it is difficult (if not impossible) to give a definition of something that relates to something that enjoys a certain characteristic only apparently. Case (B): assumptions (1) and (2) are not accepted by the interlocutor. In this case, Aristotle or the dialectician developing the commonplace must argue for them. It is, then, necessary to understand how it could be argued for (1) and (2) as the lack of an adequate support undermines the effectiveness of the refutative argument.

Some Platonic evidence to support (1) might come from the claim, often found in the dialogues, that Ideas are paradigms or standard samples of certain properties (see *Euthphr.* 6E4, *Prm.* 132D2). For example, in *R.* X, 596E–597B, Plato distinguishes between the product of a painter, which is *what appears* a bed, from that of the carpenter, which is some bed, and that of the god, which *is* a bed. We could argue as follows: If an Idea had nothing but the appearance of a certain property, or if it had a trait that precludes the full realization of that property, then it would be absurd to attribute it the status of Idea; in other words, the Idea of the so-and-so cannot be only apparently so-and-so. Thus, by virtue of their status, Ideas cannot be qualified as apparent. This argument, however, is not immune to criticism; for example, our opponent might well grant that a sophist is someone who has knowledge of what is apparently true. This is a case of knowledge of what is apparently so-and-so. If it is true to say that the object of knowledge are Ideas, as Plato seems to admit in the *Republic*, this might induce us to introduce Ideas of what is apparently so-and-so. Furthermore, in *Sph.* 236A, Plato talks about an artist who reproduces images that appear to be beautiful. Suppose that it is true to say that an artist in reproducing an image is copying from a model, i.e. from an Idea (*R.* X, 596B–C; 'The makers look towards the appropriate Idea in making the beds or tables we use, and similarly in the other cases—surely no craftsman makes the Idea itself'). It follows that in the case of images that are apparently so-and-so, the artist is copying from the Idea that is apparently so-and-so. Even though a Platonist might have an answer to this criticism, he should at least be faced with it in this context.

There is another problem. The inference from the assumption (1) that there are not Ideas of anything apparent is threatened by the failure of distinguishing between two different types of predication, namely definitional and ordinary predication. Since this distinction is introduced and discussed in the commentary on *Top.* VI.6, 143^{b}11–32 (see *ad loc.*), it suffices to repeat that definitional predication occurs when the predicate is either the whole defining expression (e.g. 'A human is a rational animal'), or a part of it (e.g. 'A human is an animal'), or the name of the kind to be defined itself (e.g. 'A human is a human'). Ordinary predication occurs when the *denotatum* of the subject instantiates a characteristic indicated by the predicate (e.g. 'Socrates is a human', 'Human is a species'). With this distinction in mind, let us consider whether the Idea of the apparently pleasant is apparent. Two answers are possible. First, if the copula expresses definitional predication, then the answer will be affirmative. In this case, the qualification 'apparently pleasant' is the name of the kind to be defined itself in the proposed definition of the Idea of apparently pleasant. Second, if the copula expresses ordinary predication, then the answer will be negative. For the Idea of the apparently pleasant does not have the characteristic of being pleasant nor that of being apparently such. Let us look at another example in order to have a better understanding of this distinction. Consider the Idea of movement and ask whether it is in movement. In the case of definitional predication, it will be true to say that it is in movement; for 'movement' is the name of the kind to be defined itself. In the case of ordinary predication, it will not be true to say that it is in movement. For the Idea of movement, in so far as it is an Idea, is motionless. Since there are different ways to distinguish between types of predication or levels of predicates (see, e.g., Owen 1968b, pp. 108–16), one might ask whether there are reasons for preferring and adopting an interpretation based on the distinction between definitional and ordinary predication. This distinction is to be favoured because it is already present in the philosophical and historical context of the *Topics*. According to a well-established interpretative line originated by M. Frede, in the *Sophist* there is evidence for attributing to Plato something like the distinction between definitional and ordinary predication (see Frede 1967, pp. 30–5; Frede 1992, pp. 309–401; Meinwald 1991, pp. 67–8; Mann 2000, pp. 178–9; Crivelli 2012, pp. 122–33. Three passages of the *Sophist* are usually mentioned in order to credit Plato with this distinction of types of predication: 250C6–7, 255E3–6, and 257D14–258C6).

This analysis shows that the argument involving premise (1), i.e. 'There cannot be Ideas of anything apparent', could be challenged by an interlocutor who understands and uses the distinction between different types of predication. It is difficult to say whether Aristotle or the interlocutor is aware of this conceptual tool. On the one hand, this passage does not mention it and makes a rather unrefined point about predication (see also *Top.* VI.6, 143^{b}14–17, 23–32, and commentary *ad loc.*). On the other hand, there are other places in the *Topics* where Aristotle introduces a more sophisticated theory of predication that could be interpreted as pointing to the distinction between definitional and ordinary predication (*Top.* V.7, 137^{b}2–8). Should we conclude that we are facing a severe tension in Aristotle's work? The answer is no: there is a way to make sense of the differences in the outlined strategies. Aristotle's choice of a specific line of argument is probably influenced by the type of interlocutor he is confronting. If he aims at refuting someone who adopts a naïve Platonic standpoint, he will not need to use a sophisticated theory of predication. But there are other circumstances, however, where the interlocutor might be a more refined Platonist; for example, he might have read, say, the *Sophist*, and hence could be able to distinguish between different types of predication. In this case, Aristotle is justified in adopting more sophisticated tools. To sum up, the analysis of assumption (1) shows that the problems it involves are sufficiently controversial to question the result of refutative strategy outlined in this commonplace.

Let us turn to (2), namely the thesis that 'An Idea is spoken of relatively to an Idea'. Is Aristotle suggesting that *every* Idea is relative to an Idea? It is unlikely that Aristotle is making such a general claim. It is more plausible that he is restricting his attention to Ideas of relative properties since this chapter concerns specific rules for rejecting proposed accounts of relatives. More specifically, the discussion is introduced by saying: 'If what is being defined is a relative either with respect to itself or with respect to the genus, examine whether the definition does not mention that in relation to which it is said, either itself or with respect to the genus' (146^a36–146^b1). Some debate as to whether the Platonic or Academic class of relative entities (*pros ti*) has the same extension as the Aristotelian class can be found in Owen 1957, pp. 107–10, and Fine 1993, pp. 171–82.

Something like the claim that 'An Idea is spoken of relatively to an Idea' seems to occur in other (non-Aristotelian) contexts. In particular, let us consider the objection raised by Parmenides in Plato's homonymous dialogue at 133C3–134A1. The details of this objection need not be reported and it suffices to mention the general line of the argument. Parmenides says to the young Socrates: 'Things in us do not have their power in relation to the Ideas, nor they (*sc.* Ideas) have theirs in relation to us; but, I repeat, Ideas are what they are of themselves and in relation to themselves, and things that belong to us are, in the same way, what they are in relation to themselves' (133E4–134A1; the same point is made at 133C3–5 and at 134D4–7). One of Parmenides' examples is: 'Mastery-itself is what it is of slavery-itself; and in the same way, slavery-itself is slavery of mastery-itself' (133E3–4). The cases presented by Aristotle have the same structure as Parmenides' example, even though they do not mention the Ideas of mastery and slavery, but those of appetite, wish, pleasure, and good. According to Aristotle, if the interlocutor accepts that an Idea is related only to an Idea, he is committed to the claim that appetite-itself is for the pleasant-itself, and, analogously, wish-itself is for the good-itself (147^a8–9). But there is an important difficulty for those who accept assumption (2), namely that 'An Idea is spoken of relatively to an Idea'. Consider knowledge-itself: it is correlative to truth-itself (134A3–4). By contrast, knowledge in us will be knowledge not of truth-itself, but of truth in our world. It follows that truth-itself is not knowable by us. In the *Parmenides*, a further step is made (134B–C), namely that knowledge in us is not knowledge of the Ideas (which are identified with the truth-itself). This objection is described as 'the greatest difficulty', to which Socrates offers no reply. As a last remark, it is worth noticing that similar formulations of the thesis expressed in (2) are part of at least one argument criticizing Platonic Ideas that we find in the *Peri Ideôn*, fr. 3 Ross = Alex. Aphr. *in Metaph.* 83.26–8: 'If the equal is equal to an equal, there will be more than one Idea of equal. For the equal-itself is equal to an equal-itself. For if it were not equal to something, it would not be equal at all' (see Fine 1993, pp. 188–90).

In conclusion, it should be observed that the argument at 147^a5–11 is not successful against any interlocutor whatsoever, but it depends on what one is ready to accept. If the interlocutor is not aware of a sophisticated theory of predication and accepts that an Idea is relative only to an Idea, then Aristotle or the dialectician can successfully deploy their line of attack. By contrast, if the interlocutor is already acquainted with more refined forms of predication and holds that an Idea can be relative not only to an Idea but also to a sensible particular, then the line of attack is open to objections and requires further argumentative moves.

CHAPTER 9

Introduction: In chapter 9, Aristotle explains how to use rules derived from a number of different patterns of argument, based on the relations obtaining between coordinates (*sustoicha*) and between opposites (*antikeimena*). What does Aristotle mean by these terms and what is their function in the context of the *Topics*? Generally speaking, *sustoicha* are coordinate elements that are grouped together in virtue of the fact that they possess a common linguistic root. More precisely, in *Top.* II.9, 114^{a}27–9 Aristotle says: 'Things of this sort are called coordinates; for example, just things and the just (*sc.* are coordinate) with justice, and courageous things and the courageous with courage'. It is not clear whether Aristotle uses 'coordinates' to indicate cognate linguistic expressions or to refer to things whose names are cognate linguistic expressions. In this context, coordinates are closely related to the so-called *ptôseis*. The literal translation of *ptôseis* is 'cases', in the sense of 'grammatical cases' or 'inflections'. Aristotle, however, employs *ptôseis* to indicate also grammatical modifications of nouns or adjectives. Examples of grammatical modifications are 'justly', which is derived from 'justice', and 'courageously', which is derived from 'courage' (see also *Top.* VI.10, 148^{a}10–13). Furthermore, according to Aristotle, 'It seems that whatever is expressed as a case is also a coordinate' (*Top.* II.9, 114^{a}33–4). A detailed analysis of coordinates and cases is not within the limit of this commentary. Nevertheless, it is important to understand what their function is. It is possible to employ coordinates to form patterns of argument to be used in the exchanges with the interlocutor. Aristotle tells us: 'If any element whatsoever within the same coordinate group has been shown to be good or praiseworthy, the remainder are also shown to be so' (*Top.* II.9, 114^{a}38–114^{b}1). For example, if you are examining whether being praiseworthy belongs to just things, you can see whether being praiseworthy belongs also to justice. For, in so far as just things are coordinate with justice, being praiseworthy must belong to all. In case of a discrepancy, the questioner can reject the answerer's claim.

Consider now opposites. When we read the refutative strategies sketched in this chapter (especially in the second part), it is important to keep in mind Aristotle's classification of opposites. This classification can be found in his early logical works (for example in *Categories* 10; in *Topics* II.8 and V.6) as well as in the *Metaphysics* (see, e.g., X.3, 1054^{a}23; 4, 1055^{a}38; 7, 1057^{a}33). According to Aristotle (see in particular *Topics* II.8), there are four kinds of opposition (*antithesis*) or opposites (*antikeimena*). Things can be opposed (*i*) as contraries (*enantia*), (*ii*) as affirmation and negation (*kataphasis* and *apophasis*), (*iii*) as possession and privation (*hexis* and *sterêsis*), and (*iv*) as relatives (*pros ti*). (For the translation of *hexis* with 'possession', see 'The value of *hexis*' in 'Terminological Clarification'; see also the commentary on 147^{a}12–22, below). This fourfold classification is often used in the *Topics*, and this might be the reason why in this chapter Aristotle does not present it in a systematic way but seems to take for granted that the reader is familiar with it. Each kind of opposition allows us to establish a rule that can be applied in the analysis of proposed definitions. Although it is possible to obtain constructive and refutative rules, in the context of the analysis of definitions we find refutative strategies only (apart from a rare example in 147^{a}30–1; see, below, the commentary *ad loc.*). Particular examples of these rules are discussed below in the commentary. In some cases, the rules are not clearly formulated, and this leads to interpretative problems (see, e.g., 147^{a}23–4).

The patterns of argument based on coordinates and opposites have a wide range of application since they can be employed in the discussion of all four predicables (accident, unique property, genus, and definition). There are other patterns of argument serving the same purpose, i.e. developing a strategy to examine the interlocutor's claim about any of the four predicables, based on more, less, and equal; these are not dealt with in this chapter (Smith 1997, xxx–xxxiv, provides a helpful overview of these patterns of argument).

This chapter is structured as follows: (1) 147^{a}12–22 contains a discussion of refutative strategies that are based on coordinates and on one type of opposites, namely contraries. (2) 147^{a}23–8 is concerned with another type of opposites, namely relatives. (3) 147^{a}28–147^{b}4 discusses rules based on opposites in general. (4) 147^{b}4–17 deals with the case of contraries that are said by privation, whereas (5) 147^{b}17–25 contains an analysis of the case of contraries that are *not* said by privation. (6) 147^{b}26–148^{a}9 analyses proposed accounts of things said by privation.

147ª12–22: The chapter begins with a discussion of the rules for examining attempted definitions of *hexis* (for the translation of *hexis*, see 'The value of *hexis*' in 'Terminological Clarifications'). In the rendering of this passage, the majority of translators adopt 'state' or 'possession'. On the one hand, in Pickard-Cambridge 1928, in Forster 1960, and in Barnes 1984, vol. 1, we read 'state (of anything)'; similarly, in Tricot 1950 we find 'état'. On the other hand, in Brunschwig 2007 'possession' is preferred. In order to translate the occurrences of *hexis* in *Top*. I.15, 106ª21–8 and II. 7, 114ª7–25, Smith chooses 'state', but in the commentary he uses interchangeably 'state' and 'possession', which he considers synonyms (see Smith 1997; his translation of *Top*. II. 7, 114ª7–25 can be found in the excerpts at pp. 165–6). There are some main advantages in translating *hexis* with 'possession'. First, it preserves uniformity of translation, as in a subsequent portion of this chapter (147ᵇ26–148ª2) *hexis* is explicitly contrasted with *sterêsis* ('privation'), and when *hexis* is related to 'privation', it is best to translate it with 'possession'. Second, when translators adopt 'state', they must translate *tou echontos* (147ª12–13) accordingly. So, they must choose something like 'of what has the state' or 'of what is in the state', and similar phrases if they adopt 'condition', rather long phrases instead of the one word which we find in the Greek text. Third, in colloquial English the expressions 'what is in a state' and 'what has a condition' convey meanings that are inappropriate for the context. By contrast, if we translate *hexis* with 'possession', we can easily adopt 'of the possessor' for *tou echontos*, thereby remaining closer to the Greek formulation.

At 147ª12–13, *hexis* ('possession') is not explicitly contrasted with *sterêsis* ('privation'). The relation discussed in these lines is that between a possession and the possessor. This relation will provide a basis for formulating the rules for the present commonplace. In order to have a better understanding of Aristotle's point, we need to analyse the phrase at 147ª13–14: 'Similarly also in other cases of this sort'. What are the 'other cases of this sort'? The answer can be found in the sentence that concludes and summarizes the cases mentioned in this first part of chapter 9 (147ª12–22), cases which must be analysed according to 'the rules derived from ... coordinates (*sustoicha*)' (147ª21–2). We should therefore understand possession and possessor as coordinates in the same linguistic group (*hexis* is etymologically linked to the verb *echô*). This will prompt the trained dialectician to use specific rules to analyse the interlocutors' proposed definitions (more on these rules below).

At first reading, it is unclear what 'the pleasant thing' (*to hêdu*) and 'the person who feels pleasure' (*ho hêdomenos*) are meant to illustrate ($147^a 14$–15). There are two possibilities. They could be an instance of the relation between possession (*hexis*) and possessor (*echon*). But it is difficult to see how *to hêdu* can be a possession. Perhaps one might argue that if *to hêdu* is a glass of wine, then one could possess a glass of wine. This reading seems to stretch the sense of the passage in an unnatural way. Furthermore, there are pleasant things like one of Schubert's piano sonatas, which can hardly be a possession, and the person who feels pleasure in hearing it can hardly be its possessor. Alternatively, the example concerning *to hêdu* and *ho hêdomenos* refers to the phrase 'all the cases of this sort'. As we know, they are cases of coordinates. This means that *hêdu* and *hêdomenos* are coordinates belonging to the same linguistic group, which is composed of the cognates of *hêdonê* ('pleasure').

At $147^a 15$, Aristotle makes a general remark concerning the definitions of coordinates. The justification for this has to be inferred from what he says at $147^a 17$–21. At first, he offers an example and then he briefly explains it. Aristotle's view is that, in certain cases, when the interlocutor proposes a definition, somehow he offers elements which define other things as well. What is Aristotle's idea? Suppose that the interlocutor puts forward an account of courage as the ethical virtue that allows us to stand firm in battle. Consider now a coordinate of courage, e.g. the courageous. The idea is that in the definition of courage it is possible to find elements that enter into the definition of the courageous. For the courageous is the virtuous person who stands firm in battle. More precisely, let D be the definition of x, and let $x_1, x_2, \ldots, x_n$ be the coordinates of x. Then $D_1, D_2, \ldots, D_n$ will be the definitions of $x_1, x_2, \ldots, x_n$ respectively. Furthermore, $D, D_1, D_2, \ldots, D_n$ contain a variation in the expression similar to that between $x, x_1, x_2, \ldots, x_n$. When the dialectician examines D of x, he must check whether D_1 of x_1, D_2 of $x_2, \ldots, D_n$ of x_n are successful. If there is a discrepancy between D of x and another definition, say D_2 of x_2, then D must be rejected or revised. It is unclear, however, how the rules should be applied: at this stage of the argument there is no precise indication of how the elements of the proposed accounts must be used to refute the interlocutor.

At 147ª17–21, we find two occurrences of *gar* ('for' or 'since'), which introduce some explanations. The first occurrence (147ª17) refers to the immediately preceding claim (i.e. 'To speak generally, in definitions of this sort the person who defines happens, in a way, to define more than one thing') and introduces a justification based on some examples. In particular, these examples are meant to illustrate the idea that if the interlocutor defines knowledge (*epistêmê*), he will have the means to find the definitions of the following: ignorance (*agnoia*), what has knowledge (*to epistêmon*), what lacks knowledge (*to anepistêmon*), to know (*epistasthai*), and to be ignorant (*agnoein*). Aristotle, however, explains neither how to look for the definitory elements nor how to formulate these definitions. The only hint can be found below at 147ª22, when he says that one should use 'the rules derived from contraries and coordinates'. And since Aristotle's intent in book VI is refutative, these rules ought to be used to criticize the interlocutor's proposed definitions. Two questions open up: (1) What *precisely* are the relations holding between the six items mentioned above? (2) How should the dialectician apply the suitable rules to this specific context? A diagram will help us to find the answers.

epistêmê (KNOWLEDGE)	*agnoia* (IGNORANCE)
to epistêmon (WHAT HAS KNOWLEDGE)	*to anepistêmon* (WHAT LACKS KNOWLEDGE)
epistasthai (TO KNOW)	*agnoein* (TO BE IGNORANT)

Diagram I

As for question (1), the diagram shows there are two basic types of items. In the left-hand column, there are items referring (or involving a reference) to knowledge. In the right-hand column, there are those that refer (or involve a reference) to ignorance, i.e. the contrary of knowledge. Every item in the right-hand column is in a relation of contrariety with the item on the same line in the left-hand column. Furthermore, all the items in the left-hand column are coordinates as they belong to the same linguistic group. Are the items in the right-hand column also coordinates? This case is not straightforward, and some difficulties arise. At first sight, they do not seem to instantiate the relation of being coordinates since, clearly, they do not belong to the same linguistic group. On the one hand, *agnoia* ('ignorance') and *agnoein* ('to be ignorant') are composed of a negative prefix, i.e. privative *alpha*, and a linguistic form linked to the verb *gnôrizein* ('to know'). On the other, *to anepistêmon* is constituted by a negative prefix and a word linked not to *gnôrizein* but to *epistasthai* ('to know' or 'to understand'). There are two options. (A) The items in the right-hand column *are not all coordinates* because they do not belong to the same linguistic group. (B) The items in the right-hand column *are all coordinates*. In this case, we need to modify the definition of being a coordinate because the merely linguistic criterion of belonging to the same linguistic group is too tight. Which option should be favoured? Option (A) has the disadvantage that it introduces an asymmetry between the two columns: according to option (A), the items in the left-hand column are all coordinates, whereas those in the right-hand column are not. With option (B) there is also a price to pay, however, as the criterion for being a coordinate must be revised, and the text provides no hint as to how. The question of which option should be favoured therefore remains open. Aristotle might have thought that it was not worthwhile to go into his example in great detail and that it sufficed to hint at some basic moves to show the general procedure. Even without a suitable characterization of coordinates that also fits the items in the right-hand column, it is possible to sketch Aristotle's envisaged procedure and to go through each stage of the example.

Consider now question (2). The suitable rules are those derived from coordinates and contraries. Some remarks concerning the rules derived from coordinates have already been made. At a later stage in the chapter we find a formulation of a rule derived from contraries. When this rule is applied to the context of definitions, it says that 'The contrary account of the contrary will be based on one combination of the contraries' (147^a32-3). For the moment, there is no need to analyse the details of this formulation (see commentary on $147^a29-147^b4$). It suffices to provide a brief illustration of the general idea concerning the application of the rules. Let us introduce some abbreviations. *Def. (K)* stands for the definition of a given kind *K*; *Def. (contrary K)* indicates the definition of the contrary of *K*; *Def. (K-coordinate)* stands for the definition of the coordinate of *K*; *Def. (contrary K-coordinate)* indicates the definition of the contrary of the coordinate of *K*. Consider first *Def. (K)* and apply to it the rule derived from contraries: we shall find *Def. (contrary K)*. Now we can look again at *Def. (K)* and, by working with an intuitive concept of coordinates, we can derive *Def. (K-coordinate)*. At this point, by an application of the rule derived from contraries, we obtain *Def. (contrary K-coordinate)*. If the application of the rules gives rise to an unsatisfactory or problematic result, this will provide a reason to reject or challenge the original account granted by the interlocutor.

147^{a}23–8: Whilst the last lines of the preceding portion of text contain an analysis of contrariety, this section concerns another type of opposition—opposition of relatives. The rule expressed at 147^{a}23–4 ('Furthermore, in the case of the relatives, examine whether he gives an account of the species as relative to a particular case of that relative to which he gives an account of the genus') is not easy to understand: the Greek syntax is complex and the translation reproduces its complexity. The expression 'a particular case' (*ti*) indicates (not an individual member of a genus, but) a subordinate species. What is the rule that Aristotle wants to establish? Suppose that *S* is a species of *G* and the interlocutor has given an account of *G* as relative to *K*. The dialectician must examine whether the interlocutor has given an account of *S* as relative to a particular case of *K*. Then the claim at 147^{a}24–5 introduces a sort of ontological ground for asserting Aristotle's rule. It says: 'If belief is relative to believable, a particular belief is relative to a particular believable' (in this context, 'a particular belief' stands for a species of belief, e.g. true belief; 'believable' stands for what is believed, namely the object of belief). Aristotle's idea is that the nature of relatives could provide the motivation that lies behind this rule. His views on the ontological status of relatives can be found in the preceding chapter: in *Top.* VI.8, 146^{b}3–4, Aristotle says that 'The substance of each relative is in relation to something else since for each of the relatives to be was precisely the same as to be in a certain relation to something' (see commentary *ad loc.*). The claim about the nature of relatives introduced in chapter 8 differs from the one in the present context since it is expressed in a general way. Perhaps

Aristotle thought that there was no need to repeat the more general claim and that it was sufficient to offer a particular case.

The relations instantiated in the example at 147^{a}24–5 can be visualized by using a diagram.

Belief	Believable
A particular belief	A particular believable

Diagram II

The items in the left-hand column are the kinds to be defined. In the first line there is a genus, whereas in the second line there is a species that is subordinate to, and less generic than, the genus in the first line. Both kinds are relatives, and, as Aristotle claims, the definition of a relative must mention its correlative (see, e.g., *Topics* VI.8, 146^{a}36–146^{b}1). The items in the right-hand column are the kinds that are the correlatives of the kinds to be defined. In particular, every member of the right-hand column is the correlative of the member on the same line of the left-hand column.

At 147^{a}26–7, the rule is instantiated by a second example. The application of the rule follows the pattern illustrated above. Does Aristotle formulate a good rule that allows us to reconstruct a valid strategy to refute the interlocutor? The rule works well when it is used in the context of mathematical relations. But there is a problem when it is applied to mental states and their objects. For Aristotle assumes that two different mental states have two different objects and he suggests defining a mental state in relation to its object. This, however, is dubious: it cannot be ruled out that a mental state could be defined not by referring to its object, but by looking at the type of relation it has to its object. In this case, two mental states might have the same object but differ because they are *differently related* to it. For example, hope and fear might be taken to be different mental states that are differently related to the same object (one can hope that *p* and fear that *p*). Something analogous can be said with respect to knowledge and belief. When in *R.* V, 477D2–4 Plato says that 'What is set over the same thing and does the same I call the same power', he seems to commit himself to the view that two powers can be reciprocally distinct either because they are set over different things or because they do something different to their objects. It should be mentioned that there are notorious difficulties in the reconstruction of Plato's argument at this point, but the analysis of these difficulties cannot be dealt with here. Note that modern philosophical logic takes knowledge and belief to target objects of the same types, namely propositions.

147ª29–147ᵇ4: The commonplace discussed here is connected with the relation of opposition. It concerns the definitions of opposites of all types (see the Introduction to this chapter). At 147ª29–31, Aristotle briefly examines the relation between the definition of one member of the pair of opposites and the definition of the other member. Then, he offers an example that we can visualize as follows:

Double	Half
What exceeds by an equal amount	What is exceeded by an equal amount

Diagram III

The items in the first and second line of the left-hand column are (respectively) one opposite, which is a thing to be defined, and its supposedly successful definition. The items in the first and second line of the right-hand column are (respectively) the other opposite, which is another thing to be defined, and its granted definition. How does the dialectical strategy unfold? The correct account of double is 'what exceeds by an equal amount'; the granted definition of half is 'what is exceeded by an equal amount'. Since the granted definition of half, i.e. 'what is exceeded by an equal amount', is the opposite of the supposedly successful definition of double, i.e. 'what exceeds by an equal amount', the granted definition of half is successful. In more general terms, let A and B be opposites. One must check whether the granted account of B is opposite to the successful definition of A. If it is so, then the granted account of B is correct (or it is a good starting point for a complete definition of B). Two brief comments on this example must be made. First, the rule is applied to the case of relatives, in particular to what we call mathematical relations. It might well be the case that Aristotle chooses this example because it is simple, unproblematic, and rather easy to understand. Second, the example seems to be constructive as it starts with a supposedly successful definition of double and it concludes by showing that the granted definition of half is successful. This is a rare case of a constructive example in book VI of the *Topics*, which is mostly refutative. That said, this example can be used to devise a parallel but refutative strategy. If the interlocutor grants an account of half that is not opposed to the successful definition of double, then the granted account must be rejected.

At $147^a31-147^b4$, Aristotle tries to show how the rule concerning accounts of opposites, which was just applied to the case of relatives, can be adapted to examine accounts of contraries. The modified rule, which contains a new and more complex requirement, says that 'The contrary account of the contrary will be based on one combination of the contraries' (147^a32-3). In other words, the account that is contrary to the given account (e.g. productive of good) and is of the contrary (e.g. harmful) will be based on one combination of contraries (e.g. either productive of evil or destructive of good). Before analysing the details of the rule's formulation, let us look at Aristotle's example by using a diagram.

Beneficial	*Harmful*
What produces a good	What produces an evil or What destroys a good

Diagram IV

Every member of the right-hand column is the contrary of the member in the same line of the left-hand column. We need to understand how the modified rule is applied to the example. The aim is to establish whether 'what produces a good' expresses the correct account of beneficial. In order to do so, we need to consider the account of the contrary of beneficial, i.e. harmful. How is the account of harmful obtained? It is obtained by looking at the granted account of beneficial, i.e. 'what produces a good', and by replacing some items (one at a time) with its contrary. Clearly, if we want to form the contrary account, we must replace one item at a time. Let us begin by replacing 'a good' with its contrary, i.e. 'an evil'. The result is 'what produces an evil': this is one contrary account of harmful according to one combination of contraries.

Then, replace 'what produces' with its contrary, i.e. 'what destroys'. The result is 'what destroys a good': this is another contrary account of harmful according to another combination of contraries. Thus, we have obtained two accounts of harmful. If neither of them is the contrary of beneficial, then its originally granted account (i.e. 'what produces a good') will not be its successful definition. If we replace both contraries at the same time, the result will be (e.g.) 'harmful is what destroys an evil'. And this is not the contrary account of harmful. It must be noted that this example is at variance with the previous ones since the member of the second line on the left-hand column has two contraries. This difference is unexpected: when, at 147^{a}31–2, Aristotle says, '*likewise also* in the case of contraries', he seems to suggest that there is a close parallelism between the example concerning opposites and the one about contraries. Perhaps we should understand the adverb 'likewise' in a loose way as indicating that there is not too close a similarity between the two cases. This difference might induce us to think that the rule concerning contraries (i.e. 'The contrary account of the contrary will be based on one combination of the contraries', 147^{a}31–2) should not be regarded simply as a modification of the rule concerning opposites. Rather, it seems to be a new and different rule.

It is helpful to introduce a more general formulation of the specific rule concerning contraries. Let C and D be two contraries. Let *Def. (C)* be the proposed account of C. Let *Def.^{1}(D)* and *Def.^{2}(D)* be two accounts of D obtained from *Def. (C)* by replacing one of its components with its contrary. That is to say, when we try to establish the contrary of *Def. (C)*, we may choose one among different combinations of contraries. This is because, according to Aristotle's standard theory of definition, the defining expression mentions at least two items. Then, in order to establish whether *Def. (C)* is the correct account of C, we must look at the contraries of *Def. (C)*, namely *Def.^{1}(D)* and *Def.^{2}(D)*. If neither *Def.^{1}(D)* nor *Def.^{2}(D)* is the contrary of C, then *Def. (C)* will not be the correct account of C. It must be observed that here Aristotle uses the relation of contrariety in a loose and unusual way. Definitions are said to be contrary not only to definitions but also to the things to be defined. That is to say, *Def.^{1}(D)* and *Def.^{2}(D)* must be contrary both to *Def. (C)* and to C.

In some passages of the corpus, Aristotle seems to assume that every contrary has exactly one contrary (see, e.g., *Metaph.* X.4, 1055^{b}19–20 and 5, 1055ᵇ30; this view seems to be presupposed in the discussion in *Cael.* I.2, 269ᵃ9–10). But in other passages he allows a contrary to have more than one contrary (see, e.g., *Ph.* VIII.7, 261ᵇ15–16 and *Top.* II.7, 113ᵃ14–15). The text we are presently commenting on is in line with the passages in the latter group, and the example is close to that in *Top.* II.7, where Aristotle says: 'Clearly, then, from what has been said, the same thing has more than one contrary. For the doing of good to one's friends has as its contrary both the doing of good to the enemies and the doing of evil to the friends' (113ᵃ16–18). Aristotle's advice to the dialectician is that he must 'select therefore whichever of the two contraries is useful in attacking the thesis'.

147ᵇ4–25: In this portion of text, Aristotle distinguishes between (i) the case where one contrary is said *by privation* (*sterêsei*) of the other (147ᵇ4–17) and (ii) the case where neither contrary is said by privation of the other (147ᵇ17–25). In this context, the term 'privation' (*sterêsis*) is used in a general way as it does not refer to the technical concept of privation that enters into the relation between possession and privation.

Consider (i), namely the case where one contrary is said *by privation* (*sterêsei*) of the other (147ᵇ4–17). The example chosen to introduce the discussion concerns the pair of contraries equality (*isotês*) and inequality (*anisotês*). It is interesting to note how Aristotle explains why inequality is the contrary by privation of equality. At 147ᵇ6, he says that 'non-equal things (*ta mê isa*) are called unequal (*anisa*)': the concept of privation is here expounded by that of negation (the same example occurs also in *APr.* I.46, 51ᵇ25–8; more on this passage below). Thus, the contrary that is said by privation is expressed by a term with a negative particle prefixed.[2] What is Aristotle trying to suggest?

---

[2] In general, negative particles can be used in different ways within propositions. One typically distinguishes between (1) propositional negation (e.g. 'It is not the case that Socrates is pale' is the negation of 'Socrates is pale'), (2) predicate negation (e.g. 'Socrates is-not pale' is the negation of 'Socrates is pale'), (3) term negation (e.g. 'Socrates is non-pale' contains 'non-pale', which is the term negation of 'pale'). Modern logic acknowledges only propositional negation, namely type (1), which is, however, foreign to Aristotle's perspective. Aristotle acknowledges only predicate negation, namely type (2), and term negation, namely type (3). In his view, type (2) is the only case of negation.

It would be difficult to believe that he is trying to reduce contrariety to a genuine case of negation. For this goes against Aristotle's standard theory of contrariety, which is a type of opposition that is different from the opposition between affirmation and negation. Aristotle refers to the contrariety by privation. A case of contrariety by privation would be a case that is intermediate between genuine negation and genuine privation. Here is a tentative explanation of the theory that lies behind these distinctions. There is *genuine negation* in the case where, for every x, either x is A or x is-not A. For example, for every x, either x is odd or x is-not odd. It is clear that what is not a number will not be odd. There is *genuine privation* in the case where for every x of the suitable type k and at any suitable time t, either x has A or x is deprived of A. Consider, for example, an animal (i.e. something that is of the adequate type k): when the right moment arrives in its development, either the animal has sight (i.e. is sighted) or it is deprived of sight (i.e. is blind). It is obvious that a two-hours-old puppy will be neither sighted nor blind since the right moment of its development has not yet arrived. There is *contrariety by privation* in the case where for every x of the suitable type k, either x is A or x is not-A (where not-A is the contrary by privation of A). Consider something that is of the adequate type k, for example distribution of goods: the distribution of goods either is equal or is not-equal (i.e. is unequal), where unequal is the contrary by privation of equal. The logical relation between equal and not-equal is explained in *APr.* I.46, 51^{b}25–8: 'Nor are "to be not-equal (*to einai mê ison*)" and "not to be equal (*to mê einai ison*)" the same: for the one has a certain underlying subject, what is not-equal (*mê isôi*), and this is the unequal (*anison*); but the other has none. This is why not everything is either equal (*ison*) or unequal (*anison*), but everything is either equal (*ison*) or not equal (*ouk ison*)'. It must also be observed that there are passages in the corpus where it is said that, in the case of privation, it is crucial to add the condition that x must be of the suitable type k. For example, in *Metaph.* X.4, 1055^{b}8–11, Aristotle says: 'There is nothing in the middle of a contradiction, but there is in the case of some privations: for everything is either equal or not equal but not everything is either equal or unequal, but if it is, *it is only in the sphere of that which is receptive of the equal*'.

At 147^{b}7–9, Aristotle observes that there is an asymmetry between the ways in which each contrary must be defined. On the one hand, the contrary said by privation (e.g. inequality) must be defined through the other contrary (e.g. equality). On the other hand, the other contrary (e.g. equality) must *not* be defined through the contrary said by privation. Then Aristotle adds that if this asymmetry condition is not respected, each of the two contraries will be known through both (147^b8–9). The Greek formulation of the last clause is '*hekateron di' hekaterou gnôrizesthai*', and its literal translation is 'Each of the two is known through each of the two'. But the literal translation, although possible, sounds harsh in English. The majority of translators choose to render '*di' hekaterou*' as 'through the other', and the entire clause becomes 'Each of the two is known through the other'. However, this is not equivalent to the original Greek text since it expresses only part of its meaning. I am inclined to think that Aristotle has in mind something stronger than the idea that 'Each of the two is known through the other'. Consider the pair of contraries *a* and *b*, where *b* is said by privation of *a*. Then *b* is defined through *a*. Suppose that someone makes the mistake of defining *a* as the privation of *b*, in other words he does not respect the asymmetry condition. Let us first show that *a* is known through both *a* and *b*:

(1) *a* is defined (by mistake) through *b*.
(2) *b* is defined (correctly) as the privation of *a*.
(3) Hence (by substituting *b* with its definition), *a* is defined through *a*.
(4) Thus, *a* is defined through *b* and through *a*.
(5) Since to know *a* is to give the definition of *a*, *a* is known both through *a* and through *b*; in other words, one contrary is known through both.

Let us then show that *b* is also known through both *a* and *b*:

(1) *b* is defined (correctly) through *a*.
(2) *a* is defined (by mistake) as the privation of *b*.
(3) Hence (by substituting *a* with its definition), *b* is defined through *b*.
(4) Thus, *b* is defined through *a* and through *b*.
(5) Since to know *b* is to give the definition of *b*, *b* is known both through *a* and through *b*; in other words, the other contrary also is known through both.

In conclusion, each of the two contraries is known through both (147^b8–9).

Although it is evident that knowing each contrary through both is an unwelcome consequence that stems from the failure to respect the asymmetry condition, in this text Aristotle does not explain why it is so. There are (at least) three possible options. First, Aristotle might assume that the unwelcome consequence (i.e. knowing each contrary through both) leads to a circular definition. He might then assume that the problems concerning circular definitions are sufficiently intuitive and need not be made explicit. But if this is the case, then it is not clear why Aristotle immediately adds as a different point that 'The person who gives a definition in this way necessarily uses the very thing that is being defined' (147^b12–13). For this does not seem to be a different point, and the mistake of using the thing that is being defined appears to be the same as that of using a circular definition. Given that the first option meets some problems, we must find an alternative.

Second option. Aristotle might think that the unwelcome consequence (i.e. knowing each contrary through both) leads to an infinite regress. Consider the situation where a is known both through a and through b, and, similarly, b is known both through a and through b. Suppose that we want to attain knowledge of a. Since a is known both through a and through b, before reaching knowledge of a we must attain knowledge of b. Then, since b is known both through a and through b, before reaching knowledge of b we must attain knowledge of a. We are, therefore, back to the situation where we were at the beginning and the process will go on *ad infinitum*. The general principle underlying this reconstruction is that if x is known through y, then knowledge of x can be attained only by attaining knowledge of y. In other words, knowledge must be based on knowledge. This principle is at work (for example) in an argument proposed by Plato in his *Theaetetus*: it is an assumption of the so-called dream theorist in Socrates' dream as it is presented towards the end of the *Theaetetus* at 201D8–204E. For a discussion of the principle that knowledge must be based on knowledge, in a Platonic context, see Fine 1979.

Third option. Aristotle might be concerned with the problem of definitional priority, whereby what is mentioned in the account's defining part must be epistemologically prior to (i.e. more familiar than) what is to be defined. In this case, he might assume that we are acquainted with one of the fundamental requirements of definitions in the *Topics*. This requirement is explicitly stated in *Top*. VI.4, 141^{a}27–32: 'The definition is given for the sake of one's becoming familiar with what is said, and *we become familiar not on the basis of just any things but on the basis of things that are prior and more familiar, as in demonstration*' (see commentary *ad loc.*). In this case, knowing each contrary through both, and hence defining each contrary through both, will lead to the impossible result that the thing to be defined is more familiar than itself. When the condition of definitional priority is not respected, the proposed account is unsuccessful.

The second and the third option outlined above seem equally attractive. Perhaps there is a slight preference for the third since it is formulated using interpretative elements that are explicitly found in the *Topics*.

At 147^{b}12–17, Aristotle introduces a second unwelcome consequence that stems from the failure to respect the asymmetry condition. This second unwelcome consequence consists in using 'the very thing that is being defined', that is to say, it consists in obtaining circular definitions. Aristotle briefly deals with this case also in *Top*. VI.4, 142^{a}34–142^{b}2 ('Another way of failing to define is if he has used the thing that is being defined: it escapes notice when the name he uses is not the same as that of what has being defined, for example, if he has defined the sun as the star that appears by day. For the person who uses day uses sun'). In chapter 4, the problem of circular definition is described as a general one, whereas in chapter 9 it concerns more specifically definitions of contraries. The strategy to detect or to prove the presence of circular definitions is the same in all cases: it consists in replacing the name with the definition (compare 147^{b}13–14 with 142^{b}2–6). There are instances where the presence of circularity is obvious, for example in the definition of equality as 'the contrary of privation of equality' (147^{b}15–16). These are easy cases and, in order to refute the interlocutor, the dialectician need not be highly trained in substitutions of linguistic expressions. But there are other instances where the circularity is not evident. Then, Aristotle's suggested strategy requires both good knowledge of the language and the ability to substitute linguistic expressions. The person who is able to discover the hidden circularity in the definition will probably be an expert dialectician.

Consider now (ii), namely the case where *neither* contrary is said *by privation*. Aristotle alerts us to the fact that it is possible to obtain circular definitions in this case too. The argument at 147^{b}17–21 is difficult to unfold and assess. The example illustrating type (ii) of contrariety employs the pair whose members are good and evil (see also *Cat.* 10, 11^{b}35–7). The reconstruction of the argument must start from the analysis of the two occurrences of 'in the same way' (*homoiôs*) at 147^{b}18 and 20. When at 147^{b}18 Aristotle says that 'The account has been given *in the same way*', he means that the proposed definitions of contraries of type (ii) are formulated *in the same way* as the proposed definitions of contraries of type (i). That is to say, one of the two definitions is expressed by using a phrase like 'the contrary (*sc.* by privation) of …'—the other, of course, will not. When at 147^{b}20 Aristotle says that 'The account of contraries of this sort must be given *in the same way*', he indicates that in the case of contrariety of type (ii) *both* contraries are defined *in the same way*. He probably means that with contraries of type (ii) it is not the case that one contrary is definitionally prior to the other (more on this below). How does Aristotle's argument unfold? Suppose that s and t are contraries such that neither is said by privation of the other. Then:

(1) The account of s is 's is the contrary of t'.
(2) The account of s and the account of t must be given *in the same way*.
(3) Therefore, the account of t is 't is the contrary of s'.
(4) The account of s is 's is the contrary of the contrary of s'.
(5) Hence, the expression used to refer to the thing to be defined occurs in the defining part.

Sentences (1) and (2) are assumptions. Sentence (3) follows from (1) and (2). Sentence (4) follows from (1) and (3) by substituting a name with its account. Sentence (5) is the conclusion and is an immediate consequence of (4). But this conclusion is perplexing: it indicates that we obtain a circular definition, and, as we know, a circular definition (at least in this context) is not successful. What is the step that allows us to derive (5)? The crucial and problematic step leading to (5) is (1). So, if we want to avoid conclusion (5), we need to reject premise (1).

The logic of the argument is clear. But, as often happens with *reductio* arguments, we only learn that a certain premise is false without an explanation of why it is so. What is wrong with premise (1)? We can address this question by reflecting on some differences between the two types of contraries. In the case of contraries of type (i), it is possible to define the privative contrary through the other one (let us call it the 'positive' contrary): see 147^{b}7–9, above. The positive contrary is definitionally prior since it must be mentioned in the definition of its privation. In the case of contraries of type (ii), neither seems to be in a privileged position and to deserve more being mentioned in the definition of the other. In this sense, their accounts must be given in the same way, as premise (2) says. In other words, neither contrary is definitionally prior. Hence, if it were correct to define *s* as the contrary of *t*, as premise (1) says, then it would also be correct to define *t* as the contrary of *s*, as premise (3) says. It follows that contraries of type (ii) cannot be defined in the same way as those of type (i). In proposing the definition of one contrary of type (ii), we cannot mention the other contrary. For example, evil cannot be defined as the contrary of good. If there is a successful definition of evil, it must not mention the contrary of evil, i.e. good. To sum up, if the interlocutor thinks that contraries of type (i) and contraries of type (ii) can be defined in the same way, then he will make the mistake of proposing a circular definition.

147^{b}26–148^{a}2: Having discussed the problems concerning proposed definitions of pairs of contraries, Aristotle focuses on the things said by privation and examines their accounts. Two main mistakes can occur in these accounts. The first is discussed at 147^{b}26–8 and the second is introduced at 147^{b}28–9 (for the translation of *hexis*, see 'The value of *hexis*' in 'Terminological Clarifications').

The first mistake is the easiest to understand and to detect. It consists in the failure to mention in the definition *that of which* the thing to be defined is a privation. The expression '*that of which*' is generic and Aristotle distinguishes three cases. They are indicated by (a) *tês hexeôs* ('of the possession'), (b) *tou enantiou* ('of the contrary'), and (c) *hotououn estin hê sterêsis* ('whatever the privation is of') (147^{b}27–8). More precisely, in case (a), '*that of which*' refers to the possession (*hexis*) in the situation where the thing to be defined expresses a privation. Here 'privation' is the technical term indicating that which enters in the specific relation between privation and possession. For example, '*that of which*' could refer to sight in the case of the pair sight and blindness. In case (b), '*that of which*' indicates the contrary (*enantion*) of what is said by privation (see 147^{b}4–17, above). For example, it indicates equality when we deal with the pair of contraries equality and inequality. In case (c), '*that of which*' refers to anything whatsoever which the thing to be defined is a privation of; that is to say, it refers to another form of privation that is not covered by cases (a) and (b), but we are not told what it is.

The second mistake is more difficult to explain. In Aristotle's words, it consists in the failure to mention 'that in which *it* is by nature, either at all or the first thing in which *it* is by nature' (147^{b}28–9). This formulation is obscure: it is not clear what the referent of the two occurrences of '*it*' is. The context suggests that, in both cases, the pronoun 'it' indicates the thing to be defined, i.e. what is said by privation. Then Aristotle observes that there are two further specifications that should not fail to be mentioned in the definition. If one of them is not expressed, the proposed definition cannot be accepted. The first is that in the defining part we ought to find *that in which* the thing to be defined is by nature, but nothing at all is mentioned. Here it is highly likely that the adverb 'at all' (*haplôs*) modifies the verb (*mê*) *prosethêken*, literally 'he does (not) add at all'. In other words, this is the case where one or more items in the definition are by nature in something, but this is not expressed at all (e.g. when the interlocutor says that ignorance is privation of knowledge, but he fails to mention any of the things in which ignorance and knowledge are by nature). The second specification is that the definition must mention *the first thing in which* what is to be defined is by nature. This is the case where the thing to be defined is by nature in a number of things and its definition must mention the first of them (i.e. the first in the order of nature; see the example at 147^{b}31–4, below).

At 147^{b}29–34, three examples illustrate the mistakes described in the first part of this portion of text. In particular, lines 147^{b}29–30 elucidate the first mistake. Lines 147^{b}30–1 refer to the first specification of the second mistake. Lines 147^{b}31–4 shed light on the second specification of the second mistake. Let us try to have a better grasp of the latter and more complex case (i.e. failing to mention in the definition *the first thing in which* the thing to be defined is by nature). Following Aristotle's suggestion, suppose that the pair ignorance and knowledge are related as privation and possession (i.e. ignorance is privation of knowledge). If in his attempted definition of ignorance the interlocutor says that ignorance is privation of knowledge but does not add *the first thing in which* ignorance is by nature, he falls into the second mistake. At first sight, it might seem perplexing to claim that there is a first thing in which not only knowledge but also ignorance (a privation) is by nature. This, however, is Aristotle's view in *Cat.* 10, 12^{a}26–8: 'Each of them (*sc.* privation and possession) is spoken of in connection to whatever the possession occurs in by nature'. One must remember that for Aristotle privations in the technical sense are not simply absence of a characteristic but amount to something more 'positive'. Although it is true to speak of ignorance as being *by nature* in connection to a human being or to a soul, these are not *the first thing* in which ignorance is by nature. For, according to Aristotle's general theory of the soul, the first thing in which ignorance is by nature is the rational part of the soul (for Aristotle's definition of the soul see *De An.* II.1; for the distinction between rational and non-rational part see, e.g., *EN* I.13 and VI.1–2). There is, however, a problem with this example that employs the concept of ignorance and knowledge. Aristotle seems to take it for granted that ignorance and knowledge are related as privation and possession (see especially 147^{b}29–30). But at the very end of this chapter, Aristotle concludes that 'ignorance is *not* said by privation of knowledge' (148^{a}9). Is Aristotle flatly contradicting himself? There are (at least) two ways to reconstruct Aristotle's line of thought that do not lead to a flat contradiction. According to Waitz's interpretative line (Waitz 1846, vol. 2, p. 501), Aristotle is implicitly referring to the distinction in *APo.* I 16, 79^{b}23–4 between 'ignorance in virtue of negation (*kat'apophasin*)' and 'ignorance in virtue of a disposition (*kata diathesin*)'. Ignorance in virtue of negation can be defined in terms of privation, whereas it is wrong to define ignorance in virtue of a disposition in terms of privation. When Aristotle introduces ignorance at 147^{b}29–30, he has in mind 'ignorance in virtue of negation (*kat'apophasin*)', which is to be defined in terms of privation. At the later stage of the argument, Aristotle is justified in saying that ignorance is not said by privation of knowledge (148^{a}9) since in this case he has in mind 'ignorance in virtue of a disposition (*kata diathesin*)', which cannot be defined in terms of privation. As we shall see later, there are reasons to resist the suggestion that, in this chapter of the *Topics*, Aristotle has in mind the distinction between the two types of ignorance. We can then turn to an alternative explanation that does not saddle Aristotle with the charge of being inconsistent. One might think that Aristotle is not proposing a correct account but is simply offering lines of attack to criticize unsuccessful definitions. In this instance, the important point is to illustrate the clause '*the first thing in which* it (*sc.* the thing to be defined) is by nature'. Thus, it does not really matter whether or not it is true that ignorance is privation of knowledge. The important point is that the example serves the purpose of illustrating well the mistake so that the dialectician or any listener will be able to grasp the strategy to be applied in these cases. Moreover, if it is correct to say that there is a Platonic target in Aristotle's subsequent criticism that ignorance is privation of knowledge (see Cherniss 1962, pp. 25–6), then the Academics, who constituted a large part of Aristotle's audience, would understand well the examples at 147^b29–34.

At 147^b28, *homoiôs* means 'similarly to what comes immediately before', and the example at 147^b28–148^a2 illustrates the last of the cases. Note that this is the standard case of privation and possession that we find in, e.g., *Cat.* 10, 12^a26–7. This last example does not seem to add anything substantial to what has already been said.

148^a3–9: In the last portion of this chapter, Aristotle draws the attention to proposed accounts that are wrongly framed in terms of privation. More precisely, it concerns the mistake of giving an account in terms of privation when the thing to be defined is not said by privation (148^a3–4). This passage presents textual and exegetical difficulties: see 'Notes on the Text' *ad loc.*, where the reasons for the emendation of *mê* ('not', 148^a5) are discussed.

The choice between maintaining or deleting *mê* ('not') leads to two main interpretative options of the example at 148^a4–6. Option (A): we maintain the presence of the negative particle *mê*. The resulting translation is: 'a mistake of this sort would seem to occur in the case of those who do *not* say ignorance in virtue of a negation'. According to a suggestion put forward in Waitz 1846, vol 2, p. 503 (followed by Tricot 1950 and Cherniss 1962, p. 26), Aristotle here refers to the distinction between two types of ignorance, namely ignorance in virtue of a negation (*kat'apophasin*) and ignorance in virtue of a disposition (*kata diathesin*). The first type of ignorance is explicitly mentioned at 148ª5, whereas the second remains implicit. This interpretative line is based on the fact that this distinction is present in *APo.* I.16, 79ᵇ23–4: 'Ignorance—what is called ignorance not in virtue of a negation (*kat'apophasin*) but in virtue of a disposition (*kata diathesin*)—is an error coming about through deduction' (translated by Barnes 1993; in his commentary, p. 151, Barnes follows Waitz's reading, whereby this distinction is at work in *Top.*, VI.9, 148ª3–9). According to this reconstruction, Aristotle would be saying that those whose account is *not* concerned with ignorance in virtue of a negation, i.e. those whose account is concerned with ignorance in virtue of a disposition, make the mistake described at 148ª3–4 (i.e. 'Although it [*sc.* the thing to be defined] is not said by privation, he has defined it by means of privation'). For ignorance in virtue of negation can be defined in terms of privation, whereas it is wrong to define in terms of privation ignorance in virtue of a disposition. This interpretation has a main advantage that makes it attractive: it gives a good sense to the text as it is transmitted by the majority of manuscripts. But it presupposes that the reader is already familiar with this distinction so that he will immediately understand the outlined strategy. Unfortunately, the distinction is not explicitly drawn in these lines and, to the best of my knowledge, is not mentioned in any passage of the *Topics*.

Option (B): we accept Brunschwig's emendation and delete the negative particle *mê* ('not'). The resulting translation is: 'A mistake of this sort would seem to occur in the case of those who say ignorance by negation'. Note that here the expression *kat'apophasin* ('by negation') does not function as an adjective attached to *agnoia* ('ignorance'), thereby introducing a special type of ignorance (i.e. ignorance in virtue of a negation). Rather, *kat'apophasin* ('by negation') has the role of an adverb that modifies the verbal form *tois legousin* ('to those who say') and therefore it introduces an incorrect way of defining ignorance.

What is the interpretation to be preferred? There are a number of reasons to prefer option (B). First, it has the advantage that it reads the expression *tois kat'apophasin tên agnoian legousin* ('to those who say ignorance *by negation*') in a way that is parallel to other similar expressions in this chapter. In particular, consider the two following clauses: (a) 'In giving an account of what is said *by privation*' (*to kata sterêsin legomenon apodidous*; 147ᵇ26) and (b) 'Although it is not said *by privation*' (*mê legomenou kata sterêsin*; 148ᵃ3). In both instances, 'by privation' modifies the verbal forms derived from 'say'(*legô*) and does not qualify a noun as suggested in option (A). Second, option (B) does not require that the reader (or the dialectician who is being trained by Aristotle) be acquainted with the technical distinction between the two types of ignorance outlined in the *Analytics*. Third, if the distinction between the two types of ignorance were presupposed in this passage, then there would be no need to add the argument at 148ᵃ6–9 proving that it is a mistake to define ignorance *tout court* in privative terms; for the reader would already know it. It is interesting to give a closer look to this last argument in chapter 9. It is based on the analysis of the linguistic use of the verb *agnoein* ('to be ignorant'). Aristotle observes that *agnoein* is employed to indicate the mental state of those who are in error, but it is not appropriately used in all cases of those who do not possess knowledge; for instance, inanimate things and children, who do not possess knowledge, are not said to be ignorant. This leads to the conclusion that we cannot define ignorance in privative terms. As a final remark, it must be noted that, at 148ᵃ8–9, the expression *kata sterêsin* ('by privation') is used in an adverbial form modifying *legetai* (it is said): this further confirms the choice of adopting option (B).

CHAPTER 10

Introduction: Three different subjects are addressed in this chapter. (1) 148^{a}10–13 discusses briefly a commonplace concerning grammatical inflections or, as I shall call them, modifications. (2) 148^{a}14–22 focuses the attention on whether the proposed definition fits a Platonic Idea. (3) 148^{a}23–148^{b}22 analyses commonplaces against proposed accounts of homonyms. This analysis occupies the longest stretch of text in this chapter. These lines raise several questions concerning Aristotle's dialectical method and the relation between dialectic and eristic. At first sight, chapter 10 seems to lack unity since there is no thematic continuity between the discussions of the first and the second commonplace. The first concerns grammatical modifications and the second deals with some difficulties arising from the Platonic theory of Ideas in a definitional context. It is possible to solve the problem of the unity if we think that the division between chapter 9 and chapter 10, as we find it in the editions, is not appropriate. The first commonplace of chapter 10 is linked to the discussion in the first part of chapter 9 (see especially 147^{a}21–2). More on this below, in the discussion of the first commonplace.

148^{a}10–13: *Ptôseis* (lit. 'cases'; 148^{a}11) are grammatical modifications of nouns or adjectives. Grammatical modifications are discussed also in *Top.* I.15, 106^{b}29–107^{a}2 and II.9, 114^{a}26–36. In my translation, I render *ptôseis* as 'modifications' because, properly speaking, in this context Aristotle does not discuss what we call 'grammatical cases', rather he focuses on certain types of modifications (see also the Introduction to chapter 9). At 148^{a}11–13, the examples concern the adjectives *ôphelimon* ('beneficial') and *poiêtikon* ('productive') as well as their modifications, namely *ôphelimôs* ('beneficially'), *poiêtikôs* ('productively'), *ôphelêkos* ('he who has been beneficial'), and *pepoiêkos* ('he who has been productive'). Note that, although the translation of *ôphelimôs* and *poiêtikôs* with 'beneficially' and 'productively' is not very elegant, it has the advantage that it reproduces in English the etymological link between the adjectives and the adverbs. This link plays an important role in the refutative strategy. As for *ôphelêkos* and *pepoiêkos* (perfect active participles), they must be translated with a periphrasis and not with a single term as we find in the Greek formulation: this will enable us to express fully the meaning of the clause. For the addition of <is defined as> (148^a11) and <will be defined as> ($148^a12, 13$), see 'The translation of *hoion ei*' in 'Terminological Clarifications'. When at 148^a10-11 Aristotle invites the dialectician to examine whether similar modifications in the account correspond to similar modifications in the name, he hints at the refutative strategy, but he does not develop it. What is, then, this suggested strategy? Consider two rules for commonplaces introduced in *Top.* II.9. According to the first rule, 'If any element whatsoever within the same coordinate series (*sustoichian*) has been shown to be good or praiseworthy, the remainders are also shown to be so' ($114^a38-114^b1$). For example, if you are examining whether being praiseworthy belongs to just things, you can see whether being praiseworthy belongs also to justice: since just things are coordinate (*sustoicha*) with justice, being praiseworthy must belong to both. But, in this rule, the procedure to adopt in the cases of grammatical modifications is not shown. The second rule deals exactly with this situation. It says that '*Justly* will be also called *praiseworthily* derived from the same modification from *praiseworthy* as *justly* is from *justice*' (114^b2-5). Suppose it was established that *beneficial* is *productive* of health. Then *beneficially* will be not *productive* of health, but *productively* of health. This is because *productive* must undergo the same grammatical transformation as *beneficial*. How is the rule to be applied in the refutation of a definition? Aristotle puts forward a test that the dialectician ought to apply to a proposed definition. Suppose that the interlocutor grants that beneficial is productive of health. Then the dialectician must check the grammatical modifications: it must be the case that beneficially is productively of health, that he who has been beneficial is he who has produced health, etc. If any of the derived definitions of the modifications is unsuccessful, the original definition cannot be accepted. It must be observed that in *Top.* II.9 the commonplace concerning coordinates and that regarding grammatical modifications are examined one after the other. In *Top.* VI, however, the order of the arguments is different: the commonplace regarding coordinates is developed at the beginning of chapter 9, whereas the discussion about grammatical modifications is found at the beginning of chapter 10. It occupies a few lines and then a totally different commonplace is introduced. One might have the impression that the passage concerning grammatical modifications is misplaced, but there is no textual evidence to prove this. Alternatively, one might think that Aristotle was somewhat inattentive in his ordering of the commonplaces. A further possibility consists in assuming that the commonplace concerning grammatical modifications belonged to the end of chapter 9: Aristotle might have forgotten to mention it after the discussion of coordinates at the beginning of the chapter and then mentioned it later. The division in chapters chosen by the editors might be responsible for inappropriately making it the beginning of chapter 10.

148^{a}14–22: The second commonplace of chapter 10 is directed against Platonic Ideas. Why are Platonic Ideas discussed immediately after grammatical modifications? The passage in *Top.* VII.4, 154^{a}12–20, which according to the majority of commentators refers to the text under discussion, might help to shed some light on this. Aristotle begins by saying that commonplaces based on coordinates and grammatical modifications are the most useful in the greatest number of occasions. He then goes on to consider the remaining commonplaces and selects among them the ones that are more effective. In particular, he says: 'Look attentively at the individual, and, in the case of the species, examine whether the account applies, since the species is synonymous. This sort of inquiry is helpful against those who posit that there are Ideas' (154^{a}15–20). For our present discussion, it suffices to observe that the order of the commonplaces (according to their effectiveness) outlined in *Top.* VII.4, 154^{a}12–20 corresponds to the organization of the commonplaces in the first part of *Top.* VI.10 (or, according to the division suggested above between chapters 9 and 10, it corresponds to the organization of the commonplaces at the end of chapter 9 and at the beginning of chapter 10). In particular, the commonplace at 148^{a}10–13 concerns grammatical modifications and it coincides with one of 'the most useful in the greatest number of occasions' (154^{a}12–13). Then, the commonplace at 148^{a}14–22 relates to the difficulties raised by Platonic Ideas in a definitional context and invites the dialectician to examine whether the definition of the species fits the species *qua* Ideas. This has a correspondence with the commonplace introduced in *Top.* VII.4, 154ª17–18 (for the details of the arguments in *Top.* VII.4, 154ª12–20 see Brunschwig 2007, p. 97, n. 1). It is interesting to note that the passage in VI.10 under discussion explains Aristotle's cryptic claim that 'this sort of inquiry is helpful against those who posit that there are Ideas' (VII.4, 154ª18–19).

The discussion of the commonplace in 148ª14–22 has two main parts. In the first (148ª14–18), a particular example is offered. In the second (148ª18–22), a more general case is introduced. In these portions of text, Aristotle explores a refutative strategy that aims at showing some difficulties involved in the attempt to define Platonic Ideas. Other arguments concerning the problems raised by Ideas in a definitional context can be found in *Top.* VI.6, 143ᵇ11–32, and VI.8, 146ᵇ36–147ª11 (see commentary *ad loc.*).

The portion of text at 148ª14–18 is analysed by several commentators who offer different interpretations of Aristotle's argument (see, in particular, Cherniss 1962, pp. 2–5; Düring 1968, p. 216; Owen 1968b, pp. 112, nn. 2 and 116–18; De Vogel 1968, p. 94; Brunschwig 2007, p. 73, n. 3). Aristotle's strategy consists in seeing whether some characteristics included in the definition apply to the corresponding Idea. The reason why they are included in the definition is that they hold of the individuals under the kind to be defined and contribute to distinguishing them from anything else. Aristotle claims that some of the characteristics included in the definition *do not* apply to the corresponding Idea. He considers the property of being mortal, which is included 'in the definition of animals' (148ª16), i.e. in the definition of several animal species. This property, however, cannot hold of the Idea of human or of any animal species: Ideas are immortal and eternal (148ª15–18). It is easy to see that, in his argument, Aristotle attributes to his Platonic interlocutor a naïve stance on the sort of predicates that could hold of Ideas. If the interlocutor were able to draw some distinctions between different forms of predications, he could resist Aristotle's attack and the suggested strategy would not work. For example, as in other similar cases (*Top.* VI.6, 143ᵇ11–32, and VI.8, 146ᵇ36–147ª11), if an interlocutor were to introduce a conceptual tool that points to the distinction between definitional and ordinary predication, then he would be able to avoid the unwelcome consequence of the objection. (The details of this distinction are discussed in the commentary on *Top.* VI.6, 143^{b}11–32, and on *Top.* VI.8, 146^{b}36–147^{a}11.) If we ask whether the Idea of human is mortal, the appropriate answer is the following: in the case of ordinary predication, the Idea of human *is not mortal*. In the case of definitional predication, the Idea of human *is mortal* because the predicate (i.e. 'mortal') conveys the nature of the characteristic the Idea imparts on the individuals that partake of it. Is Aristotle justified in attributing to his Platonic interlocutor an unrefined theory of predication? In this context, there is no evidence for saying whether the interlocutor is aware of this distinction. But in another passage of the *Topics*, Aristotle credits his Platonic opponent with a distinction that points to a more sophisticated theory of predication. In *Top.* V.7, 137^{b}3–8, Aristotle draws a distinction between properties holding of Ideas in so far as they are Ideas and properties holding to Ideas in so far as they are the bearers of properties they impart to the individuals that partake of them ('In as much as motionless does not belong to human-itself *qua* human, but *qua* Idea, it could not be a property of humans to be motionless'; 137^{b}6–8). Is Aristotle adopting different and irreconcilable strategies? There is a way to rescue him from this charge. Aristotle's choice of a specific line of attack is probably influenced by the type of interlocutor he is confronting. For example, if he is suggesting a strategy to refute an interlocutor who adopts a naïve Platonic standpoint, he will not need to use a sophisticated theory of predication. It would not be appropriate to silence the interlocutor with philosophical distinctions that are difficult for him to follow. But in other cases, the interlocutor might be a more refined Platonist (for example, he could have read Plato's *Sophist* and hence he could be acquainted with more complex philosophical distinctions). In these circumstances, Aristotle will be perfectly justified if he employs subtler conceptual tools (see Schiaparelli 2017).

At 148^{a}15–16, Aristotle says that 'Plato defines by adding "mortal" to the definition of animals'. But there is no passage in Plato's writings where he professes the view that the property of being mortal must be included in the definitions of animal species. Perhaps a similar definition was discussed in the Academy and was part of the oral tradition. There are two possible readings of lines 148^{a}15–16. According to the first, the verbal form *prosaptôn* ('adding') refers to Plato, who is the subject of the immediately preceding clause. That is to say, the person who adds 'mortal' to the definitions of animal species is Plato (this is the reading adopted in my translation). According to the second reading, the verbal form *prosaptôn* does not refer to Plato but to an interlocutor who introduces the particular example of including 'mortal' in the definitions of animals. In other words, the clause 'When Plato defines' describes a general Platonic procedure, whereas the sentence 'He who adds "mortal" to the definition of animals' contains an example that is not necessarily Platonic. This reading has the advantage that it implies that definitions containing 'mortals' may not belong to Plato and may be brought in by an interlocutor. This is in line with the fact that there is no passage providing evidence in support of the idea that Plato encouraged and accepted the formulation of animal species' definitions containing 'mortal'. This second reading, however, is grammatically more difficult, and, for this reason, I am not inclined to favour it. It is interesting to note that in *Sph.* 246E5–6, the Visitor and Theaetetus attribute this position to the Giants: 'VISITOR: "... do they say that anything is a mortal animal?" THEAETETUS: "Of course they do"'.

At 148ª18–22, Aristotle extends his criticism of Platonic Ideas to the more general situation where the predicates mentioned in the definitions are those indicating the power of affecting something (*poiêtikon*) and the power of being affected by something (*pathêtikon*). Even in these cases, according to Aristotle's refutative line, there would be a discrepancy between the characteristics of the individuals falling under the species to be defined and the properties holding of Ideas. Aristotle credits his Platonic interlocutor with the view that Ideas can have neither the power of affecting something nor that of being affected by something since Ideas are unchangeable. Hence, the interlocutor, who is trying to define Ideas, would face serious difficulties. The position attributed to the Platonic interlocutor is reminiscent of a view discussed in *Sph.* 248A4–E8. The Visitor and Theaetetus propose to the Giants and to the Friends of the Forms the characterization of being whereby 'To be is either to have the power of affecting something or the power of being affected by something' (248C7–8). This characterization is accepted by the Giants. It is not clear, however, whether it is accepted by the Friends of the Forms. On this point, there is a vast debate among commentators: see, e.g., Jowett 1892, iv, 380; Ross 1951, pp. 110–11; Moravcsik 1962, pp. 39–40; McCabe 1994, p. 204; Crivelli 2012, pp. 88–90. For our purposes, it suffices to observe that Aristotle's text seems to favour a possible interpretation of the *Sophist*: Plato is saying that knowledge, soul, intellect and movement are fully real. Ideas too are fully real, but they are not in movement, i.e. they do not change, and so they do not have the power of affecting something or being affected by something.

Let us assess Aristotle's attitude towards his Platonic interlocutor and the means he employs to refute him. There are two alternatives. (1) One might think that the argument put forward in this text is not good as it purposively deceives the opponent. This is, for example, Cherniss's interpretative line (Cherniss 1962, pp. 3–5): he accuses Aristotle of offering eristic and not dialectical arguments in his criticisms against Plato's theory of Ideas. This interpretative line is known as the 'reductive thesis' and says that, in this as well as in other occasions, dialectic is reduced to mere eristic (the expression 'reductive thesis' was introduced by Owen in his 1968b, p. 104). (2) One might, rather, think that dialectic does not collapse into eristic: they remain two different ways of interacting with your opponent. On the one hand, dialectic is a method of inquiry that does not admit of sophistic trickery. On the other hand, eristic explicitly envisages the use of specious reasoning with the only goal of gaining victory in the debate. This is an important distinction at a theoretical level: it allows Aristotle to formulate rules of reasoning that are proper to each method. It is possible to distinguish two sub-cases of this second alternative. (2.1) The distinction between dialectic and eristic remains, but we wonder whether it is possible to respect it fully in the practice of dialectic. It could happen that when Aristotle passes from a theoretical to a practical level and suggests particular lines of attack, he partly lowers the bar of using methods of reasoning that belong to eristic (Owen 1968[a], pp. 106–7). In other words, it may happen that in the dialectical exchange there are practical constraints that lead the dialectician to press his points in an 'unorthodox' way. In this case, there might be a gap between the rules prescribed by the method and their practical application to certain cases. This is a feature that seems to emerge from the practice of dialectic as it is described in *Topics* book VIII (see Brunschwig 2007, p. 43, n. 2, and p. 103, n. 5). Should we conclude that Aristotle behaves like a sophist? This is not necessarily the case. For example, he might be aware of the fact that his interlocutor is able to draw subtle philosophical distinctions. Still, he aims at setting particularly provocative questions. In this way, he is encouraging his interlocutor to examine thoroughly his tacit assumptions and reformulate them more clearly. So, the interlocutor will be led to refine even more his conceptual tools. The aim of the dialectical exchange is not, on this view, victory at all costs but might include a refinement of some of the interlocutor's theses. The refinement thus obtained will bring an important improvement in the interlocutor's philosophical view. (2.2) One might claim that there is no deceiving manoeuvre in Aristotle's argument. The target of his criticism is not a refined theory of Ideas that Plato upheld. Rather, Aristotle is objecting to a certain version of this theory: this could well be an unsophisticated form where, for example, there is no distinction between different types of predicates. This unsophisticated version was probably accepted by some members of the Academy. In this case, Aristotle would start his discussion from the premises that *they* accepted. He would then deduce paradoxical conclusions in order to show them that their theses are untenable. This is not eristic but standard dialectical practice. Which alternative should be favoured? Nowadays hardly anyone believes that (1) is a successful interpretative line, for it discredits completely Aristotle's dialectical strategies. Thus, (2.1) and (2.2) are definitely more promising. Perhaps (2.2) has the advantage that it takes into account the variety of theses discussed in the Academy.

For the textual problems at 148^{a}20–2, see 'Notes on the Text' *ad loc.*

148^{a}23–37: Aristotle begins here a long discussion of homonymy in definitions. This discussion, which is long and contains many intricate arguments, occupies the rest of chapter 10. It should be noted that homonymy in connection with definitions is considered also in *Top.* I.15, where Aristotle observes that the analysis of homonymy is helpful not merely in detecting general ambiguities but also in examining proposed definitions (see Smith 1997, pp. 92–9; Ward 2008, pp. 64–75). A further discussion of homonymy is carried out in *Top.* VI.2, 139^{b}19–31 (see commentary *ad loc.*). In the present discussion, Aristotle does not distinguish between homonyms which are a matter of chance (*apo tuchês*) and those which are not, as he does in *EN* I.6, 1096^{b}26–7. The general idea developed here in the second half of chapter 10 is the following: if the interlocutor grants an account that is common to all the things falling under a homonymous kind, then he makes a mistake. For things sharing a common account corresponding to a shared name are not homonyms but synonyms. Aristotle's remark is in line with his well-known description of synonymy and homonymy at the beginning of the *Categories*: 'When things have only the name in common and the definition of being which corresponds to the name is different, they are called homonymous' (1.1^{a}1–2); and 'When things have the name in common and the definition of being which corresponds to the name is the same, they are called synonymous' (1.1^{a}6–7). The concepts of synonymy and homonymy are name-relative in at least two respects. First, homonyms and synonyms are entities that fall under the same name; second, these entities are synonyms (or homonyms) just if they share (or fail to share) the same definition which corresponds to the name (*kata tounoma logos*, *Top.* VI.10, 148^{a}24–5, and *Cat.* 1.1^{a}4, 7)—in other words, the account picks out the way or sense in which the shared name applies to entities.

At 148^{a}25–6, Aristotle intends to sketch an argument to be used against the interlocutor who grants an account that is common to all the things said by homonymy. There is a difficulty in the translation of *homoiôs*. Its standard translation is 'in the same way', meaning 'in the same sense'. But at 148^{a}26, where Aristotle says *homoiôs epi pan to homônumon epharmottei*, the adverb *homoiôs* cannot mean 'in the same sense': a shared name *does not* apply in the same sense to its homonymous instances. One therefore needs an interpretation of *homoiôs* which is different from 'in the same sense' and gives Aristotle a good argument. One way of doing this is to take *homoiôs* as 'to the same extent'. One might doubt that *homoiôs* means 'to the same extent', but a parallel passage in *Top.* II.10, 115^{a}15–24 (especially lines 17–19) seems to display the same argument form as the clause under examination, and there *homoiôs* unequivocally means 'to the same extent'. According to my preferred interpretation, Aristotle's argument is based on the following general principle: (*E*) if a definition *x* applies *to the same extent* (*homoiôs*) to *a* as to *b*, and x does not apply to a, then it does not apply to b either. At 148ª26, the claim that the definition applies to everything to the same extent is introduced by *ei dê* ('if indeed'). It indicates that, in the dialectical exchange imagined here, the interlocutor is committed to this point.

At 148ª26-37, there is an example illustrating the mistake of granting an account that is common to the things said by homonymy. The example is complex: it concerns the (unsuccessful) definition of life proposed by Dionysius. A thorough study of the identity of Dionysius the Dialectician and of the philosophical school he belonged to can be found in Primavesi 1992.

At 148ª27-8, Aristotle attributes to Dionysius the definition of life (*zôê*) as 'a change natural to and present in a food-sustained kind' (*kinêsis genous threptou sumphutos parakolouthousa*). Let us call it D_L. The Greek formulation of the defining expression of life is convoluted and does not lend itself to being translated into stylistically good English. The general idea can be rephrased by saying that life consists in a process of change which is a fundamental feature of kinds which have the power of nutrition. Aristotle analyses D_L by making use of the principle (E) stated above (i.e. 'If a definition x applies *to the same extent* to a as to b, and x does not apply to a, then it does not apply to b either'; 148ª25-6). He observes that D_L applies *to the same extent* to the life of animals as to the life of plants. Here the expression 'to the same extent', which I have used to translate *homoiôs* at 148ª26, corresponds to *ouden mallon ê* (lit. 'no more than', 148ª28-9) (I shall come back later to the delicate question of the meaning of *ouden mallon ê*). But, Aristotle continues, the life of animals and that of plants are two different forms of life (*hetera ... hetera*, 148ª30-1); that is to say, they are homonyms. It follows that D_L does not apply at least to one of them. Hence, by virtue of (E), it applies to neither. To be more explicit, the argument may be spelled out as follows. To begin with, D_L does not apply to both animals and plants. Therefore, either it does not apply to animals or it does not apply to plants. Suppose it does not apply to animals: since it applies to animals and plants to the same extent, it follows, by (E), that it does not apply to plants either, so it applies neither to animals nor to plants. The case in which D_L does not apply to plants is to be treated similarly. This shows that D_L has to be rejected. It must be noted that the argument that refutes

Dionysius' definition of life is an example illustrating the general strategy sketched in the preceding lines (148ª23–6). For this reason, *ouden mallon ê* must have the same value (whatever it may be) as *homoiôs*.

In this text, Aristotle claims that life is a homonym since different forms of life belong to different living beings. He does not justify further his view and seems to assume that it would be easily accepted by any interlocutor. The motivations for this view can be found in the *De Anima*, where he says: 'Now this word (*sc. zôê*: 'life') is said in many ways and, provided any one alone of these is present in something, we say that it is alive' (II.2, 413ª22–3). Even though it is not possible to specify the details of Aristotle's psychological theory, the philosophical background of the *De Anima* allows us to say that different forms of life correspond to the different types of souls Aristotle individuates (413ª30–413ᵇ12). From the point of view of the refutation, it must be observed that the opponent could well refuse to accept the basic tenets of Aristotle's psychological theory. This shows that the argument is not totally exempt from criticism (see Shields 1999, pp. 177–9). In other words, an interlocutor holding a different conception of life will have the means to challenge some premises of Aristotle's argument.

At 148ª31–7, there is an interpretative difficulty. In the Greek text, there is no explicit grammatical subject for the expressions: '... has intentionally given' (*kata proairesin apodounai*, 148ª31–2), '... saw the homonymy' (*sunorônta tên homonumian*, 148ª34), '... wished to give the definition' (*boulomenon ton horismon apodounai*, 148ª34–5), '... has inadvertently given' (*lathein ... apodonta*, 148ª35–6), '... has done' (*pepoiêken*, 148ª36–7), and '... has made a mistake' (*hêmartêken*, 148ª37). There are two possibilities. (1) The subject could be a generic interlocutor engaged in the dialectical exchange. In this case, the pronoun 'someone' or a different impersonal form can be understood in the Greek text. This reading is adopted by the majority of translators. (2) The subject could be Dionysius, i.e. the proponent of the definition of life just discussed (148ª26–8). In this case, the pronoun 'he' must be understood in the text (see Primavesi 1992). The grammatical question remains open: there are not enough elements to establish who the subject is. But this does not affect the philosophical implications of the passage.

At 148ª31–6, a distinction between two cases in drawn. First case (148ª31–3): it is possible that the proponent of D_L offered his definition intentionally (*kata proairesin*) because he thought that life is a synonym, i.e. it is said according to a single form (*kath'hen eidos*). Second case (148ª33–6): it is also possible that the proponent of D_L was aware of the fact that life is a homonym, but he inadvertently failed to formulate the definition accordingly and offered an account that is common to all forms of life. In Aristotle's opinion, the proponent of D_L is equally mistaken in both cases. In the first case, it is clear why he is at fault: he lacks the knowledge that the thing to be defined is a homonym. Thus, on this basis, he could not suggest the successful definition. In the second case, the proponent of D_L has the knowledge that the thing to be defined is a homonym but fails to give the appropriate defining expressions. It is clear that the mistake described in the first case is not of the same order as that in the second case. Aristotle, however, is not interested in the motivation that led a proponent of D_L to offer this definition: whatever the motivation, what counts in the framework of the dialectical exchange and for the purpose of the refutation is that the definition is faulty. It is rather unlikely that Aristotle has a personal interest in Dionysius and wants to provide some explanations of how he could offer his definition.

148ª37–148ᵇ4: It is not easy to assess the content of this brief portion of text. Let us begin by reconstructing Aristotle's arguments. At 148ª37, he observes that some homonyms are difficult to detect. (A similar point is made also in *Top.* I.15, 107ᵇ6–7: 'But frequently, in definitions themselves, the homonym escapes notice; for this reason, you should also examine definitions'). This observation, which is simple and fair, provides the ground for sketching two different strategies. The first is a strategy for the dialectician acting as a questioner (148ª37–148ᵇ3). In asking questions to his interlocutor, the questioner must deal with the homonym as if it were a synonym. In other words, the questioner must offer no indication of the fact that the kind to be defined is a homonym and the answerer will believe that it is a synonym. The answerer will then try, but fail, to offer a single account for the kind to be defined. This failure is incompatible with the supposed fact that a synonym is being defined. For example, suppose that the kind to be defined is dog. The interlocutor is not aware of the fact that dog is a homonym: it might be a terrestrial quadruped (dog_1) or a fish (dog_2) (see LSJ, s.v. *kuôn*, I and IV; the homonymy of *kuôn* is employed by Galen in his *On linguistic fallacies*, see Schiaparelli 2002, pp. 76–7 and 107–8). Since the definition of dog_1 does not pertain to dog_2, the interlocutor will fail to define in the way that is appropriate for synonyms (*kata tropon*, 148^{b}2). That is to say, given that the interlocutor believes that dog is a synonym, he will not be able to offer a single definition that applies to all cases as would be appropriate. The second strategy is for the dialectician acting as respondent and very little is said about it (148^{b}3–4). Aristotle observes that in the case where the respondent must defend himself from the questioner's attack, he must spell out the homonymy of the kind to be defined. Hence the questioner will not be able to refute him by using the strategy just outlined since this strategy relies on the homonymy remaining undetected.

In this passage there are two features that are unexpected and unusual in the context of the *Topics*. (A) Aristotle recommends a strategy for the respondent. (B) The strategy for the questioner suggested at 148^{a}37–148^{b}3 seems to be sophistic rather than dialectical. Let us begin with (A). To the best of my knowledge, this is the first time in *Topics* VI where Aristotle suggests a strategy for the respondent. It has to be noticed that his remark is extremely concise. It is possible that Aristotle simply added it as an interesting afterthought that occurred to him after having sketched the strategy for the questioner. This need not imply that Aristotle intended to develop this idea elsewhere. But it is also possible that he is anticipating a thought that will be expanded in chapters 4 and 5 of *Topics* VIII, where 'The task of the good answerer as well as that of the good questioner are illustrated' (159^{a}16–18). Aristotle observes that he is the first to be concerned with the rules that the good answerer should follow when he is engaged in a dialectical exchange aiming at testing and inquiry (*peiras kai skepsêôs*; 159^{a}33). In other words, the conciseness of the remark concerning the answerer's strategy might be due to the fact that Aristotle has just begun thinking about it. On the role of the answerer in a dialectical debate and on the rules most suited to him, see Brunschwig 1984/85, pp. 37–9. As for (B), the situation is far from simple. The strategy for the questioner raises some doubts about his intellectual honesty. In choosing to conceal the homonymy, he seems to set a trap for the respondent. This controversial strategy has received attention from a number of scholars. They tend to accuse Aristotle of launching a line of attack that is by no means dialectical but sophistic. Is this interpretation correct? It is hard to deny that the concealment of the homonymy is not a helpful move: it will certainly put the respondent in an unfavourable situation and the questioner can take advantage of it. But before labelling this procedure as unqualifiedly sophistic, we should compare it with the sophistic refutation that hinges on homonymy. In this case, the questioner is responsible for *purposively* concealing the homonymy and for leading the respondent to an apparently false conclusion by posing him further deceiving questions. The questioner's aim is to gain victory at all costs, even at the cost of producing an apparent refutation. The sophistic refutation due to homonymy is illustrated in Aristotle's *SE* 4, 165^{b}30–166^{a}36. There is a precedent in Plato's *Euthd.* 276c3–7; 276d7–277b2. (See Dorion 1995, pp. 221–2; Fait 2007, p. 110.) The situation described in the passage of the *Topics* under discussion is different, i.e. not sophistic, for a number of reasons. (i) In the *Topics*, the questioner does not *purposively* conceal the homonymy and does not lead the answerer to believe that there is a synonymy using treacherous questions. Rather, the answerer does not realize that there is a homonymy because 'some homonyms escape notice' (*enia lanthanei tôn hômonumôn*; 147^{b}37). In other words, it is a simple fact concerning the nature of language that homonymies are difficult to detect. It is for this reason that the answerer can be mistaken. (ii) If it were a sophistic context, nothing would exclude that it could be more advantageous for the respondent not to reveal the presence of the homonymy. Thus, in this case, the clause 'in answering we must ourselves draw the distinction' (*hautôi d'apokrinomenôi diaireteon*; 143^{b}3–4) could not be justified. (iii) In the case where the homonymy is difficult to detect, it is not convenient for the questioner to begin drawing distinctions concerning the homonymous kinds since he could meet unexpected problems and might lack a strategy to solve them. For example, the respondent might stubbornly refuse to admit that there is a homonymy and argue that there is a synonymy instead. (iv) In the dialectical debate, it is certainly not the questioner who has the role of drawing distinctions between the many ways something is said. (v) In these lines, i.e. 148^{a}37–148^{b}4, the questioner might be trying *to test* the respondent's knowledge concerning homonyms. In this respect, the questioner would be making use of *peirastikê* or the 'art of examining'. Aristotle talks about this examinational procedure in *Topics* VIII.5, 159^{a}25–37, and in some chapters of the *Sophistici Elenchi* (2, 165^{b}4–7; 8, 169^{b}23–9; 11, 171^{b}3–6 and 172^{a}21–4). In chapter 8 of the *SE*, Aristotle specifies that '*Peirastikê* is a part of dialectic; and this may deduce a false conclusion because of the ignorance of the answerer'. Then he clearly distinguishes this procedure from the use of sophistic arguments. He adds: 'Sophistic refutations, on the other hand, even though they deduce the contradictory of his (*sc.* the interlocutor's) thesis, do not make clear whether he is ignorant; for even men of knowledge are entangled by these arguments' (169^{b}23–9). In chapter 11 of the *SE*, Aristotle outlines the difference between the procedure of *peirastikê* and the method used in mathematics: 'Dialectic is at the same time an art of examination (*peirastikê*) as well. For the art of examination is not an accomplishment of the same kind as geometry, but one which people may possess, even though they have no knowledge. For it is possible even for one without knowledge *to hold an examination* (*peiran labein*) of the one who is without knowledge'. Furthermore, if it is true to say that when Aristotle mentions the strategy for the respondent at 148^{b}3–4 he has in mind the discussion in *Topics* VIII.5, 159^{a}33 (see above), then there is a further reason to believe that he is recommending a strategy that belongs to the examinational function of dialectic. For he clearly refers to the rules that the answerer must follow when he is engaged in arguments for the sake of testing (*peira*) and inquiry. There is a vast literature about *peirastikê*, its goals, its function, and its relation with dialectic and with scientific knowledge: see, e.g., Moreau 1968, pp. 80–1; Moraux 1968, p. 288, n. 3; Irwin 1988, p. 138; Brunschwig 1990, pp. 256–61; Bolton 1999, pp. 80–7, pp. 92–4, and *passim*; Dorion 1995, pp. 297–9; Smith 1997, pp. 128–9; Sim 1999b, pp. 197–8; Berti 2004, *passim*; Fait 2007, pp. xxxii–xxxiii; Ward 2008, p. 50; Reeve 2012, pp. 150–4.

148^{b}4–10: In this passage, there is an attempt to establish an honest dialectical requirement whereby both parties must know the concepts involved in the suggested definition in order to start the discussion. Let us analyse the initial clauses. The text is composed of two parts: 'some answerers say, on the one hand, that *(i)* the synonym is a homonym when the given account does not apply to everything, and, on the other hand, that *(ii)* the homonym is a synonym if it applies to both' (148^b4–7; the division of the text in two parts is mine). It is likely that Aristotle has in mind the following situations.

(i) Suppose that there is a dialectical exchange whose purpose is to define a kind named x. The answerer grants the definition y. The questioner points out that y does not apply to x_1, which is one of the things falling under x. The answerer defends his position by claiming that the things that fall under x are homonyms: this is the reason why there is no single definition that applies to all of them. At this point, the questioner must avail himself of the fact that the things falling under x are synonyms, but if this was not granted at the beginning of the discussion, it will be difficult to obtain this concession at this stage of the argument. Suppose, for example, that the opponent has to define the kind named by 'animal'. The answerer grants a definition. The questioner points out that the granted definition does not apply to the species human. Then, the answerer will reply that the things falling under 'animal' are homonyms and that there is no single definition which applies to all. He will point out that, although his proposed definition does not apply to the species human, it applies to other things falling under 'animal'. If at the beginning of the refutation it was not agreed that things falling under 'animal' are synonyms, then it will not be possible to obtain an agreement on this at such a late stage in the argument.

(ii) Suppose, now, that there is a dialectical debate concerning the kind z. The answerer grants the defining expression w. The questioner observes that w applies not only to z but also to the species z_1. Then the answerer claims that z and z_1 are synonyms. The questioner must avail himself of the fact that z and z_1 are not synonyms but homonyms. However, if their homonymy was not granted at an earlier stage of the debate, it is hard to obtain this concession at this point in the argument. For example, let the debate be about the species *zôion* (in Greek *zôion* is equivalent to 'animal' and to 'portrait'). The answerer grants a defining expression. The questioner observes that the granted defining expression

applies to animal as well as to portrait. Then the answerer will defend his granted defining expression by claiming that animal and portrait are synonyms. In order to carry out his refutation, the questioner should avail himself of the fact that animal and portrait are homonyms. But if there is no preliminary agreement, the respondent can insist upon the synonymy of the things falling under *zôion*.

At 148^{b}7–9, Aristotle suggests two ways to come to a prior agreement. More precisely, the two ways apt to establish a mutual consent are indicated by the expressions *prodiomologêteon* and *prosyllogisteon*. The verbal form *prodiomologêteon* (lit. 'It must be agreed beforehand') indicates precisely the necessity of reaching a common consent through a prior agreement. Before analysing the details of this requirement, it must be observed that the need for a common ground, which guarantees the mutual understanding in the dialectical exchange concerning definitions, is not a novelty. For example, in Plato's *Meno* 75C–D, Socrates explicitly says that a definition should contain terms that both parties know. The expression *prodiomologêteon* is not often used by Aristotle. He briefly discusses preliminary agreements in *APr.* I.45, 50^{a}29–38, which, as we know, is a formal-logical context. In the background of this chapter in *Topics* VI, however, the motivation for establishing a preliminary agreement seems to be rather intuitive. This requirement can be described as something that stems from the need for a verbal accord in a daily exchange between speakers. The second way to reach a common consent is by a *prosyllogism*. Recent translations of prosyllogism are 'prior deduction' (Smith 1989) and 'preliminary syllogism' (Striker 2009). The expression *prosyllogisteon* is uncommon in Aristotle's corpus. We find two occurrences in *APr.* I.25, 42^{b}5, and I.28, 44^{a}22. In this context, it is employed to refer to arguments with intermediate conclusions. In other words, it indicates syllogisms which serve the purpose of deriving propositions that, at a later stage, will be used as premises.

In the context of this passage, on what should the questioner and the respondent agree? They should have the same view on whether the kinds to be defined are synonyms or homonyms, 'whichever of the two it may be' (148^{b}8–9). This clause can be interpreted in three ways. First, it could be intended as 'whichever of the two it may be *regardless what they really are*'. In other words, according to this reading, it does not really matter whether, as a matter of fact, the kinds to be defined are synonyms or homonyms. The important thing is that, in virtue of a preliminary agreement, both parties consider the kinds to be defined either synonyms or homonyms (see Brunschwig 2007, p. 75, n. 1). So, it can happen that what they agree on calling synonym might in reality be a homonym, and vice versa. Second, it can be understood as 'whichever of the two it may be in conformity with what they really are'. The agreement on whether the kinds to be defined are synonyms or homonyms must follow accurately what reality is like. Then both parties will call synonym what as a matter of fact is a synonym and they will call homonym what as a matter of fact is a homonym. Third, the clause may be reformulated as 'whichever of the two it may be in this context'. Here the question of whether the kinds to be defined are really homonyms or synonyms is not even asked. Questioner and answerer have a verbal agreement that does not concern how things really are. What is the best interpretative option? I am inclined to think that it is the third. This is because the text fails to indicate clearly what the interlocutors' stance on how things really are is. This failure speaks against the first and second options. Moreover, the interlocutor is more prepared to accept a view that is not ontologically loaded. This view can be shared by any respondent independently of his philosophical background.

When at 148^{b}9–10 Aristotle says, 'For they are more prepared to agree when they do not foresee the result', he has in mind the procedure of the *concealment of the conclusion* (see Brunschwig 2007, p. 245, n. 1). Broadly speaking, it consists in failing to reveal the conclusion to the interlocutor before the end of the exchange. Two texts in *Topics* VIII give us a more precise idea of this procedure:

> *T1* : The premises through which the deduction comes about are called necessary; those obtained besides these are of four kinds. They are either for the sake of induction and giving the universal, or to give the bulk of the argument, or *for the concealment of the conclusion*, (*pros krupsin tou sumperasmatos*) or to render the argument clearer.... Premises for concealment are *for the sake of the contest* (*agónos charin*), but since this entire sort of business is directed at someone else, it is necessary to use them too. (155^{b}20–8)

T2 : When you are concealing, give *preliminary deductions* (*kruptonta de prosyllogizesthai*) of the premises from which the deduction of the initial thesis is going to come about. And get *as many of these as possible*. This would result if you were to deduce not just the necessary premises, but even some of the ones useful for getting them. Next, *do not state the conclusions*, but instead deduce them all together later on (for in so doing, you would *stand further off the initial thesis*). (156^{a}7–11)

Several important points emerge from these lines. Let us consider those pertaining to our discussion. *(a)* The concealment of the conclusion is obtained by using a certain type of premises. More precisely, in his refutative argument, the dialectician must deduce not only the necessary premises (those without which the conclusion cannot be drawn, i.e. those which are needed to draw the conclusion) but also further premises, which are useful for establishing the necessary premises. Aristotle's suggested procedure can be reconstructed thus: suppose that the questioner wants to derive the conclusion Q. Now, Q can be reached only through P^1 and P^2. The questioner cannot ask directly that P^1 and P^2 be conceded since the interlocutor would see what the questioner aims at; he would, therefore, refuse his assent. Rather, the questioner should try to obtain the assent to P^3, P^4, P^5, P^6. The assent to P^3 and P^4 will allow him to deduce P^1, whereas the assent to P^5 and P^6 permits the derivation of P^2. But the interlocutor does not realize this, and hence he concedes P^3, P^4, P^5, P^6. *(b)* In some cases, the questioner can even forgo asking directly any of P^3, P^4, P^5, P^6, and he will obtain the assent to even further premises (e.g. P^7 and P^8) from which he will derive it. The result will be like a long chain of arguments. One can observe that, in this circumstance, the conclusion Q is even better concealed. *(c)* There is an explicit link between the use of preliminary deductions and the concealment of the conclusion. This link reinforces the interpretation according to which at 148^{b}9–10 Aristotle has in mind the strategy of the concealment of the conclusion. *(d)* The strategy of hiding the conclusion from the interlocutors' sight through the formulation of many premises is a procedure mentioned in connection with an agonistic aim; that is to say, it is used in competitions in order to gain victory over the adversary. But 'arguments used in competition and contest (*tôn agonistikôn kai eristikôn*)' are the subject of the *Sophistici Elenchi* (2, 165^{b}10–11), where apparent refutations are analysed. Should we conclude that even in the *Topics* Aristotle is recommending a sophistic strategy? Someone might think that in his remarks at 148^{b}9–10 Aristotle is suggesting to the questioner the use of fallacious arguments. This might eventually lead to the belief that dialectic and eristic share common strategies: undoubtedly, it would be an unwelcome consequence for dialectic. Furthermore, it would introduce a severe tension between this text and Aristotle's claim that fallacious arguments are not appropriate to dialectic (*Top.* I.18, 108^{a}33–4). It is possible, however, to show that the concealment of the conclusion, as it is presented in *T1* and *T2*, does not amount to a sophistic refutation, namely to what seems to be a genuine refutation, but is a fallacy instead (*SE* 1, 164^{b}20–1). From a formal logical standpoint, if you increase the number of the premises in a valid argument, you will not affect its validity. The listener will experience some difficulties in understanding how the argument unfolds, but he is by no means deceived or trapped in a fallacious reasoning. The questioner conceals the conclusion not because he wants to entrap the opponent, but because he wants to obtain an honest answer. Were the opponent in a position to foresee the conclusion, he would give biased answers in order to avoid the refutation.

148^{b}10–22: If no preliminary agreement is reached, then there are some refutative strategies that the questioner could follow. At 148^{b}10–16, Aristotle outlines the procedure to deal with the case described above, i.e. the case where 'Some of the answerers say that … the synonym is a homonym when the given account does not apply to everything' (148^{b}4–6). The text is extremely compressed and the stages of the refutation are difficult to unfold. A reconstruction can be offered by adding some elements that remain implicit in these lines. Consider the interlocutor's claim that 'The synonym is a homonym due to the fact that the account given does not apply also to this' (148^{b}10–12). In other words, the respondent considers what is in fact a synonym as a homonym because, among the synonyms that share a common name, there is a particular case to which the proposed defining expression does not apply. What should the questioner do? He should apply the following strategy. Suppose that *n* is a name indicating the species that must be defined, and that the respondent offers f as an account of this species. The questioner finds a case k to which (*epi touto*, 148^{b}11) n applies but f does not (I use 'to apply' to mean 'to be true of'). The answerer claims that f does not apply to k because the items (namely, $k, s_1, \ldots, s_n$) to which n applies are homonyms with respect to n (148^{b}10–12). At this point, the questioner must check whether a different account f_1 applies to k and to all of $s_1, \ldots, s_n$ (148^{b}12–13). How is f_1 obtained? Very likely, f_1 is the questioner's proposed account of k (*ho toutou logos*, 148^{b}12: *toutou* refers back to *epi touto* at 148^{b}11). Suppose that f_1 applies to k and to all of $s_1, \ldots, s_n$. Then, $s_1, \ldots, s_n$ and k will be all synonyms contrary to what the opponent claimed (148^{b}12–14). Suppose, instead, that f_1 does not apply to all of $s_1, \ldots, s_n$ (*ei de mê*: 'otherwise', i.e. 'in the case where it does not apply'; 148^{b}14). Then, f_1 will apply only to some but not to others. Let $s_1, \ldots, s_i$ be the cases to which f_1 applies; and let $s_{i+1}, \ldots, s_n$ be those to which it does not. Therefore, f will apply to $s_{i+1}, \ldots, s_n$. Hence $s_1, \ldots, s_i, s_{i+1}, \ldots, s_n$ will be homonyms. But this is contrary to what the interlocutor implicitly assumed, namely that $s_1, \ldots, s_i, s_{i+1}, \ldots, s_n$ are all synonyms with respect to n: for he was committed to k being the only case generating homonymy.

At 148^{b}18–22, Aristotle deals with another case that concerns homonymy and that is different from the instances analysed so far. Consider the name 'donkey' ('*onos*'), which applies in different ways to different things (as Aristotle points out in *Top.* I.15, 107^{a}19, it applies to certain animals and to certain engines). Suppose the interlocutor is asked to define what a donkey is. His answer is that a donkey is an animal of a certain sort. The questioner points out that the proposed definition does not apply to engines. Instead of admitting that donkeys are homonyms (which would imply a mistake on his part), the interlocutor replies that the name 'donkey' does not apply to engines. How can the questioner demolish this view? Aristotle's reply does not correspond to any of the strategies developed in this chapter for the cases of homonymy and synonymy. More precisely, he does not sketch a line of attack aimed at demolishing the interlocutor's specific view. Rather, he proposes to counter the adversary's argument with a general remark concerning the function of language. The questioner ought to point out that the interlocutor's view is not in line with the 'traditional and common language' (148^b19–21). The idea is that a language, which is accepted and shared by a community of speakers, has some rules that must be respected. It is not admissible to attempt a reform of the natural language during a dialectical debate; for this debate is grounded on the linguistic use established by the speakers. It is the linguistic use that fixes the application of, e.g. 'donkey' to certain animals and certain engines.

It interesting to look at Aristotle's last remark, namely '*In certain cases*, we must not speak like the many' (148^b21–2). Aristotle seems to soften his previous claim concerning the reform of natural language. It is possible that he is here concerned with specific instances where the language spoken by the majority of people is not adequate. Which are those specific instances? One might reasonably suppose that Aristotle has in mind some scientific context where new or complex theories must be introduced. In this context, new expressions need to be found or new ways of using existing terms need to be established. Even though these interpretative suggestions are not explicitly present in 148^b21–2, they are perfectly in line with Aristotle's way of dealing with ordinary language in a scientific or specialized context.

CHAPTER 11

Introduction. The chapter has three main parts. (1) 148^{b}23–32 contains a commonplace concerning the definition of complexes (*ta sumpeplegmena*) and proposes a rule to deal with such cases. (2) 148^{b}33–149^{a}7 analyses definitions of composites (*ta suntheta*) and discusses the problems arising in the case where the defining part contains as many elements as the expression indicating the kind to be defined (although 149^{a}5–7 addresses the issue introduced at 148^{b}33, it deserves a separate analysis). (3) 149^{a}8–28 deals with a number of difficulties associated with the substitution, in a definition, of the name with another name or with its account. This part can be divided into four subsections. (3.i) 149^{a}8–13 discusses the mistake of substituting a name with another name that is not 'the same in meaning'. (3.ii) 149^{a}14–20 tackles the problems occurring in the substitution of the name indicating the genus. (3.iii) 149^{a}20–4 contains an objection to the criticism set out in the immediately preceding subsection. (3.iv) 149^{a}24–8 considers the case where there is a replacement of a name with its account. It must be observed that there are some difficulties in the interpretation of some commonplaces discussed in this chapter. This is because, as is well known, the distinction between the ontological and linguistic levels is not always respected by Aristotle and there is often a shift between them.

148^{b}23–32: The first commonplace of chapter 11 concerns the method for analysing and refuting definitions of certain complexes (*tôn sumpeplegmenôn tinos horos*); for example, the definition of finite straight line. This portion of text contains (A) linguistic and (B) philosophical problems that need to be discussed.

(A) At a linguistic level, consider the proposed definition of finite straight line, namely 'Limit of a surface having limits whose intermediate point intercepts the view of the limits' (*peras epipedou echontos perata, hou to meson epiprosthei tois perasin*; 148^{b}27–8). This formulation might well be technical, but it is not elegant, as the term 'limit' occurs three times (*peras, perata, perasin*). The verb *epiprosthei*, which I have translated as '(it) intercepts the view of', belongs originally to the fields of astronomy and optics. This verb and its cognates are not frequently used by Aristotle and its main occurrences are in the *De Caelo* (II.13, 293^{b}21–5; II.14, 297^{b}25–30) and in the *Metereologica* (I.5, 342^{b}5–10). The two passages of the *De Caelo* offer us the context to understand the proposed definition of finite straight line. According to the first passage (II.13, 293^{b}21–5), 'Some of them consider that it is possible that there are several bodies so moving, which are invisible to us *owing to the interposition* (*dia tên epiprosthêsin*) of the earth. This, they say, accounts for the fact that eclipses of the moon are more frequent than eclipses of the sun; for in addition to the earth, each of these moving bodies can obstruct it'. According to the second passage (II.14, 297^{b}25–30), 'The shapes which the moon itself each month shows are of every kind—straight, gibbous, and concave—but in the eclipse the outline is always curved; and since it is *the interposition of the earth* (*tên tês gês epiprosthêsin*) that makes the eclipse, the form of this line will be caused by the form of the earth surface, which is therefore spherical'. The two passages show that *epiprosthei* and its cognate forms are employed to allude to eclipses. In the context of the *Topics*, the general idea is that a finite straight line is compared to a path of vision. If a body stands on any intermediary point of this path, then it will prevent the sight of one of the two extremities. It goes without saying that the situation is symmetric and one can choose any of the two extremities as the point of observation. In my translation, I follow Brunschwig's suggestion in giving to the occurrences of '*to meson*' (148^{b}27, 148^{b}30, 148^{b}31) the meaning (not of 'the middle point', but) of 'any intermediate point'. The use of *epiprosthei* and the relation between the definition of the finite straight line proposed in the *Topics* and in Plato's *Parmenides* 137C are discussed in Mugler 1956, Tréheux 1957, and Brunschwig 2007, p. 76, n. 1.

(B) At a philosophical level, there is a question to be asked: what are these complexes? Before answering, let us observe that Aristotle does not explain them but offers an example: at 148^{b}26–7, he individuates a finite straight line as one of these complexes. This example comes from the field of geometry like several other instances discussed in the *Topics* (see, in particular, book VI chapter 4, 141^{b}19–22, where proposed definitions of a point, a line, a surface, and a solid are criticized and rejected. In the case under discussion, the geometrical species to be defined is not a line *simpliciter* but a line of a certain type, i.e. the line that is qualified as finite and straight; see commentary *ad loc.*). There are two main types of answer concerning the nature of the complexes.

(B1) The complexes in question are extralinguistic entities. An entity can be complex in two ways. (i) Any species is ontologically complex because it consists in the combination of a genus and a differentia. In this case, the commonplace described here is very general since it can be applied to every species. The only case where it could not be applied would be that of the *summa genera*. (ii) An entity can be complex in the way a white person or a musical person are. To use modern jargon, we say that accidental composites are complex extralinguistic entities. Which option is Aristotle's? In this context, he does not take sides on this issue and seems to leave both options open. One might observe that the example of the finite straight line does not favour the accidental composites reading, since a finite straight line is not an accidental composite. One, then, is tempted to conclude that what Aristotle has in mind is the complexity that belongs to species in so far as they are composed of genus and differentia. Nevertheless, two points can be raised against this conclusion. First, the use of *sumpeplegmenon* to indicate the combination of a genus and a differentia is not at all common in Aristotle's writings. Second, the immediately following passage seems to support the idea that the composites introduced here are more like accidental composites. Perhaps, then, there is a third option: (iii) at an ontological level, both species and accidental composites are composites. It is possible that Aristotle uses *sumpeplegmenon* in a wider way so as to include species and accidental composites. Option (iii) seems to be more promising than (i) and (ii) since it fits well with the example of the finite straight line and with the fact that, particularly in the logical works, *ta sumpeplegmena* are accidental composites.

(B2) The complexes in question are linguistic expressions (phrases or sentences). Some linguistic expressions are simple, e.g. 'line', and other linguistic expressions are complex, e.g. 'finite straight line' (see *Cat.* 2, 1^{a}16–19). It has to be observed that a complex entity can be signified by a simple linguistic expression: for example, one can use 'cloak' to signify an ontological complex item (see *De Int.* 11, 20^{b}12–19).

It is difficult to choose between (B1) and (B2). As noted in the Introduction to this chapter, above, there is often a shift between the ontological and linguistic levels. Such a shift may be observed in the commonplace presently under consideration and generates a problem for its interpretation.

In the argument at 148ᵇ23–32, Aristotle offers a method for testing a proposed definition in the case where the kind to be defined is referred to by an expression containing two or more linguistic items. Aristotle's idea is that there is a correspondence between each item of the expression referring to the kind to be defined and the elements contained in the defining part. Let the kind to be defined be referred to by the expression '*a b c*'. Then, the defining part will mention the account of *a*, i.e. '(*def. a*)', the account of *b*, i.e. '(*def. b*)', and the account of *c*, i.e. '(*def. c*)'. That is to say, the granted definition will be: '*a b c* is (*def. a*) (*def. b*) (*def. c*)'. Suppose we remove '(*def. c*)' from the defining part and '*c*' from the expression referring to the kind to be defined. The remaining elements, i.e. '(*def. a*) (*def. b*)', will exhaustively define the kind indicated by '*a b*'. If it is not so, then the initially granted definition, i.e. '*a b c* is (*def. a*) (*def. b*) (*def. c*)' will not successfully define *a b c*. Hence the initially granted definition must be rejected.

148ᵇ33–149ᵃ4: The discussion concerns proposed definitions of composites (*suntheta*). What does qualify as a composite (*suntheton*) in this context? It is likely that the term *suntheton* is here employed in a similar way to 'complex' (*sumpeplegmenon*; 148ᵇ23). For example, Alexander of Aphrodisias uses them interchangeably (*in Top.* 476, 21). At the beginning of the chapter, 'composite' indicates the expression used to refer to a kind to be defined, an expression that is composed of one or more elements; later 'composite' will be employed to indicate the combination of items occurring in the defining expression. Aristotle is not likely to be using 'composite' in a philosophically loaded way (e.g. to indicate the composite of matter and form, as in *Metaph.* V.24, 1023ᵃ31).

The second commonplace argues against the idea that there could be successful definitions where the defining part contains as many elements as the expression indicating the kind to be defined. The key word is *isokôlos* (lit. 'formed by an equal number of elements'). Aristotle places emphasis on the property of being formed by an equal number of elements when he attempts the description of the meaning of *isokôlos* in relation to the present context (148^{b}34–6). He suggests that *isokôlos* is said of an account (*logos*) when 'the components are exactly as many as the names and verbs in the account (*en tôi logôi*)'. But this is not very clear.

One possible way of understanding Aristotle's words is the following: '*isokôlos* is said of the proposed definition in its entirety (*logos*) when the components (*sc.* of the expression indicating the kind to be defined) are exactly as many as the names or verbs in the defining part (*en tôi logôi*)'. In this interpretative suggestion, the first occurrence of *logos* (148^{b}34) is replaced b '*proposed definition in its entirety*' for two main reasons. (a) It is a *proposed* definition since it is a proposal of the interlocutor and, as Aristotle is attempting to show, it is subject to some fatal criticisms. Hence, it cannot qualify as a definition *tout court*, namely as a successful definition. (b) It is a proposed definition *in its entirety* because the relation expressed by *isokôlos* and predicated of *logos* needs at least two elements to be instantiated. The only two plausible candidates apt to satisfy this relation are the expression indicating the kind to be defined and the defining part: they constitute the definition in its entirety. As for the second occurrence of *logos* (*en tôi logôi*, 148^{b}35), it cannot indicate the proposed definition in its entirety. In this case, *logos* indicates one of the terms satisfying the relation of *isokôlos*: it indicates the defining part. This is confirmed by the following points. (i) It is reasonable to understand 'the components' (*ta sunkeimena*; 148^{b}35) as 'the components of the expression indicating the kind to be defined' since the commonplace discussed in these lines is about composite expressions indicating the kind to be defined. So, the second occurrence of *logos* cannot indicate the expression referring to the kind to be defined, but it indicates the defining part. (ii) Aristotle's examples show that, in general, names and especially verbal forms occur in the defining part rather than in the expression referring to the kind to be defined. This is, for example, a feature of the proposed defining expression of the kind finite straight line, namely 'limit of the surface having (*echontos*) limits whose intermediate point intercepts (*epiprosthei*) the view of the limits' (148^{b}26–8). Therefore, when Aristotle mentions 'the names and verbs *en tôi logôi*', he intends to say 'the names and verbs in the defining expression'.

(See below for a discussion of what names and verbs are in this context.) This suggested interpretation, however, can be criticized because it assigns different values to the two occurrences of *logos* in the same sentences.

Another possibility is to understand the first occurrence of *logos* as indicating not the proposed definition in its entirety but the defining expression only. Then, the interpretative suggestions concerning the remaining part of the sentence are left unchanged. Consider the clause that immediately precedes the first occurrence of *logos*, namely 'Whether the account (*ho logos*) that was given' has an equal number of elements (*isokôlos*) as what is being defined (*tôi horizomenôi*)' (148^{b}33–4). In this instance, *logos* clearly indicates the defining expression since the other term of the relation of being *isokôlos* is explicitly mentioned as 'what is being defined' (*tôi horizomenôi*). This suggests that when Aristotle puts forward the characterization of *isokôlos logos* at 148^{b}34, he still has in mind the defining expression, and 'what is being defined' remains understood. Although this alternative interpretation requires the addition of something that is not present in the text, it does not fall into the mistake of the other reading. That is to say, the advantage of this alternative interpretation consists in the fact that it assigns the same value to the two occurrences of *logos* in the same sentence, namely the defining expression.

The remaining lines of this passage, i.e. 148^{b}36–149^{a}4, explain why a definition where the defining part and the expression referring to the kind to be defined are *isokôloi* cannot be successful. The general idea is that the replacement of a name with another name does not yield a definition. The argument comes in several steps. (i) The fact that the interlocutor does not change the number of names induces us to see that nothing else but a replacement of names has taken place. More precisely, all or some names are replaced with other names. It is possible that the replacement involves some names but not others, which remain the same (148^{b}36–149^{a}1). (ii) Suppose that there is a replacement of a name with another name (and not with its account). Were this to be allowed to amount to a definition, then even in the case of simple items like mantle and cloak the replacement of mantle with cloak would amount to a definition. But, clearly, this is false (149^{a}3–4). (iii) Hence, in order to obtain a definition, names must not be replaced by other names; rather, they must be replaced by their accounts. This procedure concerns either all or most of the names occurring in the expression referring to the kind to be defined (149^a1–3). Some of the items can be primitive and hence indefinable.

Let us spend a few words on Aristotle's use of 'names' (*onomata*) and 'verbs' (*hremata*). At 148^b35–6 ('The components are exactly as many as the names and verbs in the account') Aristotle distinguishes names from verbs. This distinction is in line with the doctrine expounded in chapter 2 and 3 of the *De Interpretatione* (it must be said, though, that in the latter treatise Aristotle offers a detailed analysis of what names and verbs are). Then, at 149^a2, Aristotle uses 'names' in a wider way so that it covers also verbs. The wider use of 'names' corresponds to Plato's use of 'name' in *Soph.* 261D. In Greek, the term *onoma* can mean (1) name (as opposed to verb), but also (2) word. Since every verb is also a word, the second meaning of *onoma* can be extended to verbs (see Crivelli, 2012, p. 223, and n. 3 for bibliographical references).

Does Aristotle's argument at 148^b36–149^a4 work as a refutative strategy against a proposed definition where the expression referring to the kind to be defined and the defining part are composed of exactly the same number of elements? From the premises stated in the argument it is possible to develop a refutative line that will demolish a proposed definition with the aforementioned characteristics. Some of the argument's assumptions might be difficult for an interlocutor to accept. In particular, the assumption that 'The person who defines must give an account instead of the name' is introduced but not supported. This might be taken for granted by those who are familiar with Socrates' and Plato's requirements for successful definitions. But someone might have a different theory of definition whereby, in order to define, it is not necessary to replace a name with its account. In this case, the opponent can refuse his assent to some basic premises and, hence, the refutation will not go through.

149^a5–7: This short portion of text refers back to the immediately preceding lines, in particular to the criticism of proposed definitions where names are replaced not with an account (as is required) but with other names. Consider, now, the cases where the names in the expression referring to the kind to be defined are substituted by more unfamiliar names (*agnôstotera onomata*) in the defining part. This type of substitution is even more unwelcome than that of the ordinary cases where names are replaced with other names that have the same degree of familiarity. But what does it mean for a name, or in general for a linguistic expression, to be familiar? And what does the property of being *more* familiar amount to? The epistemological notion of familiarity is mentioned several times in book VI; see, e.g., 1, 139^{b}14; 2, 140^{a}9 and 140^{a}11; 3, 141^{a}13; ch. 4, *passim*. This notion is expressed by the Greek verb *gnôrizein* ('to become familiar with') and by its cognates. In the *Topics*, we find many occurrences of the adjective *gnôrimon* ('familiar'), of its comparative and superlative forms *gnôrimôteron* and *gnôrimôtaton*, and of privative expressions like *agnôston* ('unfamiliar') and its comparative *agnôstoteron*. Generally speaking, a linguistic expression is said to be *familiar* when one already has a certain understanding of its meaning. In other words, a linguistic expression is familiar when one is acquainted with its meaning since one has already come to know it. Possibly, one is also able to use it correctly. A linguistic expression is said to be *unfamiliar* when one has never encountered it or has only a vague understanding of its meaning. Consider, for example, the English 'caparison' ('an ornamental covering spread over a horse's saddle'). There are two main possibilities: (i) one has never heard that expression so that one is completely ignorant about it; (ii) one is able to relate it to horses but does not know anything else about it. In both cases the speaker would hardly be able to use it. Therefore, in both cases, 'caparison' is unfamiliar. The property of being *more familiar* is a relation between two (or more) linguistic expressions, say E^1 and E^2. In this context, the idea is that one has encountered E^1 and one is already familiar with its meaning. As for E^2, one has no (or very little) knowledge of its meaning. Suppose, then, that E^1 and E^2 are so related that the first can be used to become clear about the second. In this sense, E^1 is more familiar than E^2. In a definitional context, it is a fundamental requirement that the defining part mention things that are more familiar than the kind to be defined. This requirement is discussed at length at the beginning of *Top.* VI.4; in particular, Aristotle says that 'The definition is given for the sake of one's becoming familiar with what is said, and we become familiar with something not on the basis of just any things, but on the basis of things that are prior and more familiar' (141ª27–9). The same requirement is summarized at the end of chapter 11 (149ª26–7). The complex details of this reasoning are analysed in the commentary on chapter 4 and in Schiaparelli 2011. For the purposes of our discussion and for a better comprehension of the remaining part of the chapter (149ª8–28), it suffices to observe that one of the aims of the definition is the improvement of our understanding. That is to say, we improve our understanding of the species to be defined by looking at its genus and differentia, which are more familiar than the species. In this sense, the respect of the requirement of familiarity should guarantee the attainment of one of the definition's aims.

Consider the example at 149ª6–7. If in his attempt to define a species an interlocutor replaces 'white person' (*anthrôpos leukos*) with 'pale mortal' (*brotos argos*), he will fall into a 'greater mistake' (*meizôn amartia*; 149ª5). The greater mistake occurs when the interlocutor makes the substitution by using more unfamiliar names. It should be noted that *brotos argos* is an expression belonging to archaic and poetic jargon. For example, the term *brotos* is used by Parmenides in his poem when he writes about the 'opinion of mortals (*brotôn doxai*), in which there is no reliance' (DK 28 B 1, 30). The reason why the replacement of 'white human' with 'pale mortal' cannot be accepted is twofold: no definition is offered, and (even worse) the expression chosen for the substitution is less familiar than that which it replaces (149ª7). The discussion of the criterion of familiarity continues in the following lines.

149ª8–28: The remaining portion of text in chapter 11 addresses some difficulties mainly arising in the procedure of 'the substitution of names' (*en têi metallagêi tôn onomatôn*, 149ª8), that is to say, in the procedure of replacing a name occurring in the expression indicating the kind to be defined with a different one in the defining part. At first reading, one might think that this discussion introduces a tension. For it seems that here Aristotle is allowing the possibility of substituting names in the account, whereas previously (149ª3–4) he rules it out because he considers it an inadequate procedure for establishing a definition. But this tension can be eased. Aristotle is not changing his mind about the fact that a mere substitution of names does not yield a successful definition. Rather, he thinks that it is important to establish rules concerning the cases where the substitution is permitted. What are these cases? They cover the instances where the substitution of names aims not at establishing successful definitions but at providing helpful clarifications. In this way, the result of the substitution is in line with one of the fundamental goals of the definition, which is that of improving the understanding of the kind to be defined through familiar expressions (see commentary on 149^{a}5–7). The formulation of rules which guarantee a successful definition prevents, for example, the mistake of substituting a name with another name having a different meaning, and that of replacing an unfamiliar name with one that is even more unfamiliar (see below). The portion of text in 149^{a}8–28 can be divided into four subsections.

(1) Lines 149^{a}8–13 discuss a difficulty concerned with 'sameness in meaning' (*tauton sêmainei*, 149^{a}8). It concerns the case where, in a phrase, a name is substituted with another name. Once the substitution has been performed, the resulting phrase must have the same meaning as the original one (for the resulting phrase is supposed to be the defining part and the defining part must have the same meaning as the expression indicating the kind to be defined). For this reason, he instructs the dialectician to verify that the replacing name has the same meaning as the one it replaces. In other words, Aristotle's principle is that if $a+b = a+c$, then $b = c$. The example used to illustrate this case concerns the replacement of 'knowledge' (*epistêmên*) with 'supposition' (*hupolêpsin*) in the phrase 'theoretical knowledge' (*theôretikên epistêmên*, 149^{a}9–10). But, Aristotle argues, this is not a good substitution since 'knowledge' does not mean the same as 'supposition'. It follows that 'theoretical knowledge' does not mean the same as 'theoretical supposition'.

According to Alexander of Aphrodisias (*in Top.* 479, 12–15), knowledge and supposition have different objects. More precisely, knowledge is of things that are unchangeable and eternal, whilst supposition is of things that are misleading and changeable. Alexander's interpretation is correct if he means to say that the objects of supposition *include* things that are misleading and changeable. In the *Topics* and in the *De Anima*, *hupolêpsis* indicates a cognitive attitude that is more general than *epistêmê*. See, for example, *Top.* II.8, 114^{a}18: 'Knowledge is a supposition'; see also *De An.* III.3, 427ᵇ24–6: 'There are also varieties of supposition itself: knowledge (*epistêmê*) and belief (*doxa*) and understanding (*phronêsis*)'. In other words, *hupolêpsis* is predicated more widely than *epistêmê*. Moreover, knowledge corresponds to a mental state that is always true, whereas supposition corresponds to a mental state that can be false. For these reasons, *epistêmê* cannot be replaced by *hupolêpsis*. It is not easy to find an adequate English translation for *hupolêpsis*: it has a wide semantic spectrum and it covers notions that need to be expressed with different English words. There is no agreement among scholars concerning the rendering of *hupolêpsis*. Other options: 'conception' (Pickard-Cambridge 1928), 'conceiving' (Forster 1960), 'supposal' (Hamlyn 1968), 'belief' (Barnes 1984, vol. 1), 'jugement' (Tricot 1950), 'croyance' (Bodéüs 1993), 'représentation' (Brunschwig 2007), 'Annahme' (Wagner and Rapp 2004), 'opinione' (Colli 1970), 'supposizione' (Zadro 1974).

It is possible to raise an objection against Aristotle's argument since there are cases where the substitution, in a phrase, of a name with a name that has a different meaning *does preserve* the sameness of meaning of the entire compound where it occurs. Consider 'snub nose'. This expression has the same meaning as 'concave nose'. But 'snub' and 'concave' do not have the same meaning. For 'being concave' indicates the property of being-curved-inwards that can be possessed by objects of various sorts, including non-noses (e.g. concave lenses), whereas 'being snub' expresses a property peculiar to a nose and indicates its being short and turned up at the end. We can speak of concave noses and of snub noses, and we can speak of concave lenses, but we do not talk about snub lenses.

(2) Lines 149ᵃ14–20 discuss the problems occurring with the substitution of the name indicating the genus. The rule involved in this commonplace tells us that if there is a replacement of one of the names in the defining part, what has to be replaced is not the name indicating the genus but that expressing the differentia. The example mentioned above, which concerns the replacement of 'theoretical knowledge' (*theôretikên epistêmên*) with 'theoretical supposition' (*hupolêpsin theôretikên*, 149ᵃ9–10), is useful in illustrating this case too. On the one hand, the replacement of 'knowledge' with 'supposition' is a change in the name of the genus. On the other hand, the differentia is indicated by

'theoretical' and is left unchanged. According to Aristotle, 'theoretical' is more unfamiliar than 'knowledge'. Since the replacement should concern the more unfamiliar expression, 'theoretical' ought to be changed and 'knowledge' ought to remain unchanged. The justification for recommending the replacement of the name of the differentia and not that of the genus seems to be contained in the argument at 149^{a}16–20. This argument, however, is far from being clear and seems to miss its target. At 149^{a}18, Aristotle claims that the genus is 'most familiar of all' (*pantôn de gnôrimôtaton to genos*). He probably means that the genus is the most familiar item in the definition. The fact that the genus is more familiar than the species is established in *Top.* VI.4, 141^{b}28–34.

> The genus and the differentia carry the species to destruction with them, so that these are prior to the species. They are also more familiar; for when the species becomes familiar necessarily the genus and the differentia also become familiar (for the person who becomes familiar with human becomes familiar also with animal and terrestrial), but when the genus or the differentia becomes familiar it is not necessary that the species should also become familiar, so that the species is more unfamiliar. (141^{b}28–142^{a}4, see commentary *ad loc.*)

Then, at 149^{a}19–20, Aristotle adds that 'It (*sc.* the differentia) is more unfamiliar (*sc.* than the genus)'. The claim that the genus is more familiar than the species and the differentia is not sufficient to establish that the interlocutor 'should have made the substitution not of the genus but of the differentia' (149^{a}18–19). Most likely, the argument relies on the assumption concerning the requirement of familiarity, i.e. that, in a definitional context, the defining part must mention things that are more familiar than the kind to be defined in order to improve our understanding of the kind to be defined (see the commentary on 149^{a}5–7, above; this requirement is also mentioned at the end of this chapter, at 149^{a}26–7). But, one might object, even if we supply the assumption concerning the requirement of familiarity, the argument at 149^{a}16–20 does not succeed in establishing the initial point. For, the objection continues, in order to deal appropriately with the commonplace under discussion, Aristotle ought to prove not that the *differentia* has to be replaced, but that *its name* must be substituted. How strong is this objection? As we saw above (in the Introduction and at the end of the commentary on 148ᵇ23–32), in this chapter the distinction between the linguistic and ontological levels is often blurred. In Aristotle's arguments, it is not rare to find an oscillation between linguistic expressions and the entities they signify. So, Aristotle could well be speaking about the replacement of the genus or the differentia, even though what is replaced is the name of the genus or the name of the differentia. In the light of this, lines 149ᵃ18–19 could be read as a concise way to express the thought that the interlocutor should have made the substitution not of the name of the genus but of that of the differentia. More on this in the following section.

(3) Lines 149ᵃ20–4 contain an objection to the criticism set out in the immediately preceding section (149ᵃ14–20). The objection is meant to destroy the argument recommending the substitution of the name of the differentia and not that of the genus. The objection begins by labelling the argument it criticizes as 'ridiculous' (*geloion*, 149ᵃ20). This way of introducing the criticism is rather strong. Then the attention is focused on the linguistic level (as in 149ᵃ14–17) and not on the level of the entities signified by the linguistic expressions (as suggested by the most natural reading of 149ᵃ17–20). According to the new line of argument, there is no good reason why the more familiar name should be the one expressing the genus and not the one expressing the differentia. In the case where the differentia (and not the genus) is expressed by the more familiar name, it is permissible to maintain the name of the differentia and replace that of the genus. As it stands, this objection seems perfectly legitimate. Suppose that I am familiar with the genus animal; suppose also that someone, who is putting forward the definition of human, expresses the genus animal by using a name whose meaning escapes me. My familiarity with the genus animal is not affected because a different name appears in the defining expression. Still, my understanding of the species human is not improved because I am not familiar with the name of the genus used by the interlocutor. In order for my understanding of the species to be improved, I must become aware that the unfamiliar name means nothing else than animal. The fact that an entity can be familiar even though its name can be obscure points towards a distinction between two types of familiarity (or unfamiliarity):

(1) Familiarity (or unfamiliarity) with entities (e.g. genera, species, and differentiae).
(2) Familiarity (or unfamiliarity) with names of entities.

It is easy to see that if an entity is unfamiliar, its name also is unfamiliar. But the converse does not hold. Suppose that, when reading Darwin's *On the Origin of Species*, I come across the description of a species which lives on a remote island of the Pacific and of whose existence I am completely unaware. The name used to refer to this species will be unfamiliar. By contrast, suppose that, when reading a book about botany, I come across the Latin name used to classify a certain tree. It so happens that the Latin name is unfamiliar to me, but the tree grows in my garden and I am familiar with it. This shows that if the name is unfamiliar, it does not follow that the entity is unfamiliar.

It is not easy to assess the objection contained in these lines (149^{a}20–4). One might think that Aristotle becomes aware of some difficulties present in his previous argument at 149^{a}14–20; he, then, he criticizes his own line of thought and suggests how to improve it. Alternatively, the objection might be not a self-criticism but the answer to a question coming from the audience. But, in these cases, it is unclear why Aristotle ignores the objection in the subsequent lines (146^{a}24–8). Brunschwig suspects that lines 149^{a}20–4 are spurious (2007, p. 77, n. 2): see discussion in 'Notes on the Text' *ad loc.*

(4) Lines 149^{a}24–8 consider the case where there is a replacement not of a name with another name (as in 149^{a}5–24) but of a name with the account (i.e. the replacement of the name of *x* with the account of *x*). This brief discussion probably refers back to lines 149^{a}1–3, where Aristotle recommends that, in a definition, it is appropriate to replace names with accounts. As noted above, Aristotle does not develop here the criticism sketched in the immediately preceding lines (149^{a}20–4). Nevertheless, he maintains the view introduced at 149^{a}18–20, whereby the differentia is more unfamiliar than the genus. Aristotle uses the corresponding claim that 'The differentia is less familiar than the genus' (149^{a}27–8) as one of the premises of the argument outlined in the final section of the chapter. The other premise is nothing other than the requirement of familiarity: 'The definition is given for the sake of becoming more familiar with the thing' (149^{a}26–7; see

commentary *ad loc.*). On the basis of these premises, Aristotle concludes that, in a case where a substitution is performed in the defining expression, it is the account of the differentia, rather than that of the genus, that must be offered. It is easy to see that this is a very concise argument where no justification in support of the premises is offered. The argument depends on two previous discussions: one about the requirement of familiarity and the other concerning the relation between genus and the differentia. Both discussions are put forward in *Top.* VI.4. If the interlocutor does not accept the results established in *Top.* VI.4, he will probably refuse his assent to the premises of the argument under scrutiny. This is not the only occasion when Aristotle relies on the results of his discussions in *Top.* VI.4, which plays a foundational role with respect to the strategies outlined in the following chapters.

CHAPTER 12

Introduction: Chapter 12 can be divided into five parts. (1) 149^{a}29–37 deals with the problems arising from the substitution of a proposed differentia by its account. (2) 149^{a}38–149^{b}3 discusses the case of proposed definitions that must be rejected because they contain a categorial mistake. (3) 149^{b}4–23 analyses a commonplace concerning definitions of relatives and focuses on the case where the correlative has a wider extension than that of its relative. (4) 149^{b}24–30 is concerned with the mistake of defining the thing 'in a good or perfect state' rather than the thing *tout court*. (5) 149^{b}31–9 shows that a definition must mention what is choice-worthy for its own sake and not what is choice-worthy for the sake of something else. It is hard to find an interpretation that gives unity to this chapter since it contains a discussion of commonplaces that are not related one to the other. In this respect, chapter 12 is different from the preceding chapters; in particular, it cannot be read as chapter 5, which contains an analysis of the commonplaces concerning the genus, or as chapter 6, which offers an extensive discussion of the commonplaces regarding the differentia. At most, in chapter 12 one can find a certain continuity between two discussions, namely the commonplace concerning relatives (149^{b}4–23) and the one concerning proposed account of things in 'good or perfect state' (149^{b}24–30). In both cases, the proposed definition can be criticized because it is not extensionally adequate as it includes too much or too little.

149^{a}29–37: These lines contain the discussion of certain difficulties arising in the analysis of a differentia's proposed definition. These difficulties are associated with the replacement of a differentia with its account. It is interesting to observe that here Aristotle explicitly talks about the possibility of defining the differentia. Since the preceding chapter concerns the mistakes that can occur in case of a replacement of a name with an account, some scholars suggest that lines 149^{a}29–37 (containing the first commonplace of chapter 12) belong to chapter 11.

At line 149^{a}31–2, there is a problem in the clause *epidioristeon to pôs meson echonta* ('we must further determine in what way it has a middle'): see the discussion in 'Notes on the Text' *ad loc.*

The commonplace described at lines 149ª29–37 has three main stages. (i) 149ª29–30 contains the general formulation of a mistake that can be found when testing a differentia's proposed definition. A mistake occurs if an element of the differentia's proposed account is shared with things other than the differentia to be defined. (ii) 149ª30–5 illustrates the mistake with an example that is based on the replacement of the term indicating the differentia with an account. (iii) 149ª35–7 develops an alternative refutative strategy which is grounded on the disambiguation of a term that is said in many ways.

(i) 149ª29–30. What is wrong with an element of the proposed account being shared with things that are different from the differentia being defined? Simply that in a successful definition the defining part must counter-predicate (i.e. adopting modern jargon, it must be coextensive) with the expression indicating the kind to be defined (see, e.g., *Top.* VI.1, 139ª31–2, and 12, 149ᵇ22–3).

(ii) 149ª30–5. The presentation of the example is very compressed. There are two complex expressions, namely (a) 'odd number' (*peritton arithmon*) and (b) 'number that has a middle' (*arithmon meson echonta*). In (a), 'odd' expresses the differentia of the genus indicated by 'number'. In (b), the genus remains the same, whereas the differentia 'odd' is replaced by 'having a middle'. It is clear that (b) results from (a) by the substitution of the differentia with its proposed account. The difficulty is that the characteristic of having a middle is shared with other things that are not odd. In other words, the characteristic of having a middle has a wider extension than that of being odd. For example, if we consider the field of geometry, we can see that a line and a solid are things that have a middle. It would not be true, however, to say that they are odd. In this sense, 'having a middle' and 'odd' cannot be replaced one with the other *salva veritate*. At this stage, Aristotle does not explain how the characteristic of having a middle belongs to a line and to a solid. He proceeds to put forward an alternative refutative strategy. It is interesting to observe that, strictly speaking, it is not correct to talk about *to meson* ('the middle') in the case of a line *simpliciter*; for an infinite line has no mid-point. Aristotle is perfectly aware of this (148ᵇ30–1), and he is probably using 'line' to mean 'finite straight line' (see *Top.* VI.11, 148ᵇ25–30). Likewise, not all solids will have a mid-point, but a regular solid does: the mid-point will coincide with its centre (see the definition of sphere offered in *Metaph.* VII.8, 1033^{b}14: 'a sphere is a shape equidistant from its mid-point', *esti sphora to ek mesou schema ison*; see also Hero, *Deff.* 77: the mid-point of a sphere is called its centre).

(iii) 149^{a}35–7. An alternative refutative strategy is put forward. The formulation of this strategy is extremely concise and does not offer all that is needed for a full refutation. Aristotle's argument requires that every item in the expression indicating the kind to be defined corresponds to an item in the defining part. It begins by supposing that the expression 'having a middle' (*meson echon*) is said in many ways (*pollachôs legetai*). Then, it must be determined what these ways are, but no further indication is present in the text. Perhaps Aristotle thinks that it could be sufficient to alert the dialectician to the presence of an ambiguity. The dialectician, then, should be able to deal with a case of this sort without other instructions. It is plausible to suggest that (i) in the case of a whole number 'having a middle' is said in the sense (m.i) 'having a unity that stands in the middle between a first group of unity and a second one of the same size' (e.g. $7 = 3 + 1 + 3$); (ii) in the case of a finite line, 'having a middle' corresponds to (m.ii) 'having a mid-point'; (iii) in the case of a solid, 'having a middle' is said in the sense of (m.iii) 'having a centre'. At line 149^{a}37, what is the subject of 'has not been defined' (*ouch hôristai*)? There are two possible candidates. One is the differentia. In this case, Aristotle might be drawing a general conclusion that refers to the argument sketched at the beginning of the passage (149^{a}29–30). The other candidate is the differentia expressed by 'odd'. In this case, the dialectician can argue that the differentia 'odd' has not been defined either because the proposed defining part 'having a middle' is not coextensive with the expression indicating the kind to be defined or because it has not been specified that 'having a middle' is said in many ways and it has not been shown what the appropriate way to be used is. At 149^{a}36–7, we find the term *epitimêsis* ('criticism'), which is rarely used in the *Topics* (there are only three occurrences). The criticism consists in pointing out that it is has not been specified in which way 'having a middle' is said (149^{a}35–6). The deduction has been displayed in the first part of the paragraph ('For example, ... So this would not be a definition of odd'; 149^{a}30–5).

149^a38–149^b3: The commonplace analysed in these lines considers the possibility that the opponent grants an account containing a particular categorial mistake. According to Aristotle's general presentation of the commonplace, this happens if the species to be defined is 'among the things that are' (149^a38), whereas what is indicated by the defining expression (i.e. its alleged essence) is 'not among the things that are'(149^a39). In Greek, this opposition is expressed by affirming or denying the membership in the group of the things that are. 'Of the things that are' translates '*tôn ontôn*' which is the genitive neuter plural participle of the verb *einai* ('to be'). The outline of the refutative strategy shows that here the verb *einai* is used existentially. A more colloquial translation of the clause *ouk an eiê chrôma puri memeigmenon leucon d'esti* (149^b2–3) would be 'colour mixed with fire does not exist, but white exists' (rather than 'colour mixed with fire is not, but white is'). As it stands, the commonplace's initial presentation is not easy to grasp. At 149^a39–149^b1, the example of a proposed, but unsuccessful, definition containing the mistake under scrutiny helps us to have a better understanding of this commonplace. Aristotle supposes that the opponent's granted account is: (1) white is a colour mixed with fire. Then, in the argument at 149^b1–3, he aims at refuting sentence (1). How? This is a reconstruction of the argument's steps. At 149^b1–2, Aristotle states that (2) it is impossible for something incorporeal to be mixed (*memeichsthai*) with a corporeal entity. He tacitly assumes that (3) fire is a corporeal entity and that (4) colour is something incorporeal; from this it follows that (5) it is impossible for a colour to be mixed with fire. Hence, (6) a colour mixed with fire does not exist (149^b2–3), but (7) white exists (149^b3). Thus, (1) must be rejected since it is an instance of the case where the thing to be defined (i.e. white) exists, but what is indicated by the defining expression (i.e. colour mixed with fire) does not exist. Is this a good argument? Sentences (1) and (2) are the premises explicitly stated in the text. Sentences (3) and (4) are also premises: although they remain implicit, they are perfectly reasonable assumptions that could be accepted by a respondent on the basis of simple experiences in daily life. If the respondent, who has granted (1), accepts (2), (3), and (4), then he must also accept (5), which depends on them. Sentence (7) is conceded on the basis of experience. Furthermore, if (7) were not true, it would not be possible to ask for an account of white. The problematic premise is (2). One might intuitively accept that it is impossible for corporeal and incorporeal items to mix. Or one might even have an argument supporting the view that corporeal and incorporeal items could not mix; for example, in *GC* I.10, 327^{b}15–19, Aristotle argues that a corporeal entity cannot be mixed with the colour white, which is something incorporeal (see Williams 1982, pp. 142–4). Nevertheless, someone could refuse his assent to (2) either because he has a metaphysical position according to which corporeal and incorporeal items could mix (Aristotle himself in a fragment of the *Peri Ideôn* reports that Eudoxus explained the participation of perceptible particulars to Forms as a mixture; see Alex. Aphr. *in Metaph.* 97, 27–9), or because he has no view on this subject. In this case, the dialectician following this strategy would not be able to reject the initially granted account (1).

149^{b}4–23: This is one of the several commonplaces concerning proposed definitions of relatives that are presented in *Topics* VI (see 6, 145^{a}13–32; 8, 146^{a}36–146^{b}19; 9, 147^{a}23–8). It is helpful to remember that, according to Aristotle, a definition of a relative must mention its correlative. What is the characteristic trait of this discussion about relatives' proposed accounts? The general idea is contained in the initial presentation of the commonplace (149^{b}4–5), but it is phrased in a way that makes it difficult to grasp. The literal meaning of the Greek expression *en pleiosi perilabontes* is 'by including (*sc.* it) in many things' (see, e.g., the English translations by Pickard-Cambridge 1929, Forster 1960, and Barnes 1984, vol. 1). This rendering, however, does not capture entirely the core of the mistake described here. It is helpful to see how Aristotle uses a variant of this expression elsewhere in the corpus (see Bonitz 1870, p. 582B). In *Cat.* 5, 3^{b}21–3, Aristotle observes that the genus has a wider extension than any of its species; for example, 'in speaking of animal one takes in more (*epi pleion perilambanei*; 3^{b}22) than in speaking of human' (Ackrill 1963, translation slightly modified). In other words, the genus animal extends more widely than the species human, as it also contains animals other than humans. If we take the *Topics*' expression *en pleiosi perilabontes* in this way, we can understand what the respondent is doing: he is granting an account where the correlative mentioned in the relative's proposed defining expression has an extension that is too wide. So, the characteristic trait of this discussion about relatives' proposed accounts consists in offering a correlative that extends more widely than the relative; that is to say, it also contains elements that are the correlatives of other relatives. The example given by Aristotle confirms this interpretation. But before offering an example illustrating this commonplace, Aristotle observes that, in this circumstance, the respondent can be wrong in two ways: (i) he can be wrong *entirely* (*holôs*), or (ii) he can be wrong *partially* (*epi ti*). These ways of being mistaken will be explained in the illustration of the example below.

At 149^{b}6, the example concerns a proposed definition of medicine as 'knowledge of a thing that is' (*epistêmê ontos*; for the rendering of *epistêmê* with 'knowledge' see commentary on *Top.* VI.5, 142^{b}30–143^{a}11). One can object that medicine is not a relative and that it is not clear why it is mentioned in the context of relatives' definitions. The answer to this objection can be found at the beginning of *Top.* VI.8, where Aristotle offers the following instruction to the dialectician: 'If what is being defined is *a relative either with respect to itself or with respect to the genus*, examine whether the definition does not mention that in relation to which it is said, either itself or with respect to the genus' (146^{a}36–146^{b}1). For a definition to be successful, it must mention either the correlative of the thing to be defined (if it is a relative) or that of its relative genus (see commentary on *Top.* VI.8, 146^{a}36–146^{b}9). So, we should understand medicine as a species of knowledge. In the *Topics*, there are (at least) three other proposed accounts of medicine: (1) 'Medicine is knowledge of how to produce health and of dieting' (II.3, 110^{b}18–19); (2) 'Medicine is knowledge of things that are healthy for an animal and for a human' (VI.3, 141^{a}19–20); (3) 'Medicine is (*sc.* knowledge) of producing health and disease' (VI.5, 143^{a}3). Nothing is said about whether (1) is successful, whereas (2) and (3) are criticized on different grounds (see commentaries on the passages in chapters 3 and 5).

At 149^{b}6–12, there is a complex chain of arguments that are not easy to unfold. Let us attempt their reconstruction. The argument at 149^{b}6–8 explains the two ways of being wrong. (i) In the extension of the correlative there is *no element* connected with the relative; then the respondent is entirely wrong. That is to say, he has completely missed the target. (ii) In the extension of the correlative there are *some elements* that are connected with the relative and *others which are not*; then the respondent is only partially wrong. In other words, he has not missed the target completely, but he has individuated a correlative that is too wide as it contains also elements that are not connected with the relative. The argument at 149^{b}8–10 is introduced by *gar* ('for'), but it is not clear what it is meant to explain. There is a philological problem at 149^{b}9: see 'Notes on the Text' *ad loc*. A likely possibility is that the argument explains why it is mistaken to give an account of medicine as 'knowledge of a thing that is'. In this case, medicine should be knowledge of all (*pantos*), *sc*. the things that are. Then, the clause 'If indeed it is said to be of what is in itself and not incidentally' (*eiper kath'hauto kai mê sumbebêkos ontos einai legetai*, 149^{b}9–10) tells us why medicine should be knowledge of all the things that are: it is because it is said to be knowledge of what is *in itself* and not *incidentally*. The thought that in a definitional context the relative is not said *incidentally* in relation to its correlative will be developed at 149^{b}12–23 (more on this below). At 149^{b}10, Aristotle observes that the characteristic of being said in itself in relation to its correlative is not peculiar to knowledge but holds also of the other relatives (*epi tôn allôn echei tôn pros ti*). Then, at 149^{b}11, the sentence 'For every knowable is so-called in relation to knowledge' is meant to justify with an example the general thesis that a relative is said in relation to every instance of its correlative. It must be observed, however, that at this stage of the argument Aristotle would, rather, need to say that knowledge is so-called in relation to every knowable. But, at the moment, this remains understood. It will be explicitly stated at 149^{b}12 in the form of a general claim: 'All relatives reciprocate (*sc*. with respect to their correlatives)'. The relation of reciprocation between relatives and correlatives is expressed by the Greek verbal form *antistrephei*. The verb *antistrephô* can be used in several ways depending on the context where it occurs. (i) It can be used in a general dialectical context, where it is applied to arguments: it means that, once the necessary changes are made, an argument can be suited for constructive as well as for destructive purposes (see, e.g., *Top*. II.2, 109^{b}25–6). (ii) It can be employed in the syllogistic system, where it is applied to premises in order to transform a syllogism in one of the figures to a syllogism in another figure (see, e.g., *APr*. I.45, 50^{b}25). (iii) It can be used in the discussion of the predicables in order to express the relation between the predicables and the subject they are predicated of; for example, the genus does not reciprocate with its species (see, e.g., *Top.* IV.6, 128^{a}38 and 128^{b}4). (iv) In the passage under scrutiny, it is employed to express the relation between relative terms. It indicates the rule that whenever a relative term r is said of its correlative t, then t is also said of r. There is a parallel in *Cat.* 7, 6^{b}28 and 34–5: 'All relatives are said in relation to correlatives that reciprocate ... knowledge is called knowledge of what is knowable, and what is knowable (*sc.* is called) knowable by knowledge'.

At 149^{b}12–23, there is a new line of thought. It refers back to 149^{b}8–10 and justifies the claim 'It must be knowledge of all if indeed it is said to be of what is *in itself* (*kath'hauto*) and not *incidentally* (*kata sumbebêkos*)'. Thus, the successful definition is the one where the relative is spoken of *in itself* and not *incidentally*. What does it mean, in a definitional context, to say that a relative is spoken of *in itself* and not *incidentally*? The answer is not easy, and the present text of the *Topics* gives us very little clue. Here is a plausible guess. In the case at hand, the expressions '*incidentally*' and '*in itself*' are not used to indicate the standard distinction between attributes that belong essentially or incidentally to a subject. Rather, the adverbial form '*incidentally*' introduces the idea of a relative that is related to an 'improper' correlative, as is suggested in *Cat.* 7, 7^{a}31–7^{b}1. In particular, at 7^{a}31–4, Aristotle says: 'Again, if that in relation to which a thing is spoken is properly given, then when all the other things that are incidental are stripped off and that alone is left to which it was properly given as related, it will always be spoken in relation to that' (Ackrill 1963, translation slightly modified). There is no need to unfold all the intricacies of this complex passage. In order to clarify the points that are helpful for the present discussion, it suffices to elaborate on one of Aristotle's examples (7^{a}34–9). Consider the relative slave, which is properly related only to master. If in his account of slave someone mentions master as the only proper correlative, he will give an account *in itself* of master. But if in his account of slave someone says that the correlatives are human, two-footed, and (say) white, he will give the improper correlative of slave. Although it is undeniable that a master is a human, two-footed, and (perhaps) white, a slave is not properly spoken in relation to these. So, if in his account of slave someone mentions the correlatives human, two-footed, and white, he will give an account *incidentally* of slave. For human, two-footed, and white are related to slave only *incidentally*.

The line of thought at 149^{b}12–23 consists of two separate arguments that are both introduced by *eti* ('furthermore'; 149^{b}12 and 18). Both arguments take the form of a *reductio ad absurdum* and the thesis to be rejected is the same, namely: '(It is) by producing the account not *in itself* but *incidentally* that he gives the account correctly' (149^{b}13–14; see also 149^{b}17–18; at 149^{b}19, the expression *toiouton logon*, 'an account of this sort', indicates an account given *incidentally*). The two arguments sketch two independent strategies; each comprises both a general outline of the refutation and an example of it.

(1) A consequence of giving the account incidentally is that *each* relative will be said in relation not to one correlative, but to several. This happens because the same correlative can have a number of attributes and everything that is mentioned in the proposed defining expression as a complement of the relative must count as its correlative. But at least some relatives do not have many correlatives. For example, knowledge has only one correlative, namely the knowable. Similarly, a slave has only one correlative, namely a master. Hence, an account that is given incidentally cannot be accepted as a successful definition of a relative that has only one correlative.

(2) Another consequence of giving the account incidentally is that the account will be common and not proper. Suppose that the opponent grants that the definition of medicine is 'knowledge of a thing that is'. But 'a thing that is' does not single out medicine since other branches of knowledge are of a thing that is too. It follows that by saying 'knowledge of a thing that is' the opponent will not indicate a definition of any specific branch of knowledge. This happens because it is a necessary requirement of a definition that it be proper (*idion*) and not common. This requirement is stated also elsewhere, see, e.g., *Top.* VI.1, 139^{a}31–2. It must be observed that *idion* is used here in the weak sense, i.e. it indicates a property that is coextensive with its subject, but nothing is said as to whether it indicates the essence (see commentary on *Top.* VI.1).

Are these good refutative strategies? Their analysis shows that even if they are presented in a compressed way there seems to be nothing wrong with them. It can hardly be denied, however, that they contain some sophisticated argumentative moves. They are sophisticated because they are based on a rather refined understanding of the nature of relatives. If the opponent is completely untutored in this matter, he will not be in a position to follow the refutation. Then the dialectician would have a hard time in leading his opponent to concede certain assumptions, and, in the end, the opponent will not understand why the proposed definition is rejected. Perhaps it is possible to justify the presence of these strategies by pointing out that in the Academy there might have been some discussions concerning the nature of relatives and their complex connections with the correlatives. If this is the case, then Aristotle was speaking in a context where the audience had already a sufficient understanding of the issue and, therefore, was able to appreciate the sophisticated argumentative moves. In other words, Aristotle was talking to people who could grasp the reasons why certain proposed definitions would not withstand the objections. But there is another possibility that explains Aristotle's choice of refutative strategies. Aristotle might have had in mind a specific audience which was composed of people who had followed his lectures on the relatives. In particular, he might have had in mind those who were familiar with the content of the *Categories* and could grasp certain distinctions concerning the nature of relatives and their correlatives. To sum up, the strategies outlined in (1) and (2) are not to be used indiscriminately but with a special concern for the context of the discussion. But Aristotle gives us no warning of this.

149^b24–30: In this passage there are three main textual problems: see 'Notes on the Text' *ad loc*. What does it mean to define 'the thing in a good or perfect state' (*to pragma eu echon ê tetelesmenon*; 149^b24–5)? And why is this a mistake? None of these questions are answered directly in the text. There are only two examples illustrating definitions of something in a good or perfect state, namely (a) 'A rhetorician is one who has the capacity to see what is persuasive in each argument and to omit nothing' (149^b26–7), and (b) 'A thief is one who purloins secretly' (149^b28–9). Aristotle then explains that if they are the sort of persons described in (a) and (b), they will be a good rhetorician and a good thief respectively (149^b28–9).

At the end of the commonplace's presentation (149ᵇ29–30), there is an interesting remark: a thief is not one who purloins secretly, as suggested in (b), but (b.i) 'He who wishes (*ho boulomenos*) to purloin secretly'. The text leaves us with two tasks. First, it ought to be understood what has to be included in the definition of a rhetorician *tout court*. Second, the difference between (b) and (b.i) should be grasped. Let us begin with the first task. It must be observed that the proposed definition (a) ascribes a certain capacity to the rhetorician. Moreover, (a) is an example of a definition of something in a good or perfect state. Someone 'who has the capacity to see what is persuasive in *each* argument and to omit *nothing*' is a perfect rhetorician. There are rhetoricians who are not perfect because they have the capacity to see what is persuasive in *most* but not all arguments. This capacity makes them rhetoricians nevertheless. This is in line with the description of the rhetorician in *Top.* I.3, 101ᵇ8–10: 'The rhetorician will not convince under all circumstances, nor the physician heal; however, if he leaves out nothing that is possible, then we shall say that he has a sufficient grasp of his craft'. And in *Rh.* I.1, 1355ᵇ9–10, Aristotle says: 'It is clear, then, that its (*sc.* rhetoric's) function is not simply to succeed in persuading, but rather to discover the persuasive facts in each case'. A successful definition of the rhetorician must give us a criterion apt to pick out all rhetoricians, that is to say, a successful definition will pick out the good and the not-so-good rhetoricians. To adopt a different jargon, a successful definition must be extensionally adequate. A definition of the rhetorician that captures only good rhetoricians is not extensionally adequate and, hence, is mistaken.

Let us move to the analysis of the differences between (b) 'A thief is one who purloins secretly' and (b.i) 'A thief is he *who wishes* to purloin secretly'. The thief defined in (b) will be the good thief, as Aristotle explains. For every time he tries to steal, he is successful, and sometimes he tries to steal. By contrast, the thief described in (b.i) merely *wishes* to carry out his actions, but this does not imply that he carries them out successfully. But, as it stands, (b.i) is not sufficiently clear: what does it mean to say that one wishes to get hold of things secretly? There are two options. Option (α): it means that one has a desire to get hold of things secretly, but one does not act on his desire. Obviously, one can hardly be called a thief. So, if this is the correct way to understand it, (b.i) cannot be accepted since it is not extensionally adequate. In other words, (b.i) captures in its extension those that are thieves as well as those that are not. Option (β): saying that one wishes to get hold of things secretly means something stronger than simply having the desire to do it. It means that someone has the desire to steal and acts on his desire; that is to say, when one wishes to steal, one tries to do it. Then, sometimes one is successful and at other times one fails. If we give this meaning to the expression 'he who wishes to purloin secretly', then (b.i) has more chances to be a successful definition of the thief *tout court*. Clearly, (b.i) is extensionally more adequate than (b) since (b.i) captures the good thieves, namely the successful ones, as well as the not-so-good thieves, namely those who try to steal but, at times, fail to achieve their aim.

149ᵇ31–9: The last commonplace of chapter 12 deals with concepts that are discussed at length in ethical contexts; but Aristotle's full-fledged ethical theory, as it is found in his *Nicomachean Ethics* and *Eudemian Ethics*, need not be presupposed here. The key concepts are expressed by 'what is choice-worthy for its own sake' (*to di'hautō haireton*) and 'what is choice-worthy for the sake of something else' (*to di'allon haireton*). Some translators render *haireton* as 'desirable' (see, e.g., Barnes 1984, vol. 1, and Tricot 1950, who uses the French form 'désirable'). The translation 'choice-worthy' is perhaps to be preferred since it captures the concept of choice that is present in the Greek verb *haireô*. Aristotle illustrates here some mistakes that the dialectician's respondent can make when he attempts to define something that is choice-worthy for its own sake. This portion of text can be divided into two parts: (1) 149ᵇ31–4, and (2) 149ᵇ35–9.

(1) At 149ᵇ31–4, there is a general presentation of the commonplace, an outline of the strategy that the dialectician should adopt, and two examples. Here the important distinction between 'what is choice-worthy for its own sake' and 'what is choice-worthy for the sake of something else' is introduced. Regrettably, it is left unexplained. It might be supposed (a) that, according to Aristotle, the distinction is sufficiently intuitive to be grasped without explanation, or (b) that the intended audience should already have an understanding of it. These alternatives are equally plausible. This terminology occurs in an earlier passage,

namely in the discussion concerning the predicable accident, but it does not help us to settle this issue: 'Furthermore, what is choice-worthy for its own sake is more choice-worthy than what is choice-worthy for the sake of something else, e.g. health is more choice-worthy than gymnastics; for the former is choice-worthy for itself, the latter for something else' (*Top.* III.1, 116ª29–31). What is the strategy outlined in 149ᵇ31–4? Aristotle's advice to the dialectician consists in a relatively straightforward strategy: if the thing to be defined is choice-worthy for its own sake whereas the proposed account describes it in a way that implies its being choice-worthy for the sake of something else, then this proposed account cannot be accepted. Although Aristotle does not explicitly say so, the reason why the proposed account cannot be accepted is that it amounts to a misdescription. How can one identify the cases where the description implies that the thing to be defined is choice-worthy for the sake of something else? Aristotle gives us no general recipe but only offers some examples: he mentions the cases where the thing to be defined is described as 'productive of something' (*poiêtikon*), as 'achieving something' (*praktikon*), or in some other way that implies its being choice-worthy for the sake of something else.

(2) At 149ᵇ35–9, there is an argument discussing a mistake that is closely related to the case examined in the immediately preceding lines. An interlocutor might point out that, in some circumstances, the same thing could be described as choice-worthy both for its own sake and for the sake of something else. It is interesting to observe that this remark might have been suggested by the example of justice at 149ᵇ33. The interlocutor could have been familiar with the beginning of *Republic* II, where there is a classification of kinds of good in three groups (357B–D): (i) There is a kind of good that we welcome for its own sake; (ii) There is a kind of good we like for its own sake but also for the sake of what comes from it; (iii) There is a kind of good we do not choose for its own sake but for the sake of what comes from it. Plato notoriously puts justice in group (ii) (358A).

Let us look closely at the argument in lines 149ᵇ35–9. According to Aristotle, if the proposed definition mentions what is choice-worthy for the sake of something else, but not what is choice-worthy for its own sake, there is a mistake (149ᵇ35–7). The justification of this view is contained in the last lines of the chapter (149^b37–9). Here is a tentative reconstruction of the argument:

(1) The best (*to beltiston*) of each thing is above all in the essence (149^b37–8).
(2) Being choice-worthy for its own sake is better (*beltion*) than being choice-worthy for the sake of something else (149^b38).
(3) In the case of what is choice-worthy both for itself and for the sake of something else, what makes it choice-worthy for its own sake is more a part of its essence than what makes it choice-worthy for the sake of something else.
(4) In the case of what is choice-worthy both for itself and for the sake of something else, it is a mistake to put in its essence what makes it choice-worthy for the sake of something else and to omit what makes it choice-worthy for its own sake (149^b35–7).
(5) The definition indicates the essence.
(6) In the case of what is choice-worthy both for itself and for the sake of something else, the definition should have indicated what makes it choice-worthy for its own sake rather than what makes it choice-worthy for the sake of something else (149^b39).

Sentences (1) and (2) are assumptions and are explicitly stated in the text. Note that, in the Greek formulation of (1), the expression 'the best of each thing' (*hekastou ... to beltiston*) occupies an emphatic position at the beginning of the sentence. This suggests that (1) is equivalent to:

(1.i) It is the best of each thing that is above all in the essence (and not the worst).

Sentence (3) is needed by the argument but remains implicit: it follows intuitively from (1) and (2). Perhaps something could be added to ease the intuitive derivation of (3) from (1) and (2). Suppose that an object o has two characteristics, say F and G. Suppose also that F is better than G. Since between F and G the better characteristic is F, and since the essence contains above all what is best, it is more appropriate to put F rather than G in the essence of o. Sentence (4) is explicitly stated in the text, and it follows from (1) and (3): there seems to be nothing difficult in this. Sentence (5) is an assumption that is not explicitly mentioned in the text. But this is not a problem since the point it makes is stated several times in the *Topics* (see, e.g., I.5, 101^b38) and constitutes one of the basic tenets of Aristotle's philosophy. Sentence (6) contains the conclusion of the argument: it is explicitly formulated in the text and it seems to follow unproblematically from the acceptance of (4) and (5).

Despite the efforts aiming at improving it, this argument remains a difficult piece of reasoning. A respondent might still refuse his assent to assumptions (1) and (2), and he might not accept the derivation of (3). He would be right in asking for an explanation or a clarification of the viewpoints presented here. Perhaps it is possible to shed some light on Aristotle's claims by looking at two passages of this treatise.

The first passage is at *Top.* VI.5, 143^{a}9–11, where Aristotle offers the following advice to the dialectician: 'Consider whether he has given an account not in relation to the better but to the worse if there are several things in relation to which what is being defined is said; for every branch of knowledge and capacity seem to be of the best' (for a detailed analysis see commentary *ad loc.*). For example, although medicine can be described as knowledge of how to produce health and disease, it must be defined in relation to the best, i.e. to the capacity of producing health. This passage shows that there is at least one other occasion where Aristotle recommends that the definition should mention what is best.

The second passage is at *Top.* VI.8, 146^{b}10–12: 'In each thing the end is the best or that for the sake of which all the others are. (*sc.* In a definition) One must therefore mention either the best or what comes last, for example appetite is not for the pleasant but for pleasure since it is for the sake of this that we choose the pleasant' (see commentary *ad loc.*). This passage can be read as reinforcing assumption (1) and its equivalent (1.i). It tells us that in the definition one finds the best or what comes last; since we know that the definition reveals the essence, we can conclude that the best or what comes last is part of the essence.

These passages, however, are helpful only for those who already have an Aristotelian training and share certain basic tenets of the Aristotelian doctrine. It remains very difficult to interpret the argument at 149^{b}35–9 in a way that makes it effective to non-Aristotelian interlocutors. Unfortunately, any attempt that could be made to improve the argument and to make it acceptable to interlocutors with different philosophical backgrounds would turn out to be highly speculative.

As a final remark, it ought to be noted that this commonplace and the conceptual *apparatus* used to explain it seem to undermine the internal coherence of the chapter. In (1), in (1.i), and in the passages from the *Topics* quoted above we are told that what is best is contained in the essence and it must be captured in the definition. One might think that there is a tension between these requirements and the immediately preceding commonplace (149^{b}24–30) where Aristotle says that it is a mistake to define 'the thing in a good or perfect state' rather than the thing *tout court*. Although at first sight this sounds like a fair objection, the analysis of the concepts involved in the two commonplaces resolves the apparent tension. On the one hand, in the commonplace at 149^{b}24–30 the target of the criticism is a definition mentioning a capacity possessed at a highest degree (see, e.g., the case of the rhetorician). On the other hand, in the commonplace at 149^{b}31–9 the recommendation of making sure that the examined definition mentions what is best does not deal with a capacity's degree. This is because what is best concerns not having a capacity at the highest degree but the goal of a capacity.

CHAPTER 13

Introduction: Chapter 13 has a salient feature: it does not discuss standard definitions where the defining part is expressed in terms of the genus and (one or more) differentia of the species to be defined. Standard definitions are the subject of chapters 1–12. The commonplaces analysed in chapter 13 concern a different way of framing the definition and they point to an alternative understanding of the relation between the species to be defined and the defining elements. The species is conceived of as a whole and the defining elements are its parts. This leads Aristotle to explore certain aspects of the relation between parts and whole. If we think about this relation in terms of classical mereology, we can distinguish two fundamental ways of describing it. On the one hand, the whole is nothing but its parts. On the other hand, the whole is a unit resulting from the combination of its parts. It is possible to find an anticipation of this distinction in Plato's *Theaetetus*. Plato's ideas seem to constitute a precedent for the Aristotelian discussion, and at least part of the Platonic analysis could well be in the background of Aristotle's investigation. In the refutation of Socrates' dream (201C–205E), Theaetetus and Socrates are considering the possibility that knowledge is true opinion with an account (*logos*). They agree on the fact that certain things have an account, whereas others do not. Complex things have an account and are knowable. This is the case of the syllables: for instance, the syllable 'SÔ' has an account because if one is asked what it is, one can correctly answer: 'it is *sigma* and *omega*'. By contrast, simple things do not have an account and are not knowable. This is the case of the letters: for instance, the letter 'S' has no account because if one is asked what it is, there is no correct account one can offer (such an account should have mentioned the components, but there are none). Then Socrates distinguishes two alternatives. (1) The syllable is identical to its letters. (2) The syllable is a unit coming from the letters. At this point, Socrates shows how a paradox follows from the acceptance of either thesis. Consider the first alternative and suppose you want to know a syllable. Then you must know the letters. But the letters are unknowable since they are simple and do not have an account. So, the syllable is unknowable. Consider now the second alternative. Can the syllable be known? By being a unit resulting from the letters, the syllable is simple and does not have an account. So, in this case too, the syllable is unknowable. The analysis of the paradox and Plato's precise view on parts and wholes reach far beyond the aims of our discussion (for an informative debate see, e.g., Harte 2002). For our purposes, it suffices to observe that Socrates' alternatives seem to be present in the Aristotelian classification of the ways to understand the relation between parts and whole. Just as Socrates offers a dilemma whose horns are (1) the syllable is its letters, and (2) the syllable is a unit arising out of its letters, so also Aristotle opens chapter 13 by considering whether the species to be defined is described as (1) these things, (2) something arising from these things, or (3) this thing with this thing. The first two options of the Aristotelian tripartite distinction seem akin to the two alternatives outlined by Socrates.

This tripartite distinction gives a structure to the chapter. (1) 150^a1–21 analyses a proposed defining expression that is formulated as 'these things' and contains a conjunction of two elements (e.g. 'justice is temperance *and* courage', 150^a3–4). (2) 150^a22–150^b26 examines a proposed definition that is expressed as '*a* is what is composed of these'; the granted defining expression describes a combination of parts (e.g. 'shamelessness is *composed of* courage and false opinion', 150^b3–4). (3) 150^b27–151^a19 investigates accounts where the proposed defining expression is formulated as 'this thing with this thing' (e.g. 'courage is bravery *with* correct reasoning', 151^a3–4). The chapter is entirely refutative and the examples it contains do not seem to stand up to scrutiny. Is this due to the fact that Aristotle's examples are ill-chosen? Or is it because all non-standard definitions, namely definitions that are not framed in terms of genus and differentia of the kind to be defined, must be criticized and rejected? The text does not offer an explicit solution to this problem. Although in *Topics* VI Aristotle does not commit himself to the view that there can be successful definitions where the kind to be defined is described as a whole whose parts are mentioned in the defining expression, it could be helpful for him to conceive of an alternative form of definition since the standard one has some limitations.

Even though it does not belong exclusively to this chapter, an interesting feature shapes the discussion of each of the three parts.

It happens very often that, at first, Aristotle puts forward a commonplace, but then he seems to change his mind and offers a counterexample to this commonplace. The result is that some refutative strategies are subject to refinements and hence their original formulations must be abandoned. The text offers no hint as to why Aristotle changes direction in this way. The explanation could be that Aristotle jotted down some problems which occurred to him (or to an audience member) at or close to the time of writing this part of the *Topics*. Another option is that he may have begun to revise this part of the *Topics* at some later times but did not complete the revision. Aristotle's discussion of the commonplaces in this chapter is particularly concise and only some refutative strategies are illustrated with examples.

150^{a}1–21: Aristotle's first task consists in distinguishing three main groups of commonplaces that he develops in chapter 13. At 150^{a}1–2, he instructs the dialectician to see whether in the account granted by the interlocutor the proposed defining expression takes one of the following forms: (1) it is phrased as 'these things' (*tade*); (2) it is formulated as 'what is composed of these' (*to ek toutôn*); (3) it is expressed as 'this with this' (*tode meta toude*).

Lines 150^{a}2–7 contain a first general description of the unwelcome consequence that follows when an interlocutor grants an account where the proposed defining expression is phrased as 'these things'. The example at 150^{a}3–4 shows that attempting to define something as 'these things' corresponds to framing the defining part as a conjunction of different elements. What happens if the interlocutor grants an account of a species whose defining expression mentions the conjunction of two other species? Suppose that the granted definition of justice is the conjunction of temperance and courage. Suppose also that there are two individuals: one has temperance (without courage) and the other courage (without temperance). It follows that the same thing, i.e. justice, 'belongs to both and neither' (*amphoin kai mêdeteôi huparchein*, 150^{a}3). When the two individuals are taken together, they possess the conjunction of temperance and courage; hence they have justice. But when the two individuals are taken separately, neither of them possesses the conjunction of temperance and courage; hence, neither of them will have justice. At 150ª5–6, the unwelcome consequence is rephrased as 'both and neither will be just' (*amphoteroi dikaioi esontai kai oudeteros*). This way of rephrasing the unwelcome consequence makes its alleged absurdity more evident. But Aristotle is aware of this refutative strategy's limits and expands on them in the immediately following lines.

Lines 150ª7–11 contain a possible objection to the preceding refutative strategy, an objection which leads to a refinement of the argument sketched at 150ª2–7. Aristotle shows that there are instances when it is not absurd to say that two individuals taken together enjoy a certain characteristic which neither of them enjoys on their own. It is possible that two individuals taken together possess a hundred drachmae and that, at the same time, neither possesses them. For it could well happen that one has seventy drachmae in his hands, whilst the other has only thirty. It would only be an absurdity if it were possible to show that 'contraries belong to them' (*tanantia huparchein autois*, 150ª10). This is the conclusion that the dialectician must draw if he wants to refute his opponent successfully.

Lines 150ª11–14 explain how the refinement illustrated above (150ª7–11) can be applied to improve the strategy introduced at 150ª2–7. There will be a successful refutation of the granted account 'justice is temperance and courage' if the dialectician is able to infer the absurd thesis saying that 'both will have justice and injustice' (*amphô ... dikaiosunên kai adikian hexousin*, 150ª12–13). It is easy to see that this is nothing other than an instance of the more general claim, 'contraries belong to them' (*tanantia huparchein autois*, 150ª10). For the refutation to go through, it must be assumed that the granted definition of justice is framed in terms of the conjunction of courage and temperance (exactly as in 150ª3–4). Then, on this basis, the respondent must concede that the account of injustice will be expressed by the conjunction of cowardice and intemperance. Suppose that there are two individuals: one has temperance and cowardice, whilst the other has intemperance and courage. When they are taken together, they will have justice (since the conjunction of courage and temperance belongs to them) but they will also have injustice (since the conjunction of cowardice and intemperance belongs to them too). But this is absurd. Hence, the respondent will be refuted.

Lines 150ᵃ15–21 contain further instructions to a dialectician whose opponent grants a conjunctive definition. In this case, the dialectician will find it useful to develop the lines of reasoning showing that a whole and its parts are not the same thing. For, according to Aristotle, the interlocutor who concedes a conjunctive definition appears to identify the parts with the whole they constitute. It is not clear, however, what the common trait is between, on the one hand, a conjunctive definition and, on the other, an identification of the whole with its parts. Perhaps Aristotle has in mind something along the following lines: the interlocutor who defines justice as temperance and courage appears to claim that whenever there are temperance and courage there is also justice. But this claim is false. At most, one can say that it is a certain type of combination between temperance and courage that results in justice. The best arguments against the identification of the whole with its parts are those that employ examples where the whole is clearly different from its parts because it requires a specific mode of combination. The case of the house is one of these examples: it is easy to see that although the bricks are the parts of the house, a heap of bricks is not identical to a house. The dialectician can develop an objection against a conjunctive definition which is based on an example of this sort. On the concept of mode of combination see the commonplace at 150ᵇ22–5, below, and the commentary *ad loc.*; see also *Top.* VI.14, 151ᵃ20–31.

150ᵃ22–5: The second part of the chapter begins here. Having dealt with the refutations of proposed conjunctive definitions, namely the cases where the defining expression is formulated in terms of a conjunction of (at least) two elements (in Greek *tade*, 150ᵃ1, or *tauta*, 150ᵃ22; lit. 'these things'), Aristotle addresses the instances where the proposed definition is expressed in terms of *something being composed of these things* (in Greek *to ek toutôn*, 150ᵃ1 and 150ᵃ22; lit. 'what is from these'). He offers a brief outline of several cases which show an increasing degree of complexity. The first is contained in this portion of text (150ᵃ22–5). It concerns situations where a species cannot be defined as the composition of two elements. This happens, for example, if the components mentioned in the defining expression are a line and a number (150^{a}25). Aristotle seems to think that there is no species whose essence can be formed by the combination of a line and a number. He seems to introduce here a basic and general requirement concerning certain ontological characteristics that the components mentioned in the defining expression must possess. Among these components, there must be some sort of ontological homogeneity that allows them to be unified in a single thing (150^{a}24–5). It is not clear, however, what Aristotle means when he talks about unification in a single thing. Still, it is evident that numbers and lines cannot be unified in a single thing. By parity of reasoning, one might be tempted to add that an adagio by Beethoven and a glass of wine cannot constitute a unity.

150^{a}26–33: This portion of text concerns a further case where the proposed definition is incorrectly framed in terms of *something being composed of these things* (*to ek toutôn*). There are two possible related mistakes: (A) lines 150^{a}26–30, and (B) lines 150^{a}30–3. The mistake described in (A) consists in proposing an account where the species to be defined is by nature *primarily* in a single thing, whilst the elements mentioned in the defining expression are not. What does this mean? No example illustrates this point and no justification is offered. Some hints can be found in a commonplace discussed in *Top*. VI.6, 145^{a}28–32 (see commentary *ad loc.*). For our purposes, it suffices to indicate the general idea involved in that commonplace. Consider, for example, three proposed accounts of wisdom: (1) 'Wisdom is an excellence of a human', (2) 'Wisdom is an excellence of the soul', and (3) 'Wisdom is an excellence of the rational faculty'. Accounts (1) and (2) must be criticized and rejected, whereas account (3) is a promising starting point for a successful definition of wisdom because, according to Aristotle, wisdom is *primarily* an excellence of the reasoning faculty (see VI.6, 145^{a}30–1: *prôtou gar tou logistikou aretê hê phronêsis*). Suppose, now, that an interlocutor has granted an account of wisdom in terms of something being composed of these things, namely 'wisdom is composed of courage and temperance' (see Alex. Aphr. *in Top*. 487, 9–15). How can the dialectician refute it? He can begin by observing that wisdom is in a single thing as its primary subject, i.e. in the rational faculty, whereas courage and temperance are each in a different thing as their primary subject; that is to say, courage is in the spirited faculty as its primary subject and temperance in the appetitive as its primary subject. The dialectician can then argue that (i) 'The whole is necessarily in the things in which the parts are' (150^a29–30). In this case, the whole corresponds to the species to be defined, e.g. wisdom, and the parts are the components mentioned in the defining expression, e.g. courage and temperance. It follows that (ii) 'The whole is not primarily in one thing, but in several' (150^a30). In our example, wisdom will not be in the rational faculty as its primary subject but in the spirited and appetitive faculty. Thus, (iii) 'Clearly, that thing would not be composed of these' (150^a28–9). Hence the proposed account, 'Wisdom is composed of courage and temperance', is mistaken and cannot be accepted.

The mistake outlined in (B) concerns a slightly different situation. Although the whole and the parts are in a single thing as their primary subject (and hence they pass the immediately preceding test), they are not in the same thing. No example is offered. Suppose, then, that the interlocutor has granted the following account: (4) 'Wisdom is composed of courage and magnanimity'. Both courage and magnanimity are in a single thing as their primary subject. Still, this is not sufficient. Although wisdom is in a single thing as its primary subject, and courage and magnanimity also are in a single thing as their primary subject, the primary subject of wisdom is different from the primary subject of courage and magnanimity; for the single primary subject of wisdom is the rational faculty, whilst the single primary subject of courage and magnanimity is the spirited faculty. Hence account (4) cannot be accepted. We might wonder whether the mereological principle which this argument relies on is acceptable. Aristotle claims that if a whole x is in y as its primary subject, then each part of x is in y as its primary subject. This is a strong principle which lies at the basis of this commonplace and constitutes the grounds for criticizing the proposed definition. The text, however, does not provide us with a motivation to accept it. The interlocutor has no obligation to endorse it and he could, for instance, choose an alternative principle, namely if a whole x is in y as its primary subject, then each part of x is in a part of y as its primary subject. This alternative principle would block the dialectician's objection. Therefore, as it stands, this commonplace is not sufficiently explained, and it leaves open the possibility that a respondent might refuse to accept the questioner's strategy.

150ᵃ33–6: A third possibility of mistake is concisely described in these few lines. It concerns the case where it is a consequence of a proposed account that the destruction of the whole brings with it the destruction of the parts. But, according to Aristotle, this is wrong. The relation between parts and whole, as it is understood by Aristotle in these lines, is characterized by two factors: (a) when the parts are destroyed, the whole also is destroyed, but (b) when the whole is destroyed, the parts can continue to exist. The following example illustrates Aristotle's notion of the relation between parts and whole: consider a syllable and its letters. The syllable is the whole and the letters are its parts. When you remove a letter, the syllable is no longer there but the letter can continue to exist. In this case, the elimination of a part is sufficient for the destruction of the whole. This, however, is not always the case. Consider a different example coming from the field of biology: a human corresponds to the whole and his hand to one of its parts. (1) If a human has a hand cut off, he does not cease to exist. And this is contrary to (a) above; for the whole can continue to exist even though a part is destroyed. (2) If a human dies, his hand ceases to function as a hand: in Aristotle's view, it is not the same hand as the one belonging to the living human. And this is contrary to (b) above; for when the whole is destroyed, a part is also destroyed. It is interesting to observe that there is another case where the parts and the whole behave precisely as in the biological example. Consider a genus and its species: the species are to be conceived of as parts of the genus, which corresponds to the whole. When a species is destroyed, the genus can continue to exist. For instance, when a certain group of dinosaurs became extinct, the genus animal continued to exist. In the light of the two counterexamples, it is tempting to conclude that the mereological account adopted by Aristotle in this commonplace (150ᵃ33–6) is flawed. Thus, if he wants to answer the objections coming for the counterexamples illustrated above, the dialectician must be able to revise this refutative strategy.

150ᵃ36–150ᵇ18: This portion of text presents four general mistakes concerning proposed definitions taking the form 'what is composed of these' (*to ek toutôn*). There is a series of arguments dealing with the relations obtaining between some characteristics of the whole and some of the parts. These arguments are contained in the following subsections: (a) 150^{a}36–150^{b}1; (b) 150^{b}1–6; (c) 150^{b}7–13; (d) 150^{b}14–18.

(a) 150^{a}36–150^{b}1. The dialectician must look into whether the characteristic of being good or that of being evil are possessed by the parts and by the whole. The presentation of the argument is very compressed. *Prima facie*, the text seems to illustrate two cases: 'The whole is good or evil whereas the parts are neither, or conversely the parts are good or evil whereas the whole is neither' (150^{a}38–150^{b}1). But a deeper analysis shows that four cases must be considered. There are two interpretative options for these cases. The first option reads the text as follows: (1) The whole is good but the parts are not so, i.e. they can be evil or neither good nor evil; (2) The whole is evil but the parts are not so, i.e. they can be good or neither good nor evil; (3) The parts are good but the whole is not so, i.e. it can be evil or neither good nor evil; (4) The parts are evil but the whole is not so, i.e. it can be good or neither good nor evil. The second option offers an alternative reading: (1*) The whole is good but the parts are neither good nor evil, i.e. they are neutral; (2*) The whole is evil but the parts are neither good nor evil, i.e. they are neutral; (3*) The parts are good but the whole is neither good nor evil, i.e. it is neutral; (4*) The parts are evil but the whole is neither good nor evil, i.e. it is neutral. The first interpretation looks more satisfactory from a logical perspective, but it is hard to see it in the Greek text. The second interpretation is closer to the Greek text, but it is logically unsatisfactory. It is difficult to choose between them since no example is offered in the text. But the choice can be left open because in (c) 150^{b}7–13 Aristotle challenges his proposed strategy and offers a counterexample.

(b) 150^{b}1–6. There is a modification of the case sketched in (a). Aristotle invites the dialectician to examine the degree to which the parts and the whole possess the characteristic of being good and that of being evil. The argument is compressed, and the example helps to shed some light on the formulation of the general thesis. Aristotle's ideas can be reconstructed as follows. Consider the degree to which part x is good and the degree to which part y is evil. Suppose that the degree to which x is good is greater than the degree to which y is evil. In this situation, there are two possibilities: (1) The whole composed of x and y is good unqualifiedly (*haplôs agathon*, 150^{b}6); (2) The whole composed of x and y is more good than evil (*mallon agathon ê kakon*, 150^{b}6). Thus, if in the proposed definition the whole is not unqualifiedly good or if it is not more good than evil, then the proposed definition must be criticized and rejected. The thought behind Aristotle's argument can be better understood with the help of an analogy. Suppose that x and y are two equal parts of water. Say that the degree to which something is hot (or cold) is measured by the number of degrees Celsius by which it exceeds (or it falls below) the human body's temperature (e.g. 37 °C). If the degree to which x is hot is greater than the degree to which y is cold (e.g. if x is 10 °C above 37 °C and y is 5 °C below 37 °C), then the mixture of x and y must be either hot or at least more hot than cold (e.g. it must be 5 °C above 37 °C). Although this analogy involves precisely measured quantities, a numerical structure in not essential to the line of argument sketched by Aristotle. The mathematical framework, however, helps to clarify his point.

(c) 150^{b}7–13. Aristotle shows that the refutative strategies outlined in (a) and (b) are underdetermined and must be refined. At 150^{b}7–8, there are two possible readings of the Greek text. The clause *mê hekateron hêi kath'hauto agathon ê kakon* can be translated with (e) 'Each of the two is not a good or an evil in itself'. This is equivalent to: (e*) 'Each of the two is neutral in itself'. The alternative rendering is (f) 'Each of the two is not a good, or an evil in itself'. In (f), the presence of the comma between 'good' and 'or' marks the difference between the two readings. This becomes clearer when we paraphrase (f) as (f*) 'Each of the two is not a good in itself, or each of the two is not an evil in itself'. Translation (f) is to be preferred because at 150^{b}8–10 Aristotle says: 'Many of the productive things are good not in themselves but when mixed, *or, conversely, each of the two is good* but when they are mixed they are evil or neither'. Here the expression 'in themselves' means 'taken on their own', i.e. 'not combined'.

Lines 150^{b}8–13 help to explain how the dialectician can understand and apply the revised strategy. Consider the case of 'many of the productive things' (*polla ... tôn poiêtikôn*, 150^{b}8). Although it is unclear what Aristotle means by using the expression 'many of the productive things', the context suggests that they are

319

something like medications or therapies. In this case, it can happen that the parts are not good when taken on their own, but their mixture can be good. The reverse can also happen, namely the parts can be good when taken on their own, but what results from mixing them can be evil or neither good nor evil (*oudeteron*, 150^{b}10). Then an example, which completes the illustration of this case, is added. Consider what happens with certain substances that produce health and disease (*epi tôn hugieinôn kai nosôdôn*, 150^{b}11). Some medications prescribed to restore health are good if they are taken separately. But a cocktail resulting from their mixture can be bad for the health and make the patient ill. Even though in these lines (150^{b}7–13) Aristotle does not speak of the degree to which part *x* is good and the degree to which part *y* is evil, his argument can be applied to this case too. Suppose that the degree to which part *x* is good is greater than the degree to which part *y* is evil. Their mixture, however, can be more evil than good or as good as evil. This argument, which remains implicit in the text, can be used to criticize the refutative strategy outlined in (b) 150^{b}1–6.

In the *Topics*, Aristotle often uses examples from the field of medicine, and on several occasions objections to certain strategies are formulated on the basis of cases discussed in medicine (see Brunschwig 2007, p. 82, n. 5).

(d) 150^{b}14–18. At first, there is a concise outline of a refutative strategy (150^{b}14–15). Then, this strategy is criticized (150^{b}15–18). There is a problem with the translation of lines 150^{b}16–17 that will be discussed below. What does it mean to say that 'Although it is composed of better and worse, the whole is not worse than the better and better than the worse'(150^{b}14–15)? Consider a proposed definition of a whole which is composed of a better and a worse part. The following rule must be observed: if in the proposed definition it is not the case that the whole turns out to be both better than the worse part and worse than the better part, then this definition must not be accepted. This suggests that the whole must be worse than the better part and better than the worse part. But no explanation and no illustration of this case are offered in the text. It is useful to elaborate on a sketch of an example offered by Pacius 1597, p. 446. A proposed definition of an alloy of silver and gold should characterize the alloy (i.e. the whole) as being worse than the better part (i.e. the golden part) and as being better than the worse part (i.e. the part in silver). Aristotle, however, does not pursue this strategy further, and he raises an objection. *Prima facie*, the text containing this objection does not seem to make sense to an English reader. Although from a syntactical viewpoint the Greek formulation can easily be translated into English, its word-by-word translation offers a line of reasoning that does not work as an effective criticism. It seems to say that in the case in which the components are *not* good when taken on their own (*mê kath'hauta êi ta ex hôn sungkeitai agatha*), *nothing* prevents the whole from *not* being good (*ouden kôluei to holon mê ginesthai agathon*). This, however, cannot be right since there is one negation too many. In Forster's translation, the first occurrence of the negative particle *mê* is expressed in the connective 'unless', while the second is not translated: '*Unless* the component parts are themselves good; but there is nothing to prevent the whole being good' (Forster 1960). The rendering by Pickard-Cambridge 1929 is maintained *verbatim* in Barnes 1984, vol. 1: '*Unless* the elements compounded are in themselves good; *if they are not*, the whole *may very well not* be good'. In this case, both negative particles *mê* are translated, the expression 'if they are not' is added (probably following the reading of other manuscripts), and the phrase 'nothing prevents' (*ouden kôluei*) is not explicitly translated: perhaps it is expressed in the modalization of the verb *ginesthai* ('may very well be'). It seems to me that there are five options helping us to solve this difficulty. (1) It is possible to delete the occurrence of *mê* at 150^{b}16; then the translation would be: 'If the things of which it is composed are in themselves good, but nothing prevents the whole from *not* being good'. (2) It is possible to delete the occurrence of *mê* at 150^{b}17; then the translation would be: 'If the things of which it is composed are *not* in themselves good, but nothing prevents the whole from being good'. (3) The text at 150^{b}15–17 may not be complete. The full text could be something along the following lines: 'This is not necessary if the things of which it is composed are not in themselves good *or are not in themselves evil*, but nothing prevents the whole *from not being an evil or* from not being a good'. In other words, two possibilities would be mentioned: (a) If the parts are not in themselves good, nothing prevents the whole from not being an evil, and (b) If the parts are not in themselves evil, nothing prevents the whole from not being a good. The fact that the text is not complete could be explained in two ways: (3.i) Something dropped out of the original text; (3.ii) Aristotle is writing in an extremely concise way. (4) One might choose to attach importance to the adversative conjunction *alla* ('but', at the beginning of 150^{b}17) so that it would acquire a stronger meaning. The idea is that *alla* would introduce an antecedent that remains implicit. The implicit clause's content would express the opposite of what is stated in the antecedent mentioned in the immediately preceding line (150^{b}16). This suggestion would result in the following translation: 'This is not necessary if the things of which it is composed are not in themselves good, *but if they are*, nothing prevents the whole from not being a good'. Perhaps this might have been the reasoning behind Brunschwig's translation of 150^{b}15–17 : 'Ou alors : cela non plus n'est pas nécessaire, si ce n'est pas par elles-mêmes que sont bonnes les choses dont il y a combinaison; *car autrement*, rien n'empêche le tout de ne pas être bon' (Brunschwig 2007). (5) The occurrence of *mê* at 150^{b}17 is redundant and does not have the value of a genuine negation; for this reason, it must not be translated into English.

The analysis of these options shows that (5) is to be preferred. Consider (1) and (2): the choice of deleting one negative particle requires a harsh emendation of the Greek text. To the best of my knowledge, no manuscript supports this emendation (see *apparatus* in Brunschwig 2007, p. 83). The same argument holds for option (3.i): in the manuscript tradition, nothing favours the idea that the expressions suggested above (i.e. 'or are not in themselves evil', and 'from not being an evil') were, at some point, omitted. As for (3.ii), although it might look attractive because it does not involve an alteration of the transmitted text, it remains highly speculative. If option (4) cashes out Brunschwig's understanding of the passage, it strikes us as appealing and ingenious; nevertheless, it shares with (3.ii) the lack of explicit support and, therefore, it remains speculative too. What are the advantages that make option (5) the most attractive alternative? First, it requires no emendation and offers a good interpretation of the text as it is handed down by the manuscript tradition and printed by modern editors (Bekker 1831, Waitz 1846, Strache and Wallies 1923, Ross 1958, and Brunschwig 2007; the textual variant discussed by the editors in their *apparatus* does not concern the occurrences of the negation). Second, the use of a redundant *mê* after *kôluô* ('forbid') is perfectly possible in ancient Greek and is attested in Smyth 1956, p. 622, § 2740. The use of *mê* as a 'pleonasm after verbs of negative results signifying "to forbid"' is described also in LSJ, *s.v. mê* B.5b. There is a similar use of the particle *ne* ('not') in French and Latin. For example, the sentence 'La pluie...empêche qu'on *ne* se promène' (Racine) is equivalent to the English 'The rain prevents us from walking'. Analogously, 'Plura *ne* scribam dolore impedior' (Cicero) is rendered in English as 'I am too troubled to write more'. In none of these cases does the particle *ne* express a genuine negation. Third, it must be observed that there are similar cases where the Greek prose allows for 'an idiomatic use of a negation too many'.[3] This idiomatic use can be found in some passages in Plato: *Prt.* 344C4 and 352D1–3 (Denyer 2008, p. 162, 181); *Phd.* 72D2–3. In *Ap.* 32B5, the sentence *ênantiôthen humin mêden poiein para tous nomous* means 'I was opposed to your acting contrary to the law': here the negation *mêden* looks illogical but is idiomatic. In *Grg.* 508A8–B2, the Greek reads *exelekteos dê houtos ho logos humin estin, hôs ou dikaiosunes kai sôphrosunês ktêsei eudaimones hoi eudaimones* (word-by-word translation: 'We must refute the argument that it is not the possession of justice and temperance that makes happy people happy'). Here, the theory to be refuted is that virtue does make us happy, but still there is the negation *ou*.

At 150ᵇ18, the phrase 'precisely as in the cases just mentioned' concludes the discussion of the commonplace with a back-reference to 150ᵇ11–13. It indicates that the refutative strategy outlined at 150ᵇ15–18 can also be illustrated by the case of 'things producing health and disease' and by the example of 'Some remedies (*sc.* that) are such that each of the two is good but if they are both given as mixed, they are an evil'. In other words, Aristotle suggests that, in this case too, the characteristics possessed by the parts when they are taken on their own might well fail to determine the characteristic of the whole in a purely mathematical way.

---

[3] I owe this expression and all the examples below to Nicholas Denyer.

150ᵇ19–21: A further mistake arises if the interlocutor grants an account where the whole *is synonymous* with one of the parts of which it is composed. It is not clear how 'being synonymous' is used here. It could be used in a weak or non-technical way: it would correspond to 'sharing the name' and the question whether the definition is also shared would not be addressed. Alternatively, 'being synonymous' could be used in a strong or technical way; in this case, it would be equivalent to 'sharing both the name and the definition that corresponds to the name' (this is Aristotle's description of synonymy in the *Categories*: 'When things have the name in common and the definition of being which corresponds to the name is the same, they are called synonymous'; 1,1ᵃ6–7). There are other passages in the *Topics* where 'being synonymous' is employed in the technical way; see, for example, I.15, 107ᵇ4; IV.4, 125ᵇ5–7; VI.10, 148ᵃ24–5 (see commentary *ad loc.*). Since the technical use is already present in book VI of the *Topics*, one might be inclined to think that Aristotle is employing it in this chapter too.

The case of the syllable and its letters is meant to illustrate the fact that the whole fails to share both name and possibly definition with any of its parts. But the example is ambiguous. It can mean that a specific syllable, say 'ba', fails to be synonymous with any of its letters, namely with 'b' and 'a', with respect to the name 'syllable' ('ba' is called a 'syllable' but 'b' and 'a' are not called 'syllable'). But it can also mean that a syllable is synonymous with neither of its letters with respect to its specific name ('ba' is called '"ba"' but neither 'b' nor 'a' are so called). Why should one believe that the whole could be synonymous with one of its parts? This happens if one adopts a model of definition that is different from the one examined in these lines. Consider, for example, the definition of human as 'two-footed rational animal'. Here the species human and the genus animal have the name in common (they are both called 'animal') and they share the same definition. But if one chooses to frame the definition in terms of parts and whole, one must not mention the genus. In other words, the model of definition in terms of parts and whole is different from that of the definition by genus and differentia and does not share (at least some of) its characteristics. In particular, it does not mention the genus that is synonymous with the species to be defined.

150^b22–6: This is the last in Aristotle's series of possible mistakes concerning proposed definitions where something is defined as 'what is composed of these' (*to ek toutôn*). (Note that in translating 150^b22–6, I understand *einai* after the second occurrence of *to* at line 23 and after the occurrence of *to* at line 24.) It is a general mistake occurring every time the whole is defined in terms of the combination of its parts. If the expression 'composed of these' is taken by itself, it is underdetermined and is not sufficient to indicate the essence of the composite. Consider, for example, the case mentioned in the commentary to the preceding lines (150^b19–21). If the defining expression of clay and that of blood contain merely a list of their components, then the same account, namely 'What is composed of earth and water', would be common to both composites. How could one distinguish between the essence of clay and that of blood? Aristotle's suggestion is that something must be added in the defining expression; that it to say, the defining expression must specify 'the mode of combination' (*ton tropon tês suntheseôs*, 150^b22). What is a 'mode of combination'? The example of the house at 150^b25–6 helps us to understand better Aristotle's thought. The idea seems to be that a house is not simply the combination of, say, bricks, stones, and tiles. For a disorganized heap of bricks, stones, and tiles does not make a house. The components must be put together in a certain *ratio* (a specific quantity of bricks, stones, and tiles is needed) and according to a certain structure. And the concept of structure is closely connected with that of form. To anyone who is familiar with Aristotle's later ontology, as it is contained in the *Metaphysics*, it cannot escape one's notice that the case of the house is one of the stock examples used to introduce or illustrate the concept of form and that of formal cause. For instance, in *Metaph.* VII.9, 1034^a24, Aristotle claims that 'The art of building is the form of the house'; in *Metaph.* VII.17, 1041^a26–8, he says: 'And why are certain things, e.g. stones and bricks, a house? It is evident that we are seeking the cause'. Even though the example of the house in the *Topics* might seem to go in the direction of something like the formal cause, there is no sufficient evidence to say whether Aristotle already has this concept in mind. More on the notion of combination will be said in *Top.* VI.14, 151^a20–31.

150^b27–32: The third and last part of chapter 13 addresses the cases where the proposed defining expression takes the form 'this with this'. At the beginning of this part, Aristotle proposes to apply a linguistic test to the granted accounts. The goal of the test consists in seeing whether the expression 'this with this' corresponds either to 'these things' or to 'what is composed of these'. If it does, the dialectician can use one of the refutative strategies introduced in the first or in the second part of the chapter respectively (150^a2–21 and 150^a22–150^b26). At 150^b28–30, an unproblematic example illustrates how the questioner could proceed. It is crucial that the interlocutor concedes that 'this with this' is equivalent either to 'these things' or to 'what is composed of these'. Then, the questioner can choose the appropriate strategy among the relevant commonplaces.

One might be surprised to find a further discussion of granted accounts taking the form 'these things' and 'what is composed of these' in the analysis of proposed defining expressions containing the expression 'this with this'. Thus, one might be inclined to think that this introduces a tension since, in the preceding part of chapter 13, 'these things' and 'what is composed of these' are presented as two separate cases. In this section of the chapter, however, they appear to fall under the general case of 'this with this'. The tension can be eased by observing that 'this with this' has a wider semantic spectrum than 'these things' and 'what is composed of these'. So, it is only at a linguistic level that 'this with this' might seem to cover the other two cases. As will become clear in the sequel of the text, Aristotle distinguishes six linguistic uses of 'this with this', namely: (i) 'these things', (ii) 'what is composed of these', (iii) 'being in the same thing apt to receive them', (iv) 'being at the same time', (v) 'being in the same place', and (vi) 'this through this'.

150^b32–151^a13: The presentation of commonplaces concerning proposed definitions expressed in the form of 'this with this' begins here. The refutative strategy's first move consists in distinguishing in how many ways 'this with this' is said. We already know that it can correspond to (i) 'these things', and to (ii) 'what is composed of these'. Lines 150^b34–151^a1 mention three other ways: (iii) 'in the same thing apt to receive them' (*en tini tautôi dektikôi*); (iv) 'in the same place' (*en topôi tôi autôi*); (v) 'at the same time' (*en chronôi tôi autôi*). At 150^{b}35–6, there is an example of (iii) and it can be understood in two ways. It can serve a merely illustrative purpose, namely showing how one can say that one thing is with another, e.g. justice is with courage in the soul. But it can also have a refutative value. It could imply that 'justice and courage are in the soul' is a case of an incorrect account. The dialectician can argue that this account is wrong because justice and courage are *not* present in the *same faculty* of the soul: justice is present in the rational faculty, whereas courage is in the spirited faculty. It follows that the thing apt to receive justice and courage is not the same. Lines 151^{a}1–6 offer a deeper analysis of (v). It can happen that, although two things can exist at the same time, the interlocutor fails to see that each of them is related to a different thing. Aristotle's example concerns the proposed definition of courage as 'bravery with correct reasoning'. The explanation of this example is contained in lines 151^{a}4–6 and seems unproblematic. Although the same individual can have bravery with correct reasoning at the same time, it does not follow that he possesses courage as well. Lines 151^{a}6–13 contain a further refinement of the strategy outlined at 151^{a}1–6. Satisfying the requirement of being related to the same thing is necessary but not sufficient, as there might be cases where the result is not a successful definition. For this reason, another requisite must be added, and this is illustrated with an example. Suppose that bravery and correct reasoning, which are the components mentioned in the defining expression, are both related to medicine. Still, their combination will not describe the essence of courage. Not only must the things occurring at the same time be related to the same thing, but also their *relatum* must be connected with the kind to be defined in a suitable way. The text suggests that, in the case of courage, the common *relatum* of the two co-occurring items, namely bravery and correct reasoning, should be the end of courage (*telos*, 151^{a}13). That is to say, in order to be courageous a person must possess bravery and correct reasoning at the same time and in relation to something like 'the dangers of war' (151^{a}12), which is the end of courage. This is not the only case where the dialectician should look for the end in the interlocutor's granted account. The importance of expressing the end in a proposed definition is also stated in the commonplace in *Top.* VI.8, 146^{b}9–11: 'Or see whether a thing said in relation to something is not defined in

relation to its end: in each thing the end is the best or that for the sake of which the others are. One must therefore mention either the best or what comes last.' On the concept of end and how it is employed in the *Topics*, see commentary on chapter 8, 146ᵇ9–12.
Nothing is said concerning the second way in which 'this with this' is said, namely when it is used as 'in the same place'. Perhaps Aristotle has something like the following in mind. It is perfectly plausible to imagine a situation where someone asks a friend, 'What can you tell me about Jim?'. The answer is 'Jim is with Tim'. Here the expression 'Jim is with Tim' is equivalent to 'Jim and Tim are in the same place, e.g. in the same office'. Examples concerning individuals are the most intuitive since it is customary to think about individuals as being in the same place. It is, however, possible to conceive of natural kinds as being in the same region. For instance, a zoologist can claim that marmots are with tree squirrels, and the reason for saying this is that they inhabit the same mountain region, e.g. the Alps. Other examples of 'being in the same place' can be found in Alexander of Aphrodisias and Pacius, but they are more problematic than the text they intend to clarify (Alex. Aphr. *in Top.* 491, 16–18; Pacius 1597, pp. 446–7).

151ᵃ14–19: These lines contain the last commonplace outlined in chapter 13. It concerns a case that is not covered by the preceding analysis of the expression 'this with this' (150ᵇ27–151ᵃ14). It is introduced by an example of a proposed definition: 'Anger <is defined as> pain with the belief of being under-esteemed' (*hê orgê lupê meth'hupolepseôs tou oligôreisthai*, 151ᵃ15–16). For the addition of 'is defined as' see 'The translation of *hoion ei*' in 'Terminological Clarifications'. This example has received attention by modern scholars and commentators (see, e.g., Aubenque 1957, where there is an extensive discussion of possible accounts of anger, and Brunschwig 2007, p. 85, n. 1). In the *Topics*, there are two further commonplaces illustrated by examples concerning anger and its characteristics: the first is in IV.5, 125ᵇ20–7 and the second in IV.6, 127ᵇ26–36. There are conceptual and terminological similarities between the second of these commonplaces and the claim at 151ᵃ14–16; for at 127ᵇ30–3 Aristotle says: '... Both the pain and the belief seem to be predicated in the essence of anger; for the angry person both feels pain and believes that he is being under-esteemed' (*tês orgês hê lupê kai hê hupolepsis en tôi ti esti katêgoreisthai dokei lupeitai gar ho orgizomenos kai hupolambanei oligôreisthai*; accepting Brunschwig's emendation, see his 1967, p. 109, n. 1). Then, in *Rh.* II.2, 1378ᵃ30–1, Aristotle defines anger as 'the desire of revenge accompanied by pain for being manifestly under-esteemed (*orexis meta lupês timôrias dia phainomenên oligôrian*). Furthermore, in *De An.* I.1, 403ᵃ28–403ᵇ1, Aristotle discusses two types of definition of anger: 'The natural scientist and the dialectician would define each of these affections differently, for example what anger is (*orgê ti estin*). The dialectician will define it as desire for retaliation (*orexin antilupêseôs*), or something of this sort, while the natural scientist will define it as boiling of the blood and heat around the heart. Of these, one describes the matter and the other the form and the account' (translated by Shields 2016). The account of anger proposed in *Top.* VI.13, 151ᵃ14–16 bears a close resemblance to the definition put forward by the dialectician in the *De Anima*. But the difference between the various types of definition and the question whether the correct account is given by the dialectician or by the scientist is not what is at stake in the discussion of the commonplace. Rather, the point made by Aristotle here concerns the linguistic use of the particle 'with' (*meta*). At 151ᵃ16–19, he emphasizes that the phrase 'with the belief' (*meth'hupolepseôs*) is equivalent to 'through the belief' (*dia tên hupolepsin*). Hence it does not correspond to any of the five uses of 'this with this' (*tode meta toude*) listed above. This suggests that none of the strategies outlined in chapter 13 are adequate to deal with expressions containing 'through this' (*dia tode*). Very likely the dialectician should find the means to address these cases elsewhere. The preposition *dia* followed by a term in the accusative indicates a causal relation. 'Through' has perhaps the advantage that it is less philosophically loaded than 'because of', which is used to convey Aristotle's technical notion of cause. Since there is no evidence to say whether, in the *Topics*, Aristotle is employing the term 'cause' in a technical way, I am more inclined to adopt 'through' in my translation. A final terminological remark: at 151ᵃ15, the Greek word *diairesin* ('division') indicates not the process of dividing, but the result of a division in classes, that is to say a classification.

CHAPTER 14

Introduction: This is the last chapter in book VI. It can be divided into four sections: (1) 151^{a}20–31, (2) 151^{a}32–151^{b}2, (3) 151^{b}3–17, and (4) 151^{b}18–23. The sentence at 151^{b}24 is a conclusion to the entire book VI. The discussions in (1) and (2) concern specific rules for attacking proposed definitions. In (1), Aristotle examines a commonplace on the basis of the relation between parts and whole. In this respect, section (1) could well belong to the preceding chapter, which analyses the relation between the kind to be defined and its defining elements in terms of the relation between the whole and its parts. Section (2) develops a commonplace that deals with contraries and establishes that if two contraries belong by nature to the same subject, neither of them ought to enter into the definition of the subject. Section (3) contains three parts: (A) 151^{b}3–7, (B) 151^{b}7–11, and (C) 151^{b}12–17. The analyses of proposed definitions in (3) and (4) are more general. They do not deal with commonplaces based on specific concepts. Rather, they contain general strategies that help the dialectician to find the means for refuting a proposed definition when he is at a loss and is not in a position to apply the specific commonplaces discussed throughout book VI.

151^{a}20–31: The first commonplace concerns composites and is connected to the discussion in the preceding chapter. The commonplace in *Top.* VI.13, 150^{b}22–6 describes a mistake that can occur when the whole is defined in terms of a combination of its parts. There Aristotle claims that 'the essence of each composite is not what is composed of these, but what is composed of these *in this way*' (150^{b}23–5). Similarly, at the beginning of chapter 14 Aristotle instructs the dialectician to look into whether the person who grants an account fails to specify 'what sort of combination it is' (*poia sunthesis*; 151^{a}22).

At 151^{a}20–1, there is a first example: 'An animal is a combination of the soul and the body' (*tês psuchês kai tou sômatos sunthesin zôion*). This example serves an introductory and illustrative purpose. It offers us an instance of an account where a whole, e.g. an animal, is defined in terms of the combination of its parts, i.e. soul and body. At this stage, nothing more is said on this example: there is no indication as to whether this account of animal must be retained or rejected. It will be briefly discussed at the end of this section, namely in the argument at 151^{a}29–31 (more on this below). At 151^{a}22–3, the second example gives us an instance of two proposed accounts that must be refuted as they contain the mistake under scrutiny. These accounts are: (a) Flesh is a combination of fire, earth, and air; (b) Bone is a combination of fire, earth, and air. Lines 151^{a}23–6 explain why (a) and (b) cannot be accepted. The explanation comes in two stages (each stage is introduced by an occurrence of *gar*;151^{a}24 and 25). In the first stage, Aristotle explains what mistake has been made by proposing (a) and (b). Both (a) and (b) only speak of combination (of fire, earth, and air), which, Aristotle says, is not sufficient. The second stage explains why something must be added to the concept of combination of elements (i.e. fire, earth, and air) in order to obtain the successful definition of either flesh or bone. Aristotle appeals to the process leading to the generation of either flesh or bone: 'When they are combined in such-and-such way flesh comes to be, and when in such-and-such way bone' (*houtôsi men suntethetôn sarx, houtôsi d'ostoun*, 151^{a}26; the understood verb is *ginetai* and it can be supplied from the end of the preceding sentence). Each process involves a different combination of the elements. It is because the process of generation of flesh requires that the elements be combined in such-and-such way that the successful definition of flesh is: (a*) Flesh is the combination *in such-and-such way* of certain elements, i.e. fire, earth, and air. The choice of the examples of flesh and bone is not arbitrary. It is motivated by the fact that flesh and bone are two different things but are composed of the same elements. The only feature distinguishing flesh from bone is the way in which the elements are combined. But here Aristotle does not pursue further the thought that, in a definitory context, the type of combination must be specified. Rather, he challenges the view that either flesh or bone is a combination without offering any reason for his change of direction.

At 151^{a}26–9, Aristotle's concise argument is based on the relation of contrariety. He claims that every combination has a contrary, namely a decomposition, or dissolution (*dialusis*; 151^{a}28). But neither flesh nor bone has a contrary (151^{a}28–9). Hence neither flesh nor bone is a combination (151^{a}26–7). This suggests that a proposed definition attributing to either flesh or bone the characteristic of being a combination must be criticized and rejected. The argument is based on an intuitive thought: putting together, or combining, is contrary to dividing, or dissolving. Aristotle thinks that every type of combination has a dissolution that is contrary to it. As is well known, however, Aristotelian substances do not have a contrary. Thus, they cannot be a type of combination. But one could also argue in a different way: substances can be reduced to contraries, in particular to combination and dissolution. Aristotle gives us reason to think that some of his predecessors endorsed this type of argument: see *Ph.* I.5, 188ᵃ27–30 and 188ᵇ15–21. The philosophers who thought that substances can be reduced to contraries could contest Aristotle's claim that 'Nothing is contrary to either of the things mentioned (e.g. flesh and bone)'. In support of Aristotle's view, however, it must be observed that the question 'What is the contrary of flesh or bone?' has no reasonable answer. The philosophers who raised the aforementioned objection are therefore obliged to acknowledge that the ordinary way in which we speak and categorize the world is deeply misleading. Their way of arguing is utterly different from the Aristotelian approach, which is based on respecting our ordinary way of thinking and speaking.

At 151ᵃ29–31, the last argument of this section is difficult to unfold. The main problem stands in the interpretation of the expression *homoiôs pithanon* ('equally plausible' or 'plausible to the same degree') that occurs in the first premise (151ᵃ29–30). There are three possible readings of the first premise and they allow three reconstructions of the entire argument. The second premise and the conclusion are left unchanged.

(1) In the first reading, *homoiôs* modifies *pithanon* and has a wider scope than the quantifiers *pan* ('every') and *mêden* ('none', i.e. 'every ... not'). Then, the argument can be formulated as follows:

(*p*) That every composite is a combination is *equally plausible* as (*ê*) that every composite is not a combination.
(*q*) Some composites are not a combination (as the counterexample of animals shows).
(*r*) Hence, the other composites also are not a combination

(2) In the second reading, *homoiôs* modifies (not *pithanon*, but) *sunthesin einai* ('... is a combination') and its scope is narrower than that of the quantifiers. In this case, the argument's structure is the following:

- (*p**) *It is plausible* that every composite is a combination *to the same degree* or (*ê*) that every composite is not a combination *to the same degree*.
- (*q*) Some composites are not a combination (as the counterexample of animals shows).
- (*r*) Hence, the other composites also are not a combination.

(3) In the third reading, *homoiôs* modifies *pithanon* (i.e. 'with the same degree of plausibility'), and its scope is narrower than that of the quantifiers. This gives us the following reconstruction:

- (*p***) Every composite is a combination *with the same degree of plausibility* or (*ê*) every composite fails to be a combination *with the same degree of plausibility*.
- (*q*) Some composites are not a combination (as the counterexample of animals shows).
- (*r*) Hence, the other composites also are not a combination.

Each reading has strong as well as weak points, and it is not at all easy to decide which is the most attractive. Reading (1) has an advantage over (2) and (3); namely it reads the Greek text in its most natural way. For the expression *homoiôs pithanon* is not divided, the adverb *homoiôs* ranges over the entire sentence, and the particle *ê* is used to mark a comparison. But the result is a poor argument because the conclusion (*r*) does not logically follow from premises (*q*) and (*p*). Reading (2), although it might look appealing at a first glance, presents a difficulty which seems insurmountable: in (*p**), the division of *homoiôs* from *pithanon* is unlikely. For this reason, I am inclined to discard it. Reading (3) also puts some strain on the Greek formulation of the first premise, but not as much as reading (2). Reading (3) keeps together the expression *homoiôs pithanon,* it places it within the scope of the quantifiers, and it gives to the particle *ê* the value of a disjunction. Reading (3) has an important advantage over (1) since it allows the reconstruction of a reasonable argument. How does the conclusion (*r*) follow from premises (*q*) and (*p***)? Since (*p***) contains a disjunction, we must show that (*r*) follows from each disjunct and from (*q*). Consider the first disjunct and formulate the argument in this way: if a composite *x* and a composite *y* are combinations with the same degree of plausibility as one another, and one of the two is not a combination, the other also is not a combination. Consider, now, the second disjunct and develop the argument as follows: if a composite *x* and a composite *y* fail to be combinations with the same degree of plausibility as one another, and one of the two is not a combination, the other also is not a combination. Although this shows that (*r*) can be derived from each of the disjuncts in (*p***) and from (*q*), it is still possible to raise doubts about the validity of the argument due to the presence of the epistemic operator *homoiôs pithanon*. The occurrence of this operator does not guarantee validity: if *x*'s being F is as plausible as *y*'s being F, and *x* is F, it does not follow that *y* is F. Even though there are reasons to remain hesitant, reading (3) is preferable to (1) and (2).

Something must be said about the case of animals mentioned at 150^{a}30–1, where it is claimed that animals are composites but not combinations. This serves as a counterexample to invalidate any attempt to define a composite as a combination, and it does so by supporting the second premise, i.e. (*q*). This presupposes that the account mentioned at the beginning of the chapter (150^{a}20–1), namely 'An animal is a combination of the soul and the body', cannot be a successful definition. Why is an animal composite but not a combination? It seems to me that the reason for claiming that an animal is not a combination can be found above at 151^{a}28: 'For every combination there is a contrary dissolution'. But there is no dissolution contrary to an animal. Thus, an animal is not a combination. Nevertheless, an animal is composite (of soul and body). One might object that 'to be composite' and 'to be a combination' are synonymous expressions. But there is a subtle difference. If I say: 'An animal is a combination', I am implying that combination is the genus under which animal falls, and, according to Aristotle, this is wrong. No such implication can be found in the claim 'an animal is composite'.

151^{a}32–151^{b}2: Perhaps it is the preceding hint to the role of contraries in a definitional context (151^{a}26–9) that leads to the discussion of the second commonplace of chapter 14, which deals with contraries too. But it is also possible that Aristotle might want to develop this commonplace for some independent reasons. It is helpful to begin the analysis of this section with some linguistic remarks. At 151^{a}32, the verb *huparchein* (lit. 'to belong') does not express the relation of *belonging predicatively* to something. This happens, for example, when we say that quadruped belongs to horse, which is equivalent to claiming that horse is a quadruped. Rather, in this context, *huparchein* being construed with *en* plus dative is used to indicate that *something is in something*. Then, the meaning of the clause *homoiôs en tini pephuken huparchein* is '*to be* equally *in something* by nature'. This construction is found in, e.g., *Cat.* 5, 2^{a}14–15: 'The species *in which* the things primarily called substances *are* (*en hois eidesin hai prôtôs ousiai legomenai huparchousin*) are called secondary substances'. At 151^{a}35, after *eirêken*, we must supply the word *horismon* ('definition') from the previous sentence (151^{a}34). At 151^{a}35, the expression *homoiôs ... pephuke ginesthai en* is a stylistic variant of *homoiôs en tini pephuken huparchein*, and both are rendered as 'to be equally in something by nature'. The logical use of *huparchein* (meaning 'to belong predicatively') does not seem suitable to the present context where Aristotle is using *huparchein en* to mean something like 'to occur in' or 'to be present in' (this is a metaphysical notion rather than a logical one).

Consider a subject in which contraries are equally present by nature. The general rule stated at 151^{a}32–3 tells us that a proposed definition where the subject is defined in terms of one contrary must be criticized and rejected. For example, as suggested below at 151^{b}1–2, consider the soul as the subject in which the pair of contraries knowledge and ignorance are equally present by nature. If an interlocutor attempts to define the soul by mentioning in the defining expression either knowledge or ignorance, then he will fail to offer a successful definition. Aristotle tells us that this way of defining something has an unwelcome consequence; that is to say, the same thing will have more than one definition (151^{a}33–4). Why does it follow that the same thing will have several definitions? And why is this unacceptable? The first problem is addressed at 151^{a}34–6: Aristotle asks a rhetorical question whose expected answer is negative. Since contraries are *equally* present by nature in the subject to be defined, the proposed definition mentioning one contrary will not be more informative than the account containing the other contrary. For example, 'substance receptive of knowledge' is no more a definition of the soul than 'substance receptive of ignorance'. In the context of this argument, the adverb *homoiôs* has a strong value and corresponds to something like the English expression 'in the same way'. Aristotle is saying that knowledge and ignorance have the same claim to be part of the essence of the soul. Since there is no reason to favour one of the attempted accounts, both could be retained. But this is not possible. In this passage, however, Aristotle does not explain why there cannot be more than one definition of the same thing. He might believe that this is sufficiently intuitive and need not be justified. Or he could believe that it is not necessary to repeat the reasoning introduced in *Top.* VI.4, 141^a34–141^b1 (see commentary *ad loc.*). It must be observed that the argument at 151^a32–151^b2 shares a feature with that of the immediately preceding section (151^a20–31) and with many other arguments in book VI; for the concept of comparison, which structures the refutative strategy, is central to all of them.

Something more needs to be said about the example of the pair of contraries knowledge and ignorance introduced by Aristotle at 151^b1–2. Perhaps this is not a very good choice. Although it is true to say that knowledge and ignorance are contraries, there might be a reason to favour the presence of knowledge in the account of the soul. One can argue that knowledge enjoys a certain teleological priority, thus it is more apt to be mentioned in the proposed defining expression. In other words, knowledge, but not ignorance, is the positive end that should be attained by the soul. This idea is in line with what Aristotle says in other chapters of book VI. For example, in *Top.* VI.5, 143^a9–10, he invites the dialectician to examine 'Whether he (*sc.* the interlocutor) has given an account not in relation to the better but to the worse, if there are several things in relation to which what is being defined is said'. Aristotle explains that if the interlocutor's account mentions not the better but the worse, the account is mistaken and must be criticized. It is for this reason that even though medicine can be described as a capacity productive of health and disease (143^a3), its definition must mention the good result only (i.e. health). According to the view presented here, 'Every body of knowledge and capacity seems to be for the best' (143^a10). Moreover, in *Top.* VI.8, 146^b11–12, Aristotle suggests that, in a definition, one should mention the end in relation to which the kind to be defined is said, and 'In each thing the end is the best or that for the sake of which all other things are' (see commentaries on *Top.* VI.5 and on *Top.* VI.8 *ad loc.*).

151ᵇ3–17: There are four occurrences of verbal forms of *anairein* (*anairethentos* 151ᵇ6; *anaireitai* 151ᵇ7; *anairousi* 151ᵇ13; *anêirêmenos* 151ᵇ16). Aristotle employs this verb when he discusses commonplaces aimed at destroying the interlocutor's proposed definition; see, e.g., *Top.* VI.4, 142ᵃ14: 'it is possible to destroy (*anairein*) the definition in a way that will meet most agreement'. But it is difficult to translate all the occurrences of verbal forms of *anairein* with the same English verb 'to destroy'. For this reason, I maintain the translation 'to destroy' for three occurrences only (151ᵇ6, 151ᵇ7, 151ᵇ16), but I adopt 'abolish' for the occurrence at 151ᵇ13.

This portion of text can be further divided in three parts: (A) 151ᵇ3–7, (B) 151ᵇ7–11, and (C) 151ᵇ12–17. As anticipated in the introduction to this chapter, there is a characteristic common to these parts and to lines 151ᵇ18–23 that immediately follow them. They all sketch refutations that do not fall under the classifications contained in the rest of book VI. For example, here we do not find specific strategies that examine the details of how, say, the genus or the differentia appear in the proposed account. Rather, the lines of attack presented here are intended to help the dialectician who is at a loss and is not able to find an appropriate commonplace to refute the opponent's proposal.

In (A) 151ᵇ3–7, Aristotle offers a suggestion to the dialectician who is not able to see a mistake in the proposed definition in its entirety and hence cannot formulate an attack against it taken as a whole (*pros holon*, 151ᵇ3). This happens when the proposed definition taken as a whole is not familiar (*mê gnôrimon einai to holon*, 151ᵇ4). In this context, *gnôrimon* ('familiar') is used in a non-technical way, that is to say, it indicates the fact that the dialectician is not sufficiently acquainted with the entire proposed definition. The adjective *gnôrimon* and its comparative form *gnôrimôteron* can also be used in a technical way, as in *Top.* VI.4, 141ᵃ26–31 and 141ᵇ3–4. In that context, Aristotle argues that, in a successful definition, the defining expression must mention things that are prior to and more familiar unqualifiedly than the kind to be defined (for the technical meaning of *gnôrimon* see commentary on chapter 4). When it is not possible to find a refutation to demolish the suggested account as a whole, one should consider its parts and attack one of them. The description of the strategy, however, is compressed and no example is offered. We are merely told that two requirements must be satisfied: (i) One of the proposed definition's parts is familiar, and (ii) This part has not been formulated well ($151^{b}5$–6). What is a part of a definition? Consider the preceding commonplace that deals with contraries ($151^{a}32$–$151^{b}2$). In the example of the soul's suggested account, there is a problem with a part of the defining expression. For, according to Aristotle's analysis, one part of the defining expression, i.e. knowledge, is no more apt than its contrary, i.e. ignorance, to reveal the essence of the soul. In this case, by criticizing the presence of one contrary in the defining expression, the dialectician is attacking not the proposed definition taken as a whole but a part of it. Then, lines $151^{b}6$–7 contain a justification of this strategy: when it is shown that a part does not stand up to scrutiny, the entire account is refuted.

In (B) $151^{b}7$–11, the attention is drawn to proposed definitions that are unclearly formulated. Obscure definitions are also discussed in chapters 2 and 3 of book VI, where they receive a detailed analysis. At $151^{b}8$, I render *dêloun* as 'to make clear' and not as 'to indicate' (like in the other occurrences of this verbal form) in an attempt to offer a translation that sounds more natural to an English reader. It looks as if in chapter 14 Aristotle has in mind something other than a careful classification of various forms of obscurity: he conceives of cases where the proposed account is unclear, but the dialectician is not able to attack it on the basis of any of the specific commonplaces already discussed. How should the dialectician proceed in these cases? The suggested strategy is contained in lines $151^{b}7$–9, but it is expressed in a rather convoluted way. When he is faced with an unclear definition, the dialectician's first task should consist in improving the proposed account, possibly by rephrasing some of its parts with the aim of making them clear. This will enable him to find a suitable refutative strategy (*echein epicheirêma*). He should then proceed to the examination of the granted account, in its rephrased formulation, as indicated by the strategy. Lines $151^{b}9$–11 justify the procedure outlined in the immediately preceding passage (151^{b}7–9). Some commentators believe that this justification is needed in order to prevent a possible objection (see Pacius 1597, p. 447). One might claim that the interlocutor could refuse to assent to the reformulation of the originally granted account. So, Aristotle's envisaged procedure could not be applied and the dialectician will not succeed in refuting the opponent. This can be prevented if we endorse the following rule of the dialectical debate: the answerer must either accept the questioner's rephrasing of the account or offer a formulation which expresses clearly what is indicated by the proposed definition. On other occasions, I translate the verbal forms of *dêloô* by forms of 'to make clear'. In this way, it is possible to keep the etymological link with the adjective *dêlos* ('clear'). But in semantical contexts (where *dêloô* is used to indicate what a linguistic expression reveals or 'makes clear' to an ideally competent listener) the mechanical translation of *dêloô* by 'make clear' yields unwelcome results. For instance, at 151^{b}10–11, the clause *auton diasaphêsai ti pote tugchanei to dêloumenon hupo tou logou* is best translated as 'He himself presents clearly whatever the thing indicated by the account is'. There would be no need to present clearly something that has already been made clear.

In (c) 151^{b}12–17, the commonplace concerns the prospect of formulating a new definition while discarding the old account since it is not possible to keep both. This discussion has two parts: (i) 151^{b}12–15 and (ii) 151^{b}15–17. Part (i) introduces a comparison between laws and definitions. According to the view presented here, the debates in the Athenian assemblies, where laws are discussed, have something in common with the dialectical debates where definitions are examined. The discussion of an established law *L* may bring about the need to amend it. When this happens, a new and more adequate law, say *L**, replaces *L* that was previously established. In other words, if a better law *L** is found, *L** is introduced and *L* is abolished. This is what Aristotle says. There are, however, two objections. First, it is not the case that, in general, when a better law is found, it replaces the preceding one. Aristotle should have said that when a law is judged to be better by a majority in the assembly, then it replaces the one previously established. Second, at 151^{b}13, in speaking of laws Aristotle says, 'if the introduced one *is better*', whilst at 151^{b}15, in speaking of definitions, he says, 'if it *appears to be* *better*'. This discrepancy weakens the analogy. Perhaps one might understand an occurrence of something like the qualification 'it appears' in the case of the laws too (more on 151^{b}15 is said below). Aristotle suggests to the dialectician that he follow the same procedure adopted by the legislators. Suppose that, in a dialectical debate, the questioner cannot find a suitable refutation for the interlocutor's proposed definition *D*. Then, the questioner can formulate a different definition, say *D**.

Part (ii) justifies the choice of this strategy. Consider now the case where the questioner's suggested definition *D** appears to be better than the previously proposed account *D*. What does it mean to say that *D* appears to be better* than *D*? In the clause 'If it appears to be better and to indicate more what is being defined' (*ean ... phainêtai beltiôn kai mallon dêlon to horizomenon*, 151^{b}15–16), the particle *kai* (lit. 'and') has an epexegetic value and means 'that is to say'. In other words, *D* appears to be better* than *D* when *D** indicates the thing to be defined more than *D*, i.e. when *D** discloses the essence of the thing to be defined more than *D*. Since each kind does not have more than one definition, *D* must be abolished, whilst *D** must be retained. Nothing more, however, is said about the claim that for each kind there cannot be many definitions. But this should not be the source of a worry. Elsewhere in book VI, Aristotle has already tried to establish the view that for each kind there is only one definition since the definition expresses the essence and each kind has only one essence (see, in particular, *Top.* VI.4, 141^{a}34–141^{b}1). Moreover, in 151^{a}34, Aristotle seems to assume that his audience is already acquainted with this argument.

It is interesting to note that the question whether and how existing laws should be improved and changed is reminiscent of a debate that was present in Athens (at least) at the time when Aristotle was philosophically active. This debate is mentioned in Aristotle's *Politics* II.8, 1268^{b}26–8: 'It has been doubted whether it is or is not expedient to make any changes in the laws of a country, even if another law be better' (translated by Jowett, in Barnes 1984, vol. 1). There were well-known arguments in favour of changing the laws as well as against. The discussion in Brunschwig 1980 offers a detailed reconstruction of both types of argument. What Aristotle says here in the *Topics* is not sufficient to establish his position on this subject.

It remains to observe that the verb *phainêtai* ('it appears', 151^{b}15) can be understood in two ways. (a) *Phainêtai* has a factive value. It is equivalent to 'it is manifest' and implies that what appears is true. (b) *Phainêtai* has a neutral value. It is equivalent to 'it seems' or 'it appears', but it does not imply that what appears is true. In his translation, Brunschwig (2007) opts for (a): 'Si en effet elle (*sc.* la formule) est manifestement meilleure ... '. This reading has the advantage that it puts the claim about definitions at 151^{a}15 ('it is manifestly better') on the same footing as that about laws at 151^{a}13 ('the introduced one is better'). Moreover, this reading is supported by the presence of *dêlon* (151^{a}16), which has a factive value. But, perhaps, the dialectical context favours reading (b), which gives the value of an *endoxon* to the premise of the argument. For example, in *EN* VII.1, 1145^{b}3–4, when Aristotle says that 'We must set out the appearances (*ta phainomena*)', he refers to the *endoxa* (Owen 1961, p. 85). For this reason, I am more inclined to opt for (b).

The logic of the argument underlying the refutative strategy can be summed up as follows. The dialectician is at a loss because he cannot find a commonplace that enables him to refute the interlocutor's proposed account. Then, he suggests an alternative definition which appears to be more apt to indicate the essence of the kind than the interlocutor's account. But it is not possible to keep both definitions. Hence, the better (i.e. the dialectician's) definition is to be chosen and the other (i.e. the opponent's) rejected.

151^{b}18–23: In the immediately preceding passage, we find the thought that, as part of his refutative strategy, the dialectician himself should formulate an alternative and better definition than the account proposed by the interlocutor. This thought is central to this section of the text too. In this case, however, it is developed in a different way. Aristotle introduces here the concept of a model (*paradeigma*, 151^{b}20–1). What is the role of a 'model definition'? Presumably, it is an example that should be observed by all those who aim at putting forward a successful definition. Moreover, the 'model definition' should be compared to the interlocutor's suggested account. Then, there are two simple ways to detect a fault in the interlocutor's account. The comparison shows that (a) the interlocutor's account fails to mention a fundamental element, or (b) it contains more than what is needed. Starting from (a) or (b), the dialectician can formulate different and more specific refutations in order to criticize the interlocutor's account. When Aristotle introduces the concept of a model for the definition, he might be implying that for each kind there is 'the perfect' definition. But he might also be implying that it is always possible to find a definition that is better than the one previously granted. It seems to me that, in this context, there is nothing in favour of either one or the other claim. So, both options can be left open.

Those who are familiar with Aristotle's syllogistic theory might see a parallel between some requirements for a successful definition and certain characteristics that a syllogism must have. On the one hand, a successful definition must contain all the fundamental elements that indicate the essence of the kind to be defined, and it must not be redundant. On the other hand, a syllogism must neither lack a premise nor contain more premises that needed.

It is easy to see that the refutative strategy suggested here (151^b18–23) is in line with the unifying theme of the second part of chapter 14. For, in this second part, Aristotle helps the dialectician who is not able to find a specific commonplace to destroy the opponent's granted account.

151^b24: The last sentence of chapter 14 is the conclusion of the entire book VI, which discusses commonplaces that are helpful to destroy proposed definitions. As some commentators observe (see, e.g., Brunschwig 2007, p. 87, n. 2), this conclusion seems to suggest that there is nothing more to add about the predicable definition. But this is not what happens since in book VII (especially in chapters 1–3), Aristotle deals with themes that concern definitions.

TERMINOLOGICAL CLARIFICATIONS

1. 'GENUS', 'SPECIES', AND 'KIND'

As a general convention, I translate *genos* with 'genus' and *eidos* with 'species'. There are two uses of 'species': (1) a relative use (when we speak of a species falling under a genus); (2) an absolute use (when 'species' is not relative to 'genus'). A far as the relative use of 'species' is concerned, 'genus' is its correlative: a is a species of b if and only if b is a genus of a. Note that the same thing can be a genus or a species in different contexts. For example, living being is a genus of animal and animal is a species of living being. But animal is a genus of man, and man is a species of animal. I adopt 'kind' as a blanket term covering anything that can be called 'genus' or 'species'. My use of 'kind' corresponds to the absolute use of 'species'.

2. NOTE ON THE VALUE OF *Ê*

In book VI, there are many occurrences of the particle *ê*, which can be used in several ways. (1) It can introduce a claim that looks like an objection raised by the answerer against the immediately preceding view put forward by the questioner. In certain cases, this objection could be seen as a criticism that Aristotle himself makes to his own position. In this way, *ê* would mark a change of direction and the claim it introduces would be the starting point of a new argument. (2) It can introduce a claim that helps the answerer to reject a premise, which the questioner asks him to grant. (3) It could be used to indicate an exception to a general rule or a further detail that must be added to the given rule. (4) It can introduce another stage in the argument. (See Brunschwig 2007, p. 45, n. 6; p. 61, n. 8.)

3. THE VERB *APODIDONAI* AND ITS FORMS

In a definitional context, Aristotle uses the forms of *apodidonai* (lit. 'to give back') to mean 'to give an account', 'to give a definition'. In these cases, *apodidonai* is equivalent to *horizein*, 'to define'. Occasionally, in my translation I adopt the short form 'to give' and I understand 'an account'; see, for example, *Top.* VI.8, 146^{b}8–9, in the clause *tôi horismôi apodidosthai* the presence of 'an account' would be redundant. Then, in *Top.* VI.8, 146^{b}8–9, I translate *apodidedotai* as '(it) is defined' in order to preserve the syntax and the word order of the Greek text.

4. THE VALUE OF *HEXIS*

It is impossible to find a single English word that translates the Greek *hexis*. The semantic *spectrum* of *hexis* does not correspond to any English expression. For this reason, in some contexts *hexis* is adequately translated with 'possession' and cannot be rendered as 'state' or 'condition' (142^{b}12; 147^{a}12, 13), whereas in other contexts the roles are reversed (143^{a}16; 144^{a}10, 13, 14, 15, 17).

5. THE TRANSLATION OF *HOION EI*

In the majority of cases, when the expression *hoion ei* is not followed by a verb in a finite form, an occurrence of something like 'he has said' or 'he has defined' must be understood. See, for example, VI.4, 142^{a}35–142^{b}1: *hoion ei ton hêlion astron hêmerophanes hôrisato*. For this reason, at 139^{b}32–3 I added 'he has said'; at 141^{a}16 and at 142^{b}31–2, I supplied 'he has defined...as'. Analogously, at 145^{b}35–6 I wrote 'has been defined as' (here the subject is in the nominative case). At 147^{a}14, the presence of *hoper* requires an understanding of an occurrence of *esti*. At 147^{a}24–7 and 33–5, the examples are not instances of the interlocutor's granted account but illustrations of the general rule, and the verb *esti* is understood.

NOTES ON THE TEXT

In what follows the names of the MSS are as in Brunschwig's edition.[1]

TOPICS VI.2

139^{b}33. There are two textual problems. (1) Although it does not represent a difficulty for the understanding of the passage, the first problem is worth noticing. The majority of MSS read γῆν after ἀμετάπτωτον ἢ τήν, and this reading is accepted by all editors. There is only one MS, namely **C**, where ὕλην takes the place of γῆν. (2) The second problem is more controversial. On the one hand, most MSS read τιθήνην after ἢ τὴν γῆν. This reading is adopted by Bekker 1831, Waitz 1846, Strache and Wallies 1923, and Ross 1958. On the other hand, the two most important MSS, namely **A** and **B**, as well as **M**, have τιθηνητικόν instead of τιθήνην. This reading is accepted in Brunschwig's edition (see his 2007, *apparatus*, and p. 43, n. 6). There seems to be no difference between the meaning of τιθήνην and that of τιθηνητικόν as they both indicate 'nurse' or 'wet nurse'. For example, in Tricot 1950 τιθήνην is rendered as 'nourrice', and in Brunschwig 2007 the same rendering is adopted for τιθηνητικόν. It must be observed that the expression τιθηνητικόν seems to be a *hapax* and it cannot be found in LSJ. Perhaps, in this context, one might expect to find the singular feminine form τιθηνητική (or τιθηνητικήν in the accusative). This reading is present in the second hand of **B** only and it can be considered an attempt to normalize the text.

140^{a}7. The expression οὔτε κυρίως ('neither properly') is bracketed for deletion in Brunschwig 2007, but it is accepted by Bekker 1831, Waitz 1846, Strache and Wallies 1923, and Ross 1958. Although οὔτε κυρίως is present in many MSS, it does not appear in **A**, which is one of the most important MSS. The absence of this expression in the text is supported by Alexander of Aphrodisias' commentary (see Brunschwig 2007, *apparatus*, and p. 44, n. 3). According to Brunschwig, beside the philological

---

[1] See SIGLA in Brunschwig 2007, p. LXI.

reasons in favour of deleting οὔτε κυρίως, there is another consideration. Since at the beginning of this section the question whether or not the expression under scrutiny must be taken literally is left open and it will be discussed below at 140ᵃ13–16, it seems more reasonable not to exclude this possibility from the start.

140ᵃ13. At the beginning of line 140ᵃ13, Brunschwig's edition (2007) reads οὔτε κυρίως εἴωθε λέγεσθαι ('it is not customary to call it so properly'). On the one hand, this occurrence of κυρίως ('properly') is attested in the most authoritative MSS, i.e. **A** and **B**. By having εἴωθε κυρίως, Alexander of Aphrodisias' quotation supports this reading (*in Top.* 426, 26; Brunschwig 2007, *apparatus* and p. 44, n. 3). Also, in the editions by Bekker 1831 and Waitz 1846 we find this occurrence of κυρίως ('properly'). It is maintained in the translations by Pickard-Cambridge 1928 and by Forster 1960. On the other hand, it is not retained in the texts edited by Strache and Wallies 1923 and Ross 1958. It does not appear in the translation by Tricot 1950, in the Revised Oxford Translation (Barnes 1984), or in Wagner and Rapp 2004. Perhaps the logic of the argument flows better if we accept Brunschwig's text. Aristotle begins the discussion of this *topos* by introducing cases that are instances neither of a homonymy nor of a metaphor. He explains that these cases are worse than metaphors since they lack the cognitive value possessed by metaphors. Then he states that the way of speaking involved in these cases cannot be taken literally as it does not correspond to the traditional use of language. Finally, he sketches the refutative argument and shows that the account is inadequate both (a) if the interlocutor is speaking literally (the definition of image does not apply to the law) and (b) if he is not speaking literally (the understanding of the thing to be defined, i.e. the law, is not improved).

TOPICS VI.3

140ᵇ29–30. There are two possible readings of the text that are accepted by modern editors. On the one hand, Bekker 1831, Waitz 1846, Strache and Wallies 1923, and Ross 1958 print γίνεται οὖν ὅρος τῆς ἐπιθυμίας ὄρεξις ἡδέος ἡδέος (lit. 'Thus a definition of the appetite becomes desire for the pleasant for the pleasant'). But this reading faces a difficulty since it is hard (if not impossible) to understand how one can arrive at the desired conclusion of Aristotle's argument. From the proposed definition of appetite as 'desire for the pleasant' (τὴν ἐπιθυμίαν ὄρεξις ἡδέος, 140ᵃ27–8) and from the added premise that 'appetite is of the pleasant' (ἐπιθυμία ἡδέος ἐστίν, 140ᵃ28), it does not follow that the definition of appetite is 'desire for the pleasant for the pleasant' (ὅρος τῆς ἐπιθυμίας ὄρεξις ἡδέος ἡδέος, 140ᵃ29–30).

On the other hand, in Brunschwig 2007, the phrase ὅρος τῆς ἐπιθυμίας ('definition of the appetite') is bracketed for deletion and the proposed text is γίνεται οὖν ἡ ὄρεξις ἡδέος ἡδέος ('thus desire for the pleasant comes to be for the pleasant'). This reading has (at least) two advantages. First, it avoids the interpretative problem arising from the text printed by the majority of the editors. Second, it fits better in Aristotle's discussion of the present *topos*. In Brunschwig's proposed text, it is clear that the sentence 'the desire for the pleasant is for the pleasant' contains a repetition of the same expression. But it is also clear that this repetition does not amount to a double predication. This is important because in the immediately following lines Aristotle distinguishes between repetition of the same name and double predication. He then adds that there is no absurd consequence in the repetition of the same expression and he criticizes the use of the double predication in a definitional context. Brunschwig's conjecture is partly based on MSS **A** (before the correction of a copyist who misunderstood the text) and **B**. The justification for this emendation, the history of the transmission of the text, and the complex state of the textual evidence can be found in Brunschwig 2007, p. 47, *apparatus* and n. 3; and in his 2003, pp. 57–9.

141ᵃ17–19. There is no *consensus* among the editors on the text to be printed. Bekker 1831 and Waitz 1846 write: τὸ γὰρ δίκαιον συμφέρον τι, ὥστε περιέχεται ἐν τῷ συμφέροντι. περιττὸν οὖν τὸ δίκαιον ὥστε καθόλου εἴπας ἐπὶ μέρους προσέθηκεν ('For the just is something expedient so that it is included in the expedient. Thus, the just is redundant; so that having mentioned the universal, he has added the particular'). This text is accepted by Ross 1958 with a minor change: at 141ᵃ18, an occurrence of γάρ ('for') is present in the last clause, ὥστε γὰρ καθόλου εἴπας ἐπὶ μέρους προσέθηκεν. Strache and Wallies 1923 delete the clauses ὥστε περιέχεται ἐν τῷ συμφέροντι. περιττὸν οὖν τὸ δίκαιον, and print τὸ γὰρ δίκαιον συμφέρον τι, ὥστε καθόλου εἴπας ἐπὶ μέρους προσέθηκεν. Similarly, in Brunschwig 2007, the following clauses are bracketed for deletion: ὥστε περιέχεται ἐν τῷ συμφέροντι. περιττὸν οὖν τὸ δίκαιον. His proposed text is τὸ γὰρ δίκαιον συμφέρον τι, ὥστε γὰρ καθόλου εἴπας ἐπὶ μέρους προσέθηκεν. There is no justification for this emendation. It seems to me that Strache and Wallies's and Brunschwig's deletion should be accepted for the following reason: the first of the clauses to be excised says that the just is (extensionally) contained in the expedient. But this is irrelevant for the argument. Rather, the text should say that the expedient is (intensionally) contained in the just. Perhaps there is a way to assign a role to the claim that the just is (extensionally) contained in the expedient: from this claim, one might be able to infer that the expedient is (intensionally) contained in the just. But if this is so, why does Aristotle immediately add that the just is superfluous? This does not make sense. The text resulting from Strache and Wallies's and Brunschwig's deletion has a more satisfying logical flow. It must be noted, however, that Brunschwig's proposed text differs from Strache and Wallies only in the presence of an occurrence of γάρ at 141[a]18, which I find indefensible. I therefore follow Strache and Wallies, who excise γάρ on the basis of MSS **A** and **B**, which do not print it.

TOPICS VI.4

142[a]18. Deleting the comma between δηλοῦν and καθάπερ allows one to link better the clause καθάπερ πρότερον εἴπαμεν ('as we said before') with the clause τὸ διὰ τῶν ὑστέρων τὰ πρότερα δηλοῦν ('to indicate prior things through posterior ones'): the καθάπερ πρότερον εἴπαμεν need not qualify the whole of the sentence εἷς μὲν οὖν τρόπος τοῦ μὴ διὰ γνωριμωτέρων ἐστὶ τὸ διὰ τῶν ὑστέρων τὰ πρότερα δηλοῦν ('One way, then, of failing to give a definition through more familiar things is to indicate prior things through posterior ones').

TOPICS VI.5

142[b]20. Most editors (see, e.g., Bekker, Waitz, Ross) accept the text handed down by the majority of MSS and read τόπος; I follow this reading, *pace* Brunschwig, who reads τρόπος, attested in two MSS. The word τόπος is more technical and is a fitting introduction to the following discussion. Moreover, the expression εἷς ἐστι τόπος bears a similarity with the first line of chapter 2 above (εἷς μὲν οὖν τόπος, VI.2, 139[b]19), where Aristotle introduced the first of the commonplaces concerning the obscurity in a formulation of a definition. In this last text, all the MSS read τόπος.

142ᵇ33. There are the following textual variants: (1) According to the reading handed down by the majority of the most authoritative MSS, there is no article in the nominative in the sentence οὐδὲν γὰρ ... οὐδέτερος at 142ᵇ33–4. This reading makes the text grammatically harsh and does not offer a referent to οὐδέτερος (142ᵇ34). (2) In some other MSS we find an article before ἀποδούς. There is no agreement among modern editors. Waitz maintains reading (1). Ross offers a different reading, namely (3) he thinks that two occurrences of the article must be supplied: one before τοῦ γράψαι and another before τοῦ ἀναγνῶναι. This reading is not attested in any of the MSS but agrees with what immediately follows, since it offers a clear referent to οὐδέτερος (142ᵇ34). Still, it is hard to see how two occurrences of the article could have dropped from an MS. Brunschwig restores the article before ἀποδούς in line with (2). In the translation, it is difficult to show the difference between Ross's and Brunschwig's reconstruction of the text. I have a preference for Brunschwig's solution because it is attested in some MSS and renders the text grammatically acceptable.

TOPICS VI.6

143ᵇ2. There are some textual problems. The main difficulty concerns how many and which differentiae are listed here. There are four options. (i) There are four differentiae: footed (πεζόν), winged (πτηνόν), aquatic (ἔνυδρον), and two-footed (δίπους). This reading is attested only once in a late and secondary MS, namely *Marcianus* App. iv. 5, 1320 (see Waitz 1846, vol. 2); it is accepted by Pickard-Cambridge 1928, Tricot 1950, and Zadro 1974. (ii) There are three differentiae: footed, winged, and two-footed. This reading is handed down by the majority of MSS; it is accepted by Bekker 1831 and (with hesitation) by Strache and Wallies 1923. (iii) There are three differentiae: footed, winged, and aquatic. This reading is attested only in one MS, namely V, which is a more authoritative than the *Marcianus* mentioned above. This reading is accepted by Waitz 1846, vol. 2, Ross 1958, Colli 1970, and Wagner and Rapp 2004. (iv) There are only two differentiae: footed and winged. Although it is not attested in any MS, this option was suggested by Düring 1943; it is accepted by Barnes 1984, vol. 1, and by Brunschwig 2007. There are reasons not to favour options (i) and (ii): they mention two-footed, which is a differentia of both winged and footed, and it is not coordinate with them, as the argument in the immediately preceding lines

(143^a36–143^b1) requires. It is difficult to choose between options (iii) and (iv). The arguments in favour of option (iv) are interesting and plausible: according to Brunschwig 2007, the main advantage of this reading is that it offers a convincing reconstruction of the history of the text's transmission. Nevertheless, there are more compelling philological and philosophical reasons to choose option (iii): it is attested in one authoritative MS and introduces three coordinate differentiae, which result from the division of the genus animal. The division of the genus proposed by this option is exhaustive, whereas the one suggested by option (iv) is not. The presence of the pair footed and aquatic at 144^b33–145^a1 does not constitute decisive evidence in favour of option (iv). A discussion of the philological alternatives can be found in Brunschwig 2007, p. 56, n. 2.

143^b7–8. The textual difficulty concerns the two occurrences of εἰδοποιός. In his edition, Brunschwig argues that both occurrences of εἰδοποιός are interpolated glosses, and hence he brackets them (see his 2007, p. 57, n. 1). The reasons for this emendation are accepted by Smith 2010, p. 49. Brunschwig's proposal is interesting but involves an important change to the text: the first occurrence of εἰδοποιός is attested in all MSS; the second is present in all but three of them. Is it possible to keep the text transmitted by all or most of the MSS while offering a satisfactory interpretation of the argument at 143^b6–10? Some consideration might suggest an affirmative answer. This argument is concerned with differentiae that form the species together with the genera they divide. Let us explore two possibilities. The first, and more likely, is that the restriction on differentiae forming a species (when they are added to the genus they divide) follows on from the preceding lines. So, the function of 'species-making' (εἰδοποιός) is that of emphasizing a trait of the differentiae discussed in this argument. Even if the occurrences of 'species-making' can be seen as pleonastic, this does not seem a sufficient reason to delete them: surely there are plenty of pleonasms in Aristotle. In the conclusion (143^b9), there is no need to say that the differentia is species-making (εἰδοποιός) since all the differentiae discussed in this argument are species-making. The second, and less likely, possibility is that the restriction on species-making differentiae does not follow from the preceding argument. So, both occurrences of εἰδοποιός are restrictive, for they single out a type of differentiae, namely species-making differentiae. Then in the conclusion (143^b9) 'differentia' is an abbreviation of 'species-making differentia'. One could claim that from an exegetical or philosophical viewpoint that the presence (or absence) of εἰδοποιός is of no fundamental importance to this passage since, as mentioned before, the argument concerns those differentiae that constitute the species together with the genus they divide. If this is the case, then the question is purely philological, namely whether Aristotle did use the expression εἰδοποιός to make his point perfectly explicit. Despite the two arguments set out in the preceding paragraph, the fact that the expression εἰδοποιός occurs nowhere else in the corpus with the meaning 'species-making' (it is used in *Ethica Nichomachea* 1174^{b}5 with a different meaning, i.e. '*form-making*') induces me to accept Brunschwig's emendation.

144^{b}22 and 30. The occurrences of ζῷον ('animal') are attested in all MSS; the one at 144^{b}23 is not attested in **A**, but it is retained in all the others. Brunschwig deletes all the occurrences of 'animal' (see his 2007, p. 61, n. 3). He then understands that 'footed' and 'winged' indicate not differentiae but genera, which can be divided by means of further differentiae in subordinate genera or species; e.g. footed can be divided into footed two-footed and footed four-footed. However, since this passage occupies a central place in the chapter on the differentia, the most natural way to understand expressions like 'footed' and 'two-footed', which are not qualified by 'animal' in the immediate context, is that they indicate differentiae (see above at 143^{b}1). Furthermore, when Aristotle wants to refer to footed as a genus that can be further subdivided, he explicitly mentions 'animal' (see 144^{a}34–5). Although Brunschwig's arguments are interesting, the reasons for the emendation of the occurrences of 'animal' at 144^{b}22 and 30 are not completely convincing. The text, which is transmitted by all MSS, gives us an acceptable philosophical argument and can be retained. A different case could be made for the occurrence at 144^{b}23: it could be regarded as a mere repetition of the one in the preceding line and hence there might be a stronger reason to delete it.

145^{a}15–16 and 17–18. There is a textual problem concerning the occurrences of καὶ πρακτική ('and practical') and καὶ πρακτική τινός (lit. 'and practical of something'). The majority of editors choose to keep these expressions; the translation of their text is 'For they are said to be speculative and practical and productive; each of them indicates a relative. For it is speculative of something and productive of something and practical with respect to something.' This reading introduces three differentiae of knowledge—speculative, practical, and productive. However, as argued in Brunschwig 2007, p. 62, n. 2, there are reasons to delete καὶ πρακτική and καὶ πρακτική τινός. Even if an important change to the text is introduced, the philological reasons for this emendation are convincing. As a result of this emendation, the passage will read: 'For they are said to be speculative ... and productive; each of them indicates a relative. For it is speculative of something and productive of something ... .' Here the differentiae of knowledge are only two—speculative and productive.

TOPICS VI.8

In the commentary on VI.8, 146^{a}36–146^{b}9, some of the main reasons why it is not easy to assess the account of literacy as knowledge of letters are presented and explained. In connection with that analysis, it is worth looking at a textual variant that occurs at the beginning of the clause immediately following the disputed account. The choice between two readings may influence the interpretation of this passage.

(1) At 146^{b}7, the most recent editions of the text (Ross 1958; Brunschwig 2007) read ἔδει. This reading is attested in the first of the two families of MSS handing down the text of the *Topics*, namely **A** and **B**. These are old and very authoritative MSS (see Brunschwig 1967, pp. CIV–CVIII).

(2) A variant reading hands down δεῖ instead of ἔδει. It is attested in some of the second family of MSS (e.g. **C**) as well as in the two other MSS consulted by Brunschwig for his edition (Brunschwig 1967 and 2007), namely **V** and **M**. These were not used in the previous editions of the *Topics*.

Let us consider the reading (1), which attests ἔδει. It is important to note that there are two occurrences of ἔδει in a rather short portion of text (146^{b}5–8): the first is at line 146^{b}5; the second, namely the one under discussion, is at 146^{b}7 (i.e. two lines earlier). In order to have a better grasp of the passage and of the influence of the *lectio* attesting ἔδει on the interpretation of Aristotle's thought, it is helpful to begin by analysing the first occurrence. At 146^{b}5, the expression ἔδει εἰπεῖν introduces two cases of accounts that the interlocutor ought to have given if he wanted to arrive at successful definitions: 'he ought to have said that knowledge is a belief of a knowable and that wish is a desire for a good' (146^{b}5–7). These accounts are meant to replace the unsuccessful attempts at defining knowledge as a belief that is incontrovertible and wish as a desire that is painless (146^{b}1–2). It is at this point that we find the proposed definition of literacy followed by the clause beginning with ἔδει (146^{b}7).

It is intuitive and natural to take this occurrence of ἔδει as having the same import as the one found two lines above (i.e. at 146^{b}5). There is no good reason why Aristotle should change the meaning of a word he has just introduced and that plays an important role (i.e. introducing correct lines along which a successful definition is to be framed). Thus, ἔδει introduces some requirements that the interlocutor ought to have respected, had he wanted to arrive at a successful definition. The reading attesting ἔδει at 146^{b}7 might well reinforce the interpretation, favoured in the commentary, that 'literacy is knowledge of letters' expresses an account offered by the interlocutor, an account that must be criticized and rejected by the dialectician. In other words, since 'in a definition one ought to have given either that in relation to which itself is said or whatever the genus is in relation to', and since the interlocutor did not fulfil this requirement in giving his account, the proposed definition is not successful.

Let us turn to reading (2), which attests the present δεῖ instead of the imperfect ἔδει. The clause where δεῖ is contained corresponds to the English sentence: 'For he ought to give either that in relation to which itself is said or whatever the genus is in relation to'. This may well be interpreted as following from the assumption that the proposed definition of literacy as knowledge of letters is correct and as explaining why it is so. In other words, this claim may explain what the interlocutor correctly does in his account of literacy: he mentions the correlative of the genus that is expressed by 'of letters'. Hence this variant could support an interpretation different from that of (1); for, according to (1), the proposed definition of literacy cannot be accepted. But there is a problem with the second family of MSS, i.e. those reading δεῖ. For the MSS belonging to the second family contain corrections that were originated by a desire to explain Aristotle's thought. This is one of the reasons why the second family is less authoritative than the first; and this suggests that we should not accept its reading. Nevertheless, the presence of the variant is interesting since it could be a witness to the difficulty in assessing the proposed definition of letters. Perhaps someone could have thought that δεῖ was more apt than ἔδει to confirm the adequacy of the proposed definition.

TOPICS VI.9

148^{a}5. Brunschwig deletes the negative particle μή ('not') that is accepted by all earlier editors and translators (Brunschwig 2007, p. 73, n. 1).

There is a textual basis supporting this emendation since the negation μή is not attested in some MSS and its absence is presupposed by Alexander's paraphrase. The negation μή could easily have been introduced here because of a misunderstood sentence in Alexander's commentary on the *Topics*. The choice between maintaining or deleting μή ('not') leads to two main interpretative options of the example at 148ª4–6. These options are discussed in the commentary *ad loc*.

TOPICS VI.10

148ª20–2. I follow Brunschwig's emendation in deleting τοῖς λέγουσιν ἰδέας εἶναι ('to those who say that Ideas exist'). This emendation requires that we change πρὸς δὲ τούτους ('against them') into πρὸς δὲ τούτοις ('beside such cases'); see Brunschwig 2007, p. 74, n. 1.

TOPICS VI.11

149ª20–4. Brunschwig suspects that lines 149ª20–4 are dubious (2007, p. 77, n. 2), and, in the *apparatus*, he indicates that he is tempted to delete them. In favour of keeping the text as it is transmitted, it should be observed that Aristotle does not abandon the idea that the genus is more familiar than the species. This idea is maintained not only throughout the argument in 149ª16–24 but also in the final section of the chapter at 149ª24–8. The idea of the genus being more familiar is an element of continuity in Aristotle's reasoning both in this chapter and in chapters 1 and 4. It seems to me that the main problem for the interpretation of lines 149ª20–8 is the blurring of the distinction between linguistic and extra-linguistic levels.

TOPICS VI.12

149ª31–2. The problem concerns the clause ἐπιδιοριστέον τὸ πῶς μέσον ἔχοντα ('we must further determine how it has a middle'). This clause is present in **A, B, u,** and it is accepted by the editors. This clause, however, is not handed down by other MSS and it seems that Alexander had not read it. It is also absent from the Latin translation of Boethius. Brunschwig argues that it is a 'clumsy anticipation' of the phrase διοριστέον τὸ πῶς μέσον ἔχον ('we must define how it has a middle') at line 149ᵃ36, and he suggests deleting it (see Brunschwig 2003, pp. 60–1; Brunschwig 2007, p. 78, nn. 1, 2, and *apparatus*). In my translation, I accept Brunschwig's emendation. It is hard to make sense of the clause ἐπιδιοριστέον τὸ πῶς μέσον ἔχοντα ('we must further determine how it has a middle') when it is read in the argument developed at 149ᵃ29–35.

149ᵇ9. All MSS except A read ὄντος ('of what is') after κατὰ συμβεβηκὸς ('incidentally'). This reading is accepted by Bekker 1831, Waitz 1846, Strache and Wallies 1923, and Ross 1958. It is also accepted by the majority of the translators: Pickard-Cambridge 1928, Rolfes 1949, Tricot 1950, Forster 1960, Colli 1970, Zadro 1974, Wagner and Rapp 2004. But Brunschwig (2007, p. 79 *in apparatu*, and n. 1) follows the reading of MS A and does not print ὄντος. He thinks that the absence of ὄντος in two parallel clauses in the sequel of this passage (149ᵇ13 and 149ᵇ17–18) speaks in favour of its absence also at 149ᵇ9. Even Brunschwig, however, admits that ὄντος, although absent from the text, must be understood as a complement of the verb εἶναι at 149ᵇ10 (he translates: 'il faut en effet qu'elle le soit de tout étant, si c'est par soi et non par accident qu'elle est dite *l* 'être). But understanding ὄντος in this way feels linguistically unnatural: it puts an undue and implausible pressure on the reader. For this reason, I follow the majority of the editors and translate the text with ὄντος.

149ᵇ24–30: In this passage, there are three main textual problems. (1) At line 149ᵇ26, the reading handed down by the majority of MSS (and the most authoritative ones) has the participle δυνάμενος between μὲν ὁ and τὸ ἕν. This reading is accepted by all editors apart from Brunschwig, who deletes δυνάμενος. The reasons for this emendation, which is based on Alexander's paraphrase, can be found in Brunschwig 2003, pp. 61–3, and 2007, p. 79, n. 1. (2) At line 149ᵇ27, all MSS and all editors read θεωρεῖν after πιθανὸν, but Brunschwig prints the text quoted by Alexander, i.e. θεωρῶν. (3) At the same line, 149ᵇ27, the most authoritative MSS read παραλείπειν after μηδέν. This reading is accepted by Bekker 1831 and by Waitz 1846, whilst Strache and Wallies 1923, Ross 1958, and Brunschwig 2007 print παραλείπειν. It is difficult to choose among the alternative readings and each of them has something that can be said in favour of it. In particular, Brunschwig's detailed justification in support of his choice is very attractive. Nevertheless, one wonders whether it is possible to keep the text as it is preserved in the most important MSS while giving a good sense to the passage. Let me offer the following reading, which lies behind my proposed translation. (1) At 149^{b}26, let us retain the participle δυνάμενος between μὲν ὁ and τὸ ἕν. (2) At 149^{b}27, let us read θεωρεῖν; this infinitive depends on δυνάμενος. (3) At 149^{b}27, let us read παραλείπειν; in this way, this infinitive also depends on δυνάμενος. My reading has two strong points. It has a philological advantage since it respects the text preserved in the most important MSS. It also has an interpretative merit since it allows us to cash out the two infinitives in the same way as they both depend on the participial form ὁ δυνάμενος. The need to offer a text with an interpretative advantage might have been the reason why Bekker printed the infinitive παραλείπειν instead of the participle παραλείπων.

APPENDIX

The Predicables' Logical Relations

The following formal argument enables one to see why any two positively related classes stand in one of the four relations that constitute the predicables.[1]
As usual:

∩	stands for	set theoretical intersection
−		set theoretical complement
⊆		set theoretical inclusion
⊂		proper set theoretical inclusion
∘		proper overlap
∅		the empty set

The following principles function as background assumptions:

X ∩ −Y=∅ ↔ X ⊆ Y (*dictum de omni*)
X ⊆ Y ↔ X ⊂ Y v X=Y (definition of inclusion)
A ∘ B ↔ (A ∩ B ≠ ∅ & A ∩ −B ≠ ∅ & B ∩ −A ≠ ∅) (definition of proper overlap)

The argument that two positively related classes must by linked by one of the Aristotelian predicables is as follows:

1. A ∘ B ↔ (A ∩ B ≠ ∅ & A ∩ −B ≠ ∅ & B ∩ −A ≠ ∅) (definition of proper overlap).
2. ¬ A ∘ B ↔ ¬(A ∩ B ≠ ∅ & A ∩ −B ≠ ∅ & B ∩ −A ≠ ∅) (from 1 by contraposition).
3. ¬ A ∘ B ↔ (A ∩ B=∅ v A ∩ −B=∅ v B ∩ −A=∅) (from 2 by De Morgan's Laws).
4. ¬ A ∘ B ↔ (A ∩ B=∅ v A ⊆ B v B ⊆ A) (from 3 by *dictum de omni*).
5. ¬ A ∘ B ↔ (A ∩ B=∅ v A ⊂ B v A=B v B ⊂ A v B=A) (from 4 by the definition of inclusion).
6. ¬ A ∘ B ↔ (A ∩ B=∅ v A ⊂ B v A=B v B ⊂ A v A=B) (from 5 by symmetry of identity).
7. ¬ A ∘ B ↔ (A ∩ B=∅ v A ⊂ B v B ⊂ A v A=B) (from 6 by idempotency of disjunction).

---

[1] Thanks to Paolo Crivelli for some suggestions about the formalization.

8. $\neg A \circ B \to (A \cap B = \emptyset \vee A \subset B \vee B \subset A \vee A = B)$ (from 7 by weakening of the biconditional).
9. $A \circ B \vee A \cap B = \emptyset \vee A \subset B \vee B \subset A \vee A = B$ (from 8 by the principles of disjunction and conditional).
10. $A \cap B = \emptyset \vee A \circ B \vee A \subset B \vee B \subset A \vee A = B$ (from 9 by permutation of disjunction).
11. $A \cap B \neq \emptyset \to (A \circ B \vee A \subset B \vee B \subset A \vee A = B)$ (from 10 by the principles of disjunction and conditional).

SELECT BIBLIOGRAPHY

I. Editions

Bekker, Immanuel 1831 *Aristotelis Opera*, vol. 1 (Berlin: Georg Reimer)
Brunschwig, Jacques 1967 *Aristote:* Topiques Livres *I–IV* (Paris: Les Belles Lettres)
Brunschwig, Jacques 2007 *Aristote:* Topiques Livres *V–VIII* (Paris: Les Belles Lettres)
Ross, W.D. 1958 *Aristotelis Topica et Sophistici Elenchi* (Oxford: Clarendon Press)
Strache, Ioannis, and Maximilianus Wallies 1923 *Aristotelis Topica cum libro De Sophistici Elenchi* (Leipzig: Teubner)
Waitz, Theodorus 1846 *Aristotelis* Organon, vol. 2 (Leipzig: Hahn)

II. Commentaries and Translations

Alexander of Aphrodisias 1891 *Alexandri Aphrodisiensis in Aristotelis Topicorum libros octos commentaria, Commentaria in Aristotelem Graeca ii pars iii.*, Maximilianus Wallies (ed.) (Berlin: Georg Reimer)
Barnes, Jonathan (ed.) 1984 *The Complete Works of Aristotle: The Revised Oxford Translation*, vol.1 (Princeton: Princeton University Press)
Colli, Giorgio (ed.) 1970 *Aristotele*: Organon, 3 vols (Bari: Laterza)
Forster, E.S. 1960 *Aristotle:* Posterior Analytics *and* Topica, translated by Hugh Tredennick and E.S. Forster (Cambridge, MA, and London: Harvard University Press)
Pacius, Julius 1597 *In Porphyrii Isagogen et Aristotelis Organum Commentarius Analyticus* (Francofurti: Apud Heredes Andreae Wecheli, Claudium Marnium, & Iohan. Aubrium); reprinted 1966 (Hildesheim: Georg Olms)
Pickard-Cambridge, W.A. 1928 *Aristotle:* Topics in W.D. Ross (ed.) *The Works of Aristotle Translated into English*, vol. 1 (Oxford and London: Oxford University Press and Humphrey Milford)
Rolfes, Eugen 1919 *Aristoteles:* Topik, *Neu Übersetzt und mit Einer Einleitung und Erklärenden Anmerkungen* (Leipzig: Felix Meiner)
Segurado e Campos, J.A. 2007 *Aristóteles:* Tópicos, *Tradução e notas* (Lisboa: Imprensa Nacional-Casa da Moeda)
Tricot, Jules 1950 *Aristote:* Topiques. Organon *V. Traduction et notes* (Paris: Vrin)

359

Wagner, Tim and Christoph Rapp 2004 *Aristoteles, Topik* (Stuttgart: Reclam)

III. Books and Articles

Ackrill, J.L. 1963 *Aristotle's* Categories *and* De Interpretatione: *Translated with Notes.* Clarendon Aristotle Series (Oxford: Clarendon Press)
Ackrill, J.L. 1965 'Aristotle's Distinction between *Energeia* and *Kinêsis*', in Renford Bambrough (ed.), *New Essays on Plato and Aristotle* (London: Routledge & Kegan Paul), 121–41; reprinted in Ackrill 1997, 142–62
Ackrill, J.L. 1981 'Aristotle's Theory of Definition: Some Questions on *Posterior Analytics* II. 8–10', in Berti (ed.), 359–84; reprinted in Ackrill 1997, 110–30
Ackrill, J.L. 1997 *Essays on Plato and Aristotle* (Oxford: Clarendon Press)
Annas, Julia 1976 *Aristotle's* Metaphysics *Books M and N: Translated with Introduction and Notes.* Clarendon Aristotle Series (Oxford: Clarendon Press)
Apostle, H.G. 1952 *Aristotle's Philosophy of Mathematics* (Chicago: University of Chicago Press)
Aubenque, Pierre 1957 'Sur la définition aristotélicienne de la colère', *Revue Philosophique de la France et de l'Étranger* 147, 300–17
Balme, D.M. 1987 'Aristotle's Use of Division and Differentiae', in Allan Gotthelf and James G. Lennox (eds), *Philosophical Issues in Aristotle's Biology* (Cambridge: Cambridge University Press), 69–89
Balmes, Marc 2002 'Predicables de los *Tópicos* y Predicables de la *Isagoge*', *Annuario Filosófico* 35, 129–64
Barnes, Jonathan 1970 'Property in Aristotle's *Topics*', *Archiv für Geschichte der Philosophie* 52, 137–55
Barnes, Jonathan 1975 *Aristotle's* Posterior Analytics: *Translated with a Commentary.* Clarendon Aristotle Series (Oxford: Clarendon Press)
Barnes, Jonathan 1993 *Aristotle's* Posterior Analytics: *Translated with a Commentary*, second edition. Clarendon Aristotle Series (Oxford: Clarendon Press)
Barnes, Jonathan 2003 *Porphyry's* Introduction. Clarendon Later Ancient Philosophers Series (Oxford: Clarendon Press)
Berg, Jan 1983 'Aristotle's Theory of Definition', in Vito Michele Abrusci, Ettore Casari, and Massimo Mugnai, *Atti del Convegno Internazionale di Storia della Logica, San Gimignano, 4–8 Dicembre 1982* (Bologna: CLUEB), 19–30

Berti, Enrico 1962 *La filosofia del primo Aristotele* (Padova: Cedam)
Berti, Enrico 1977 *Aristotele: dalla dialettica alla filosofia prima* (Padova: Cedam)
Berti, Enrico 1981 (ed.) *Aristotle on Science. The Posterior Analytics, Proceedings of the Eighth Symposium Aristotelicum held in Padua from September 7 to 15, 1978* (Padova: Editrice Antenore)
Berti, Enrico 2003 'L'Essere e l'Uno in *Metaph. B*', in Vincenza Celluprica (ed.), *Il Libro B della* Metafisica *di Aristotle. Atti del Coloquio, Roma* 30 *Novembre–1 Dicembre 2000* (Napoli: Bibliopolis), 105–25
Berti, Enrico 2004 *Nuovi Studi Aristotelici*, vol. 1 (Brescia: Morcelliana)
Bird, Otto 1964 *Syllogistic and its Extensions* (Englewood Cliffs, NJ: Prentice-Hall)
Bobonich, Christopher 2007 'Plato on *Akrasia* and Knowing Your Mind', in Bobonich and Destrée (eds), 41–60
Bobonich, Christopher, and Pierre Destrée (eds) 2007 Akrasia *in Greek Philosophy. From Socrates to Plotinus* (Leiden: Brill)
Bodéüs, Richard 1993 *Aristote. De l'âme* (Paris: Flammarion)
Bolton, Robert 1990 'The Epistemological Basis of Aristotelian Dialectic', in Deveraux and Pellegrin (eds), 185–236
Bolton, Robert 1994 'The Problem of Dialectical Reasoning in Aristotle', *Ancient Philosophy* 14, 99–132
Bonitz, Hermann 1870 *Index Aristotelicus* (Berlin: Georg Reimer)
Bostock, David 1988 'Pleasure and Activity in Aristotle's Ethics', *Phronesis* 33, 251–72
Bostock, David 1994 *Aristotle's* Metaphysics *Books Z and H*. Clarendon Aristotle Series (Oxford: Clarendon Press)
Bronstein, David 2010 'Meno's Paradox in *Posterior Analytics* 1.1', *Oxford Studies in Ancient Philosophy* 38, 115–41
Bronstein, David 2016 *Aristotle on Knowledge and Learning* (Oxford: Oxford University Press)
Brown, Lesley 1993 '*Thaetetus*: Knowledge, Definition, Parts, Elements and Priority', *Aristotelian Society Supplementary Volume* LXVII, 229–42
Brunschwig, Jacques 1973 'Sur quelques emplois d' OPSIS', in *Zetesis. Album amicorum door vrienden en collega's aangeboden aan Prof. Dr E. de Strycker ter gelegenheid van zijn vijfenzestigste verjaardag.* (Antwerp and Utrecht: De Nederlandsche Boekhandel), 24–39
Brunschwig, Jacques 1980 'Du mouvement et de l'immobilité de la loi', *Revue International de Philosophie* 34, 512–40
Brunschwig, Jacques 1984/85 'Aristotle on Arguments without Winners or Losers', *Wissenschaftskolleg zu Berlin-Jahrbuch*, 31–40

Brunschwig, Jacques 1986 'Sur le systyème des «prédicables» dans les *Topiques* d'Aristote', in *Energeia. Études aristotéliciennes offertes à Mgr A. Jannone* (Paris: Vrin),145–57

Brunschwig, Jacques 1992 'Note sur la conception aristotélicienne de l'accident', in *Methexis. Études néoplatoniciennes présentées au professeur E.A. Moutsopoulos* (Athènes: C.I.E.P.A), 67–80

Brunschwig, Jacques 1995 'Rhétorique et dialecique, «Rhétorique» et «Topiques»', in David J. Furley and Alexander Nehamas (eds), *Aristotle's Rhetoric. Philosophical Essays* (Princeton: Princeton University Press), 57–96

Brunschwig, Jacques 1999 'Homonymie et contradiction dans la dialectique aristotélicienne', in Philippe Bütten, Stéphan Diebler, and Marwan Rashed (eds), *Théories de la phrase et de la proposition de Platon à Averroès* (Paris: Éditions Rue d'Ulm), 81–101

Brunschwig, Jacques 2003 'Do we need new Editions of Ancient Philosophy?', in R.W. Sharples (ed.), *Perspectives on Greek Philosophy S.V. Keeling Memorial Lectures in Ancient Philosophy 1992–2002* (Aldershot: Ashgate), 50–69

Burnyeat, Myles 1981 'Aristotle on Understanding Knowledge', in Berti (ed.), 97–139

Burnyeat, Myles 2001 *A Map of* Metaphysics *Zeta* (Pittsburgh: Mathesis)

Burnyeat, Myles 2008 '*Kinêsis* vs. *Energeia*: A Much-Read Passage in (but not of) Aristotle's *Metaphysics*', *Oxford Studies in Ancient Philosophy* 34, 219–92

Burnyeat, Myles 2012 'Episteme', in Benjamin Morison and Katerina Ierodiakonou (eds), *Episteme etc.: Essays in Honour of Jonathan Barnes* (Oxford: Oxford University Press), 3–29

Burnyeat, Myles, et al. 1979 *Notes on Book Zeta of Aristotle's* Metaphysics (Oxford: Sub-faculty of Philosophy)

Casari, Ettore 1984 'Note sulla logica aristotelica della comparazione', *Sileno* 10, 131–46

Cavini, Walter 1989 'Modalità dialettiche nei *Topici* di Aristotele', in Giovanna Corsi, Corrado Mangione, and Massimo Mugnai (eds) *Atti del Convegno Internazionale di Storia della Logica, Le teorie della modalità* (Bologna: CLUEB), 15–46

Charles, David 1986 'Aristotle: Ontology and Moral Reasoning', *Oxford Studies in Ancient Philosophy* 4, 119–44

Charles, David 1991 'Teleological Causation in the *Physics*', in Judson (ed.), 101–28

Charles, David 2000 *Aristotle on Meaning and Essence* (Oxford: Oxford University Press)

Charles, David (ed.) 2010 *Definition in Greek Philosophy* (Oxford: Oxford University Press)

Charlton, William 1970 *Aristotle's* Physics *Book I and II. Translated with Introduction, Commentary, Note on Recent Work, and Revised Bibliography.* Clarendon Aristotle Series (Oxford: Clarendon Press)

Cherniss, Harold 1962 *Aristotle's Criticism of Plato and the Academy*, 2 vols (New York: Russell & Russell)

Chiba, Kei 2010 'Aristotle on Essence and Defining-Phrase in his Dialectic', in Charles (ed.), 203–51

Cleary, John J. 1995 *Aristotle and Mathematics* (Leiden: Brill)

Cohen, S. Marc 1981 'Proper Differentiae, the Unity of Definition and Aristotle's Essentialism', *New Scholasticism* 55, 229–40

Corcilius, Klaus 2011 'Aristotle's definition of non-rational pleasure and pain and desire', in Jon Miller (ed.), *Aristotle's* Nicomachean Ethics: *A Critical Guide* (Cambridge: Cambridge University Press), 117–43

Crivelli, Paolo 2004 *Aristotle on Truth* (Cambridge: Cambridge University Press)

Crivelli, Paolo 2012 *Plato on Falsehood* (Cambridge: Cambridge University Press)

Crivelli, Paolo 2017 'Being-said-of in Aristotle's *Categories*', *Rivista di Filosofia Neo-Scolastica* 3, 531–56

Denyer, Nicholas (ed.) 2008 *Plato:* Protagoras (Cambridge: Cambridge University Press)

De Pater, W.A. 1965 *Les* Topiques *d'Aristote et la dialectique platonicienne. Methodologie de la définition* (Fribourg: Éditions Saint-Paul)

Deslauriers, Marguerite 2007 *Aristotle on Definition* (Leiden and Boston MA: Brill)

Deveraux, Daniel, and Pierre Pellegrin (eds) 1990 *Biologie, logique et métaphysique chez Aristote* (Paris: CNRS Éditions)

De Vogel, C.J. 1968 'Aristotle's Attitudes to Plato and the Theory of the Idea according to the *Topics*', in Owen (ed.) 1968a, 91–102

DK = Diels, Hermann, and Walther Kranz (eds) 1952 *Die Fragmente der Vorsokratiker*, 3 vols (Berlin: Weidmann)

Dorion, Louis-André 1995 *Aristote:* Les réfutations sophistiques (Paris et Laval: Vrin et Presse de l'Université de Laval)

Duncombe, Matthew 2015 'Aristotle's Two Accounts of Relatives in *Categories* 7', *Phronesis* 60, 436–61

Düring, Ingemar 1943 *Aristotle's* De Partibus Animalium. *Critical and Literary Commentary* (Göteborg: Göteborg University Press)

Düring, Ingemar 1968 'Aristotle's Use of Examples in the *Topics*', in Owen (ed.) 1968a, 202–29

Ebert, Theodor 1977 'Aristotelischer und traditioneller Akzidenzbegriff', in Günther Patzig, Erhard Scheibe, and Wolfgang Wieland (eds) *Logik, Ethik, Theorie der Geisteswissenschaften XI. Deutscher*

Kongress für Philosophie, Göttingen 5.–9. Oktober 1975 (Hamburg: Meiner), 338–49

Ebert, Theodor 1998 'Aristotelian Accidents', *Oxford Studies in Ancient Philosophy* 16, 133–59

Fait, Paolo 1998 'L'éristique mise en formules. Étude critique de: *Aristote, Les réfutations sophistiques* par Louis-André Dorion (Paris, 1995)', *Dialogue* 37, 131–54

Fait, Paolo (ed.) 2007 *Aristotele. Le Confutazioni Sofistiche* (Bari: Laterza)

Fine, Gail 1979 'Knowledge and *logos* in the *Theaetetus*', *Philosophical Review* 88, 366–97

Fine, Gail 1993 *On Ideas: Aristotle's Criticism of Plato's Theory of Forms* (Oxford: Oxford University Press)

Frede, Michael 1967 *Prädikation und Existenzaussage: Platons Gebrauch von '...ist...' und '...ist nicht...' im Sophistes* (Göttingen: Vandenhoeck & Ruprecht)

Frede, Michael 1981 'Categories in Aristotle', in O'Meara (ed.), 1–24; reprinted in Frede 1987, 29–48

Frede, Michael 1987 *Essays in Ancient Philosophy* (Oxford: Clarendon Press)

Frede, Michael 1992 'Plato's *Sophist* on False Statements', in Richard Kraut (ed.) *The Cambridge Companion to Plato* (Cambridge: Cambridge University Press), 397–424

Frede, Michael, and Günther Patzig 1988 *Aristoteles* Metaphysics Z: *Text, Übersetzung und Kommentar*, 2 vols (München: C.H. Beck)

Gambra, J.M. 2003 'La théorie aristotélicienne de la différence dans les *Topiques*', *Philosophie antique* 3, 21–54

Gentzler, Jyl (ed.) 1998 *Method in Ancient Philosophy* (Oxford: Oxford University Press)

Gill, Mary Louise 1989 *Aristotle on Substance: The Paradox of Unity* (Princeton: Princeton University Press)

Goldin, Owen M. 2004 'Atoms, complexes, and demonstration: *Posterior Analytics* 96^{b}15–25', *Studies in History and Philosophy of Science* 35, 707–27

Goodwin, William W. 1879 *Syntax of Greek Moods and Tenses* (Boston: Ginn & Heath)

Gourinat, Jean-Baptiste, and Juliette Lemaire (eds) 2016 *Logique et Dialectique dans l'Antiquité* (Paris: Vrin)

Granger, Herbert 1980 'Aristotle and the Genus–Species Relation', *Southern Journal of Philosophy* 18, 37–50

Granger, Herbert 1984 'Aristotle on Genus and Differentia', *Journal of the History of Philosophy* 22, 1–23

Grene, Marjorie 1974 'Is Genus to Species as Matter to Form? Aristotle and Taxonomy', *Synthese* 28, 51–69
Grote, George 1872–80 *Aristotle*, 2 vols (London: Murray)
Hadgopoulos, Demetrius 1976 'The Definition of the "Predicables" in Aristotle', *Phronesis* 21, 59–63
Hamlyn, D.W. 1968 *Aristotle's* De Anima, *Books II and III (with certain passages from Book I)*. Clarendon Aristotle Series (Oxford: Clarendon Press)
Hardie, W.F.R. 1980 *Aristotle's Ethical Theory*, second edition (Oxford: Clarendon Press)
Harte, Verity 2002 *Plato on Parts and Wholes: The Metaphysics of Structure* (Oxford: Oxford University Press)
Heath, Thomas 1949 *Mathematics in Aristotle* (Oxford: Clarendon Press)
Heath, Thomas 1956 *Euclid. The thirteen books of* The Elements, *translated from the text of Heiberg with introduction and commentary*, second edition (New York: Dover)
Hintikka, Jaakko 1973 *Time and Necessity: Studies in Aristotle's Theory of Modality* (Oxford: Clarendon Press)
Hintikka, Jaakko 1974 *Logic, Language Games and Information: Kantian Themes in the Philosophy of Logic* (Oxford: Clarendon Press)
Huby, Pamela M. 1962 'The Date of Aristotle's *Topics* and its Treatment of the Theory of Ideas', *Classical Quarterly* 12, 72–80
Hussey, Edward 1983 *Aristotle's* Physics. *Books III and IV*. Clarendon Aristotle Series (Oxford: Clarendon Press)
Irwin, Terence 1977 *Plato's Moral Theory: The Early and Middle Dialogues* (Oxford: Clarendon Press)
Irwin, Terence 1987 'Ways to First Principles: Aristotle's Method of Discovery', *Philosophical Topics* 15, 109–34
Irwin, Terence 1988 *Aristotle's First Principles* (Oxford: Clarendon Press)
Irwin, Terence 1995 *Plato's Ethics* (New York: Oxford University Press)
Irwin, Terence 1999 *Aristotle.* Nicomachean Ethics, second edition (Indianapolis: Hackett)
Isnardi Parente, Margherita 1966a *Techne, momenti del pensiero Greco da Platone ad Epicuro* (Firenze: La nuova Italia)
Isnardi Parente, Margherita 1966b 'Per l'interpretazione di *Topici* VI 6, 145[a]19 sgg.', *Rivista di Filologia e di Istruzione Classica* 94, 149–61
Isnardi Parente, Margherita (ed.) 1982 *Socrate-Ermodoro. Frammenti* (Napoli: Bibliopolis)
Johnson, William 1921 *Logic* (Cambridge: Cambridge University Press)
Jowett, Benjamin 1892 *The Dialogues of Plato*, third edition (Oxford: Clarendon Press)

Judson, Lindsay (ed.) 1991 *Aristotle's* Physics, *A Collection of Essays* (Oxford: Clarendon Press)
Judson, Lindsay 1997 'Aristotle on Fair Exchange', *Oxford Studies in Ancient Philosophy* 25, 147–75
Judson, Lindsay 2018 '*Physics* I.5', in Quarantotto (ed.), 130–53
King, C.G. 2021 'Adversarial Argumentation and Common Ground in Aristotle's *Sophistical Refutations*', *Topoi* 40, 939–50, https://doi.org/10.1007/s11245-020-09734-x
KRS = Kirk, G.S., J.A. Raven, and Malcolm Schofield (eds) 1983 *The Presocratic Philosophers*, second edition (Cambridge: Cambridge University Press)
Kirwan, Christopher 1993 *Aristotle's* Metaphysics *Books Γ, Δ, and E: Translated with notes*, second edition. Clarendon Aristotle Series (Oxford: Clarendon Press)
Kneale, William, and Martha Kneale 1962 *The Development of Logic* (Oxford: Clarendon Press)
Lear, Jonathan 1980 *Aristotle and Logical Theory* (Cambridge: Cambridge University Press)
Lear, Jonathan 1982 'Aristotle's Philosophy of Mathematics', *Philosophical Review* 91, 161–92
LeBlond, J.M. 1979 'Aristotle on Definition', in Jonathan Barnes, Malcolm Schofield, and Richard Sorabji (eds) *Articles on Aristotle*, vol 3: *Metaphysics* (London: Duckworth), 63–79
Lee, Edward N., Alexander P.D. Mourelatos, and Richard Rorty (eds) 1973 *Exegesis and Argument: Studies in Greek Philosophy presented to Gregory Vlastos* (*Phronesis Supplementary Volume 1*) (Assen: Van Gorcum), 393–420
Lennox, James 2001 *Aristotle: On the Parts of Animals Books I–IV. Translated with an Introduction.* Clarendon Aristotle Series (Oxford: Clarendon Press)
LSJ = Liddell, H.G., Robert Scott, and H.S. Jones 1985 *A Greek–English Lexicon* (*With a Supplement, 1968*), ninth edition, reprint (Oxford: Clarendon Press)
Madigan, Arthur SJ 1999 *Aristotle* Metaphysics *Book B and K 1-2, Translated with a Commentary.* Clarendon Aristotle Series (Oxford: Clarendon Press)
Malink, Marko 2007 'Categories in *Topics* I.9', *Rhizai* 4, 271–94
Mann, Wolfgang-Reiner 2000 *The Discovery of Things. Aristotle's Categories and Their Context* (Princeton: Princeton University Press)
Mansion, Suzanne 1979 '«Plus connus en soi», «Plus connus pour nous». Une distinction épistémologique importante chez Aristote', *Pensamiento* 35, 161–70; reprinted in Suzanne Mansion 1984 *Études*

Aristotéliciennes (Louvain-la-Neuve : Éditions de l'Institut supérieur de philosophie), 213–22

Mansion, Suzanne 1984 'Notes sur la doctrine des catégories dans les *Topiques*', in Suzanne Mansion, *Études Aristotéliciennes* (Louvain-la-Neuve : Éditions de l'Institut supérieur de philosophie), 169–81

Matthews G.B. and Blackson T.A. 1989 'Causes in the Phaedo', *Synthese* 79, 581–91

Meinwald, Constance 1991 *Plato's* Parmenides (New York and Oxford: Oxford University Press)

Mignucci, Mario 1975 *L'argomentazione dimostrativa in Aristotele. Commento agli* Analitici secondi (Padova: Antenore)

Mignucci, Mario 1986 'Aristotle's Definitions of Relatives in *Cat.* 7', *Phronesis* 31, 101–27

Moravcsik, J.M.E. 1962 'Being and Meaning in the *Sophist*', *Acta Philosophica Fennica* 14, 23–78

Moraux, Paul 1968 'La joute dialectique d'après le huitième livre des *Topiques*', in G.E.L. Owen (ed.) 1968a, 277–311

Moreau, Joseph 1968 'Aristote et la dialectique platonicienne' in G.E.L. Owen (ed.) 1968a, 80–90

Morison, Benjamin 2002 *On Location: Aristotle's Concept of Place* (Oxford: Oxford University Press)

Morrison, Donald 1993 'Le statut catégoriel des différences dans l'Organon', *Revue Philosophique de la France et de l'étranger* 183, 147–78

Moss, Jessica 2012 *Aristotle on the Apparent Good* (Oxford: Oxford University Press)

Mugler, Charles 1956 'Sur deux passages de Platon', *Revue des Études Grecques* 69, 20–34

Müller, Ian 1970 'Aristotle on Geometrical Objects', *Archiv für Geschichte der Philosophie* 52, 156–71

Natali, Carlo (ed.) 2009 *Aristotle's* Nicomachean Ethics, *Book VII. Symposium Aristotelicum* (Oxford: Oxford University Press)

Nussbaum, Martha (ed.) 1986 *Logic, Science and Dialectic: Collected Papers in Greek Philosophy* (London: Duckworth)

O'Meara, Dominic (ed.) 1981 *Studies in Aristotle* (Washington, DC: Catholic University of America Press)

Owen, G.E.L. 1957 'A Proof in the *Peri Ideôn*', *Journal of Hellenic Studies* 77, 103–111

Owen, G.E.L. 1960 'Logic and Metaphysics in Some Earlier Work of Aristotle', in Ingemar Düring and G.E.L. Owen (eds), *Aristotle and Plato in the Mid-Fourth Century—Papers of the Symposium Aristotelicum Held at Oxford in August 1957* (Göteborg: Almqvist & Wiksell), 163–90; reprinted in Nussbaum (ed.), 180–99

Owen, G.E.L. 1961 'Tithenai ta phainomena', in Suzanne Mansion (ed.) *Aristote et les problèmes de méthode* : *Papers of the Second Symposium Aristotelicum* (Louvain: Publications Universitaires), 83–103

Owen, G.E.L. (ed.) 1968a *Aristotle's on Dialectic. The Topics. Proceedings of the Third Symposium Aristotelicum* (Oxford: Clarendon Press)

Owen, G.E.L. 1968b 'Dialectic and Eristic in the Treatment of the Forms', in Owen (ed.) 1968a, 103–25

Pelletier, Yvan 1991 *La dialectique aristotélicienne. Les principes clés des Topiques* (Montréal: Bellarmin)

Peramatzis, Michail 2011 *Priority in Aristotle's Metaphysics* (Oxford: Oxford University Press)

Primavesi, Oliver 1992 'Dionysios der Dialektiker und Aristoteles über die Definition des Lebens', *Rheinisches Museum für Philologie* 135, 246–61

Primavesi, Oliver 1996 *Die Aristotelische Topik: ein Interpretationsmodell und seine Erprobung am Beispiel von Topik B* (München: C.H. Beck)

Prior, Arthur N. 1949 'Determinables, Determinates and Determinants', *Mind* 58, 1–20

Prior, Arthur N. 1968 'Now', *Noûs* 2, 101–19

Proclus 1873 *In primum Euclidis librum commentarius*, ed. G.Friedlein (Leipzig: Teubner)

Quarantotto, Diana (ed.) 2018 *Aristotle's Physics I: A Systematic Exploration* (Cambridge: Cambridge University Press)

Reeve, C.D.C. 1998 'Dialectic and Philosophy in Aristotle', in Gentzler (ed.), 227–52

Reinhardt, Tobias 2000 *Das Buch E der Aristotelischen Topik. Untersuchungen zur Echtheitsfrage* (Göttingen: Vandenhoeck & Ruprecht)

Rorty, Richard 1973 'Genus as Matter: A Reading of *Metaphysics* Z–H', in Lee, Mourelatos, and Rorty (eds), 393–420

Ross, W.D. 1924 *Aristotle's Metaphysics: A Revised Text with Introduction and Commentary*. 2 vols (Oxford: Clarendon Press)

Ross, W.D. 1949 *Aristotle's Prior and Posterior Analytics: A Revised Text with Introduction and Commentary* (Oxford: Clarendon Press)

Ross, W.D. 1951 *Plato's Theory of Ideas* (Oxford: Clarendon Press)

Rowe, Christopher 2007 'A Problem in the *Gorgias*: How Is Punishment Supposed To Help With Intellectual Error?' in Bobonich and Destrée (eds), 19–40

Schiaparelli, Annamaria 2002 *Galeno e le fallacie linguistiche* (*Il de captionibus in dictione*) (Venezia: Istituto Veneto di Scienze, Lettere ed Arti)

Schiaparelli, Annamaria 2003 'Aristotle on the Fallacy of Combination and Division in *Sophistici Elenchi* 4', *History and Philosophy of Logic* 24, 111–29

Schiaparelli, Annamaria 2011 'Epistemological Problems in Aristotle's Concept of Definition: *Topics* VI.4', *Ancient Philosophy* 31, 127–43

Schiaparelli, Annamaria 2016 'The Concept of Differentia in the *Topics*' in Gourinat and Lemaire (eds), 231–57

Schiaparelli, Annamaria 2017 'Platonic Ideas and Appearance in Aristotle's *Topics*', *Archiv für Geschichte der Philosophie* 99, 129–55

Searle, John 1959 'Determinables and the Notion of Resemblance', *Proceedings of the Aristotelian Society, Supplementary Volume* 33, 125–58

Shields, Christopher 1999 *Order in Multiplicity: Homonymy in the Philosophy of Aristotle* (Oxford: Clarendon Press)

Shields, Christopher 2007 'Unified agency and *Akrasia* in Plato's *Republic*', in Bobonich and Destrée (eds), 61–86

Shields, Christopher 2016 *Aristotle's De Anima, Translated with Introduction and Commentary*. Clarendon Aristotle Series (Oxford: Clarendon Press)

Sim, May (ed.) 1999a *From Puzzles to Principles? Essays on Aristotle's Dialectic* (Lanham, MD: Lexington Books)

Sim, May 1999b 'Dialectical Communities: From the One to the Many and Back', in Sim (ed.) 1998a, 183–213

Simons, Peter 1987 *Parts: A Study in Ontology* (Oxford: Clarendon Press)

Slomkowski, Paul 1997 *Aristotle's* Topics (Leiden, New York, Köln: Brill)

Smith, Robin 1989 *Aristotle's* Prior Analytics (Indianapolis: Hackett)

Smith, Robin 1997 *Aristotle's* Topics *Books I and VIII: Translated with Commentary*. Clarendon Aristotle Series (Oxford: Clarendon Press)

Smith, Robin 2010 Review of Brunschwig, Jacques 2007 *Aristote* Topiques *Livres V–VIII* (Paris: Les Belles Lettres), *Classical Review* 60, 48–50

Smyth, Herbert W. 1956 *Greek Grammar*. Revised by Gordon M. Messing (Cambridge, MA: Harvard University Press)

Stalnaker, Robert 2014 *Context* (Oxford: Oxford University Press)

Striker, Gisela 2009 *Aristotle's* Prior Analytics *Book I: Translated with an Introduction and a Commentary*. Clarendon Aristotle Series (Oxford: Clarendon Press)

Tréhcux, Jacques 1957 "Ἐπιπροσθεῖ", *Revue des Études Grecques* 70, 356–60

Verbeke, Gérard 1968 'La notion de propriété dans les *Topiques*', in Owen (ed.) 1968a, 257–76

Verdenius, W.J. 1968 'Notes on the *Topics*', in Owen (ed.) 1968a, 22–42

Vlastos, Gregory 1965–6 'A Metaphysical Paradox', *Proceedings and Addresses of the American Philosophical Association* 39, 5–19; reprinted in Vlastos 1981, 35–57

Vlastos, Gregory 1969 '"Self-Predication" in Plato's Later Period', *Philosophical Review* 78, 74–8; reprinted as 'Self-Predication and Self-Participation in Plato's Later Period' in Vlastos 1981, 335–41

Vlastos, Gregory 1981 *Platonic Studies*, second edition (Princeton: Princeton University Press)

Ward, Julia K. 2008 *Aristotle on Homonymy. Dialectic and Science* (Cambridge: Cambridge University Press)

Wiggins, David 1967 *Identity and Spatio-Temporal Continuity* (Oxford: Blackwell)

Wiggins, David 1980 *Sameness and Substance* (Oxford: Blackwell)

Williams, C.F.J. 1982 *Aristotle's* De Generatione et Corruptione: *Translated with Notes*. Clarendon Aristotle Series (Oxford: Clarendon Press)

Zadro, Attilio 1974 *Aristotele I Topici. Traduzione, introduzione, commento* (Naples: Luigi Loffredo Editore)

GLOSSARY

ENGLISH–GREEK

to abolish	ἀναιρεῖν	anairein
accident	συμβεβηκός	sumbebêkos
account	λόγος	logos
accurate	ἀκριβής	akribês
affection	πάθος	pathos
animal	ζῷον	zôion
the answerer	ὁ ἀποκρινόμενος	ho apokrinomenos
apparent	φαινόμενος	phainomenos
appetite	ἐπιθυμία	epithumia
to apply	ἐφαρμόττειν	epharmottein
to argue against, to attack	ἐπιχειρεῖν	epicheirein
to become familiar with	γνωρίζειν	gnôrizein
(being-) in-something	ἔν τινι	en tini
the being-just-what-it-is	τὸ εἶναι ὅπερ ἐστίν	to einai hoper estin
to belong to	ὑπάρχειν	huparchein
by privation	κατὰ στέρησιν	kata sterêsin
to carry to destruction with	συναναιρεῖν	sunanairein
commonplace	τόπος	topos
complex	συμπεπλεγμένος	sumpeplegmenos
composite	σύνθετος	sunthetos
contrary	ἐναντίος	enantios
to convert	ἀντιστρέφειν	antistrephein
coordinate	σύστοιχος	sustoichos
to correspond	ἐφαρμόττειν	epharmottein
to counter-predicate	ἀντιστρέφειν	antistrephein
to define	ὁρίζεσθαι	horizesthai
definition	ὁρισμός, ὅρος	horismos, horos
definitory	ὁριστικός	horistikos
desire	ὄρεξις	orexis
differentia	διαφορά	diaphora
disposition	διάθεσις	diathesis
to divide	διαιρεῖν	diairein
to divide by coordinate elements	ἀντιδιαιρεῖσθαι	antidiaireisthai
division	διαίρεσις	diairesis

371

equal	ἴσος	isos
equality	ἰσότης	isotês
essence	οὐσία	ousia
familiar	γνώριμος	familiar
form	εἶδος	eidos
genus	γένος	genos
appropriate genus	οἰκεῖον γένος	oikeion genos
to give (*sc.* an account)	ἀποδιδόναι	apodidonai
(grammatical) modification	πτῶσις	ptôsis
human	ἄνθρωπος	anthrôpos
Idea	ἰδέα	idea
immovable	ἀμετάπτωτος	ametaptôtos
incidentally	κατὰ συμβεβηκός	kata sumbebêkos
incontrovertible	ἀμετάπειστος	ametapeistos
to indicate	δηλοῦν, σημαίνειν	dêloun, sêmainein
in the same way	ὁμοίως	homoiôs
justice	δικαιοσύνη	dikaiosunê
knowable	ἐπιστητός	epistêtos
knowledge	ἐπιστήμη	epistêmê
letter	γραμμή	grammê
line of attack	ἐπιχείρημα	epicheirêma
literacy	γραμματική	grammatikê
living being	ζῷον	zôion
opinable	ὑποληπτός	hupolêptos
opinion	δόξα	doxa
opposed	ἀντιδιῃρημένος	antidiêirêmenos
part	μέρος	meros
to partake	μετέχειν	metechein
particular	ἐπὶ μέρους	epi merous
the person who defines	ὁ ὁριζόμενος	ho horizomenos
plane	ἐπίπεδον	epipedon
pleasant	ἡδύς	hêdus
pleasure	ἡδονή	hêdonê
point	στιγμή	stigmê
possession	ἕξις	hexis
privation	στέρησις	sterêsis
the producing factor	τὸ ποιητικὸν	to poiêtikon
the product	τὸ ποιούμενον	to poioumenon
proximate genus	ἐγγυτάτον γένος	eggutaton genos
relative	πρός τι	pros ti
solid	στερεόν	stereon

GLOSSARY

species	εἶδος	eidos
state	ἕξις	hexis
substance	οὐσία	ousia
supposition	ὑπόληψις	hupolêpsis
two-footed	δίπους	dipous
uncontrolled person	ἀκρατής	akratês
(unique) property	ἴδιον	idion
universal	καθόλου	katholou
virtue	ἀρετή	aretê
way	τρόπος	tropos
the what is	τὸ τί ἐστι	to ti esti
what is being defined	τὸ ὁριζόμενον	to horizomenon
the what-it-is-to-be	τὸ τί ἦν εἶναι	to ti ên einai
whole	ὅλος	holos
wish	βούλησις	boulêsis

GREEK–ENGLISH

ἀκρατής	akratês	uncontrolled person
ἀκριβής	akribês	accurate
ἀμετάπειστος	ametapeistos	incontrovertible
ἀμετάπτωτος	ametaptôtos	immovable
ἀναιρεῖν	anairein	to abolish
ἄνθρωπος	anthrôpos	human
ἀντιδιαιρεῖσθαι	antidiaireisthai	to divide by coordinate elements
ἀντιδιῃρημένος	antidiêirêmenos	opposed
ἀντικατηγορεῖσθαι	antikatêgoreisthai	to counter-predicate
ἀντιστρέφειν	antistrephein	to convert, to reciprocate
ἀρετή	aretê	virtue
ἀποδιδόναι	apodidonai	to give (*sc.* an account)
ὁ ἀποκρινόμενος	ho apokrinomenos	the answerer
βούλησις	boulêsis	wish
γένος	genos	genus, kind
ἐγγυτάτον γένος	eggutaton genos	proximate genus
οἰκεῖον γένος	oikeion genos	appropriate genus
γνωρίζειν	gnôrizein	to become familiar with
γνώριμος	gnôrimos	familiar
ἁπλῶς γνωριμώτερος	haplôs gnôrimôteros	unqualifiedly more familiar

373

GLOSSARY

ἡμῖν γνωριμώτερος	gnôrimôteros hemin	more familiar to us
γραμματική	grammatikê	literacy
γραμμή	grammê	letter
δηλοῦν	dêloun	to indicate, to reveal
δηλοῦν τὴν οὐσίαν	dêloun tên ousian	to make clear the essence
διάθεσις	diathesis	disposition
διαιρεῖν	diairein	to divide
διαίρεσις	diairesis	division
διαφορά	diaphora	differentia
ἴδια διαφορά	idia diaphora	proper differentia
δικαιοσύνη	dikaiosunê	justice
δίπους	dipous	two-footed
δόξα	doxa	opinion
εἶδος	eidos	species, form
εἶναι	einai	to be, to exist
τὸ εἶναι ὅπερ ἐστίν	to einai hoper estin	the being-just-what-it-is
τὸ τί ἐστι	to ti esti	the what is
τὸ τί ἦν εἶναι	to ti ên einai	the what-it-is-to-be
ἐναντίος	enantios	contrary
ἔν τινι	en tini	(being-) in-something
ἕξις	hexis	possession; state
ἐπιθυμία	epithumia	appetite
ἐπίπεδον	epipedon	plane
ἐπιστήμη	epistêmê	knowledge
ἐπιστητός	epistêtos	knowable
ἐπιχειρεῖν	epicheirein	to argue against, to attack
ἐπιχείρημα	epicheirêma	line of attack
ἐφαρμόττειν	epharmottein	to correspond, to apply
ζῷον	zôion	animal, living being
ἡδονή	hêdonê	pleasure
ἡδύς	hêdus	pleasant
ἰδέα	idea	Idea
ἴδιον	idion	(unique) property
ἴσος	isos	equal
ἰσότης	isotês	equality
λόγος	logos	account
καθόλου	katholou	universal
καθόλου εἰπεῖν	katholou eipein	to speak in general
μέρος	meros	part
ἐπὶ μέρους	epi merous	particular

GLOSSARY

μετέχειν	metechein	to partake
ὅλος	holos	whole
ὁμοίως	homoiôs	in the same way
ὄρεξις	orexis	desire
ὁρίζεσθαι	horizesthai	to define
ὁ ὁριζόμενος	ho horizomenos	the person who defines
τὸ ὁριζόμενον	to horizomenon	what is being defined
ὁρισμός	horismos	definition
ὁριστικὸς	horistikos	definitory
ὅρος	horos	definition
οὐσία	ousia	substance, essence
πάθος	pathos	affection
τὸ ποιητικὸν	to poiêtikon	the producing factor
τὸ ποιούμενον	to poioumenon	the product
πρός τι	pros ti	relative
πτῶσις	ptôsis	(grammatical) modification
σημαίνειν	sêmainein	to indicate
συναναιρεῖν	sunanairein	to carry to destruction with
στερεόν	stereon	solid
στέρησις	sterêsis	privation
κατὰ στέρησιν	kata sterêsin	by privation
στιγμή	stigmê	point
συμπεπλεγμένος	sumpeplegmenos	complex
σύνθετος	sunthetos	composite
σύστοιχος	sustoichos	coordinate
συμβεβηκός	sumbebêkos	accident
κατὰ συμβεβηκός	kata sumbebêkos	incidentally
τόπος	topos	commonplace, place
τρόπος	tropos	way
ὑπάρχειν	huparchein	to belong to
ὑποληπτός	hupolêptos	opinable
ὑπόληψις	hupolêpsis	supposition
φαινόμενος	phainomenos	apparent

INDEX LOCORUM

ALEXANDER OF APHRODISIAS
  in Metaph. 83, 26–8 233
  in Metaph. 97, 27–9 298
  in Top. 218, 37–219, 30 152
  in Top. 219, 6 155
  in Top. 222, 4–7 178
  in Top. 225, 47–226, 2 206
  in Top. 421, 27–9 65
  in Top. 423, 19–21 73
  in Top. 452, 6–11 165
  in Top. 476, 21 282
  in Top. 479, 12–15 288
  in Top. 487, 9–15 315
  in Top. 491, 16–18 328

ARISTOTLE
  Categories
    1, 1^{a}1–2 21, 265
    1, 1^{a}4 265
    1, 1^{a}6–7 21, 265, 324
    1, 1^{a}7 265, 324
    1, 1^{a}6–7 265
    2, 1^{a}16–19 281
    2, 1^{a}20–5 154
    2, 1^{a}24–5 182
    3, 1^{b}17–24 147
    3, 1^{b}20–4 171
    5, 2^{a}14–15 335
    5, 2^{b}8–12 142
    5, 3^{a}33–3^{b}9 147, 189
    5, 3^{a}33–3^{b}10 145
    5, 3^{b}21–3 298
    5, 4^{a}31 176
    6, 4^{b}20–25 109
    6, 5^{a}38–5^{b}10 138
    6, 6^{a}36–7 123, 203
    7, 6^{b}5 134
    7, 6^{b}6–7 227
    7, 6^{b}28 228, 301
    7, 6^{b}29–30 228
    7, 6^{b}34–5 301
    7, 7^{a}22–3 228
    7, 7^{a}31–4 301
    7, 7^{a}31–7^{b}1 301
    7, 7^{a}34–9 301
    7, 7^{b}10 123
    7, 7^{b}15 122
    7, 7^{b}27–31 204
    7, 7^{b}23–35 204
    7, 7^{b}27–31 204
    7, 8^{a}26–8 203
    7, 8^{a}28–31 203
    7, 8^{a}39–8^{b}1 203
    8, 8^{b}27–30 78
    8, 8^{b}27–8 182
    8, 8^{b}35–7 182
    8, 9^{a}28 176
    8, 11^{a}23–5 177
    8, 11^{a}23–36 207
    8, 11^{a}24–6 134, 203
    8, 11^{a}28–33 208
    8, 11^{a}29 134
    8, 11^{a}29–30 206
    10, 11^{b}35–7 250
    10, 12^{a}26–7 254
    10, 12^{a}26–8 253
    10, 13^{b}22–4 157
    11, 14^{a}8–10 118
    12, 14^{a}26–^{b}9 102
    12, 14^{a}29–35 118
    12, 14^{a}38–14^{b}1 111
    12, 14^{a}38–14^{b}9 102
    13, 14^{b}27–33 122
    13, 14^{b}35–15^{a}4 149
    13, 15^{a}4–7 131
  De Interpretatione
    11, 20^{b}12–19 281
  Prior Analytics
    I.1, 24^{a}16–20 172
    I.1, 24^{b}23–4 224
    I.2, 25^{a}4–5 172
    I.25, 42^{b}5 273
    I.28, 44^{a}22 273
    I.31, 46^{a}32–5 16
    I.37, 49^{a}6–7 67
    I.45, 50^{a}29–38 273
    I.45, 50^{b}25 301
    I.46, 51^{b}25–8 245, 246
    II.16, 64^{b}30–3 102
    II.23, 68^{b}35–7 107
  Posterior Analytics
    I.1, 71^{a}1 105
    I.2, 71^{b}14–16 78
    I.2, 71^{b}33–72^{a}5 102

ARISTOTLE (*cont.*)
    I.2, 72^{a}1–5 107
    I.2, 72^{b}3–4 201
    I.3, 72^{b}26–30 107
    I.16, 79^{b}23–4 253, 255
    I.24, 85^{b}27–86^{a}2 210
    I.24, 85^{b}32–8 210
    II.8, 93^{b}7–12 17
    II.8, 93^{b}38–9 17
    II.13, 96^{a}20–35 167
    II.13, 96^{a}32–5 168
    II.13, 97^{b}37–9 76
  Topics
    I.1, 100^{a}18–21 2
    I.1, 100^{a}25–7 18
    I.1, 100^{a}25–100^{b}25 2
    I.1, 100^{a}27–9 105
    I.5, 101^{a}38 7
    I.3, 101^{b}8–10 304
    I.4, 101^{b}15–28 4
    I.4, 101^{b}17–23 167
    I.4, 101^{b}19–23 64
    I.4, 101^{b}25 128
    I.5, 101^{b}37–102^{a}2 13
    I.5, 101^{b}38 57, 130, 307
    I.5, 101^{b}38–102^{a}17 57, 130
    I.5, 102^{a}1 105
    I.5, 102^{a}4–5 5, 6, 57, 67
    I.5, 102^{a}7–9 57
    I.5, 102^{a}18–26 88
    I.5, 102^{a}19–22 5
    I.5, 102^{a}31–2 5, 130
    I.5, 102^{a}31–5 161
    I.5, 102^{a}32 141
    I.5, 102^{a}32–5 141
    I.5, 102^{a}33–4 130
    I.5, 102^{b}4–5 6, 67
    I.5, 102^{b}6–7 6, 67
    I.5, 102^{b}10 6
    I.5, 102^{b}11–12 6
    I.6, 102^{b}27–33 11
    I.6, 102^{b}29–33 64
    I.7, 103^{a}27 116
    I.7, 103^{a}28 88
    I.8, 103^{b}5 116
    I.9, 103^{b}21–3 215
    I.10, 104^{a}15–16 122
    I.10, 104^{a}16 137
    I.15, 106^{b}21–8 236
    I.15, 106^{b}29–107^{a}2 257
    I.15, 107^{a}3–17 159
    I.15, 107^{a}19 277
    I.15, 107^{a}22–9 143

    I.15, 107^{b}4 324
    I.15, 107^{b}6–7 20, 268
    I.16, 108^{a}1–3 180
    I.18, 108^{a}33–4 276
    II.1, 109^{a}15–16 116
    II.1, 109^{a}20–2 67
    II.2, 109^{a}34–5 67
    II.2, 109^{b}25–6 300
    II.2, 110^{a}6 104
    II.3, 110^{b}17–20 137
    II.3, 110^{b}18 136
    II.3, 110^{b}18–19 299
    II.3, 110^{b}19–21 137
    II.4, 111^{a}8–10 104
    II.5, 112^{a}19 88
    II.6, 113^{a}4 88
    II.7, 113^{a}14–15 245
    II.7, 113^{a}16–18 245
    II.7, 114^{a}7–25 236
    II.8, 114^{a}18 288
    II.9, 114^{a}26–36 257
    II.9, 114^{a}27–9 22, 234
    II.9, 114^{a}33–4 234
    II.9, 114^{a}38–114^{b}1 234, 258
    II.9, 114^{b}2–5 258
    II.10, 115^{a}15–24 265
    III.1, 116^{a}29–31 306
    III.6, 120^{b}3–6 90
    IV.1, 120^{a}12–14 57, 153
    IV.1, 120^{a}12–15 25
    IV.1, 120^{b}12 64, 140
    IV.1, 120^{b}12–14 57
    IV.1, 120^{b}17–19 139
    IV.1, 120^{b}36–121^{a}8 134
    IV.1, 121^{a}10–20 144
    IV.1, 121^{a}12–14 153
    IV.1, 121^{a}13–14 145
    IV.1, 121^{b}3–4 153
    IV.1, 121^{b}11–14 90, 141, 153, 164, 165
    IV.2, 121^{b}29–31 15, 79, 160
    IV.2, 122^{a}3 144
    IV.2, 122^{a}5 141
    IV.2, 122^{b}7–24 153
    IV.2, 122^{b}12–17 189
    IV.2, 122^{b}16–17 163
    IV.2, 122^{b}17 142
    IV.2, 122^{b}29–123^{a}1 172
    IV.2, 122^{b}39–123^{a}1 168
    IV.2, 123^{a}11–14 90
    IV.2, 123^{a}14–19 117
    IV.3, 123^{a}23–6 90
    IV.3, 123^{a}27 141

IV.3, 123^{a}33–7 76, 78
IV.4, 124^{b}20 134
IV.4, 125^{b}5–7 324
IV.5, 125^{b}20–7 328
IV.5, 126^{a}9–10 201
IV.5, 126^{a}36 138
IV.5, 126^{b}13–19 131
IV.5, 126^{b}18 131
IV.5, 126^{b}37–8 174
IV.5, 127^{a}4 222
IV.6, 127^{b}26–36 328
IV.6, 127^{b}30–3 328
IV.6, 128^{a}20–8 163
IV.6, 128^{a}20–9 141
IV.6, 128^{a}25–8 117
IV.6, 128^{a}26–9 177
VI.6, 128^{a}38 301
IV.6, 128^{b}4 301
V.1, 128^{b}36 88
V.2, 130^{b}8 88
V.2, 130^{b}15–16 201
V.3, 132^{a}1–4 117
V.5, 132^{a}20 88
V.5, 132^{b}1 88
V.5, 133^{a}20–2 88
V.5, 134^{a}15–17 88
V.5, 134^{b}28–34 195
V.6, 136^{b}11–14 180
V.7, 137^{b}2–8 155, 231
V.7, 137^{b}3–8 261
VII.1, 152^{b}7–9 193
VII.4, 154^{a}12–20 259, 260
VII.4, 154^{a}12–13 259
VII.4, 154^{a}15–20 259
VII.4, 154^{a}17–18 260
VII.4, 154^{a}18–19 260
VII.5, 154^{a}23–8 132
VIII.1, 155^{b}20–8 274
VIII.1, 156^{a}4–7 107
VIII.1, 156^{a}7–11 275
VIII.2, 157^{a}32 74
VIII.3, 158^{b}9–12 20
VIII.4, 159^{a}16–18 269
VIII.5, 159^{a}25–37 271
VIII.5, 159^{a}33 269, 271
Sophistici Elenchi
1, 164^{a}20–1 225
1, 164^{b}20–1 276
1, 165^{a}2–3 3
2, 165^{b}4–7 271
2, 165^{b}10–11 276
4, 165^{b}30–166^{b}36 270
8, 169^{b}23–9 271

11, 171^{b}3–6 271
11, 172^{a}21–4 271
13, 173^{a}32 95
17, 175^{a}36–7 73
17, 176^{b}14–25 76
22, 178^{a}25–8 73–4
31, 181^{b}34–5 136
Physics
I.1, 184^{a}16–26 107
I.5, 188^{a}27–30 332
I.5, 188^{b}15–21 332
I.5, 188^{b}30–2 107
I.6, 189^{a}4–7 107
II.3, 195^{a}24–5 210
II.3, 195^{b}3–4 138
II.8, 199^{a}12–20 179
III.2, 201^{b}24 121
IV.3, 210^{a}14–24 129
IV.3, 210^{a}17–18 129
IV.3, 210^{a}18–19 144
IV.8, 215^{b}9 110
IV.11, 220^{a}1–21 110
IV.11, 220^{a}10–11 110
IV.11, 220^{a}27–32 111
IV.13, 222^{a}15 110
VI.1, 231^{a}24 110
VI.1, 231^{b}6 110
VI.10, 241^{a}3 110
VII.3, 246^{b}4–5 74
VIII.7, 260^{b}17–18 118
VIII.7, 261^{b}15–16 245
De Caelo
I.2, 269^{a}9–10 245
II.3, 286^{a}9 187
II.13, 293^{b}21–5 280
II.14, 297^{b}25–30 280
III.1, 300^{a}7–10 110
De Generatione et Corruptione
I.2, 317^{a}10 110
I.10, 327^{b}15–19 298
Metereologica
I.5, 342^{b}5–10 280
De Anima
I.1, 403^{a}28–403^{b}1 329
I.4, 409^{a}9 110
II.1, 413^{a}11–16 107
II.2, 413^{a}22–3 267
II.2, 413^{a}30–413^{b}12 267
III.3, 427^{b}24–6 289
III.9, 432^{a}15–17 151
III.10, 433^{a}27–9 225
Historia Animalium
I.1, 487^{a}5–6 90

ARISTOTLE (cont.)
  I.5, 490^{a}10–12 172
  De Motu Animalium
    6, 700^{b}22 201
  De Generatione Animalium
    I.18, 725^{a}14–16 90
  Metaphysics
    I.3, 983^{b}6–8 221
    I.3, 983^{b}18–28 221
    I.5, 986^{a}23–6 121
    I.9, 991^{a}20–22 77
    I.9, 992^{a}19 110
    III.3, 998^{b}17–28 165
    III.3, 999^{a}1–6 112
    III.5, 1002^{a}4–14 110
    III.5, 1002^{a}5–8 110
    IV.2, 1003^{a}33–1003^{b}15 21, 181
    V.5, 1010^{b}3–9 120
    V.7, 1017^{a}22–7 215
    V.11, 1019^{a}2–4 118
    V.13, 1020^{a}11–12 115
    V.13, 1020^{a}13 111
    V.15, 1021^{b}6–8 216
    V.22, 1023^{a}27–31 157
    V.34, 1023^{a}31 282
    V.24, 1023^{a}34 112
    V.25, 1023^{b}24 97
    V.25, 1023^{b}24–5 144
    VII.2, 1028^{b}15–22 110
    VII.3, 1029^{b}3–12 107, 114
    VII.4, 1030^{a}2–7 219
    VII.4, 1030^{a}11–12 219
    VII.8, 1033^{b}14 296
    VII.9, 1034^{a}24 325
    VII.12, 1037^{b}18–20 95
    VII.12, 1038^{a}18–20 217
    VII.12, 1038^{a}19–20 130
    VII.12, 1038^{a}27–30 217
    VII.13, 1039^{a}12 111
    VII.17, 1041^{a}26–8 325
    IX.2, 1046^{a}30–1 213
    IX.6, 1048^{b}18–35 214
    X.1, 1053^{a}30 111
    X.3, 1054^{a}23 235
    X.3, 1055^{a}38 234
    X.4, 1055^{b}8–11 246
    X.4, 1055^{b}19–20 245
    X.5, 1055^{b}30 245
    X.6, 1056^{b}25 111
    X.7, 1057^{a}33 235
    XI.1, 1059^{b}38–1060^{a}2 117
    XII.2, 1069^{b}12 175
    XIII.7, 1082^{a}25 111
    XIII.9, 1085^{b}10 111

  Nicomachean Ethics
    I.4, 1095^{b}2–3 108
    I.4, 1095^{b}4 114
    I.6, 1096^{a}23–9 159
    I.6, 1096^{a}26–7 21, 265
    I.6, 1096^{b}26–7 265
    III.2, 1111^{b}12–13 201
    III.3, 1112^{a}15–17 113
    III.4, 1113^{a}23–5 226
    III.4, 1113^{a}26–9 120
    IV.5, 1125^{b}7–10 216
    V.1, 1129^{a}6–7 192
    V.9, 1136^{b}20–1 99
    V.10, 1137^{b}34–1138^{a}1 99
    VI.5, 1140^{a}24–8 191
    VII.1, 1145^{a}35–1145^{b}10 220
    VII.1, 1145^{b}2–5 225, 341
    VII.1, 1145^{b}3–4 341
    VII.2, 1145^{b}23 220
    VII.2, 1145^{b}25–6 219
    VII.4, 1147^{b}31–4 221
    VII.8, 1151^{a}11–13 221
    VII.12, 1153^{a}7–12 214
    VII.12, 1153^{a}10 213
    X.3, 1173^{a}29–31 214
    X.4, 1174^{a}14–16 213
    X.4, 1174^{a}14–1174^{b}14 214
    X.9, 1179^{b}31 101
  Magna Moralia
    II.6, 1201^{b}5–6 201
  Politics
    II.8, 1268^{b}26–8 340
  Rhetoric
    I.1, 1355^{b}9–10 304
    II.2, 1378^{a}30–1 329
  On Ideas
    Fr. 3 Ross 233

HERO
  Deff. 77 296

PARMENIDES
  DK 28 B 1, 30 287

PLATO
  Apology
    32B5 323
  Euthydemus
    276C3–7 270
    276D7–277B2 270
  Euthyphro
    6E4 229
    11A7–9 63

Gorgias
  464A 220
  466A–472A 220
  508A8–B2 323
Hyppias Major
  298A6–7 196
Meno
  75B–E 81
  75C–D 273
  76A 115
  76A–B 112
  77B–78C 220
  80D5–7 118
  87D2
Parmenides
  132D2 229
  133C3–5 232
  133C3–134A1 232
  133E3–4 232
  133E4–134A1 232
  134A3–4 233
  134B–C 233
  134D4–7 232
  137C 280
Phaedo
  72D2–3 323
  97C–D 211
Phaedrus
  245E 89
Philebus
  26D 73
Politicus
  258B7–12 160
  258B7–21 16
  264D–E 151
Protagoras
  344C4 323
  351B–357E 220
  352D1–3 323
Republic
  I, 334A 137
  II, 357B–D 306
  II, 358A 306
  IV, 431D8 77
  IV, 437C–441C 202
  V, 477D2–4 241
  X, 596B–C 230
  X, 596E–597B 229
  X, 602E–604E 202
Sophist
  219B 73
  236A 230
  246E5–6 262
  247D8–E4 196
  248A 196, 262
  248A4–E8 262
  248C5 196, 262
  248C7–8 262
  250C6–7 231
  255D 203
  255E3–6 231
  257D14–258C6 231
  258C6 231
  261D 285
Symposium
  187B4 77
Theaetetus
  201C–205E 310
  201D8–204E 248
  202B7–8 112
  202E–206B 112
Timaeus
  29B7 77
  40B8 77
  49A6 77
  52D5 77
  88D6 77
ps. Platonic *Definitions*
  411A 73
  411B 77, 125
  412 B 83
  414B10 77

PROCLUS
  in Euc. 95.26 110

GENERAL INDEX

Note: Page references in bold are to the translation.

Academy 1, 80, 109–12, 115, 118, 219, 261, 264, 303
accident 3–4, 6–7, 11, **27**, 64, 67–9, 117, 135, 163, 306
 two definitions of the predicable accident 6, 67
Ackrill, J. 105, 109, 124, 133, 134, 144, 203, 207, 214, 298, 301
activity **44**, 57, 212–14
actuality 121
affection **40, 41**, 148, 173–6, 182, 184
Alexander of Aphrodisias 65, 73, 178, 206, 282, 288, 328
ambiguity 19–21, 73, 187, 189, 296
Anaxagoras 221
Anaximenes 221
Annas, J. 109, 111
answerer 2–3, 12, 19, 21, 63, 75, 268–73, 277, 339
Apostle, H.G. 109, 111
asymmetry 117, 239, 246–9

Barnes, J. 17 n.5, 64, 70, 74, 80, 103, 104, 105, 108, 114, 129, 133, 134, 135, 144, 184, 219, 236, 255, 289, 298, 305, 321, 340
Bekker, I. 31 n.3, 51 n.9, 66, 68, 98, 322
Berti, E. 106, 118, 130, 165, 271
Blackson, T.A. 210
Bobonich, C. 219, 220
Bodéüs, R. 289
Bonitz, H. 67, 97, 123, 138, 149, 186, 196, 210, 215, 224, 228, 298
Bostock, D. 130, 214, 218
Bronstein, D. 105
Brunschwig, J. 27 n.1, 31 n.2 and 3, 40 n.8, 51 n.9, 58, 64, 66, 68, 71, 74, 75, 80, 81, 88, 89, 90, 94, 98, 99, 106, 109, 114, 121, 129, 131, 133, 152, 157, 165, 169, 171, 176, 177, 178, 185, 196, 202, 206, 212, 227, 236, 260, 263, 269, 271, 274, 280, 289, 292, 320, 322, 328, 340, 341, 342
Burnyeat, M. 114, 130, 134, 214

Casari, E. 138
Categories 1, 19, 21, 79, 124, 154, 203, 204, 207, 235, 265, 303, 324
category 110, 122, 134, 159, 177, 178, 215–16
 categorial mistake 139, 294, 297
 categorial problem 134
causality 16, 18
cause 17–18, 105, 125, 181, 182, 185, 210–11, 222, 325, 329
Charles, D. 14 n.3, 17 n.5, 105, 214
Charlton, W. 210
Cherniss, H. 155, 227, 254, 260, 263
Cleary, J. 111
coextensivity 5, 6, 10, 25, 63, 87–9, 91–3, 172, 295, 296
Colli, G. 58, 70, 80, 152, 157, 202, 289
commonplace 3, **28, 37, 38, 42**, 72, 76, 80, 81, 83, 140–1, *passim*
 constructive commonplace 4, 12, 131, 205, 235, 300
 refutative commonplace 3, 12, 21–2, 25, 57, 66, 74, 131, *passim*
complex (*sumpeplegmenon*) **49**, 111, 281–2
composite (*sunthetos*) **49, 55**, 282, 332–4
contrary **29, 41, 46, 47**, 72, 83, 183–5, 238, 239–40, 243–5, 247–9, 250–2, 331–8
contrary by privation **46**, 245–7, 250
coordinate 22, **35, 37**, 234, 237, 240, 258
 coordinate member (or element) of a division **38**, 126, 149–50, 158
Corcilius, K. 210, 211
correlative 23, 24, **40, 41**, 123–4, 177–81, 195, 200, 206–9, 210–12, 216–19, 221, 223, 233, 241, 293, 294, 298–302
Crivelli, P. 138, 144, 154, 231, 263, 285

De Anima 214, 267, 288, 329
deduction 3, 16, 26 n.7, **28, 48, 50**, 76, 255, 273, 274–5, 296

GENERAL INDEX

definition 3–14, *passim*
  causal definition 17–18, 82, 329
  class definition 15, 19
  circular definition 127, 248–51
  incomplete definition 24, 200, 222
  mereological definition 14, 199, 317
  unclear definition 20, **56**, 72,
    101–2, 338
  successful definition 13–17, 23, 26,
    66, 92, 100, 106, 109, *passim*
  standard definition 14–15, 19, 77,
    81, 95, 198, 209, 244, 310–1
  definitional context 23–4, 72, 78–9,
    84, 133, 257, 259, 260, 286, 290,
    300, 301, 334
demonstration 2, 16, 18, **32**, 105, 249
De Pater, W.A. 139
Deslauriers, M. 217
Destrée, P. 219
De Vogel, C.J. 227, 260
dialectic 18, 25–6, 257, 263, 271, 276
dialectical method 2–4, 220, 257
dialectician 3–4, 12–13, 19, 25, 58, 66,
  75–6, 147, 164, 182, 186, 193–9,
  211, 222, *passim*, 336–7
differentia 4–5, 14–16, **29**, **33**, **37–40**,
  147–190
  differentia of substances 149,
    173, 177
  differentia of relatives 16, **40**, 148,
    176–7, 202
Dionysius **48**, 266–8
disposition **41**, 121, 148, 182,
  253, 255
division 14, **35**, **55**, 126–7, 149–52,
  329
  division of the genus by
    negation **38**, 143, 147, 152–7, 166
  method of division 15–16
Dorion, L.-A. 95, 270, 271
Duncombe, M. 203
Düring, I. 227, 260

Ebert, T. 64, 68
einai 14, 188, 198, 209, 297, 325
  einai hoper 202
eristic 257, 263–4, 276
  eristic argument 21
essence 5, 8–10, 18, 27, 30, 36, 52, **52**,
  54, 57, 65, 102, *passim* (*see also*
  what-it-is-to-be)
Euclid 109, 153

Fait, P. 73, 95, 190, 270, 271
familiar 16, **28**, **29**, **31**, **32–5**, **50**, **55**,
  56, 108, 123, 249, 286–8, 290, 337
  familiar to us *vs* familiar
    unqualifiedly **32–4**, 70, 107–9,
    112–20, 125–6, 337
  less familiar **50**, 106, 113, 287, 292
  more familiar 23, **32–5**, 101–7,
    113–20, 125–28, 204, 248–9,
    286–7, 290–1
  unfamiliar **32**, **33**, **49**, **50**, 131,
    285–8, 290–2
familiarity 103, 106, 107, 118–19,
  286–7, 291–3
Fine, G. 210, 232, 233, 248
Form **45**, 77, 120, 152, 154–5, 197,
  262, 298
Forster, E.S. 64, 70, 74, 80, 123, 133,
  185, 236, 289, 298, 321
Frede, M. 130, 147, 203, 231

genus 3–6, 10–15, 23–5, **27**, **29**, **33–7**,
  117–18, 128–46
  appropriate genus 12, 25, **27**, **36**,
    37, **39**, **40**, 61, 68, 139–40, 149–50,
    169–71
  proximate genus **36**, 61, 128, 130,
    139–45, 170, 198
  relative genus 23–4, **43**, 128, 132–6,
    176–9, 199, 200
  subordinate genus 148, 160,
    171, 172
Gambra, J.M. 147, 177
Goodwin, W. 213
Granger, H. 130

Hardie, W.F.R. 143
Harte, V. 311
Heath, T. 109, 153
homonymy 20–1, **28**, **48**, 72–6, 264–77
hoper see *einai hoper*
Huby, P. 155
Hussey, E. 110, 121, 129

Idea 15, **47**, 152, 155–156, 227–33
Irwin, T. 113, 143, 219, 220, 224, 225,
  226, 271
Isnardi-Parente, M. 89, 96

Judson, L. 143

Kirwan, C. 215

383

Madigan SJ, A. 165
Malink, M. 147, 177, 215
Mann, W.-R. 147, 231
Mansion, S. 103, 108
Matthews, G.B. 210
metaphor 20, **28–9**, 72, 76–82
Metaphysics 5, 115, 130, 165, 214, 216–18, 325
Mignucci, M. 108, 203
modification (grammatical) 22, **47**, 182, 234, 257–9
Moraux, P. 271
Moreau, J. 271
Morison, B. 129
Morrison, D. 147, 177, 217
Moss, J. 225, 226
Mugler. C, 280

negation 245 n.2
 negation (opposed to affirmation) 235
 negation (and privation) 245–6, 253–5
 see also division of the genus by negation
Nicomachean Ethics 99, 143, 159, 200, 213–14, 220, 224, 305

opinion **53**, 117, 287, 310–11
 reputable opinion 2, 220, 222, 225
opposites (commonplaces concerning opposites) 24, **34**, **46**, 102, 122, 124–7, 191, 234–5, 242–4
 classification of opposites 19, 83
opposition 24, 83, 235, 240, 242, 246
Owen, G.E.L. 157, 181, 225, 227, 231, 232, 260, 263, 341

parts and whole relation 14, **52–3**, 111, 310–318, 321–5, 330
Pacius, J. 121, 152, 193, 210, 320, 328, 339
Parmenides 232, 287
Patzig, G. 130
peirastikê 271
Plato 15, 16, **28**, **30**, **47**, 73, 77, 89, 99, 110, 118, 137, 153, 155, 160, 196, 197, 202, 228–31, 241, 248, 261–4, 306, 323
Pickard-Cambridge 64, 70, 74, 80, 184, 236, 289, 298, 321
possession **35**, **45**, **47**, 97, 127, 192, 235–7

possession and privation 157, 235, 251–4
possessor **40**, **45**, 192, 236–7
Posterior Analytics 1, 15, 17–18, 105, 114, 116, 125, 134
predicable 3–12, 21–5, 57, 64–9, 101, *passim*
 theory of the predicables 3–4, 7–9, 18, 25, 129
predication 4, **31**, 96, 144, 148, 182, 228
 counter-predication 7, 9, 93
 to counter-predicate 5, 6–10, **30**, 88, 129, 295
 definitional *vs* ordinary predication 154–6, 230–2, 261
 double predication 85, 96–8
 essential predication 141, 164
 self-predication 154
Primavesi, O. 266, 267
Prior Analytics 1, 15, 16, 172
priority 19, 101, 116–19, 150–2, 167, 181, 204
 priority requirement 23, 122
 definitional priority 248–9
 epistemological priority *vs* ontological priority 23, 102–3, 109–12, 118, 122–6, 131
 teleological priority 336
privation **31**, **46–7**, 97–8, 157, 251–5
 by privation **46–7**, 235, 245–50, 252, 254–6
 see also possession and privation
proper 12, 25, **27**, **30**, **37**, **48**, **51**, 63–8, 75, 93, 205, 302 (*see also* unique property)

quality **44**, 79, 134, 142, 176–8, 189, 200, 207, 215–17, 220, 222
quantity **44**, **45**, 82, 110, 128, 200, 215–19, 222
questioner 2–3, 19, 21, 26, **56**, 63, 173, 234, 268–77, 326, 340

Rapp, C. 71, 80, 152, 289
redundancy 70–1, 85–7, 91, 93–8, 10–3, 198, 342
Reeve, C.D.C. 271
refutation 3, 13, 21, 89, 95, 192, 194, 203, 211, 229, 258, *passim*
relatives 3, 16, 19, 23–4, **40**, **43**, **45**, **51**, 122–7, 132–6, 148, 191, 199, 207–11, 216, 227–8, 232, 235, 240–3, 298–303

definition of relatives 200–2
see also differentia of relatives
Ross, W.D. 31 n.3, 35 n.5, 51 n.9, 65, 66, 68, 108, 110, 165, 170, 263, 322
Rowe, C. 220

Schiaparelli, A. 5, 63, 177, 190, 205, 207, 227, 261, 269, 287
Shields, C. 72, 159, 165, 181, 215, 220, 267, 329
Sim, M. 271
simultaneous (by nature) 13, **34**, **35**, 122, 126
Slomskowski, P. 64, 68, 135
Smith, R. 2, 4 n.1, 58, 68, 72, 83, 101, 104, 134, 135, 144, 159, 191, 235, 236, 264, 271, 273
Smyth, H. 140, 184, 215, 323
Socrates 6, 13, 107, 112, 115, 159, 196, 219–20, 232–3, 273, 285, 310–11
Sophistici Elenchi 1, 21, 26, 73, 95, 136 n.1, 190, 225, 271, 276
soul **30**, **41**, **47**, **54**, **55**, 88–90, 151, 179–183, 193, 201–2, 253, 263, 315, 327, 330, 334–5
substance **37**, **40**, **43**, **55**, 79, 90, 110, 118, 128, 130, 149, 159, 203, 209, 217–18, 332–6
  substances and affections 174–6
  primary substance 142
  substance and accident 117
  see also differentia of substances
substitution
  of names in definitions **49–50**, 97, 191, 279, 286–93
  of a name with its account 295
Strache, J. 31 n.3, 51 n.9, 66, 68, 98, 322

Striker, G. 273
syllogism 2–3, 18, 105, 224, 273, 300, 342
synonym **48**, 265–77
synonymy 21, 265, 270, 273, 277, 324

Thales 221
Tréheux, J. 280
Tricot 64, 70, 80, 133, 152, 185, 196, 236, 254, 289, 305

unique property 3–4, 8–11, **27**, 63–4, 67–9, 87–9, 195, 235
two ways of being a unique property 5, 89, 167, 302

Verdenius, W.J. 227

Wagner, T. 71, 80, 152, 289
Waitz, T. 31 n.3, 51 n.5, 66, 68, 98, 152, 165, 253, 245, 322
Wallies, M. 31 n.3, 51 n.9, 66, 68, 98, 322
Ward, J. 72, 264, 271
what-it-is 5, 6, **35**, **47**, 63, 130, 162, 169, 215
what-it-is-to-be 4, 6, 12, 14, 16, **27**, **32**, **33**, **44**, 57, 65, 102, 105 (*see also* essence)
  what-it-is-to-be for something 7
  what-it-is *vs* what-it-is-to-be 141–2
whole *see* parts and whole relation

Xenocrates **31**, 88–9, 96–8

Zadro, A. 152, 289